D1566405

# Criteria for Competence

*Controversies in the Conceptualization
and Assessment of Children's Abilities*

# Criteria for Competence

*Controversies in the Conceptualization
and Assessment of Children's Abilities*

Edited by

## Michael Chandler
## Michael Chapman
*University of British Columbia*

**LEA** LAWRENCE ERLBAUM ASSOCIATES, PUBLISHERS
1991 Hillsdale, New Jersey          Hove and London

Lawrence Erlbaum Associates, Inc., Publishers
365 Broadway
Hillsdale, New Jersey 07642

**Library of Congress Cataloging-in-Publication Data**

Criteria for competence : controversies in the conceptualization and
   assessment of children's abilities / edited by Michael Chandler and
   Michael Chapman.
      p.      cm.
   Includes bibliographical references and index.
   ISBN 0-8058-0606-7
   1. Performance in children.   2. Cognition in children.   3. Human
information processing in children.   4. Piaget, Jean, 1896–
I. Chandler, Michael J.   II. Chapman, Michael, 1947–
BF723.P365C73   1991
155.4'13—dc20                                                    91-15637
                                                                      CIP

Printed in the United States of America
10  9  8  7  6  5  4  3  2  1

# Contents

# Introduction: Issues in the Identification of Competence

Michael Chandler
Michael Chapman
*University of British Columbia*

Detailing the sorts of competencies that regularly differentiate persons of various ages and accounting for the timing of such sequencing of abilities are central among the tasks with which developmental psychologists and closely allied professionals have been charged. This book takes up these obligations, not by attempting to catalogue the specific age of onset of such developmental milestones, but rather by addressing the prior question of how such uncertain matters are to be decided. Making some headway toward determining what should stand as criteria for competence is obviously a matter of first importance, both because doing so is decisive in arbitrating the differences that now divide competing accounts of human development, and because such practical matters are among those that our constituents most want decided. Modern parents, for example, often set their child-rearing agendas on the basis of what developmentalists assert about the talents of various age groups. So do educators and other service-oriented professionals who must decide what is timely and what is premature for persons positioned at various points across the life span. For the sake of our own disciplinary well-being and for the benefit of those onlookers whose interests we serve, deciding what is to count as evidence that a particular competence has or has not emerged is a necessary first step in getting the study of human development underway.

Without expecting perfect consensus on these critical matters, one at least might have thought that developmentalists already would have worked out among themselves how questions concerning such matters of emerging psychological competencies are to be decided. Unfortunately, no such consensus is apparent. Instead, each wave of incoming research delivers a new flotsam of increasingly divergent claims about almost any developmental milestone one might care to mention. for example, recent evidence can be found to indicate that children are able to reflect or deduce or behave intentionally somewhere between the ages of 5 months and 15 years of age, depending on which authority one happens to read. Although the most recent tide of professional opinion appears to be running in favor of those who claim to observe initial traces of any and all competence is at increasingly early ages, the exact opposite was true at least once or twice in the careers of most practicing psychologists. Given our collective uncertainty about how to decide these matters, the tide could turn again on a moment's notice.

Clearly, something is seriously amiss. How could research into questions as fundamental as when persons first acquire a sense of self or learn to reason transitively yield up answers that are seemingly so far apart? How can it be that experts who hold to such radically different views appear to be so unruffled by this same divergence of opinion? Where is the collective embarrassment one might reasonably expect in the face of such wholesale disagreement? And where are the grounds for hope that this divergence of professional opinion is on the wane?


## A BACKGROUND TO THE CONTROVERSY

Providing answers to these and related questions is the shared purpose of all of the chapters in this book. In the balance of this Introduction, the scope of this problem is documented, and some of the reasons why developmentalists have so far failed to arrive at procedures for deciding when various human competencies develop are discussed.

As a first step toward formulating a diagnosis of the reason for these radical disagreements, it is useful to draw attention to the fact that, if anything, the problem appears to be getting progressively worse rather than better. We do not mean by this bleak assessment that experts in human development have ever been complete strangers to such controversies, only that their disagreements have grown in volume and volubility rather than decreased with the passage of time. Central to any understanding of this increasing divergence of views is the wedge that Piagetian theory has driven between generations of students of the developmental course. The recent history of the field might reasonably be glossed by saying that the events preceding the cognitive revolution of the 1960s and 1970s conspired to create a broad, but premature consensus concerning just how easily and how quickly young persons come to participate in a psychological way of being that is fundamentally adult-like in its basic forms or structure. For example, the various learning theories that dominated academic psychology in the first half of this century had as their shared message the reductive claim that whatever it means to become knowledgeable or expert or well practiced is roughly the same for the young and the old. In consequence, a certain "adultopomorphism" was all but ubiquitous in the writings of most early 20th-century experimental psychologists. Similarly, many psychodynamic theorists of this same period, by reconstructing childhood through the recollections of their adult patients, were driven to the mistaken conclusion that children were no more than miniature adults. In short, there was little about the early decades of North American psychology that would have suggested that the basic competencies of young persons might be fundamentally different from those of their admittedly more knowledgeable, expert and better practiced adult counterparts.

Into this historical context of premature agreement, Piaget's theory, and all that it inspired, drove home the novel message that infants and children were not simply less schooled, but also qualitatively different from adults in more fundamental ways having to do with their basic competencies for processing and organizing experience. Newly armed with the possibility that persons of different ages might represent instances of what amounted to different psychological types, the task that whole armies of developmentalists set for themselves was to prove in just how many interestingly different ways the competencies of children different from those of adults. In these earlier exciting times reputations were quickly made by those who fell upon still another way of showing that the fundamental competencies of children were different from those of adults, or that young persons could not do something previously assumed to be within their repertoires. Whether or not these new found distinctions were overdrawn is no easy matter to decide. However, one conclusion now seems inevitable in retrospect: In a discipline where only novelty has real staying power, an earlier generation of developmentalists whose ticket to success lay in demonstrating a sizeable gap between the more and less mature, may well have been guilty of overplaying their hand. In just the same way that an entire cohort of young investigators earlier succeeded in winning their stripes by detailing the long list of things children were said to be incapable of doing or understanding, a newer generation was gathering in the wings to say it isn't so. In such a climate, asserting that children of a given age definitely lack this or that ability quickly became the psychological equivalent of bear baiting: Someone was always more than happy to try to take off the hand of anyone who had the temerity to hold out any clear declaration about missing competencies.

From this third perspective, much research was conducted during the 1970s and into the 1980s purporting to demonstrate that children acquire various cognitive competencies at a significantly earlier age than the preceding generation had thought possible. The common target of many of these studies was Piaget's theory, and their common assumption was that the assessment strategies on which this theory frequently relied unwittingly incorporated various "performance factors" (such as linguistic and memory skills) unrelated to the competencies presumably being assessed. By these lights, Piaget and his co-workers were seen to have underestimated children's true abilities and to over-estimate the ages at which they developed the forms of thinking characteristic of various developmental stages.

## SECOND THOUGHTS

Because all of the several pendulum swings described here have occurred with-in the span of a half a professional lifetime, the field is now full of advocates of every kind. There are those whose interests or inclinations caused them to remain outside of the orbit of the Piagetian theory and the cognitive revolu-tion more generally, and whose otherwise quaint views about children's early competencies now seem strangely postmodern. Then there are those faux-Piagetians for whom later has always seems better, along with their detrac-tors, who see proof of early competence in successful performances of almost any sort. And finally, there are those critics of critics ready to find faulty with all hedges thrown up against the assignment of any and all competencies to infant children. For other sciences whose revolutions have occurred at a more languid and leisurely pace, the living often joust only with theoretical oppo-nents who have long since passed from the scene. Developmentalists, by con-trast, live cheek by jowl with most of their own intellectual ancestors, who con-tinue to defend and develop their own still viable views. Little wonder that the field seems divided and that the interested reader scarcely knows whom to believe.

## OVERVIEW

Given the history of rapidly changing fashions of thought sketched in earlier, there is little reason to imagine that we have managed somehow to be present at last turn of this interpretative wheel. Nor is it the purpose of this book to attempt to initiate some new era in this revolutionary process. The more modest service we can hope to perform is to adopt a critical attitude toward the patch-work of views regarding the meaning and measurement of competence left as a legacy by those who have some before. In particular, we all currently appear to be living through a particularly undistinguished historical period within which more serious thoughts about the meaning of the concept of competence are regularly replaced by methodologic contests waged between those who imagine themselves to have discovered the new lower bound of some competence, and others eager to defend the legitimacy of some still higher or lower threshold of that same ability. Rather than attempting to choose between such alterna-tives some other second thoughts on this bad spirited enterprise seems required. This book is a compendium of such second thoughts.

An important first step in the process of rethinking the meaning of cognitive competence is to try to become clear about just what is entailed by the claim that a given individual has or lacks such an ability. In referencing such competencies do we mean only to put a name to some pattern of skills or talents already evident in that individual's problem-solving efforts? Or do we intend to speak of some otherwise hidden antecedent structure on or determinant force causally responsible for those manifest actions that represent their effects? Where do such competencies reside? Are they the private intrapsychic chattel of those individuals who manifest them? Or is it rather that such competencies somehow occupy that interstitial space created by the overlap of persons and tasks and sociocultural contexts, and make no sense as items of private property. In Part I, entitled "Metatheoretical Issues," these and related issues are taken up by Michael Chandler (chapter 1), Willis Overton (chapter 2), and John Meacham (chapter 3) by way of setting out and exploring those alternative explanatory frameworks within which concepts of competence have found a home.

Part II, "Issues in Piagetian Theory," stands as an acknowledgment of the fact that most contemporary talk about matters of cognitive competence represent either explications of or attacks on that body of developmental theory initiated by Piaget. The contributors to this section all focus attention on and seek to resolve controversies that have been triggered by evidence purporting to demonstrate the presence of some cognitive competence in children younger than those discussed by Piaget. In various ways these authors set about to show that (a) age of onset was never the issue (Leslie Smith, chapter 4); (b) the new evidence is consistent with rather than somehow antithetical to Piaget's theory (Ann Dean and James Youniss, chapter 5); (c) the newly documented abilities are precursors to rather than examples of the competencies in question (Jacques Montangero, chapter 6); or (d) cognitive competence needs to be viewed in the context of both task and sociocultural constraints (Eberhard Schröder and Wolfgang Edelstein, chapter 7). In the process, these four chapters serve to sharpen our understanding of what is entailed by the claim that particular competencies are present in some and absent in others.

Part III, entitled "Beyond Piaget," contains three chapters that owe some important allegiance to the work of the Geneva group, but go on to propose more dimensions to the problem of cognitive competence than existed in the imagination of Piaget. Among these are included efforts aimed at (a) uncovering those networks of causal relations that underpin Piagetian structures (Juan Pascual-Leone and Janice Johnson, chapter 8); (b) identifying representational systems of meaning underrepresented by most structural models of development (Irving Sigel, chapter 9); and (c) expanding the dialogic character of traditional subject–object interactions in order to leave a proper place for those subject–subject relations that constitute the third leg of the stool on which cognitive competencies are said to rest (Michael Chapman, chapter 10). Especially here, but also scattered elsewhere throughout the volume, emphasis is placed on the importance of conducting penetrating task analyses aimed at laying bare all that is involved in satisfactorily passing various assessment procedures.

Finally, in Part IV, "Modeling the Development of Competence," chapter 11 by Mark Aber and J.J. McArdle is made to stand witness for a whole constituency of novel or otherwise little known methods of data analysis especially well suited to the task of explicating cognitive competencies. Whatever such competencies are ultimately understood to be, it is obvious that they require being ferreted out somehow from a thicket of more task-specific matters that otherwise obscure their presence. The account of latent growth curve models presented in this final chapter is held out as an especially promising representative of a large class of such approaches, all of which promise to aid us in the heady task of identifying those various patterns or latent causes that competencies are understood to be.

# Part I

# Metatheoretical Issues

The three chapters that form this first section help to situate the other contributions that follow by making clear the range of alternative meanings commonly attached to the concept of competence and by offering opinions about the relative merits of these competing views. In each case, these authors proceed by winnowing away what they deem to be counterproductive readings of the competence–performance relation and by advocating in their place what they hold up as more coherent alternatives. Although importantly different in detail, the shared message contained in these chapters is that any attempt to construe psychological competence as some hidden mechanical cause secreted away within the private inner workings of other minds is automatically doomed from the outset to a future of certain incoherence and likely abuse. Instead, they each argue that competence concepts are best understood as normative explanations rather than descriptions or empirical generalizations, that serve to elucidate rather than to literally cause actual concrete performances. In each case, these authors lay stress on the ways in which competency concepts serve to pick out particular patterns characteristic of certain types of personal or interpersonal actions, and all work to situate such pattern explanations within a still broader framework of other explanatory forms.

In chapter 1, Chandler provides an organizing framework within which alternative conceptions of competence might be located. He begins this taxonomic task by rejecting at the outset any easy assumption that there are ''pure competence'' or ''pure performance'' theories to be had and by insisting instead that every theory that aspires to being complete must somehow make room for both of these fundamental notions. By applying this standard he comes to a fourfold classification scheme that divides contenders into what he terms (a) strict performance theorists, (b) straight competence theorists, and those that either (c) see performance as causally determined by competence, or conversely, (d) utilize competence concepts as a way of explaining performance.

Whereas proponents of either the first or second of these interpretive frameworks are characterized as being at least superficially attentive to matters of both competence and performance, each is quickly written off as offering only lip service to one or the other half of the competence–performance equation. For example, strict performance theorists are portrayed as accepting competence concepts as useful heuristics, but guided by the hope that such overly abstract explanatory ''conventions'' can be dispensed with as soon as additional hard data become available. In contrast, straight competence theorists are described as advocating the opposite kind of one-note explanatory tune by effectively rejecting the distinction between capacity and its use.

Having effectively dismissed half of the contenders in his working typology, Chandler focuses the balance of his chapter on the competing visions of those who either undertake to get performance out of competence, or conversely, work to get competence out of performance. By this account, the real villains of Chandler's chapter are those whom he characterizes as attempting to enlist various psychological competences in the role of antecedent causes that have manifest behavior as their consequent effects. Such interpretations, he contends, ultimately fall into incoherence for the reasons that they are altogether too deterministic to accommodate those dimensions of choice or purpose seemingly constitutive of the notion of competence, and because they naturally veer toward a kind of solipsism promoted by the fact that hidden causes of this caliber can never be measured directly.

In the place of all that has gone before, Chandler finishes by advocating the fourth in his quartet of alternative views, offering reasons as to why concepts of competence are best understood as formal attempts to reconstruct those rules or patterns thought to be already implicit in the concrete performances of particular individuals or groups. The object of such attempts at theory formation, he argues, is not to predict what particular individuals will do next, but to utilize such performances as clues to the existence of structures that give possible meaning to the particular actions in question.

Chapter 2 by Willis Overton usefully extends and elaborates Chandler's introductory remarks by arguing first, that competence must be understood as a type of explanation, not a type of description, and second, that such accounts of competence are only one among several types of explanations that enter into scientific inquiry. On these assumptions he reasons that because competence explanations offer idealized, normative accounts of the pattern or form or structure of the events being explained, they cannot be enlisted as a way of accounting for individual differences on cross-situational variabilities. Using as a spring board an earlier account by Chandler of certain important isomorphisms between (a) the ways in which young persons develop an understanding of the knowing process and (b) the history of philosophy's understanding of the knowledge acquisition process more generally, he proposes an interpretive scheme for organizing several distinct approaches to the study of the competence–performance relation. Two of these, which he associates with "positivism" and "conventionalism," generally maintain a rigid distinction between interpretation and fact, or explanation and description, and consequently leave no room for pattern explanations of the sort that coherent interpretations of competence are said to require.

Set against both of these positions, Overton identifies a further movement within contemporary philosophy of science circles that expresses a revitalized interest in rationalism and interpretationism, and that creates a place within explanations in science that involves discerning patterns rather than observing cause–effect sequences. Although such views risk opening the door onto a kind of know-nothing relativism, or a vacillation between skepticism and dogmatic over-commitment, they also provide for the possibility of a kind of post-skeptical approach to the philosophy of science that regards all knowledge as emerging out of human activity. Such activities, Overton points out, include constructing abstract patterns that plausibly and coherently systemize domains of inquiry such as those that might be of interest to developmental psychologists on the one hand, or to the young persons who are their subjects, on the other. Such abstract patterns, according to Overton, not only constitute explanations, but are themselves the competencies that represent the focus of this book. The foregoing interpretive framework allows Overton to point out interesting parallels between competency explanations and "formal" as opposed to "material" and "efficient" causal accounts, and to distinguish between hardware, procedures, and competence as interrelated levels of explanation. All of this is then brought to bear as a way of resolving controversies in the research literature on deductive reasoning.

In chapter 3, John Meacham undertakes to better contextualize certain of the issues raised by Chandler and Overton by (a) exploring the range situations in which conflicting claims regarding children's competencies are likely to arise, and (b) examining the objectives of those engaged in such controversies. He does this by introducing what he characterizes as two competing paradigms or "images of nature" that he finds at work in our cultural conceptions of both the ecology in general, and of child development in particular. From within one of these perspectives adult human beings are understood to stand apart from nature and the world of childhood, both of which are seen to require their superintendency and control. By contrast, those who operate out of the second of these views understand themselves to be a part of nature in general and the lives of their children in particular, and take as their principal objective understanding rather than dominating their human and nonhuman environments.

Although Meacham is quick to judge the position that holds persons to be a part of nature as being somehow closer to the truth, both of these views are seen to risk degenerating into tragedies of one sort of another. In the specific case of family relations, parents who see their own lives as somehow standing apart from those of their children, and who make it their business to strongly intervene in their lives, are seen to court a brand of disaster characterized by a failure to produce just those qualities of independence and responsibility that the whole project of domination was originally meant to secure. By contrast, the world view that leads parents to regard their own lives as naturally inter-mingled with the lives of their children may be generally supportive of better outcomes, but under certain circumstances can degenerate into patterns of neglect. The danger here, according to Meacham, is that those adults who are inclined to view the course of human development as a part of nature are some-times also prone to falling into the error of imagining that all of the problems of growth and development will somehow magically take care of themselves. At their worst, then, such views can function as a rationale for maintaining a passive or uncaring approach toward child rearing.

Of special relevance to the guiding theme of this book, Meacham then goes on to outline the ways in which these two contrasting "views of nature" each support different conceptions of psychological competence. According to the view that all of nature, including the children within it, is a part of "man's" privileged dominion, the primary objectives of psychological assessment are either to assay the quality or the materials one has to work with, or to monitor the effectiveness of one's previous intervention efforts. By contrast, for those committed to the view that parents and children are immersed in an inter-dependent life course, the primary goal of such assessment efforts is to better understand new ways of improving the quality of that relationship. Of special interest in this viewpoint is the fact that competence is not interpreted as some-thing that inheres only within the child, but must be located instead within the network of relationships that obtain between children and the system of potentially social supports within which they are embedded.

# Chapter 1

# Alternative Readings of the Competence–Performance Relation

Michael Chandler
*University of British Columbia*

> *The readiness is all*
> —W. Shakespeare (*Hamlet*, V.ii)

A book about criteria for competence would do well to begin with an effort to become really clear about what the referents of concepts of competence are meant to be. Awkwardly, nothing like that happens here, at least at the outset, and for much of the same reasons that a book of this sort is needed in the first place. The relevant literature is simply too riddled with contradictory claims to permit any such easy show of definitional solidarity. Among the important things about which there is no clear consensus are whether such competency concepts are best understood as observational or interpretive, descriptive or normative, technologistic or teleological; whether they represent type or pattern concepts rather than empirical generalizations; and still more importantly, whether they are intended to *elucidate* or actually *cause* concrete performances. The absence of agreement on these and other similarly fundamental questions effectively scuttles all thoughts about all introductory naming of the parts.

In the place of any such simple summary, the best that can be offered here by way of a beginning is an attempt to lay out, in some systemic way, the broad range of divergent opinions that are commonly had about the status of competency concepts and the different parts they are imagined to play in accounting for other and more manifest behavioral aspects of the human enterprise. The primary aim, then, of this introductory chapter is to set out such an in terpretive framework. Over and above fulfilling this mapping and sign-posting function, this chapter also offers examples and strong opinions about what will be held out as sensible and not so sensible claims concerning the possible meanings of competency concepts and their relation to performance and so-called performance variables.

## COMMON SENSE CONCEPTIONS OF COMPETENCE

The common sense conviction that one's own and others' concrete actions must somehow instance, or otherwise arise as a consequence of other still more persistent and perhaps deeper lying aspects of ourselves is so pivoted to our ordinary self-understanding (Harré & Secord, 1972; Heider, 1958) that any broad psychological theory that did not leave room for something like, such a competence-performance distinction simply would be dismissed as uninteresting. For this reason it would be a mistake to imagine, as is sometimes done (e.g., Wood & Powers, 1987), that the roots of contemporary interest in the competence-performance relation reach back no further than Chomsky's (1968) inaugural use of these particular terms, or Flavell and Wohlwill's (1969) introduction of them into the literature on cognitive development (Neimark, 1985). Clearly, the writings of Freud and other early psychodynamic theorists, whose work featured accounts of hidden mechanisms and unconscious processes, represent an attempt to cover some of the same ground now being he worked by so-called competence or performance theorists, as did the efforts of other more behaviorally oriented psychologists such as Clark Hull, who reluctantly undertook to redecorate their black box versions of mental life with more or less stable central state furnishings.

What does appear to be without clear precedent in such older theoretic accounts, however, and what sets much contemporary talk about competence and performance well apart from these more traditional readings of analogous form–function distinctions, is the frequently voiced modern conviction that the business of theory construction can be jobbed out by delegating the work of studying competence to some and the task of explicating performance to others. On this view Piaget and Chomsky, for example, are regularly characterized as "competence theorists" (Neimark, 1985), supposedly disinterested in the mundane behaviors of concrete subjects. Those specializing in information-processing psychologies, by contrast, are commonly cast in the role of pure "performance theories," whose job it is to look after those rules and procedures necessary for the manufacture of particular acts (Wood & Power, 1987). Having portrayed the early decades of psychology's cognitive revolution as a period marked by the proliferation of such cottage industries, the future growth potential of the field is often seen to lie in somehow merging these isolated accounts of competence and performance under the corporate umbrella of some single and more inclusive conglomerate view (see e.g., Davidson & Sternberg, 1985; Overton & Newman, 1982).

This chapter raises doubts about the necessity and workability of any such proposed merger, both because the overly specialized division of labor it is meant to remedy simply never occurred, and because the competence–performance relations that are actually envisioned by most structural and information-processing theorists are sufficiently incommensurable as to make a category mistake out of any attempt to simply run them together. Seeing why this is so requires first getting clearer about how the notions of competence and performance are differently read by representatives of these divergent theoretical stances.

## ALTERNATIVE READINGS OF THE COMPETENCE–PERFORMANCE RELATION

Although every psychological theory strives to somehow generalize beyond the details of concrete behavioral acts and, consequently, must make some provision for linking such competencies with the specific performances to which they somehow refer, evidently no single or obligatory way of doing so exists. Instead, a survey of the available literature suggests that it is possible to distinguish a minimum of four possible ways of rendering this competence–performance relation. Two of these undertake to abolish or trivialize the problem either by (a) dismissing the whole idea of psychological competencies in favor of the promissory note that all behaviors eventually will be understood as by-products of the particular environmental circumstances that gives rise to them, or (b) re-reading all performances as the direct and automatic by-product of one's true competencies. By either of these lights half of the competence–performance relation is seen simply to disappear. By contrast, neither of the remaining interpretations to be reviewed here undertakes merely to define the competence–performance problem out of existence. Instead, both proceed in their own way either to (c) explain performance as the *effect* of which competence is the partial *cause*, or (d) *explicate* competences in light of the performances that exemplify them. In what follows each of the foregoing alternatives are taken up in turn, with the eventual aim of making the case that only the last of these possibilities offers a coherent interpretive framework for characterizing the competence–performance relation.

### Strict Performance Theories

During the short-lived period between the two World Wars, serious contributors to the psychological literature held out hope for the prospect that all loose talk about central state determinants of human behavior, including cognitive competencies, would eventually give way to a more detailed understanding of the point-to-point relations thought to hold between specific behavioral responses and the unique pattern of stimuli imagined to give rise to them (Ashcraft, 1989). Although often reduced to an interim reliance on various competency descriptors as temporary heuristics, early practitioners of this "kinematic" (Macnamara, 1990) or behavioral approach tended to regard all such explanatory devises as expendable "conventions" (Overton, 1985) meant to be dispensed with as soon as enough hard facts could be collected to fill in the awkward gaps in our understanding.

This is not the place to rehearse the many reasons why such potentially elegant simplifying assumptions were eventually rejected in favor of more demanding accounts that repopulated the opaque interior of people's minds with various presumed competencies (Ashcraft, 1989). If such radical behavioral views somehow had succeeded in their purpose, however, the balance of this book would be largely unnecessary. In fact, such reductive efforts failed in their purposes and few contemporary psychologists are prepared to confine themselves to relying on such exclusively behavioral acounts, or to imagine that any sort of interesting interpretation of human practices can be gotten off the ground without making reference to some sort of internal structures or rule books or liturgies. Instead, those who survived the demise of behaviorism inherited the job of trying to understand the relation between such competences and the manifest performances that they reference. Each of the three remaining accounts discussed here represent alternative efforts to explicate such competence-performance relations.

## Straight Competence Theories

In what amounts to a kind of contemporary mirror image of behaviorism's more dated attempt to do without concepts of competence, one also can identify within the current cognitive literature an equally one-sided approach, less committed to abolishing the competence–performance distinction than to discounting it as superfluous. In effect, advocates of this "rationalist" view (Griggs, 1981) see the relation between competence and performance as so direct that any distinction between the two seems hardly worth making. Instead, such straight competence theorists simply reject the usual Aristotelian distinction between availability and accessibility (Lefebvre-Pinard & Pinard, 1985), or between capacity and its use (Goodnow & Cashmore, 1985), in favor of a more Cartesian vision in which the aptitude for using a capacity is simply understood as an integral part of that capacity itself. According to advocates of this brand of "conceptual realism" (Smedslund, 1977), all so-called "performance failure" simply are re-read as shows of incompetence, and all individual actions are seen as rational in the sense that they are said to represent the logical consequences of those working premises currently in place.

When apparent behavioral inconsistencies do arise, the available escape hatch open to those who champion such straight competence accounts simply is to argue that subjects sometimes either reject or misinterpret the tasks that confront them, and so either do nothing at all, or competently solve the wrong problem (Griggs, 1981). Although such arguments sometimes are used to good effect (see Montangero, chapter 6, this volume), they risk opening the door to still other performance considerations that effectively reduce such competency-only accounts to some variation upon one or the other of the remaining readings of the competence–performance relation discussed later.

## EXPLAINING COMPETENCE VERSUS DETERMINING WHAT COMPETENCE EXPLAINS

On the assumption that competence and performance cannot be collapsed into one another as easily as some would like to believe and to teach others (Broughton, 1981), we are left with the task of understanding these concepts in relation to one another. Two possible readings of this relationship have dominated, but remain more or less confused within the available literature. From one of these standpoints the primary task thought to require doing is to find out *what explains competence*. The alternative is to determine *what competence explains* (Flavell, 1977). Although it is possible to imagine a more symmetrical world in which "getting competence out of performance" would amount to no more than standing the process of "getting performance out of competence" on its head, this would appear not to be one of those conveniently reversible situations. Instead, these different readings of the competence–performance relation not only appear to "push in the opposite directions," (Habermas, 1988), but to belong to different and essentially incommensurate interpretive realities.

In the first of these cases, where the job to be accomplished is construed to be somehow getting overt performance out of latent competence, the usual approach taken is broadly hypothetical-deductive, and the goal is seen to be developing some explanatory framework in which competence can be counted as an antecedent *cause* of which manifest behavior is a consequent *effect* (Olson, 1978). In the second, where the line of argument runs from performance to competence, the alternative goal is to elucidate, through the construction of abstract, formal descriptions, those rules or patterns assumed to be implicit in the concrete performances of particular individuals or groups (Bernstein, 1983). The method here is "abductive" (Peirce, 1931), or "reconstructive" (Habermas, 1979), rather than empirical-analytic, and concrete behaviors, rather than being of interest in themselves, are seem primarily as *clues* to the pattern or meanings that cut across them (Fodor & Garnett, 1966). Because of these differences in goals and methods, any attempt to translate between these two explanatory frameworks is difficult if not impossible (Olson, 1978), and consequently each is discussed in turn in the sections that immediately follow.

## On Deciding What Competencies Explains

One well-rehearsed strategy that does seek to preserve the distinction between competence and performance, while remaining safely within what Lycan (1981) called the "closed casual order of the empirical world," proceeds by construing competence as a causally relevant component in a conceptual equation in which manifest performance is interpreted as some direct function of that competence plus other things. Such straight forward causal accounts, which are branded by their detractors as "technologistic" (Habermas, 1979) or "objectivist" (Smedslund, 1977) or "automation" models (Flavell & Wohlwill, 1969), and which typically regard the successful anticipation of behavioral outcomes as an end in itself (Neimark, 1985), come in two, not quite identical versions. According to the first and simplest version, so-called competence factors and performance factors are accorded conjunctive and co-equal status (Overton & Newman, 1982) and are invisioned as somehow jointly responsible for the production of concrete behaviors. According to the second, which Davidson and Sternberg (1985) perhaps too generously credit with providing an "interface" between Piagetian and information-processing psychologies, competencies are viewed as a kind of latent "power" or "know-how" capable of directly activating appropriate behaviours provided that certain opportunities and enabling conditions (e.g., motivations, specific knowledge, etc.) obtain (Cohen, 1981).

Despite the modest differences that divide the foregoing conjunctive and disjunctive conditional accounts, both effectively reduce competence to the role of a parameter assumed to be responsible for actively producing observed patterns of behavior as their effects. At least this is how, in theory, things are meant to work. Actually moving such causal models off of the drawing board and setting them to work making real-world predictions about concrete behaviors requires as a first step somehow narrowing in on the measurement of such competence, presumably by partially out of observed behaviors those effects due to performance variables (Davidson & Sternberg, 1985). It is here that things commonly begin to go badly wrong.

One such problem is that there simply are too many candidates in the role of antecedent variable, the absence of any one of which implies the same lack of successful performance. As a consequence, one can never be certain whether failure on a given testing procedure is due to the absence of a particular competence or, alternatively, should be to written off to deficits in one or another performance factor (Einhorn & Hogarth, 1981). The upshot of this is that faulty competence can never be established from studying faulty performance (Evans

& Pollard, 1981), and every causal theory that treats manifest behavior as the effect of some competence plus other things naturally veers toward solipsism. For the reason just outlined some have come to regard all versions of the competence-performance distinction as alibis (Blackburn, 1981), or explanatory dodges meant to rescue the claims of certain so-called "competency theories" from the possibility of refutation (Neimark, 1985; Sampson, 1981). Whether such accusations are warranted, as I argue in sections to follow, depends on whether there are workable alternatives to the view that competence is some form of hidden cause.

A second difficulty that arises from attempts to view competence as a mechanical causal factor in the issuance of concrete behaviors is the natural bias that such views exercise in favor of earlier and earlier attributions of competence. This consequence results from the fact that behaviors that appear to confirm the presence of some hypothesized ability are commonly read as direct manifestations of that competence, whereas those behaviors that fail to do so are easily dismissed as artifacts of various performance factors or technical measurement failures (Lopez, 1981). The effect of such asymmetric practices is that the age at which a given competency is ascribed moves systematically and inexorably downward as experimental evidence accumulates.

Finally, there are good reasons to suppose that the traditional beliefs enshrined in the everyday notion of competence simply are inconsistent with the deterministic views championed by those who insist on seeing competence as causally related to performance. At least this would appear to follow from the presumptions of a long philosophic tradition that counts among the reasons that competence sometimes goes unexpressed the fact that persons often *choose* not to exercise abilities that they unarguably possess (Brand, 1970). Unless the notion of "try," that Heider (1958), among many others (e.g., Harr*e & Secord, 1972) insist is a natural component of manifest competence concepts, can be reduced somehow to the waxing and waning of physiological drives, the whole enterprise of behaving competently take on an unexpungable quality of purpose or willfulness that strict causal accounts can scarcely accommodate.

For the reasons just outlined, it would appear that any causal theory that honors what Habermas (1979) has characterized as the "dualism of scheme and reality" either degenerates into a some kind of obligatory apriorism or proves to be untestable. In both cases natural epistemic concerns over deciding and knowing whether someone has an ability is confounded with the question of what is means to say that a person has a particular competence. The impossibility promoted by this confusion is that one can no more measure competence by holding performance constant than one can catch sight of the dark by switching the lights on suddenly (Broughton, 1981). Without some independent way of measuring competence such causal equations simply end up with too many unknowns. We are, as a result, either left with the infinite regress of seeing competence behind every fortuitous behavioral success, or giving up on its measurement entirely. Foreseeing these consequences, others have turned their attention to explaining competency rather than deciding what competence explains.

## On Getting Competence Out of Performance

In pointed contrast to those empirical-analytic efforts just outlined, which seek to attribute manifest behaviours to the inner workings of invisible competencies, one also can identify within the relevant literature an entirely different theoretical enterprise that reads the competence–performance relation the other way around, by seeking to identify some interpretive framework within which manifest behaviors can be intelligently, that is, thickly described (Nelson, 1978). Investigations housed within this contrastive research program (e.g., Piaget and other like-minded structural theorists) simply by-pass the whole antecedent-consequent system of independent and dependent variables preferred by behaviorist and information-processing theorists in favor of differently intended attempts to understand such behavioral actions by specifying their place within some formal and rationally reconstructed set of concepts or rules or schemata (Olson, 1978). That is, the object of such attempts at theory formation is not to predict what particular individuals will do next, but to utilize these particular performances as clues to the existence of some structure or structures that give possible *meaning* to the specific actions in question (Fodor & Garnett, 1966).

Not only is the primary *object* of such reconstructive efforts different from that pursued by more behaviorally oriented theorists, but so is the general direction and style of their inquiry. The methodological approach commonly followed by such structural-oriented theorists has little to do with ferreting out whatever mechanisms might be involved in the actual production of specific performances, but turns instead upon efforts to sift imaginatively through relevant behaviors with the aim of ultimately arriving at some previously unmarked pattern or relatively simply set of idealized structures and transformational rules.

Although the competency concepts that are generated by such "boot-strapping" operations are therefore at least partially empirical in *origin*, the relationships they seek to specify are logical relations of *identification* rather than empirical relations cause and effect. That is, competencies in the sense being described here are seen to specify the *kind* or *type* of individual we are dealing with, and the ensemble of specific behaviors that instance them are constitutive tokens of competencies of this type, rather than their consequent *effects* (Nelson, 1978).

Because much of what remains to be said about competencies and their relations to performance hinges on the foregoing distinction between conceptual connections of an internal or logical sort, and external or empirical relations of cause and effect, it is important to be especially clear about this difference. One way of better grasping this distinction is to remind ourselves that any sort of competence that could literally cause an action or otherwise enter into a causal relation with some concrete behavior would need to be a separate entity that either preceded that action or at any rate accompanyed it. That is, an event A can cause an event B to occur only if A and B are "numerically" distinct. If A and B were not independent or did not have separate identities in this sense, then we would be forced to conclude that A somehow caused itself, or that B is the effect of itself. Such consequences are obviously contrary to our ordinary understanding of what it could mean to talk coherently of causes and effects (Brand, 1970). Although much that has been written about the competence-performance relation has been predicted on making just such a numerical distinction between hidden inner states and their supposed behavioral effects, most of the difficulties encountered by those promoting such causal accounts come down to their failures to define competencies apart from their presumptive effects.

In sharp contrast to such causal accounts, theories of the reconstructive sort currently under discussion regularly view competencies and their associated behavioral manifestations, not as numerically distinct differences in existence, but rather as differences in the mode of manifestation of what is effectively the same existence. That is, the connections between the generative behavioral accomplishments of acting subjects and the general competencies which they exemplify are *constitutive* connections similar to those that hold between signs and their meanings in words (Harré & Secourd, 1972). For example, to complain, is *to be* discontented, and to conserve quantities across transformations in appearance is a manifestation of what being concrete operational is understood to mean in the context of a particular task. In both examples, the connection in question is a logical or conceptual and not an empirical or causal one. Talk of competencies, in this sense, is simply part of an adequate taxonomy of behaviors, not a reference to anything outside of such actions, and certainly not a reference to some second and hidden causal event. If talk of causality is somehow required, then competencies are at best *formal* causes in the classic Aristotelian sense and not mechanical (i.e., efficient + material) causes. In Habermas' (1979) terms, such competencies are part of the "causality of fate" and not the "causality of nature."

Hopefully, the foregoing remarks have served to successfully draw the distinction between theories that undertake to treat competencies as material causes and those that do not. What remains to be considered is how reconstructive theories of this final sort conceive of the problems of theory formation, theory evaluation, and the making of concrete behavioral predictions.


## THEORY FORMATION AND THEORY EVALUATION

The task of building up a reconstructive theory of human competence is not an attempt to account for events in terms of the mechanisms that produce them, but essentially a hermeneutic enterprise that consists primarily of efforts to read the performances of certain cohorts of individuals as instances of behaviors of a particular type. Obviously one could never invent such an interpretive framework or lend a common meaning to that which is implicit in a diversity of such performances by observing individuals in only one specific situation. The task facing such reconstructive theorists consequently amounts to finding some clear criteria for deciding when two or more behaviors can be referred back to a given competency or, in the case of a given individual, when a particular competency is being manifested over again. Although in some ways such attempts to typify human behaviors are similar to comparable taxonomic efforts in the natural sciences, social scientists interested in deciding when persons have performed another action of the same type are confronted with an additional difficulty that the natural scientist does not face. This second level of complexity grows out of the fact that, in trying to get clear about their own categoric rules, behavioral scientists must also somehow make room for the fact that the individuals who are the objects of their study also behave with reference to rules (Winch, 1958). Although no one is as yet very clear about what particular mixture of careful observation and creative insight is required to abduct some useful typology out of such complex admixtures, it is at least obvious that it is a task that persons manage to do, although not always with the same skill. The common starting place for such theory-building efforts is usually the ordinary folk psychology that competency theorist share with their audience. Beyond this, the candidacy of those various interpretive frameworks that have been proposed appears to be decided on the basis of how far they are judged to have gone toward making overt behavior altogether more intelligible.

Although the standards of confirmation and falsification appropriate to such reconstructive theories remain, then, somewhat unclear, it is at least the case that such theory building efforts can easily go wrong, and are no less in need of being checked out than are strictly causal theories (Bernstein, 1983). That is, reconstructive theories of cognitive competence, like theories of any type, demand some sort of empirical support. Because they are meant to account for certain regularities in manifest behavior, they disqualify themselves if the expectations they engender fail to conform to observed performances to some given degree. The open question discussed in the following section is the particular sense in which the merit of such theories hinges on their ability to generate testable predictions about the concrete behaviors of concrete individuals.


## ON PREDICTING PERFORMANCE
## FROM COMPETENCE

The preceeding paragraphs concerned the theory formation process by means of which investigators go about reading the competence-performance relation from right to left in the process of moving from direct observations to some interpretive account of those pattern concepts that elucidate and lend meaning to what would otherwise appear to be a mere random assortment of behaviors. Although such interpretive process and the taxonomies they construct are never complete, there is a point in the evolution of such theories after which the competency concepts that they generate are sufficiently well formulated and within the public domain to warrant our asking how closely they are related to the concrete actions of some particular individual or group of individuals.

Two approaches to this matter can be distinguished. One continues to read the competence-performance relation from right to left by asking whether, by their actions, given individuals can be said to possess or fulfill the conditions for membership in a particular competence type. The second undertakes to read the competence-performance relation the other way around by asking whether it is possible to predict an individual's performance from knowledge of his or her presumptive competencies. In what follows it is argued that although the answer to the first of these questions is a qualified yes, the answer to the second is an unqualified no.

The reason that reconstructive account of competence do not allow for explicit predictions regarding individual attempts at problem solving is that the pattern or type concepts to which they refer, although based on concrete particulars, have no one-to-one relation with such events. Therefore, they say nothing specific about what particular individuals will and will not do on a given occasion. Put somewhat differently, when a person somehow stays in character, and so regularly performs in certain ways *in virtue of* being the specific kind of individual he or she is, such behaviors, resembling as they do those actions that led to the original carving out of such a type concept on the first instance, support the diagnosis that we still are dealing with an individual of the sort in question. By contrast, such individuals need not, and in fact often do not, end up behaving in the ways sometimes implied by the ascription of such a competence to them. Belting the ball out of the park every 10th time at bat would certainly qualify one as a heavy hitter or home-run king, even though the best bet is that one will not repeat such a performance on the next trip to the plate. For such practical reasons the notion of actually applying competence concepts as a way of predicting the short-run future is not efficient. More importantly, because the relations between competencies and their manifestations are not contingent, but matters of identification, the whole enterprise of predicting one from the other is in some sense fundamentally incoherent. Instead, what ascriptions of competence sometimes can do is specify a set of formal restrictions on the likely range of behavioral variations of which an individual is somehow capable. Persons cannot consistently act out of character or behave as do persons of a different type without somehow forfeiting their identity. In this "weak" empirical sense, at least, there is some loose warrant for the *prima facie* presumption that to attribute a competence to an individual is to ascribe to him or her a certain likelihood of expressing a certain bounded class of behaviors, in virtue of being an individual of the type of question.

The alternative question of whether the actions of a given individual can be said to fulfill the conditions for membership in some particular competence type can be answered more simply and affirmatively. Because to show a particular pattern or type of behavior is what it literally means to possess a particular competency, anyone who regularly evidences such behavioral patterns automatically qualifies as a promising candidate. The only difficulty that arises in attempting to make such competence attributions with confidence is the practical one of knowing when one has sufficient data in hand. To characterize someone as having a particular sort of competence is not the same things as arguing that they possess a certain enumerable set of ritual behaviors that can be exhaustively assayed. Instead, a certain kind of creative expression of that competence capable of endlessly generating novel expressions of itself can be easily recognized, although not necessarily anticipated. The upshot of this line of thinking is that the list of criteria for competence is disjunctive rather than conjunctive, and there simply is no end to the ways in which an individual's credentials as a member of given competence type might be tested and on which they might conceivably succeed or fail.

For the reasons just outlined, there is no easy solution to the problem of deciding when to award and when to withhold attributions of competence that cover every possible case; nevertheless, reconstructive accounts of the sort currently under discussion do provide certain practical rules of thumb. What clearly would be advised against is any enterprise that stakes its claims regarding presumed competence on some single assessment probe. When competence is alternatively construed as a hidden cause, easily masked by recalcitrant performance factors, then even a single unambiguous behavioral success can be, and often is, taken as unimpeachable evidence for that competence on the grounds that every effect must have its cause. By insisting that competency concepts are pattern, rather than causal concepts, reconstructive accounts of the present sort manage to escape such unpalatable conclusions.

In a more positive vein, it also follows from those constructions that regard competence as a pattern concept that one need not attempt the impossible by enumerating the full intention of such concepts in order to come to some agreement about what they mean. As Wittgenstein pointed out (see Chapman & Dixon, 1987), if anything like such full coverage were required it would be impossible to learn a language. Following this lead, it can be argued that one only needs to be attentive to those criteria for competence that are sufficient to teach that concept to, for example, a child. Such potentially simplifying remarks do not imply, of course, that there may not be debate or difficulty in publicly settling any controversy over exactly what criteria must be in place before competency attributions can be made with confidence. They do, however, set out the agenda that must be followed if any chance for success is to be had. The chapters of this book are all devoted in one way or another to setting out what such criteria for cognitive competence might be.

## ACKNOWLEDGMENT

The preparation of this chapter was supported in part by Operating Grant OG0037045 from the Natural Sciences and Engineering Research Council of Canada.

## REFERENCES

Ashcraft, M. (1989). *Human memory and cognition*. Glenview, IL: Scott, Foresman.

Bernstein, R. (1983). *Beyond objectivism and relativism*. Philadelphia: University of Pennsylvania Press.

Blackburn, S. (1981). Rational animal? *The Behavioral and Brain Sciences, 4*, 331–332.

Brand, M. (1970). *The nature of human action*. Pittsburgh: Scott, Foresman.

Broughton, J. (1981). Piaget's structural developmental psychology. II. Logic and Psychology. *Human Development, 24*, 195–224.

Chapman, M., & Dixon, R. (Eds.). (1987). *Meaning and the growth of understanding: Wittgenstein's significance for developmental psychology*. Berlin: Springer-Verlag.

Chomsky, N. (1968). *Language and mind*. New York: Harcourt, Brace.

Cohen, L. J. (1981). Can human irrationality be experimentally demonstrated? *The Behavioral and Brain Sciences, 4*, 317–331.

Davidson, J. E., & Sternberg, R. J. (1985). Competence and performance in intellectual development. In E. D. Neimark, R. DeLisi, & J. L. Newman (Eds.), *Moderators of competence* (pp. 43–76). Hillsdale, NJ: Lawrence Erlbaum Associates.

Einhorn, H., & Hogarth, R. (1981). Rationality and the sanctity of competece. *The Behavioral and Brain Sciences, 4*, 334–335.

Evans, J., & Pollard, P. (1981). On defining rationality unreasonably. *The Behavioral and Brain Sciences, 4*, 335–336.

Flavell, J. (1977). *Cognitive development*. Englewood Cliffs, NJ: Prentice-Hall.

Flavell, J. H., & Wohlwill, J. F. (1969). Formal and functional aspects of cognitive development. In D. Elkind & J. H. Flavell (Eds.), *Studies in cognitive development: Essays in honor of Jean Piaget* (pp. 67–120). New York: Oxford University Press.

Fodor, J., & Garnett, M. (1966). Some reflections on competence and performance. In J. Lyons & R. J. Wales (Eds.), *Psycholinguistics papers* (pp. 135–179). Edinburgh: Edinburgh University Press.

Goodnow, J. J., & Cashmore, J. (1985). Culture and performance. In E. D. Neimark, R. DeLisi, & J. L. Newman (Eds.), *Moderators of competence* (pp. 77–98). Hillsdale, NJ: Lawrence Erlbaum Associates.

Griggs, R. (1981). Human reasoning: Can we judge before we understand? *The Behavioral and Brain Sciences, 4*, 338–339.

Habermas, J. (1979). *Communication and the evolution of society*. Boston: Beacon Press.

Habermas, J. (1988). *On the logic of the social sciences*. Cambridge, MA: MIT Press.

Harré, R., & Secord, P. (1972). *The explanation of social behavior*. Oxford: Basil Blackwell.

Heider, F. (1958). *The psychology of interpersonal relations*. New York: Wiley.

Lefebvre-Pinard, M., & Pinard, A. (1985). Taking charge of one's cognitive activity: A moderator of competence. In E. D. Neimark, R. DeLisi, & J. L. Newman (Eds.), *Moderators of competence* (pp. 191-211). Hillsdale, NJ: Lawrence Erlbaum Associates.

Lopez, L. (1981). Performing competently, *The Behavioral and Brain Sciences, 4*, 343-344.

Lycan, W. (1981). "Is" and "ought" in cognitive science. *The Behavioral and Brain Scieces, 4*, 344-345.

Macnamara, J. (1990). Ideals and psychology. *Canadian Psychology, 31*, 14-25.

Neimark, E. D. (1985). Moderators of competence: Challenges to the universality of Piagetian theory. In E. D. Neimark, R. DeLisi, & J. L. Newman (Eds.), *Moderators of competence* (pp. 1-14). Hillsdale, NJ: Lawrence Erlbaum Associates.

Nelson, K. (1978). Structural and developmental explanations: Stages in theoretic development. *The Behavioral and Brain Sciences, 2*, 196-197.

Olson, D. (1978). A structuralists view of explanation: A critique of Brainerd. *The Behavioral and Brain Sciences, 1*, 197-198.

Overton, W. F., & Newman, J. L. (1982). Cognitive development: A competence-activation / utilization approach. In T. M. Field, A. Houston, H. C. Quay, L. Troll, & G. E. Finley (Eds.), *Review of human development* (pp. 217-241). New York: Wiley.

Overton, W. F. (1985). Scientific methodologies and the competence-moderator-performance issue. In E. D. Neimark, R. DeLisi, & J. L. Newman (Eds.), *Moderators of competence* (pp. 15-41). Hillsdale, NJ: Lawrence Erlbaum Associates.

Peirce, C. (1931). *Collected papers of Charles Sanders Peirce* (C. Hartshorne & P. Weiss, Eds.). Cambridge, MA: Harvard University Press.

Sampson, G. (1981). Human rationality: Misleading linguistic analogies. *The Behavioral and Brain Sciences, 4*, 350-351.

Smedslund, J. (1977). Piaget's psychology in practice. *British Journal of Educational Psychology, 47*, 1-6.

Smedslund, J. (1981). Rationality is a necessary presupposition in Psychology. *The Behavioral and Brain Sciences, 4*, 352.

Winch, P. (1958). *The idea of social science and its relation to philosophy.* London: Routledge & Kegan Paul.

Wood, R., & Powers, C. (1987). Aspects of the competence-performance distinction: Educational, psychological and measurement issues. *Journal of Curriculum Studies, 19*, 409-424.

# Chapter 2

# Competence, Procedures, and Hardware: Conceptual and Empirical Considerations

Willis F. Overton
*Temple University*

What is competence? There are two necessary features of competence that require recognition at the outset of any discussion. First, competence is a type of explanation, not a type of description. A competence explanation is characterized by being normative and abstract. *Competence* refers to an idealization of the organization, pattern, design, form, or structure of the event or system being explained. Thus, competence is explanation from pattern or design.

The second essential feature of competence is that it is one among several types of explanations that enter into scientific inquiry. Competence is introduced into scientific discourse to explain the relatively stable, enduring components of the domain under examination (Overton, 1985, 1990; Overton & Newman, 1982). It does not explain how competence is accessed and implemented. It does not explain the origin of competence itself. Answers to these latter questions require process explanations, procedural explanations, and neurobiological explanations. A complete scientific explanation of behavior needs the totality of several types of explanation, including competence explanations.

In this chapter I locate competence as an explanation within the context of contemporary empirical scientific discourse. In this effort I clarify the nature and value of competence explanations and demonstrate their necessary relationship with other types of scientific explanation. Following discussions of the place of competence in scientific discourse, and the relationships of competence to other forms of scientific explanation (i.e., procedures, hardware, and process), I describe some findings drawn from my own research project on the development of deductive reasoning. I hope this serves as an empirical example of the heuristic value of a developmental competence-procedure approach to our understanding of developmental phenomena.

Chandler (1987) has described an important isomorphism between the history of philosophy's understanding of the nature of knowledge, and the development of knowledge in human ontogenesis. This isomorphic sequence Chandler presented as stations of epistemology. The sequence serves as a base for a further elaboration into stations of scientific knowing. At the initial station described by Chandler, both philosophical thought and the individual organism hold a naive realist position. This *objectivist* epistemology lives by the claim that "seeing is believing" and asserts that sufficient observation will yield a fixed, absolute, objective "Truth" that exists independently of the mind. The second station continues to hold to the objectivist standard but accepts the fallibility of naive and time-limited inspection. Here, "seeing" is clouded by illusion, rumor, prejudice and other "errors." Tools of logic and time are needed to sort observations into the illusory and "the real." This station is sometimes defined as *"historical" realism* (Overton, in press-a).

At the third station of epistemology, marked in philosophy by the emergence of *contemporary rationalism*, and in ontogenesis by early formal thought, the objectivist standard is abandoned. Realism is rejected in favor of a recognition that all human knowledge derives from the human activity of interpretation (Overton, in press-a). This dawning awareness of the person-relative quality of human knowledge tends initially to lead to choices that cycle between skepticism, marked by a belief in the complete uncertainty of all knowledge, and dogmatism, marked by the belief that there must be some omniscient source of truth that resides outside human interpretation.

As the rationalist position develops it leads to the fourth epistemological station that Chandler called *post-skeptical rationalism*. Here, recognition that all knowledge is constructed knowledge—and hence, never absolute—moves beyond skepticism–dogmatism to a strategy of asserting that arguable good reasons, developed in the context of agreed upon knowledge criteria, can function at various levels of plausibility as a system for choosing one belief or one action over another.

## STATIONS OF SCIENTIFIC KNOWLEDGE

These four stations of epistemology have strongly influenced the development of stations of scientific knowledge (see Overton, 1984, 1985, in press-a; Piaget & Garcia, 1986), and it is in this specific arena that the question of the scientific legitimacy of competence type explanations becomes evident. The first station of scientific knowledge corresponded to the epistemology of naive realism, and was called *positivism*. As a strategy designed to distinguish scientific knowledge from other knowing activities, positivism held that to be properly scientific any explanatory statement must be an empirical generalization induced directly from observation, and must be demonstrably capable of being reduced to observation.

The force of positivism's criterion of science was to warn the aspiring scientist—on penalty of being branded nonscientific—to avoid speculation and interpretation, and to swear fealty and devotion to description and direct observation. Not only did this station require that explanation both temporally and logically follow complete description, but explanation itself, as a generalization inductively drawn from direct observation, of necessity, had to be composed of only observationally based antecedent-consequent functional statements. Thus, explanations became known as empirical generalizations.

*Conventionalism* constituted the second station of scientific knowledge. This strategy for distinguishing science from other types of knowledge conserved the realist objectivist tenets of positivism. However, conventionalism recognized that not all features of theory could be reduced to direct observations. As a consequence, conventionalism agreed to admit nonreducible features of theory into the arena of legitimate science. But theory so defined was also understood to function only as a means of arranging the hard data of description. Thus, theories or models came to be thought of as heuristic devices that should fade in scientific importance once time and observation had led to explanatory laws based on inductive generalizations from the reality of hard data. Under this interpretation, legitimate scientific explanation remained tied to inductive empirical generalizations drawn from direct observations of antecedents and consequences.

At both of the realist objectivist stations of science a rigid distinction was maintained between theory and data, interpretation and fact, explanation and description. And it was offered as an absolute necessity that data, fact, observation, and description constituted the court of final appeal for scientific merit. This attitude engendered various methodological slogans designed to keep investigators on the path to absolute, objective Truth; "if you describe carefully enough, explanation will take care of itself," "stay close to the data, avoid speculation," "see what the data tells you," "interpretation must await further data," "we need local explanations, not universal explanation," "explanations must be tied to observables either as intervening variables, or as hypothetical constructs."

It is clear that at these realist scientific stations there has been no room for pattern or competence explanations as legitimate scientific explanation. If "competence" is even introduced at these stations it is only used to suggest that the investigator has unearthed some faint glimmer of an otherwise obscure ability hidden by measurement error. According to this interpretation, competence merely points toward an underlying ability that constitutes the reality, and that will be directly observed and described once the debris of error is cut away.

The third station of science emerged out of a renewed focus on rationalism or *interpretationism* as a viable epistemological approach. Although rationalism has a history as ancient as realism (Overton, in press-a, in press-b), its contemporary impact on science is marked by the work of Norwood Russell Hanson (1958). Hanson developed the influential argument that all data, including the data of observation, are "theory laden" (i.e., necessarily interpretative), and the corollary argument that *explanation in science involves discerning patterns rather than observing cause-effect sequences.* This argument erased the realist's clear distinction between descriptive facts and interpretations, and reintroduced pattern or competence as legitimate scientific explanation. Following from Hanson's work, Kuhn (1962, 1977) presented his now famous thesis that at every level science is controlled by interpretative paradigms and these paradigms pervade both observational data and the methodology of theory choice.

By establishing interpretation as basic to and inherent in the scientific enterprise, this station of science opened up the door of relativism, and as with the underlying epistemological station, a *skeptical-dogmatic* axis soon developed. The skeptical pole was established by Feyerabend (1978) who made radical relativism a scientific virtue. If the human activity of interpretation is a nondissectable feature of science—so the argument goes—then there is no basis for making judgments of good or bad interpretations. My interpretation is as good as yours because there are no absolute, objective criteria for deciding between judgments. Hence, "anything goes" in science as it does in other forms of knowing.

Indeed, as skepticism progresses it becomes increasingly difficult to discriminate empirical science from any other knowing activities. As a result, this pole moves through phases of its own line of development from empirical to hermeneutic science, to narrative and rhetorical knowing, to reconstructionism and deconstructionism, and into postmodern thought (see Overton, in press-a). With each new phase the skeptical pole asserts its antifoundational spirit and advances toward solipsism. An important corollary of this movement is that all types of universals are increasingly devalued in discourse because they appear to evoke the ghost of some transpersonal order that has been rejected. Thus, the historical, the contingent, the particular gain a privileged status in this system that asserts that there is no privilege. In this atmosphere there is no room for the abstract, the normative, and hence no room for competence.

In the face of the specter of on rushing solipsism, the dogmatic pole of the skepticism-dogmatic axis has arisen as a renewed faith in the methods-of-science. "Scientific method," like a religious sacrament, is accepted as the unquestioned means for achieving ultimate certainty. This amounts to a form of neo-positivism with an insistence on the absolute priority of particulars, observation, description, analysis, and induction (see Siegler & Shipley, 1987; Sugarman, 1987a, 1987b). As Kessen (1984) has pointed out this "zest for analysis and for particulars may lie close to the center of American psychology's unspoken creed" (p. 11).

As rationalism has generated a skepticism–dogmatism axis, it has also es-tablished the context for moving forward to a post-skeptical station of empiri-cal scientific knowledge. At this fourth station, the argument that all knowing emerges out of activity forms the point of origin for any inquiry into the possi-bility of constructing arguable good reasons as a foundation for a relatively stable, coherent, consistent, and plausible system of empirical scientific knowledge. The writings of Lakatos (1978) on scientific research programs, Laudan (1977, 1984) on scientific research traditions, Putnam's (1987, 1988) exploration of meaning and meaning holism, and Dennett's (1987) and Marr's (1982) analyses of strategies of scientific explanation all represent significant components of this effort.

The post-skeptical rationalist station of science begins—as do all the sta-tions of science—in the commonsense actual or manifest world (Overton, in press-a; Sellars, 1963). This manifest world is the conceptual lens that we, mere-ly through being human, employ in day to day life. Like all other stations, this one also takes as its general aim the establishment of order and organiza-tion in the chaos of contradictory experiences that emerge in this manifest world. And like other stations, this one also brings about order and organization through explanation. Thus, at all the stations of scientific knowledge science moves from the manifest image of man-in-the-world to the scientific image of man-in-the-world. However, at this rationalist station order is not established by ever intensified micro-observations and micro-descriptions designed to un-cover absolute, objective, fixed functional relationships that will yield induc-tive universal generalizations as explanations. This realist strategy has been abandoned.

At the fourth station of scientific knowledge order is brought about by con-structing *abstract patterns* that plausibly, intelligibly, and coherently systema-tize the domain of inquiry. These abstract patterns, arrived at through abduc-tive or retroductive inference process (interpretation), constitute the primary explanations of science. Causal laws are formulated within and derive their meaning from the pattern context (see Overton, in press-a). Pattern explana-tion avoids regression to skepticism-dogmaticism by being formulated and tested according to criteria that are explicitly recognized as the product of human discourse. These criteria have included scope of application, depth, logical con-sistency, fruitfulness, and empirical support.

If we now attend directly to the concept of competence, it should be clear that as abstract, normative, pattern explanation, this concept finds scientific legitimacy only at the scientific station of post-skeptical rationalism. Here, ab-stract patterns are not mere heuristic devices that temporarily substitute for real explanation, nor the symptoms of some hidden ability called competence.

Rationalism—or what Putnam (1988) called "internal realism" and Lakoff (1987) called "experiential realism"—establishes the context that lends scien-tific meaning to competence explanations. However, a more detailed analysis is needed to demonstrate the use of competence as psychological explanation, to illustrate specific features of competence, and to show how competence is related to other forms of psychological explanation. A first approximation to this effort, begins with the recognition that the primary types of explanation offered in any field have changed little since the general explanatory scheme proposed by Aristotle.

## SCIENTIFIC EXPLANATION

Aristotle asserted that any phenomenon was completely understood only when four causes or explanations were offered for that phenomenon. These four consisted of *material* cause (that which the thing is made of), *efficient* cause (that which moves a thing), *formal* cause (the form or pattern of the thing), and *final* cause (that which the thing is directed toward) (see Overton, 1985, in press-a, in press-b). Material and efficient causes are particulars and, in principle, observable. It is for this reason, of course, that they are favored by any system that accepts the realist standards. They are also causal in the traditional sense of a cause as being something that produces something. Contemporary examples of material causes include the range of neurobiological factors such as genetic, physiological, and neurological factors. Contemporary examples of efficient causes include environmental, cultural, and situational factors.

Formal and final causes are abstract universals and thus, in principle, not observable. Both are pattern explanations. Formal causes define synchronic patterns; final causes define diachronic (developmental) patterns. These explanations are not productive in a causal sense, but rather, they are principles that introduce coherence and intelligibility. When reasons are contrasted with causes in schemes of scientific explanations, formal and final explanation constitute reasons. The structure of the atom, the structure of DNA, the structure of the solar system, and the structure of the universe are examples of formal explanation drawn from the natural sciences. Kinship structures, mental structures, mental organization, structures of language, ego, and superego, dynamisms, schemes, operations, and cognitive structures are formal explanations drawn from the human sciences. The second law of thermodynamics is a contemporary example of final explanation in the natural sciences. Piaget's equilibration process, Werner's orthogenetic principle, Erikson's epigenetic principle, and Margaret Mahler's individuation-separation process are final explanations in developmental psychology.

Today the labels have changed and the terms *material, efficient, formal*, and *final* are infrequently directly discussed. However, in contemporary theories of mind and in the cognitive sciences the surrogates of the four causes—"hardware" explanation, "procedural" (also "algorithmic," "functional," and "semantic") explanation, and synchronic and diachronic "competence" (also "pattern," "design," "syntactic") explanation—continue to frame the dialogue and the debate about what constitutes adequate scientific explanation. The most significant recent change in the four explanatory types is that they have come to be thought of as related levels of analysis from the hardware, to the procedural, to the competence level (see Dennett, 1987; Marr, 1981, 1982; Searle, 1984).

Within the competence–procedure–hardware framework of scientific explanation significant questions about the nature of mind have centered around issues of whether all levels are required for adequate explanation; whether a particular level might be eliminated or reduced to other levels (P.M. Churchland, 1981; P.S. Churchland, 1986; Dennett, 1987; Searle, 1984); whether the levels themselves are best formulated within the framework of a computer metaphor or an organic metaphor (Lycan, 1987; Overton, 1990, in press-c). Thus, for example, both P.M. Churchland (1981) and P.S. Churchland (1986) take an eliminative materialist position and argue that adequate explanation can be established at the neurophysiological hardware level, and other levels are reducible to this; Searle (1984, 1990) claimed that the procedural or algorithmic level is an unnecessary interposition between the physical and the mental levels; Dennett (1987) discussed the necessity of each of the levels. It should not be surprising that those who favor reduction to causal levels are the same individuals who continue to favor the realist scientific strategies described earlier.

## FUNCTIONALISM AND SCIENTIFIC EXPLANATION

Before directly examining hardware, procedures, and competence as interrelated levels of explanation it is important to emphasize that these explanations are framed by a functional understanding of the nature of human systems of behavior and behavioral development. The explanations are all functional in nature. The patterns are *patterns of activity* and change, and the causal features attend to manifest or real-time processing in relation to inputs, outputs, and other internal states of the organism. These are all criterial features of contemporary functionalism. However, "functionalism" incorporates a variety of approaches (Garfield, 1988; Overton, 1984, 1990), and recently certain of these have come under increasing criticism (Garfield, 1988; Lycan, 1987; Putnam, 1988; Searle, 1984, 1990). The basic issue of concern is not functionalism itself, but the choice of underlying metaphor to guide further elaboration of the functionalist program.

Early functionalists in the time of William James and John Dewey drew their functionalism out of an organic metaphor. Functionalism was understood in terms of activity as it related to the inherent organization of the activity, function as related to its form or structure, adaptation as related to the forms of adaptation, ends as related to the means for their achievement. Later functionalists from the time of Angell, Carr, and Woodworth replaced the organic metaphor with the machine metaphor. Under the influence of a 19th-century physics that understood energy as being separate and distinct from structure, activity came to be understood as separate and distinct from organization, adaptation *produced* forms, activity itself was *caused by* inputs. Sometimes, as in the case of Watson and Skinner, the machine metaphor faded sufficiently into the background so that only the causal (functional) concerns with inputs and outputs were recognizable. At other times a variety of machines, from hydraulic systems, to telegraph systems, telephone switchboards, and finally digital computers have explicitly framed explanation. Today, critics of machine functionalism and a subspecies of machine functionalism called *psychofunctionalism*, are again urging the rejection of the machine metaphor (Lakoff, 1987; Lycan, 1987; Macnamara, 1986; Putnam, 1988; Pylyshyn, 1984; Searle, 1984, 1990) and a replacement by an organic metaphor (Johnson, 1987; Lakoff, 1987; Lycan, 1987; Overton, 1990).

The importance of a move to an organic metaphor as the guiding conceptual foundation for functionalism cannot be overemphasized. It is equivalent to—and in some ways identical with (see Overton, in press-b)—the move from the stations of epistemological realism to the stations of epistemological rationalism. It is only from this organic conceptual foundation that pattern explanation and causal explanation (structure and function) are joined into a unified meaningful whole. It is only from this vantage point that patterns establish meaning, coherence, intelligibility, and understanding while causality yields the pragmatics of analysis, implementation, and manifest plausibility. This type of meaning holism (Putnam, 1988) is the province of the organic, not the machine.

Organic functionalism requires hardware, procedures, and competence as an integrated organization of explanatory types. Hardware and procedures constitute the causal mechanisms according to which competence functions. The levels form a hierarchical system of explanation that is holistically regulated. Each level requires and interacts with the others but predictions made from any one level will differ from predictions made from another level.

## COMPETENCE–PROCEDURES–HARDWARE

Competence refers to the design features of the system that is being explained. The investigator beings the process of explanation by asking the functional question of what the system is for. The answer to this question constitutes the general domain of inquiry and, with proper specification, it leads to the question of the design of the system that serves this function. For example, many theories of human development—including Jean Piaget's cognitive theory and John

Bowlby's social-emotional theory—assert that "adaptation" constitutes the most general function of the human organism. Adaptation is usually defined according to some interpretation of survival, and thus the theories align themselves with a more inclusive evolutionary theory. Having taken this stance with respect to the functional question, investigators further specify more circumscribed domains of the adaptation. Piaget focuses on the adaptational value of thinking that is coherent, noncontradictory, and precise (i.e., logical reasoning). Bowlby focused on the adaptational value of behavior that maintains or strengthens bonds of close interpersonal relationships (i.e., attachment). These circumscribed domains form the specific focus of the theory (i.e., the system of propositions that will constitute explanation). After addressing the question of what the system is for, the investigator turns to the question of the nature of the design or organization that serves this function. Here Piaget (Piaget & Garcia, 1986) proposed a design that has the character of a logic system and Bowlby proposed a design that is referred to as a "behavioral attachment system" (see Hinde, 1982; Overton, in press-a; Sroufe, 1977).

The design that the theorist articulates constitutes the competence in the domain in question. This is not a thing that exists in the head of the organism. Such a position would only be appropriate to the realist who believes that all explanation is description. Competence is a type of explanation that asserts that it captures organizational features of the organism in the domain under examination. For example, in the field of the development of logical reasoning (Overton, 1990), competence or mental logical theorists claim that the rules that have been derived by logicians to represent the structure of valid arguments may be taken as a relatively adequate *model* of the normative, idealized, abstract operations of mind in this domain. The model constitutes logical competence.

A particularly critical attribute of a competence model is that it predicts universal and necessary features of the domain under investigation. For example, in logical reasoning the competence model addresses questions concerning the organism's ability to comprehend or understand valid argument forms. It predicts the psychological availability of specifically logical (i.e., necessary and universal) features of deductive reasoning. Thus, with respect to the competence model itself, the developmental investigator can ask empirical questions about the adequacy of the particular model as a general representation of the organism's logical knowledge, about the developmental timing of the availability of this logical knowledge, about precursor forms of competence that approximate this competence.

The competence model does not, however, specify the particular details of how this design is accessed and implemented. Access and implementation are questions for the procedural model or procedural explanation. Russell (1987) captured this important detail when he pointed out that the competence is not to be regarded "as 'mental representations' that the adult thinker uses when he reasons, but . . . idealizations of the system of thought to which the 'normal adult' has access. Sometimes the access is good, sometimes poor" (p. 41).

Competence thus necessarily leads to procedures, because procedural explanation offers explanation for *how* competence may be accessed, implemented, and expressed. And procedures require competence, because procedures operate as detached and empty causal mechanisms unless they are grounded in the meaning structure provided by competence (see Marr, 1981). If procedures are explored without reference to competence as they often are in experimental psychology, then we return to the standards of realist science with the hope and wish that some day in some way the generation of numerous causal mechanisms will inductively yield an explanatory synthesis.

Procedural explanation is offered to explain the manifest or real-time activities that access and implement competence. That is, procedures predict specific causal features of task solutions. As competence is directed toward understanding, procedures are directed toward successful task performance. As competence is relatively context free, procedures are context embedded. For procedural explanation the investigator proposes some algorithm or heuristic that mimics or imitates the organism's real time activity and this serves as a procedural model. The model is functional in nature in the sense that it identifies some token psychological state (e.g., logical reasoning according to truth tables) with some token behavioral state (e.g., actual truth table manipulation or some derived measure of this), or some token physical state (e.g., some neurophysiological state), and it is sensitive to inputs and outputs (e.g., the specific content of logical problems) (see Garfield, 1988).

Because the kinds of procedures that can be used to account for the access and implementation of competence are limited only by these functional criteria, the number of candidates for designation as procedures is large. If we again take logical reasoning as the domain of interest, it may be the case—as, in fact, proposed by various investigators—that the actual processing of logical problems takes place by reasoning in terms of truth tables (Osherson, 1975); by reasoning in terms of Venn diagrams (Revlis, 1975); by reasoning in terms of natural deductive procedures (Braine, 1990); by reasoning according to mental models (Johnson-Laird, 1983), by pragmatic methods (Cheng & Holyoak, 1985; Cheng, Holyoak, Nisbett, & Oliver, 1986), or by various methods employing direct experience (Griggs, 1983; Mandler, 1983). Further, procedures may reflect individual differences or individual strategies, and as a consequence, different people may at different times and under different circumstances use different procedures in the actual processing of logical problems. The empirical problem is not necessarily to choose among these alternatives, but to test, in the context of available competence, when and under what conditions the alternatives best facilitate logical reasoning.

The formal distinction between the competence and the procedural model is illustrated in the contrast between Dennett's (1987) presentation of the competence model as a "fictional notation system" and Craik's (1943) presentation of the procedural model as a "working model." About competence, Dennett (1987) stated:

> The idea of a notational world, then is the idea of a model—but not the actual, real, true model—of one's internal representations. The theorist wishing to characterize the narrow psychological states of a creature, or in other words, the organismic contribution of that creature . . . *describes* a fictional world; the description exists on paper, the fictional world does not exist, but the inhabitants of the fictional world are treated as the notional referents of the subject's representations. . . . (pp. 154-155)

On the other hand, in keeping with the actual internal representations of procedural models Craik (1943) asserted:

> By model we thus mean any physical or chemical system which has a similar relation—structure to that of the process it imitates. By "relation-structure" I do not mean some obscure nonphysical entity which attends the model, but the fact that it is a physical working model which works in the same way at the process it parallels. . . . My hypothesis then is that thought models, or parallels reality. (p. 61)

Although there is general agreement that procedures, as distinct from competence, must be modeled on actual or manifest real-time activities, Craik's limiting argument for a "*physical*" working model demonstrates an early commitment to the ideal of machine functionalism or psychofunctionalism where the test of the adequacy of a model rest on its ability to pass the test of the Turing machine. That is, within these types of functionalism a procedure is adequate or "effective" to the extent that it can be carried out by a simple machine.

Johnson-Laird's (1983) more recent work on mental models as "effective procedures" in the domain of logical reasoning is a contemporary example of a commitment to such a machine criterion of adequacy (see also Johnson-Laird, Byrne, & Tabossi, 1989). Johnson-Laird, in fact, proposed to limit psychological theory to just this test and just this level of explanation. As he said, "My proposed criterion for psychological theories is that they count as putative explanation only if it is possible to formulate them as effective procedures . . ." (p. 7). And, "My starting-point will be Craik's intuitive idea of an inner mental replica that has the same 'relation-structure' as the phenomenon that it represents" (p. 11). As stated earlier, this machine metaphor is not a necessary feature of functionalism and its use as a standard leads to an exclusionary stance with respect to explanation, and a consequent failure to consider a necessary interrelationship among levels of explanation. Macnamara (1986), who presented a type of organic functionalism in the domain of logical reasoning, argues that the very use of the term *procedures* is misleading: "A procedure is an electronic device that in the last analysis can be described completely in the language of physics. I do not call the mind's interpretative devices procedures but simply interpreters" (p. 35).

One of the most important reasons for keeping clear the formal distinction between competence (i.e., fictional notation systems) and the procedural (i.e., simulations of actual or manifest operations) models is that it highlights the often misunderstood fact that empirical tests designed to assess procedures do not count for or against any particular competence notation. For example, it is quite possible to conclude on the basis of empirical research that people rarely *actually* think in terms of truth tables. This counts against the plausibility of truth-table thinking as an effective procedure or interpreter. However, even if no one ever actually thinks in terms of truth tables, it is still quite reasonable to accept truth-table notation as the notation for the competence model of logical reasoning. The empirical test for the plausibility of the truth-table notation as an adequate competence model (see Smith, 1987) is quite distinct from the test of the truth table as a plausible procedural model.

The final and most particular level of analysis, is the *hardware* level. Here a physical strategy is employed and attempts are made to describe the physical mechanisms (e.g., neurophysiological mechanisms) that implement the design constrained procedures. Little needs to be said about this familiar level except perhaps to note that the term *hardware* itself derives from a machine metaphor and this level might perhaps simply be known as the neurobiological level of explanation.

## DEVELOPMENT AND COMPETENCE-PROCEDURE-HARDWARE EXPLANATION

The one feature still missing from this account of the hierarchical relationship among competence, procedures, and hardware explanations is any statement of how such a scheme would incorporate a developmental or change dimension. There are several potential solutions to this problem. It could be assumed that the active processes that are instances of each explanatory type are built into the system. This is the classical nativist solution. Or it could be assumed that the processes themselves are directly acquired from the environment. This is the classical empiricist solution. Both of these solutions are, in fact, generated by the machine metaphor.

The organic functionalist solution to the explanation of development calls on the diachronic dimension of pattern explanation (the Old Aristotelian final cause). It is maintained that the active processes that correspond to each explanatory type (competence, procedure, hardware)—and hence, the explanatory types in their specific instantiations—become transformed across development. Each transformation marks major development phases. The transformation are ordered and explained according to some pattern. However, here the pattern and the process corresponding to the pattern, is progressive in nature (see Overton, in press-a). Pattern-progressive explanations are explanations of development itself, whereas competence, procedures, and hardware are explanations of what has developed at any point in the developmental series.

To illustrate the developmental explanation consider Werner's (1957) Orthogenetic Principle. This explanatory principle asserts that the pattern of all developmental series is from states of globality and lack of differentiation of parts, to states of increased articulation, differentiation, and hierarchical integration. The functional process that is the direct complement to this diachronic pattern explanation is found in Piaget's (1987) equilibration process—itself framed by an adaptational context. The equilibration process asserts that pattern differentiations and integrations are constructed through the activity of assimilation/ accommodation (Overton, 1989) and lead to increasingly adaptational patterns.

When this developmental explanatory scheme is applied to a particular domain such as logical reasoning it suggests that initially there is little differentiation at a psychological level between competence, procedures, and hardware. The initial state of the organism is understood as an organized system of biological activity. Psychological organization and processes differentiate out of this neutral matrix through the assimilation/accommodation activities of the organism. Thus, both competence and procedural systems initially emerge from the organized embodied experiences of the organism—a biological level of competence, procedures, and hardware. The initial psychological (sensorimotor) development is procedural in nature, but this develops in the context of the original biological competence and it results in the acquisition of the first psychological competence. At this level there is a logic, but it is a logic defined by organized activity, not reasoning.

As the developmental process proceeds, further differentiations and integrations lead to new more adapted states that are characterized as "representational" or "conceptual" (Overton, 1989, 1990). At this new level, novel competence and procedures again differentiate. Here, the competence pattern may be referenced by a class logic notational system or some other notation. Logical thinking becomes available but the logic is fragmentary in nature and does not permit generalized systematic inference across a network valid argument forms (see Markovits, Schleifer, & Fortier, 1989). At the next level of adaptive differentiation and integration, the acquired system can be characterized as a relatively complete predicate logic system and a system of procedures that access and implement this competence. This level is identified as the level of formal deductive reasoning.

Thus far, I have demonstrated that pattern explanation is required for a complete understanding of human functioning and human development, that pattern explanation finds true scientific legitimacy only at the post-skeptical rationalist station of science, that pattern explanation is thoroughly functionalist in nature, and that pattern explanation is a part of an integrated organization of explanatory types. In the final section of this chapter I present an overview of a specific empirical research program that has been formulated and conducted within this conceptual frame.

## COMPETENCE PROCEDURES AND DEDUCTIVE REASONING: EMPIRICAL RESEARCH

For several years my students, colleagues, and I have been investigating problems related to the developmental availability of deductive reasoning competence, and real-time procedures that access and implement competence. Conditional ("If . . . then . . . ") sentences are central to deductive reasoning because they can express implication, and implication is the pivotal concept in any system of logic. Accordingly, reasoning with conditionals has been the focus of our research.

Our general working hypothesis has been that although there are early precursor forms of logical competence (i.e., a logic of action, a fragmentary class logic), the competence that permits fully systematic deductive reasoning does not become available until the adolescent years. Further, once available, a variety of real-time procedures may be required to successfully access and implement the competence. The idea of a systemic or systematic availability refers to the fact that deductive understanding (i.e., competence) involves a network of inference rather than being limited to only one or two specific types of inferences (see Smith, 1987). For example it may be the case that young children understand some form of the inference "If p, then q; p; therefore q." However, systemic deductive competence is in evidence only when this becomes the valid Modus Ponens inference rather than a promise, or a causal, or temporal sequence. This Modus Ponens inference, in turn, becomes a part of a network of inferences including the valid Modus Tollens ("If p, then q; not q; therefore not p"), as well as the invalid inference forms, Denied Antecedent ("If p, then q; not p; therefore not q") and Affirmed Consequence ("If p, then q; q; therefore p").

In an early series of studies, O'Brien and Overton (1980, 1982) examined availability (a competence issue) and the manner in which interpretation (a procedural issue) of the conditional "If . . . then . . ." sentence influences accessibility. In every day usage people may interpret "If . . . then . . ." sentences as causal, temporal, or biconditional ("If and only if") relationships, rather than as a relationship of implication. When the task is designed to evaluate the understanding of formal implication, the other types of interpretations yield the appearance of poor logical reasoning. However, the failure may be the product or poor access to the logical competence, rather than the absence of this competence.

These studies employed a contradiction training technique. Participants in Grades 3, 4, 7, 12, and college were presented with an incomplete conditional rule; "If a worker is ——— years of age, or older, then that person will receive at least $350 each week." Following the rule presentation, a series of 12 exemplars of ages and salaries were given (e.g., A 20-year-old who makes $50 per week; A 60-year-old who makes $600 per week). The task was to select, for each exemplar, what could be inferred about the missing age in the rule (i.e., "The age in the rule is more than . . . ."; "the age in the rule is . . . at most"; "Nothing at all").

During the early trials there is a tendency to make inference errors suggesting that participants fail to interpret the rule as a conditional. However, on the sixth trial, an exemplar was presented that directly contradicted such faulty interpretations. It was expected that this procedure would facilitate access, via interpretative procedures, to the appropriate logical competence for those individuals who had this competence available. The results of these studies demonstrated the availability of competence at Grade 12, and at the college level. At these age levels, the contradiction training successfully facilitated performance, and this enhanced performance generalized to other deductive reasoning tasks. The studies did not, however, show any evidence of the availability of competence at ages earlier than Grade 12, and this became an issue for later investigations.

The interpretation of the conditional sentence is a fundamental issue for procedural models of deduction. However, there are other classes of variables, both organismic and environmental, that also implicate real-time procedures. One of these is cognitive style. In an effort to analyze the role of cognitive style in accessing and implementing available deductive competence, an investigation was conducted with participants from Grades 8, 10, and 12 (Overton, Byrnes, & O'Brien, 1985). The contradiction training paradigm was again employed, but in this study the participants were also tested for Reflective–Impulsive cognitive style, by means of the Matching Familiar Figures test. As in the earlier research, it was found that the availability of deductive competence was in evidence at Grade 12, but not earlier. At this grade, contradiction training enhanced performance, and generalized to another deductive task. A reflective cognitive style was found to enhance performance at all age levels. However, for the generalization deductive task, the benefits of a reflective style were limited primarily to those who had demonstrated the availability of competence. Thus, it appears that once deductive competence is available, and interpretative procedures access this competence, a reflective cognitive style operates as a procedural support to further facilitate implementation of the competence.

The fact that the contradiction-training paradigm did not yield evidence of deductive competence prior to Grade 12 precluded any exploration of the role of interpretative procedures during childhood and early adolescence in these early studies. This led to a more direct exploration of the understanding of "If . . . then . . ." sentences, and precursors to such understandings. In order to claim a formal deductive understanding of "If p, then q" as an implication, it must be shown that the following are recognized: (a) that particular instances of the antecedent (p) and consequence (q) clause of the sentence are permissible; (b) that other instances are not permissible; and (c) that others are indeterminate. Specifically, given "If p, then q," it is the case that "p and q" is permitted, "p and not-q" is not permitted, and "not-p and q" and "not-p and not-q" are indeterminate. For example, with the sentence "If it has rained, then the grass is wet," finding an instance of "rain and wet" supports the truth of the sentence; finding "rain and not wet" falsifies the sentence' and finding "no rain and wet" or "not rain and not wet" yield uncertainty about the truth of the sentence.

An obvious precursor to a formal deductive understanding of implication is the understanding of the certainty and uncertainty of conclusions. Unless it is recognized that it is *certain* that "p and not-q" falsify the sentence, and unless this knowledge is coordinated with the certainty and uncertainty of the other instances, a formal deductive competence cannot be claimed. In an initial study (Byrnes & Overton, 1986), we examined the ability of children at Grades 1, 3, and 5, to draw certain and uncertain conclusions. It was expected, following Piaget's (1987) work on necessity, that concepts of certainty and uncertainty would first develop in nonformal concrete and causal contexts, and only later in formal deductive contexts. At each grade, the children's conclusions were evaluated in all three contexts. The *concrete* context involved a task requiring conclusions about whether objects would fit into openings in a box, the *causal* context a task requiring conclusions about pictured causal sequences, and the *formal deductive* context conditional syllogisms.

Our predictions were supported, and we found that an understanding of, and discrimination between certain and uncertain conclusions is mastered in concrete and causal context by Grade 5. However, this understanding is just beginning to emerge at Grade 5 for formal deductions. This is consistent with Piaget's position that formal competence begins to become available around 10–12 years. If this is the case, it appears that the next several years may be a period of consolidation for the formal competence, which only then demonstrates systemic availability.

In the next study (Byrnes & Overton, 1988), we focused more specifically on the understanding of "If p, then q" as a formal implication. Participants at Grades 3, 5, 8, and college level were evaluated with several procedures designed to elicit understanding of the coordination between permitted and nonpermitted instances of formal application, and distinction between the conditional and other propositional types, particularly the biconditional ("If and only if''). The findings demonstrated that a significant increase in the understanding of formal implication occurs between Grades 3 and 5, and again between Grade 8 and college level.

The results of this study again support the position that formal deductive competence begins to emerge in an incomplete form around 10–12 years of age, and then goes through a consolidation process. Another important finding of this study is that the primary improvement that occurs between Grade 8 and the college level is in the ability to distinguish the conditional from the biconditional. Because both the conditional and biconditional are formal deductive relationships, it can be speculated that the period beginning at approximately Grade 8 marks the time during which novel interpretative procedures are acquired to adequately interpret and implement the deductive competence. It may be the case, as with means–ends relationships generally, that the emergence of a novel competence initially uses old procedures, and subsequently, new procedures are acquired to meet the demands of the new competence.

When the findings of these latter two studies are considered together, a pattern begins to emerge, suggesting that the period between approximately 10 and 14 years is the time of achievement and consolidation of formal competence, and the period between approximately 14 and 18 years is the time during which novel procedures, adequate to the novel competence, are developed. This schema would also account for why the contradiction training paradigm, employed in earlier research, was unable to detect the availability of competence prior to Grade 12. This paradigm was designed to introduce a formal contradiction that would lead the person from one formal interpretation of the conditional (the biconditional), to another formal interpretation (the conditional). However, distinguishing among such formal interpretations is exactly the interpretative procedural skill that may develop only in the later adolescent years. Thus, the contradiction training paradigm may be evaluating a later developing procedural skill. Once this skill is operating (i.e., by Grade 12) it can access competence, but not before.

Following from the difficulty in detecting deductive competence in early adolescence, we began another series of studies designed to again focus on the issue of developmental availability. After examining several deductive tasks, pilot work led us to a modification of the Wason (1983) selection task. This task presents the participant with a conditional rule (e.g., ''If a person is driving a motor vehicle, then the person must be over 16 years of age''). Four cards are also presented. The participant is told that each card has information on one side about whether a person is driving, and on the other side about the age of the person. The problem is to select those cards, and only those cards, that would necessarily have to be turned over to determine if the rule is being broken (i.e., false).

The four card surfaces in view correspond to (a) the affirmation of the antecedent (p) of the rule, (i.e., A person driving); (b) the denial of the antecedent (Not-p), (i.e., A person not driving); (c) the affirmation of the consequent (q), (i.e., A person 18 years of age); and (d) the denial of the consequent) (not-q), (i.e., A person 14 years of age). The correct deductive choices for the falsification of the rule consist of selection of the p card, and the not-q card. The reason for this is that it is these, and only these cards, that could possibly yield the "p and not-q" instance that is required for deductive certainty. That is, the card "A person driving" (p), might yield "A person 14 years of age" (not-q) on the other side, thus giving a necessary falsification of the rule. Similarly, the card "A person 14 years of age," might yield "A person driving" on the other side, again showing the necessary falsification instance.

The selection task is clearly a deductive reasoning task, and one that requires coordination among the permissible and impermissible instances that define implication. Although it focuses on the certainty of the Modus Tollens inference it involves the recognition and coordination of the other inference forms as well. Thus, from a formal perspective, it is well suited for evaluating the systemic availability of deductive competence. Because the rules can be varied in terms of semantic content, the selection task also presents the opportunity to explore procedures that access and implement competence.

Our first set of studies using the selection task (Overton, Ward, Noveck, Black, & O'Brien, 1987) examined the development of deductive availability and the role of semantic content in accessing and implementing this competence. In Experiment 1, participants at Grades 8, 10, and 12 were tested on several familiar content, and several abstract content, selection problems. In Experiment 2, participants at Grades 4, 8, and 12 were tested on the familiar problems used in Experiment 1. In Experiment 3, participants in Grades 4, 6, and 8 were tested on new familiar content problems, familiar content problems with conditional clauses reversed, a meaningful but unfamiliar problem, and an abstract problem.

The findings of these studies were strongly supportive of the developmental competence-procedure model that has been described. First, at all levels, participants performed poorly when abstract problem content (e.g., "If there is a vowel on one side of the card, then there is an even number on the other side.") was used. This is consistent with Wason's (1983) suggestion, that abstract content presents the individual with an overload of information that cannot adequately be represented as a coherent whole. That is, abstract content fails to engage an adequate representational procedure and, thus, does not generally access competence, even when deductive competence is available.

An improvement in performance found for familiar and, to a lesser extent, meaningful but nonfamiliar semantic content, is understood by considering schemata (see Mandler, 1983) as a basic procedure for representational integration. According to this explanation, familiar content produces the greatest facilitation because it most readily evokes world-knowledge schemata. These schemata operate as frames or integrating devices and, thus, permit ready access to and implementation of, available competence. Meaningful but nonfamiliar material is indirectly related to world-knowledge schemata. Hence, it is less adequately integrated and less facilitative.

Abstract content fails to invoke any integrating mechanism. This explanation is also consistent with the lack of any transfer effects from familiar content to abstract content investigated in Experiment 1.

Although the nature of semantic content is an important factor with respect to the access and implementation of competence, the findings supported the position that semantic content cannot, in itself, explain performance. Poor performance in Grades 4 and 6 on even highly familiar problems; variable adequacy across conditions at Grade 8; and the consistently adequate performance at Grades 10 and 12 all suggest the developmental view that formal deductive competence becomes available in adolescence. This position was given further tentative support by findings of a developmental improvement between Grades 8 and 12 on even the abstract problem (Experiment 1) and a logically systematic responding at Grade 8 to problems that had their clauses reversed from the usual semantic order (Experiment 3).

Following from this set of selection task studies, we continued to examine the procedural role of familiarity in relationship to the developmental availability of deductive competence. In the next investigation (Ward & Overton, 1990), however, familiarity was defined in terms of the *relevance* relationship between antecedent and consequence clauses of the conditional rule. Relevance is a logical concept that refers to some identifiable meaningful relationship between the clauses. Based on ratings obtained from children at Grade 5, a group of high relevant (e.g., ''If a person is driving a motor vehicle, then the person is over 16 years of age''), and a group of low relevant (e.g., ''If a person is driving a motor vehicle, then the person is a school teacher'') conditional rules were formulated and placed into a selection task context. Participants at Grades 6, 9, and 12 were tested on these selection task problems.

It was predicted that a high propositional relevance would operate as a facilitative procedure only after deductive competence became available in adolescence. This prediction was supported. At Grade 6, logical solutions were infrequent regardless of the relevance of the rule content. At Grades 9 and 12, low relevant content continued to result in poor performance. However, performance improved significantly between Grades 9 and 12 when the content of the conditional rule involved a high degree of relevance between antecedent and consequent clause. This again suggests that prior to adolescence, deductive competence is not systematically available, and familiarity of semantic content can be considered facilitative, but it cannot explain deductive reasoning itself.

The most interesting developmental finding of this study is that the performance found at each age level for the high relevant groups very closely match the performance levels found for the familiar content problems in Experiments

1 and 2 of the earlier investigation. This consistency occurred despite the fact that the several studies involved different experimenters, different methods, and different problem content.

There are a number of ways to measure deductive success. However, consistency of completely correct deductive solutions across varying content is the most meaningful theoretical measure of the availability of deductive competence. Using the criterion of a minimum of 60% of the problems solved with a correct deductive solutions, the following emerges as the percent of individuals at each Grade level who evidence available deductive competence: Grade 4 = 14% (Experiment 2); Grade 6 = 24% (present study); Grade 8 = 42% (Experiment 2), 48% (Experiment 1); Grade 9 = 75% (Experiment 2), 80% (present study), 86% (Experiment 1). Similar results are found when scoring is computed simply in terms of number of correct solutions across all problems.

The issue of the role of familiar semantic content was pursued and expanded in a later study (Ward, Byrnes, & Overton, in press). Late adolescents were tested with selection task conditional sentences that crossed familiarity and entailment. *Entailment* refers to the case where there is a necessary rather than a contingent relationship between the antecedent and consequent clause of a conditional. Thus, a conditional statement constitutes an entailment if and only if given the statement "if p then q," it is impossible to have a situation in which, p and not-q co-occur. For example, the sentence "If it's a dog then it's a mammal" asserts an entailment relationship because it is impossible to find the case of a non-mammal dog. It was predicted that entailment as a structural feature would be a stronger determinant of correct reasoning performance than familiarity, and this prediction was supported.

The consistent, but indirect, evidence for developmental changes in the availability of deductive competence across the several studies, and the similarity of scores at each age level across the several studies, led us to undertake a longitudinal investigation to further examine the development of deductive competence (Reene & Overton, 1989). Participants at Grades 6 and 8 were tested on the high relevant selection problems from the Ward and Overton study. They were then retested a year later at Grades 7 and 9. Grades 6 and 7 did not differ in performance, whereas Grade 9 showed a significant improvement over Grade 8. Using the consistency of solution criterion described above, the percent of individuals at each grade level who evidenced available deductive competence was: Cohort 1: Grade 6 = 17%; Grade 7 = 38%; Cohort 2: Grade 8 = 38%; Grade 9 = 60%. These longitudinal findings are highly consistent with the earlier cross-sectional research. Testing on the third year of this project has been completed and the results continue to support the cross sectional studies. For Cohort 1, the Grade 7 performance level of 38% was followed by a Grade 8 performance level of 53%. For Cohort 2, the Grade 9 performance of 60% was followed by a Grade 10 performance of 67%.

In addition to scoring the selection task according to number of correct solutions, and according to consistency of correct solutions, it is possible to examine error response patterns. For example, selection of the p card and the q card yields the p,q error pattern. This pattern, which represents a matching of the selection cards to the antecedent and consequence clauses of the rule, has generally been interpreted as a failure of logical understanding. In the described studies, as would be expected, this pattern decreases directly in relation to increasing age. Another error pattern, which presents greater developmental interest is the p,q,not-q pattern. Wason and Johnson-Laird (1972) suggested that this pattern represents partial insight into the correct logical solution. Here the individual selects the correct p card, and the correct not-q card, but contaminates the solution by continuing to choose the matching q card.

Pollack, Ward, and Overton (1988) explored the hypothesis that the p,q,not-q error pattern may mark a developmental transition in the progression toward a systemic available deductive competence. In reviewing the error data from the Overton et al. (1987) study, we found that in two of the three experiments there was an inverted-U-shaped relationship between grade (4, 8, and 12) and selection of the p,q,not-q pattern. Grade 8 constituted the maximum point of the curve. This finding, along with Wason and Johnson-Laird's interpretative suggestion led to the further exploration of this pattern for individuals at Grades 4, 5, 6, 8, 9, 12, and college level. The high-relevant selection task problems from the Ward and Overton (1990) study were used in this investigation. The results supported the conclusion that there is a curvilinear relationship between grade and the p,q,not-q pattern. Grade 8 constituted the maximum point of the curve, whereas Grades 4 and college level constituted the minimum points.

This support for the hypothesis of a transition to a deductive competence led to a follow-up investigation that employed data from the first 2 years of the longitudinal study mentioned earlier. In this follow-up (Reene, Pollack, & Overton, 1989), the age-related curvilinear relationship in the production of p,q,not-q pattern was again found. The seventh and eighth grades constituted the maximum points of the curve, whereas the sixth and ninth grades constituted the minimum points.

When the findings from the last two studies are considered in the light of the Byrnes and Overton (1986, 1988) investigations, additional weight is added to the suggestion that sometime around 14 years of age (Grade 8) a transition occurs. This transition may mark the end of the consolidation of formal competence, and the beginning of the development of novel procedures designed to access this competence.

## CONCLUSION

The basic thesis of this chapter has been that an adequate scientific theory of the nature, origin, and development of any human capacity requires an integrated set of explanatory concepts. Competence models offer explanation for the universal features of understanding at different levels of development. Procedure models offer explanations for how competence is accessed and implemented in real time at various levels of development. The research program that has been described represents a continuing effort designed to explore, examine, and elaborate the empirical implications of this framework in the domain of the development of deductive reasoning.

## REFERENCES

Braine, M. D. S. (1990). The "natural logic" approach to reasoning. In W. F. Overton (Ed.), *Reasoning, necessity, and logic: Developmental perspectives* (pp. 135-158). Hillsdale, NJ: Lawrence Erlbaum Associates.

Byrnes, J. P., & Overton, W. F. (1986). Reasoning about certainty and uncertainty in concrete, causal, and propositional contexts. *Developmental Psychology, 22*, 793-799.

Byrnes, J. P., & Overton, W. F. (1988). Reasoning about logical connectives: A developmental analysis. *Journal of Experimental Child Psychology, 46*, 194-218.

Chandler, M. (1987). The Othello effect: Essay on the mergence and eclipse of skeptical doubt. *Human Development, 30*, 137-159.

Cheng, P. W., & Holyoak, K. J. (1985). Pragmatic reasoning schemas. *Cognitive Psychology, 17*, 391-416.

Cheng, P. W., Holyoak, K. J., Nisbett, R. E., & Oliver, L. M. (1986). Prgamatic versus syntactic approaches to training deductive reasoning. *Cognitive Psychology, 18*, 293-328.

Churchland, P. M. (1981). Eliminative materalism, and the propositional attitudes. *Journal of Philosophy, 78*, 67-90.

Churchland, P. S. (1986). *Neurophilosophy.* Cambridge, MA: MIT Press.

Craik, K. (1943). *The nature of explanation.* Cambridge: Cambridge University press.

Dennett, D. (1987). *The intentional stance.* Cambridge, MA: MIT Press.

Feyerabend, P. (1978). *Against method.* New York: Schocken.

Garfield, J. L. (1988). *Belief in psychology.* Cambridge, MA: MIT Press.

Griggs, R. A. (1983). The role of problem content in the selection task and in the THROG problem. In J. St. B. T. Evans (Ed.), *Thinking and reasoning: Psychological approaches* (pp. 16-47). London: Routledge & Kegan Paul.

Hanson, N. R. (1958). *Patterns of discovery.* London & New York: Cambridge University Press.

Hinde, R. A. (1982). Attachment: Some conceptual and biological issues. In C.M. Parkes & J. Stevenson-Hinde (Eds.), *The place of attachment in human behavior* (pp. 60-76). New York: Basic Books.

Johnson, M. (1987). *The body in the mind.* Chicago: The University of Chicago press.

Johnson-Laird, P. N. (1983). *Mental models.* Cambridge, MA: Harvard University Press.

Johnson-Laird, P. N., Byrne, R. M. J., & Tabossi, P. (1989). Reasoning by model: The case of multiple quantification. *Psychological Review, 96*, 658-673.

Kessen, W. (1984). Introduction: The end of the age of development. In R. J. Sternberg (Ed.), *Mechanisms of cognitive development* (pp. 1-17). New York: Freeman.

Kuhn, T. S. (1962). *The structure of scientific revolutions.* Chicago, IL: The University of Chicago Press.

Kuhn, T. S. (1977). *The essential tension.* Chicago, IL: The University of Chicago Press.

Lakatos, I. (1978). *The methodology of scientific research programmes: Philosophical papers* (Vol. 1). New York: Cambridge University Press.

Lakoff, G. (1987). *Women, fire, and dangerous things. What categories reveal about the mind.* Chicago: University of Chicago Press.

Laudan, L. (1977). *Progress and its problems: Towards a theory of scientific growth.* Berkeley, CA: University of California Press.

Laudan, L. (1984). *Science and values: The aims of science and their role in scientific debate.* Los Angeles, CA: The University of California Press.

Lycan, W. (1987). *Consciousness.* Cambridge, MA: MIT Press.

Macnamara, J. (1986). *A border dispute: The place of logic in psychology.* Cambridge, MA: MIT Press.

Mandler, J. M. (1983). Structural invariants in development. In L. S. Liben (Ed.), *Piaget and the foundations of knowledge* (pp. 97–124). Hillsdale, NJ: Lawrence Erlbaum Associates.

Markovits, H., Schleifer, M., & Fortier, L. (1989). Development of elementary deductive reasoning in young children. *Developmental Psychology, 25,* 787–793.

Marr, D. (1981). Artificial intelligence: A personal view. In J. Haugeland (Ed.), *Mind design* (pp. 129–142). Montomery, VT: Bradford Books.

Marr, D. (1982). *Vision.* Cambridge, MA: MIT Press.

O'Brien, D., & Overton, W. F. (1980). Conditional reasoning following contradictory evidence: A developmental analysis. *Journal of Experimental Child Psychology, 30,* 44–60.

O'Brien, D., & Overton, W. F. (1982). Conditonal reasoning and the competence-performance issue: A developmental analysis of a training task. *Journal of Experimental Child Psychology, 34,* 274–290.

Osherson, D. (1975). Logic and models of logical thinking. In R. J. Falmagne (Ed.), *Reasoning: Representation and process* (pp. 81–91). Hillsdale, NJ: Lawrence Erlbaum Associates.

Overton, W. F. (1984). World views and their influence on psychological theory and research: Kuhn-Lakatos-Laudan. In H. W. Reese (Ed.), *Advances in child behavior and development* (Vol. 18, pp. 191–226). New York: Academic Press.

Overton, W. F. (1985). Scientific methodologies and the competence-moderator-performance issue. In E. Neimark, R. DeLisi, & J. Newman (Eds.), *Moderators of competence* (pp. 15–41). Hillsdale, NJ: Lawrence Erlbaum Associates

Overton, W. F. (1989). Review of Piaget, J. "Possibility and necessity. Volumes 1 & 2." *Contemporary Psychology, 34,* 629–631.

Overton, W. F. (1990). Competence and procedures: Constraints on the development of logical reasoning. *In W. F. Overton (Ed.), Reasoning, necessity, and logic: Developmental perspectives* (pp. 1–32). Hillsdale, NJ: Lawrence Erlbaum Associates.

Overton, W. F. (in press-a). The structure of developmental theory. In P. van Geert & L. P. Mos (Eds.), *Annals of theoretical psychology, Vol. 7: Developmental psychology.* New York: Plenum.

Overton, W. F. (in press-b). Metaphor, recursive systems, and paradox in science and developmental theory. In P. van Geert & L. P. Mos (Eds.), *Annals of theoretical psychology, Vol. 7: Developmental psychology.* New York: Plenum.

Overton, W. F. (in press-c). Historical and contemporary perspectives of development and research strategies. In R. Downs, L. Liben, & D. Palermo (Eds.), *The legacy of Joachim F. Wohlwill.* Hillsdale, NJ: Lawrence Erlbaum Associates.

Overton, W. F., Byrnes, J. P., & O'Brien, D. P. (1985). Developmental and individual differences in conditional reasoning: The role of contradiction training and cognitive style. *Developmental Psychology, 21,* 692–701.

Overton, W. F., & Newman, J. (1982). Cognitive development: A competence-activation/utilization approach. In T. Field, A. Houston, H. Quay, L. Troll, & G. Finley (Eds.), *Review of human development* (pp. 217–241). New York: Wiley.

Overton, W. F., Ward, S. L., Noveck, I. A., Black, J., & O'Brien, D. P. (1987). Form and content in the development of deductive reasoning. *Developmental Psychology, 23,* 22–30.

Piaget, J. (1987). *Possibility and necessity. Vol. 1. The role of possibility in cognitive development. Vol. 2. The role of necessity in cognitive development.* Minneapolis: University of Minnesota Press.

Piaget, J., & Garcia, R. (1986). *Vers une logique de signification [Toward a logic of meaning.]* Geneva, Switzerland: Editions Murionde.

Pollack, R. D., Ward, S. L., & Overton, W. F. (1988). *Early adolescence: A transitional time in logical reasoning.* Paper presented at the biennial meeting of the Society for Research in Adolescence, Alexandria, VA.

Putnam, H. (1987). *The many faces of realism.* Cambridge: Cambridge University Press.

Putnam, H. (1988). *Representation and reality.* Cambridge, MA: MIT Press.

Pylyshyn, Z. W. (1984). *Computation and cognition.* Cambridge, MA: MIT Press.

Reene, K. J., & Overton, W. F. (1989, June). *Longitudinal investigation of adolescent deductive reasoning.* Paper presented at the Biennial meetings of the Society for Research in Child Development, Kansas City, MO.

Reene, K. J., Pollack, R. D., & Overton, W. F. (1989, June). *The partial insight response: Longitudinal evidence for a transitional time in logical reasoning.* Paper presented at the 19th Annual Symposium of the Jean Piaget Society, Philadelphia, PA.

Revlis, R. (1975). Syllogistic reasoning: Logical decisions from a complex data base. In R. J. Falmagne (Ed.), *Reasoning: Representation and process* (pp. 93–133). Hillsdale, NJ: Lawrence Erlbaum Associates.

Russell, J. (1987). Rule-following, mental models, and the developmental view. In M. Chapman & R. A. Dixon (Eds.), *Meaning and the growth of understanding* (pp. 23–48). New York: Springer-Verlag.

Searle, J. (1984). *Minds, brains and science.* Cambridge, MA: Harvard University Press.

Searle, J. (1990). Is the brain's mind a computer program? *Scientific American, 262*(1), 26–31.

Sellars, W. (1963). *Science, perception and reality.* London: Routledge & Kegan Paul.

Siegler, R. S., & Shipley, C. (1987). The role of learning in children's strategy choices. In L. S. Liben (Ed.), *Development and learning: Conflict or congruence* (pp. 71–108). Hillsdale, NJ: Lawrence Erlbaum Associates.

Smith, L. (1987). A constructivist interpretation of formal operations. *Human Development, 30,* 341–354.

Sroufe, L. A. (1977). Attachment as an organizational construct. *Child Development, 48,* 1184–1199.

Sugarman, S. (1987a). The priority of description in developmental psychology. *International Journal of Behavioral Development, 10,* 391–414.

Sugarman, S. (1987b). Reply to Peter Bryant. *International Journal of Behaivoral Development, 10,* 423–424.

Ward, S. L., Byrnes, J. P., & Overton, W. F. (in press). Organization of knowledge and conditional reasoning. *Journal of Educational Psychology.*

Ward, S. L., & Overton, W. F. (1990). Semantic familiarity, relevance, and the development of deductive reasoning. *Developmental Psychology, 26,* 488–493.

Wason, P. C. (1983). Realism and rationality in the selection task. In J. St. B. T. Evans (Ed.), *Thinking and reasoning: Psychological approaches* (pp. 44–75). London: Routledge & Kegan Paul.

Wason, P. C., & Johnson-Laird, P. N. (1972). *Psychology of reasoning: Structure and content.* Cambridge, MA: Harvard University Press.

Werner, H. (1957). The concept of development from a comparative and organismic point of view. In D. B. Harris (Ed.), *The concept of development: An issue in the study of human behavior.* Minneapolis: University of Minnesota Press.

# Chapter 3

# The Concept of Nature: Implications for Assessment of Competence

John A. Meacham
*State University of New York at Buffalo*

Controversy over the extent of children's abilities at various ages is certain to continue as long as the debate remains centered on an idealized notion of competence abstracted from the actual life of the child. Understanding what lies behind the controversy and making progress toward resolving it will come in part through contextualizing the controversy. The situations in which controversy over criteria for competence arise and the objectives of the principal actors in those situations must be closely examined. The controversy over criteria for assessing children's abilities does not arise in a vacuum. It arises when parents, teachers, public officials, and researchers intend to take some action toward children and, as a prerequisite to that action, attempt to assess children's abilities and then give an interpretation to the results of that assessment. The notion that the results of any assessment objectively capture the extent of a child's competence and are, in themselves, a reliable guide to action is an illusion. It is an illusion because the results of the assessment are given meaning as a function of the context in which the need for assessment and the desire for action arise.

Thus, the principal thesis of this chapter is that in order to understand the controversy over criteria for competence we must turn to an examination of the contexts in which the controversy arises and the objectives that permeate those contexts. Although there is a multitude of possible contexts, the argument is made in this chapter that these might profitably be organized into a family of only four contexts. These four are shown to be strongly associated with four images of nature, that is, images that capture how it is that we as humans conceive our relationship to the natural environment. The chapter is organized into four major sections. In the first of these, various historical and contemporary usages of the concept of nature are brought together within a conceptual framework that generates the four images of nature. In the second section, the four images are employed to shed light on the kinds of situations in which controversy over competence arises and the objectives of the actors in those situations, in particular, parent–child relationships and the contexts of child rearing. Third, some general implications for assessment of children's abilities associated with each of the four contexts are briefly set forth. In the final section, the four images are employed to elucidate the conflicting objectives and interpretations that arise in an area of heated debate over children's abilities, namely, the issue of whether or not young children are competent to provide eyewitness testimony during legal proceedings.

The motivation on the part of parents, teachers, or public officials to assess competence, whether informally or through a formal testing procedure, is often one of wanting to know whether a child's development is normal or, to introduce the particular concept on which I focus, natural. The child's abilities are assessed in order to determine whether the child's development is natural or not; if not, then some sort of intervention is likely to be proposed in order to restore the child's development to its natural course. Yet there is already a problem with my choice of terms, for what is *normal* and what is *natural* might not be the same. Only a few years ago, circumcision of male infants was a normal event in the United States; currently, however, the proportion of parents choosing to have their sons circumcised is declining. Was the normal circumcision of the 1960s a natural or unnatural part of male development? Is being uncircumcised the natural way to be today? Perhaps whether or not we conceive of some developmental event as natural is for the most part a reflection of its normality within a socio-historical context. What motivates many parents to decide in favor of circumcision is the desire that their sons appear normal, that is, not different from other males in North American locker rooms. Yet certainly there are other behaviors—using and abusing drugs, driving while intoxicated, becoming pregnant out of wedlock, and so forth—that many parents would decry as unnatural even though they have become normal events of adolescence. Assessment of children's abilities takes place, therefore, not only within a context of what is normal but also within a distinctly separate and often implicit context of what is thought to be natural in the course of development.

## THE CONCEPT OF NATURE

The answers to questions such as these, about what is right or wrong in child and adolescent development and about whether some sort of intervention is appropriate or necessary to guide development along a different course, depend on a close examination of what is implied about ourselves as humans and about our relationship to nature when we use such terms as *natural* and *unnatural*. There are, across cultures and across history, many different expressions of the concept of nature. Some of these differences can be made explicit by considering the answers to two critical questions: First, do we consider humans to be *apart from* nature or a *part of* nature? Second, is the objective of humans to understand nature, or to intervene in and control nature? This second distinction is made most clear by Habermas (1982), who similarly distinguished between communicative action oriented toward reaching understanding, on the one hand, and instrumental action oriented toward intervention in the world and achieving success, on the other. It is not that the objective of understanding is devoid of the possibility of action. The action that follows from understanding, however, is based in the cooperation of the individuals who are parties to the action, whereas the action that follows from the objective of intervention proceeds from an egocentric defining of what will constitute successful action.

## Domination of Nature

One typical and influential category of response to these two questions is that humans stand apart from nature, but nevertheless have as their objective to intervene in nature. The image that represents this category of response is referred to as the domination of nature, and is indicated in the upper right cell of the matrix shown in Fig. 3.1. This first image of the relationship of humans to nature is well-grounded in the history of Western thought (Leiss, 1972). Particularly in the 17th century and afterward, "the religious teaching that man completes and perfects the work of creation was reinterpreted along more 'activist' lines. Nature was said to require the superintendence of man in order to function well, and this was understood as meaning a thorough transformation of the natural environment, rather than mere occupation or nomadic passage" (Leiss, 1972, p. 74). The image of domination of nature is associated

|  | Objective | |
|---|---|---|
| Humans and Nature | To understand nature | To intervene in nature |
| Humans are apart from nature | 4. Neglect | 1. Domination of nature |
| Humans are a part of nature | 3. Living with nature | 2. Ecological disasters |

FIG. 3.1.  Four images of humans and nature.

with the expectation that, through the control and mastery of nature, humans
will be able to construct a utopian world of freedom from dependence on nature for food, shelter, and so forth. To control nature is understood from the
perspective of domination primarily as a technical problem, not as a problem
that raises issues of values or ethics.

Unfortunately, the image of domination of nature prepares the way for ecological disasters. Because humans are in fact a part of nature and so cannot
in the long run stand apart from nature, they cannot intervene in nature without
intervening in their own development. Humans cannot control or dominate
nature without suffering a loss of freedom as humans are, in turn, controlled
or dominated by nature. For example, our attempt to become independent
through the domination of nature by ranching and farming by intervening in
the rain forests of Brazil has resulted instead in their increasing destruction,
leaving humans increasingly dependent on the scant remaining forest to provide the oxygen vital for all animal life.

Similarly, our ability to exploit petroleum as an energy source, in the hope
that humans could thus become more independent from nature, has instead
made human societies far more dependent on the availability of petroleum and
on the laws of nature. The fates of nations and millions of people now follow
from their ability to exercise economic and military control over the world's
declining petroleum resources. The 1989 oil spill in Alaska has led to the destruction of hundreds of miles of shoreline ecosystem; the deaths of thousands
of mammals such as otters, who lose their buoyancy and their capacity to retain heat when as little as 10% of the body is covered with oil; the deaths of
hundreds of thousands and perhaps millions of migratory birds; the loss of ir-
replaceable nurseries for fish and shellfish; and consequent increases in the price
of gasoline and food for humans. Rather than gaining freedom through the
control of nature, human societies have become increasingly subject to the hard
laws of nature.

The disastrous consequences that have followed from the first image of the
relation of humans to nature stem from the naive assumption that humans can
successfully intervene in nature while continuing to stand apart from nature.
If this assumption were true, then it would indeed seem reasonable that humans could exploit and even destroy nature but suffer no ill consequences themselves. This assumption that humans stand apart from nature is flawed,
however, so that the image of domination of nature in practice degenerates
into the image of the second, lower right cell, a cell characterized by ecological
disasters (see Fig. 3.1). Because the assumption of separateness is untenable,
for humans to intervene in nature is to intervene in the ecological system out
of which both human nature and the rest of nature are mutually constructed.
The scale of human intervention in nature has increased dramatically in recent decades, so that humans themselves now constitute one of the major features of the natural environment (Leiss, 1972, p. 15).

Within the first two images of domination of nature and ensuing ecological disaster, humans implicitly are thought to be essentially good, whereas nature is lacking in intrinsic worth or, at best, is neutral. The issue of whether or not to exploit nature is not considered to be an ethical problem, but instead a practical one. Matters of feasibility, efficiency, and profit become the major concerns in extracting the value that is potential within nature. Human science and the technology of exploitation are considered to be value-neutral. There is potential value within nature, but the intervention of humans is required in order for the value in nature to be made real. Humans thus conceive of the world of nature as value-neutral, but they do this because of a particular value that they hold: the value of mastery, power, and domination over things in nature (Leiss, 1972, p. 109). Nevertheless, scant attention is given, within the image of domination of nature, to the analysis of such human goals and motives themselves (Leiss, 1972, p. 117).

## Living With Nature

A third image also exists in response to the two questions raised at the outset. This is the view that humans cannot stand apart from nature and that their objective should be to understand nature, rather than to intervene in it. In this third image, the opening questions are given answers opposite to those of the first image, so that the image of domination of nature is diametrically opposed by this third image, the image of living with nature (see Fig. 3.1). From the perspective of this image, one hopes to achieve a utopia for humans through learning to live in harmony with nature. This third image contrasts with the first image in basing its utopia on the ideal of limited consumption and relatively little control over nature versus an ideal of expanding consumption by expanding the control of humans over nature. Rather than asking what one can do with nature, one is interested in nature as it is (Leiss, 1972, p. 87).

As with the first image of domination, so with this third image of living with nature there is the potential for disaster if the assumptions implied in answering the two critical questions are not valid. In particular, if it is not the case that humans are a part of nature but instead are apart from nature, then the role of humans with respect to nature becomes a passive one. Whatever understanding of nature that might be achieved has no impact either on nature or on human development, because of the lack of any efficacious relationship between humans and nature. This fourth image is an image of neglect (see Fig. 3.1, upper left cell), for there is a failure to willingly assume any responsibility for nature: Let nature be; let nature take its course. It is assumed that to do so is the right course of action, for within this fourth image nature is considered to be intrinsically good (Leiss, 1972, p. 181). The image of neglect might at first seem inconsistent with the objective of understanding nature. The neglect is not devoid of understanding, however; it is based on the presumption that the minimal understanding that has been achieved is adequate and that no implications for intervention follow from this understanding.

It is also the case within the third image of living with nature that nature and being natural are considered to be good. But within the third image humans are a part of nature. If nature is good, then humans likewise are good. If one contemplates intervening in nature, then ethical concerns immediately arise, for to intervene in the world of nature is to intervene in a world that encompasses and is supportive of humans

## PARENTS AND CHILDREN

In order to understand the controversy surrounding assessment of children's abilities, the controversy must be contextualized. That is, we must consider those concrete situations in which controversy over criteria for competence arise and the motivations or interests of the parents, teachers, public officials, and researchers who are in a position to assess children's abilities and to provide interpretations of those assessments. In this section, the focus is that situation in which children's abilities are most frequently and directly assessed, the child-rearing situation. The images in terms of which the relationships between parents and children are viewed bear striking similarities to the images through which we view the relationship between humans and nature. I describe each of these four parallel images, and then turn to the question of how these images might guide how we go about assessing a child's psychological competence.

The four images of the relationship between parents and children can be located within a 2 x 2 matrix constructed around questions quite similar to those for the figure already discussed. First, should we consider the life courses for parents and children to be separate, such that events in one life course have little or no impact on events in the other life course? Or do we consider that parents and children share a developmental course within which their separate lives are mutually constructed?[1] Second, is the primary objective of parents to understand their children or instead to intervene in the lives of their children? Now let me turn, in clockwise fashion, to each of the four cells constructed by the intersection of the two answers to these two questions.

### Domination of Children

The image of parent–child relationships represented in the first upper right cell (see Fig. 3.2) is similar in many respects to the image previously charac-

---

[1]I use the term *life course* to refer to single lives, and the term *developmental course* to refer to two or more interdependent lives.)

| | Parents' Objectives in Lives of Children | |
|---|---|---|
| Parent and Child Life Courses | To understand | To intervene |
| Separate | 4. Neglect | 1. Domination of children |
| Shared | 3. Living with children | 2. Family disasters |

FIG. 3.2.  Relationships between parents and children.

terized as the domination of nature. Within this image, parents follow life courses that are, relative to the other images, separate from those of their children. The objective or interest of many parents is to intervene in the lives of their children and to control the children's development so that it is predictable within the context of the parents' hopes and values. Parents tend to view their children's achievements similarly to their own achievements of success in a career, a fine house and a car, opportunities for travel, and so forth. Children and their achievements become additional objects that can be accumulated in the course of a successful life. In many respects, at least in the short-run, parents are able to act comfortably within this relationship of domination of children, by virtue of their superior physical and psychological power over their children.

The answers to the two initial questions that, by their intersection, produce the image of domination of children are mutually supportive. That is, the logic of this first image of parent–child relationships is internally consistent. A first assumption of this image is that the lives of parents and their children are sufficiently separate or independent that parents can intervene without restriction, molding the children's development to suit the parents' needs, without concern for possible negative consequences for the parents' own development. The case of Joel Steinberg, the Manhattan lawyer who was convicted for murdering his 6-year-old adopted daughter, is an extreme example of this image of domination of children and separateness of life courses. Regardless of the extent of the apparent physical and psychological abuse of his daughter over several years, there were apparently no improper or even inconvenient consequences for his own life course. Only in the singular event of her death did the daughter's life course have an impact on the father's.

This first assumption, that the lives of parents and children are separate, serves to reinforce the second assumption, that the lives of the children have little intrinsic positive value or worth. Instead, they accrue value only as they can be subordinated to the purposes of the parents' lives. Within this image of domination of children, children are at best regarded as having no value or a neutral value; at worst, they are regarded as being naturally bad unless they can be molded to the purposes of the parents' lives. To be a natural child is to be valueless or bad; to be socialized, civilized, and useful within the context of the parents' lives is to be good. This second assumption, that the children in their natural state are bad and that the parents are intrinsically good, serves to reinforce the first assumption of the image of domination, the assumption that the life courses of parents and children are qualitatively different and should be kept separate. Both assumptions together support an attitude that it is all right, and perhaps even a responsibility, for parents to intervene in a strong sense in the lives of children. Within this image of domination of children, children are viewed by the parents as objects, not as persons.

Consistent with this image of domination of children is the current emphasis by certain affluent groups in the United States on creating what have been termed *superbabies* or *overstimulated children* or *gourmet babies*. Implicit in the parents' enthusiasm to arrange a variety of educational experiences for their infants and toddlers is the assumption that if they were permitted to continue to develop in a state of nature, without intervention, then the babies would develop naturally into children and adults who will be less worthy than they would be with appropriate intervention early in infancy. The parents likely would explain their actions by asserting that they have a responsibility to ensure that the best possible developmental outcome is achieved.[2]

Despite the internally consistent logic of the image of domination, one of the assumptions is flawed, namely, the assumption that parents and children can lead separate life courses. Indeed, the careful documenting of the mutual dependencies of child and parent development has been one of the major contributions of developmental psychology within the past two decades (Lewis & Freedle, 1973; Meacham, 1984b, 1985, 1987; Riegel, 1979; Sameroff, 1975; Sameroff & Chandler, 1975; Wertsch, 1985; Youniss & Smollar, 1985). There are certainly precursors of this enlightened view, for example, the work of Vygotsky (1978), who emphasized that cognitive abilities appear first in social interaction and only subsequently at the intrapsychological level. Because the assumption of separate lives is flawed, the image of domination of children in practice degenerates into the image of the second, lower right cell, a cell characterized by family disasters (Fig. 3.2). What gets carried forward from the image of domination of children is the attitude that the parents are good while the children are, in their natural state, bad, along with the attitude that parents have a responsibility to intervene actively in the lives of their children. But because the assumption of separate lives is untenable, for parents to intervene in the lives of children is for parents to intervene in the developmental

---

[2]In describing parents as I do, I do not wish to suggest that the intentions of parents are not honorable. It is likely that most parents engage in behaviors during the course of a day or week that might be typical of each of the four images of parent–child relations. But I do want to suggest that there are dominant styles of parenting that follow from how parents conceive of their relationship to their offspring.

course out of which both the parents' and the children's lives are mutually constructed.

The current superbaby or gourmet baby syndrome has encouraged parents to invest heavily in educational toys and courses of instruction that purport to give infants and preschoolers an advantage in the learning of motor and cognitive skills, including reading, arithmetic, gymnastics, swimming, violin, piano, foreign languages, and so forth. There are, of course, a number of reasons for the superbaby phenomena, including the increased affluence and decreased child-rearing time that come with having both parents work, successful marketing strategies that convey a view that all good parents are buying certain products or enrolling their children in certain courses, as well as the parents' reasonable desire to decrease the risk that their children might not develop into independent adults who will have many opportunities for leading successful and satisfying lives.

Yet there might be considerable danger in overemphasizing the development of only particular competencies as opposed to encouraging the harmonious development of a variety of competencies within the child. In fact, a number of concerns have been raised about early interventions into the lives of infants and preschoolers (Zigler & Lang, 1985, 1986). First, an overemphasis on cognitive skills, such as learning to read, might be accompanied by a neglect of opportunities in which children can learn the social skills that will be the foundation for later competence. Much learning of social skills arises not in programmed settings, but in the spontaneous interactions of children with each other and with their parents. Second, children may learn at an early age to value themselves only in terms of what they can achieve cognitively. Of course, there are many other dimensions of human worth, dignity, and expression. Third, time may be taken away from children's opportunities for spontaneous play, within which children not only construct a general understanding of their physical and social world but also develop creative and expressive skills as well as basic attitudes toward life.

Fourth, by pushing too hard on the child to become super-competent, the parents may produce a child lacking in autonomy and independence, precisely the characteristics the parents wished to forestall. This revolt of the child against the domination of the parents might reflect that the parents' emphasis on teaching skills has undermined the child's disposition to use the skills. Undue pressure to learn and failure in learning might lead the child to become anxious in learning situations and to avoid learning situations in the future (Katz, 1987). It has been suggested that overemphasizing intellectual achievement at the expense of emotional skills can lead to the development of anorexia nervosa (Langway, 1983). Thus, the superbaby syndrome, representative of the first image of domination of children, degenerates into the family disasters of the second image.

The fifth disaster, as we move from the upper right to the lower right cell of Fig. 3.2, is the disaster that has now been self-inflicted on the parents' life course. The parents have defined the criteria for success in their own lives in terms of their success in raising children who can become independent and successful adults, so that for many parents the child's successes become the major symbols of the parents' own self-worth. The parents' behavior is contradictory to the achievement of their own goals, for in dominating their children's development they deny the possibility of the child constructing a sense of autonomy, the sense that was essential to the parents' initial interest in dominating their children. Because of the interdependence of the children's and the parents' lives within the same developmental course, the disaster that has been inflicted upon the children becomes a disaster in the lives of the parents as well. Just as the image of domination of nature by humans degenerates into an image of disaster for the ecological system that includes humans, so the image of domination of children by the parents degenerates into an image of disaster for the family system that includes the parents. It is for this reason that I have not characterized this second image merely in terms of child-rearing disasters, preferring instead to make explicit the parallel between ecological systems and family systems.

## Living With Children

The image of parent–child relationships represented in the third, lower left cell (Fig. 3.2) contrasts in major respects with the image of domination of children represented in the first cell. In the present case, the life courses of parents and children are taken to be inseparable aspects of the same developmental course. The objective of the parents is not to intervene in the life of the child, any more than one might say that the parents' objective is to intervene in their own lives. Instead, the objective of the parents is to maintain and increase understanding, by the parents of the child and by the child of the parents. The orientation of the parents toward the life of the child is not one of wanting to control and predict that life, but instead a desire to share in the child's enjoyment of life, to be a participant in the child's life course, to have an appreciation of the aesthetics of the child's developmental progress, and to be the secure foundation for what must be the child's very own achievements. The parents' satisfaction comes not through the domination of children, but through the everyday interactions that are a part of living with children.

Just as the image of domination of children in practice degenerates into the image of family disasters, so the image of living with children can also in practice degenerate, into the image of neglect of the fourth, upper left cell (Fig. 3.2). This happens when the assumption of shared lives of parents and child is violated; when this assumption is violated, then the objective of mutual understanding cannot be achieved. There are many reasons why the assumption of shared lives is violated. Certainly the major and inexcusable reason in the United States is that many parents find that working outside the home for 40 hours a week at minimum wage is not sufficient to provide the basic necessities of food, shelter, clothing, and medical care. The neglect characteristic of the fourth cell might also reflect that the parents have conceptualized the child in terms quite similar to what Zigler and Lang (1986) have called a "little wildflower." As the parents of such a child, "we can relax and assume that nature has programmed the little wildflowers to bloom, and that our only task is to observe their physical, intellectual, and emotional growth" (p. 9).

Within what I have termed the *image of neglect*, the parents believe that the very best they can do for their child is to permit his or her development to proceed naturally, for what is natural is good and so to interfere with the child's natural development is bad. Nevertheless, this image has the potential to become merely a rationale for maintaining a passive approach toward child rearing, for failing to ensure an atmosphere of consistent emotional support and for refusing to accept responsibility for realization of the full developmental potential of the child. A lack of acceptance of responsibility is revealed in contemporary attitudes toward the provision of child care: "As a nation, we've had a difficult time determining whether the family, the government, or the private section is most responsible, resulting in a lack of a coherent family policy, unnecessary fluctuations in service, a waste of resources—human and financial—and a lack of equity in service distribution" (Kagan, 1987, p. 20). The interest of the parents, government, and industry, in this fourth cell of neglect, is merely to ensure that what is provided for the child does not fall below some minimal standard. It is appalling that, for example, the legislatures in the states of Texas and Florida find teacher–child ratios of 1:20 to be acceptable for preschool education (Kagan, 1987).

What is critical in distinguishing the image of neglect (upper left cell) from the image of living with children (lower left)? It is essential, for the image of living with children, that both assumptions hold, namely, the assumption that the life courses of parents and child are inseparable and the assumption that the objective of the parents is to maintain and increase understanding. If the first assumption of a shared developmental course is violated, then it will not be possible for the parents to achieve their objective of mutual understanding. In the absence of mutual understanding, any decisions and actions affecting the child's well-being are necessarily made from the perspective of the parents' needs, not necessarily because the parents do not want to do what is in the child's interest, but because the parents simply do not know what is in the child's best interest. The relationship between parents and child must be solidly within the image of the lower left cell, living with children, in order for the parents to fully apprehend the child's interest. Given this knowledge, then the parents are able to act on behalf of the mutual developmental interest of both themselves and the child. The images of domination of children and living with children are opposites in most respects, but they have in common the fact that the logic of each image is internally consistent and the assumptions are mutually reinforcing. When the assumptions on the relatedness of the parent and child life courses are violated, then each image degrades into the adjacent images of family disasters and neglect, respectively.

Why is the third image of living with children, based on the assumption of shared lives and the objective of mutual understanding, the ideal among the four images of parent–child relations? There are several reasons. Within the framework of this image, parents spend their time "developing their role as observers of their children or sympathetic onlookers fostering the children's growth" (Zigler & Lang, 1985, p. 341). The parents, in contrast to the child's school teachers, peers, and other adults in the community, are both more strongly committed to their child's development to his or her full potential and at the same time more supportive, accepting of failure, and less demanding. This is not to say that the parents are not interested in their child's learning and in the child's successes. What is important within the image of living with children is that the focus is not merely on the child's achievements, but rather on the development within the child of competencies that permit the child to enjoy an increasing participation in the mutual understanding that is the objective of the parents.

These competencies include foremost the development of communicative and social competencies, as well as the development of interest in or motivation for learning (Katz, 1987). Communicative and social competence on the part of the child are essential for the maintenance and further development of mutual understanding with the parent, as well as a motivational and a skill foundation for later learning. "The fact that parent and child share a common life and frame of reference allows them to explore events and ideas in intimate, individualistic conversations with great personal meaning" (Zigler, 1987, p. 35). The failure to acquire minimal social competence during the preschool years, including the ability to form and maintain meaningful and satisfying relationships with others, is associated with high risk of dropping out of school and of having difficulties in areas such as mental health and marital adjustment (Katz, 1987). Learning and achievement in later life not only depend upon acquiring specific skills, such as reading, but also on the development of appropriate attitudes toward learning such as intrinsic motivation, curiosity, and spontaneity (Kagan, 1987; Katz, 1987). Within the image of living with children, all these competencies are best promoted not by parents focusing on their child's productivity and achievement, but instead by parents being concerned with how to understand, appreciate and enjoy, and participate in the child's development.

## ASSESSING PSYCHOLOGICAL COMPETENCE

Each of these four images of nature and the associated images of parent–child relationships prescribes a particular perspective on the assessment of psychological competence. Let me suggest what these four perspectives are, by considering the images in the same sequence as before.

### Assessing the Child's Achievements

The first, upper right cell in Fig. 3.3 corresponds to the images of the domination of nature (in Fig. 3.1) and the domination of children (in Fig. 3.2). Assessment is done from the standpoint that nature is bad, and that children are deficient. The objective is to intervene, to manipulate, and to control, so as to improve on and exploit nature, and to improve on and exploit children. The objective or interest in assessment is twofold: First, to find children to be competent at an early age, including those who are gifted by nature, so that there is a foundation of basic abilities on which the parents' or teacher's intervention can build; and second, to assess the gains that have been made subsequent to the intervention. The first assessment of early competence is analogous to exploring for gold, uranium, or other natural resources; the second assessment is analogous to computing the profit in mining these minerals after subtracting production costs. The profit for the parents is admission of the child to a prestigious college, minus the costs of raising a superbaby. In most cases, the assessment that takes place is an implicit assessment: My child, if permitted to develop naturally without major intervention on my part as a parent, will be a failure, for what is natural has no value or worth without human effort to make real what is only potential within nature.

Corporations involved in the production of oil and the mining of precious metals have to subtract from their profits the clean-up costs and fines associat-

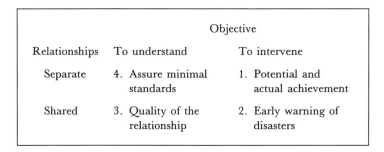

|  | Objective | |
|---|---|---|
| Relationships | To understand | To intervene |
| Separate | 4. Assure minimal standards | 1. Potential and actual achievement |
| Shared | 3. Quality of the relationship | 2. Early warning of disasters |

FIG. 3.3. What is the interest in assessing?

ed with environmental disasters (these costs are generally passed along to the consumers and taxpayers). The interest in assessing nature is to guard against damage to the environment such that clean-up costs will be incurred, for example, damage to the ozone layer through release of chemicals into the atmosphere, damage to our forests through release of acids from smokestacks, or pollution of our natural water resources through dumping of chemical wastes. The miners' canary in a cage is one example of such an assessment; bird censuses are another example, for a decline in certain bird species might indicate a collapsing ecosystem. Parents might also face substantial costs associated with the potential disasters of the second, lower right cell (Fig. 3.3); societies face similar costs associated with adults who are not independent and productive. The interest in assessment at this point is to have some preliminary warning of, and so be able to guard against, impending disasters. Screening for behavior disorders, depression, or drug abuse are examples of assessments carried out in the face of potential child-rearing and family disasters. The focus of the assessment has remained on the child, even though in this second cell the reality of the shared developmental course of parents and child has been admitted. This is because the original objective, to intervene in the lives of children, has not been exchanged for the objective of understanding children.

## Assessing the Quality of Relationships

Assessment within the context of the third, lower left cell (Fig. 3.3), which corresponds to the images of living with nature (Fig. 3.1) and living with children (Fig. 3.2), is focused not on finding qualities or traits that inhere within nature or within the child, but rather on assessing the quality of the relationship of mutual understanding within which both parents and child are immersed. From this perspective, a positive or a negative evaluation adheres neither to the child nor to the parents, but to the relationship. It is neither the life course of the parents nor that of the child that is being assessed, but the developmental course within which both are participants and contributors. That this is so stems from the assumption that humans and nature and parents and child will benefit when there is an atmosphere of mutual understanding and care and will suffer when the ecological system within which humans live and develop has been damaged. Both nature and the child are viewed as intrinsically good. There is little interest in direct intervention or exploitation, because there is a recognition that humans are dependent upon a healthy natural environment and, furthermore, that the psychological development of parents depends upon the proper development of their children. Intervention into nature or into the life of the child becomes simultaneously an intervention into one's own life. The interest in assessing children is in ensuring their participation within an atmosphere of mutual understanding: Are there adequate communication and social competencies as well as motivation for learning within the parent–child relationship? Assessment should be directed not merely toward communicative and social competence on the part of the child; instead, assessment should be directed toward ascertaining the communicative competence of the parent–child dyad.

The interest in assessment in the fourth, upper left cell (Fig. 3.3) is merely upon understanding the child. Because of the neglect of the assumption that parent and child are mutually dependent within a developmental course, however, the understanding that can be achieved from this last image is naive with respect to the child's true interests. The understanding is aloof and abstract, lacking the focus of care on a particular child. One might carry out an assessment merely to make certain that a group of children is not lacking in certain minimal standards for nutrition, safety, and stimulation from the environment. It is assumed that parents have sufficient understanding of the course of the child development to know the appropriate levels for setting such minimal standards. This appears to not be a good assumption; it appears that we have not set our standards for maintaining the integrity of our ecological system and for ensuring the safe development of children and adolescents high enough.

## CHILDREN'S COMPETENCE
## AT EYEWITNESS TESTIMONY

The issue of early competence in children is raised in dramatic and often tragic form, not only for children but also for their families and communities in the courtroom. The issue is particularly acute in cases of crimes against children, such as sexual assault and incest, and crimes for which a child might be the only witness, such as domestic violence or murder. Goodman and Reed (1986) estimate that each year hundreds of thousands of children become victims of crimes or witness crimes. In general, the prosecution will want to argue that a child is competent to testify as an eyewitness to his or her own victimization or to a crime against another person; the defense will want to argue, in many instances, that the child is not sufficiently competent at remembering and reasoning to be accepted as a credible eyewitness. How do the images of nature illuminate the question of whether or not children are competent to provide eyewitness testimony? It would be far too simplistic to suggest, for example, that the image of domination of children corresponds to the defense's view that children are not competent as witnesses, or that the image of living with children corresponds to the prosecution's view that children are indeed competent. It might also be too simplistic to argue that the apparently marked increase in the frequency of such crimes against children reflects the ascendancy of the image of domination of children within our society.

## Domination of Children

More to the point is the idea that the contrasting images of nature provide
a useful tool for considering how the legal system responds to child eyewitness
testimony and how researchers into children's memory for events respond to
conflicting research evidence (DeAngelis, 1989). In the following discussion,
the issue is not children's competence per se, for this issue cannot be decided
merely on the basis of some presumably objective evidence. Instead, the focus
is on our expectations regarding children's competence, how we respond when
these expectations are violated, and how we conceptualize children's competence. Within the legal system, children's testimony is generally thought to
be less credible than that of adults (Turtle & Wells, 1988). This belief has long
been held, according to Goodman and Hahn (1987), who cited an early review
by Whipple asserting that children make poor and even dangerous witnesses.
The presumption is that children's memories are inadequate in a variety of
ways and that children's testimony is particularly responsive to suggestions
or leading questions. In light of such beliefs, several countries, including Is-
rael and West Germany, have adopted procedures by which children may be
protected from cross-examination in the courtroom (Turtle & Wells, 1988),
and several U.S. states require competency examinations before children below a certain age are permitted to testify (Goodman & Reed, 1986). Typically, a competency examination consists of a courtroom interview and perhaps
the advice of a psychologist, with a judge making the final determination of
whether the child is competent and, as such, permitted to testify. In summary,
the view of the legal system that children are not competent to provide credible eyewitness testimony (upper right cell, Fig. 3.4) corresponds to the image
of domination of children (Fig. 3.2), within which children in their natural
state are regarded as having little value and even as bad until they can be socialized and made useful within the context of the adults' lives and world. Given
the need to choose between the testimony of a child and that of an adult, the
bias of the legal system has been against the former and for the latter, so that
children are frequently denied the full protection of the law (Dent, 1988). The
burden typically has been on the prosecution to prove that a child's eyewitness
testimony should indeed be accepted as credible.

     In fact, the parent and child life courses are not separate, as assumed with-
in the image of domination of children. Instead, their respective courses are
shared, so that child sexual assault and other crimes against children quickly
escalate into family and community disasters (lower right cell, Fig. 3.2). During the past two decades, parents and school teachers have been deluged with
television documentaries, newspaper and magazine articles, and books urging
them to take preventive steps with the children in their care so that the children might become more competent to avoid or escape from potential danger.
These steps include, for example, teaching children to "Never talk to strangers"

(Joyce, 1967) and how to respond when touched by an adult in an inappropriate place. According to Yarmey (1988), parents in Canada are now advised to "streetproof" their children: "Teach your child to report any suspicious incidents. . . . Teach your child the importance of remembering license plate numbers." In the mid-1980s the media devoted considerable attention to stories of child sexual abuse in nursery schools and child-care centers (in particular, the McMartin preschool case in California). Within a short period of time, insurance companies wary of claims of negligence against child-care providers increased their rates dramatically. Some child-care providers have responded with new regulations to ensure that children are not permitted to be alone with adults. Consistent with the images heretofore described for the lower right cell (Fig. 3.2), the interest is primarily one of wanting to avoid family and community disasters. In place of the miners' canary, the children themselves are expected to become sufficiently competent to assess whether or not a situation is dangerous; in the event of a crime, the children will now be more competent at providing eyewitness testimony, for they have been trained to notice details such as license plate numbers (lower right cell, Fig. 3.4). But just as the miners' canary does nothing to eliminate the causes of mine explosions, such training programs to increase children's competence do little to eliminate the causes of violence against children. The discussion of children's competence, whether to protect themselves or to provide credible testimony, has remained primarily a discussion only about the children; the original objective, to intervene in the lives of children, has not been exchanged for the objective of understanding children.

## Living with Children

A challenge to the conceptions of children's competence as eyewitnesses is provided by research on children's remembering that is consistent with the image of the neglect of children in the upper left cell, Fig. 3.2. (Note that the upper left and lower left cells are being discussed out of order.) As in earlier discussions of this cell, the image of neglect is not intended to reflect in any way the motivations of particular researchers. Considerable research has been conducted by psychologists highly motivated to understand and assess children's competence to remember both people and events (Meacham, 1984a). Nevertheless, relative to the other three cells, the image of the upper left cell is unique in that there is an intersection of the assumptions both that the parent and child life courses are separate and that the primary interest is not to intervene in the child's life course, but merely to understand it.

Goodman and Reed (1986), drawing on previous theory and research on the development of children's remembering abilities, have suggested that when children witness familiar, real-life events, then their remembering competence might be considered comparable to that of adult witnesses. They asked chil-

|  | Objective | |
|---|---|---|
| Relationships | To understand | To intervene |
| Separate | 4. Claim of child's competence not ecologically valid | 1. Bias against finding child competent |
| Shared | 3. Competence is in the system, not in the child | 2. Make child competent for dangerous situations |

FIG. 3.4.   Children's competence at eyewitness testimony

dren and adults to play a game with a man while otherwise alone in an experimental room; the game involved performing a series of arm movements that directed attention to the man's face. A few days later, children as young as 6 years of age answered objective questions about the game and recognized the man's face as accurately as adults did. Goodman and Reed (1986) concluded that "if 5- to 6-year-old children are questioned in a nonsuggestive manner . . . their eyewitness accuracy can equal or even exceed adults'" (p. 328). Dent (1988) summarized this and similar studies: "The most important conclusion . . . is that children as young as 6 years can be as reliable as adults when answering objective and suggestive questions" (p. 102).

Yet Goodman's report of another, very similar study of children's competence for remembering people and events "sparked fireworks" at a recent conference on the credibility of children's testimony (DeAngelis, 1989). The fireworks appeared to fly from two different directions. One line of criticism, reflecting the perspective of the upper right cell (Fig. 3.4), involved the charge that Goodman had "taken sex abuse questions and attached them to events that have nothing to do with sex abuse" (p. 8), so that the children were not motivated to withhold the truth as is often the case in real-life sex abuse when an attacker warns the child to not tell. The charge, in other words, was that Goodman's research was not ecologically valid (upper left cell, Fig. 3.4). (In fact, Goodman is well aware of the limits of her research findings; e.g., see Goodman & Reed, 1986.) Another participant neatly exposed the bias in this charge, however, referring to "the general trend among scientists in the field toward skepticism regarding children's ability to accurately report abuse" (p. 8). In summary, the recent response among research psychologists to an empirical demonstration of children's competence as eyewitnesses was structurally the same as that of the legal system to the possibility that children might be competent to provide credible testimony (upper right cell, Fig. 3.4); the burden has typically been on those who seek to prove that a child's eyewitness testimony should indeed be accepted as credible. The structural similarity stems from the salience of the image of domination of children within both the legal and the psychological professions.

A second line of criticism, also concerned with ecological validity, reflected the perspective of the lower left cell (Fig. 3.2), living with children. In order to understand this line of criticism, one should keep in mind that the principal issue with regard to children's competence to testify is whether or not they will be misled through suggestive or leading questioning into errors of intrusion or commission in their reporting of significant events. The question is whether children easily can be led to report events that *might* have happened but in fact did not. This is widely presumed to be the case; in some instances judges explicitly instruct juries that children are particularly suggestible (Goodman & Hahn, 1987). At the same conference, Clarke-Stewart and Dent reported studies directed toward describing the context within which children's testimony would be least open to suggestive or leading questions. Clarke-Stewart (as reported in DeAngelis, 1989, p. 8) found that more suggestible children were also suggestible in contexts other than the experimental setting, were more compliant, and were less knowledgeable about what it means to lie. Furthermore, their parents were "less likely to value self-direction for their children and were not as strict about the children's lying." She also found that, when a confederate asked some of the children not to tell what had happened during the experimental session, those children who subsequently did not tell were more often children without preschool experience, less knowledgeable about lying and secrets, and less socially mature, competent, and confident. Dent (as reported in DeAngelis, 1989) reported on procedures that were successful in minimizing the suggestibility of children in response to questioning: The interviewer told the child that he or she did not know what actually happened; the children were explicitly instructed to say "I don't know" if they didn't know the answer to a question; the children were assured that the interview wasn't a test so that it didn't matter whether they remembered a lot or a little; and so forth. Dent also reported individual differences among interviewers, with those who were trained and practicing school teachers obtaining high levels of accuracy in the children's testimony.

One might ask in what ways the research procedures and the findings reported by Clarke-Stewart and by Dent correspond to the image of living with children (Fig. 3.2). First, the competence of the child to provide eyewitness testimony is not conceived as located solely within the child him or herself, as is the case for the image of domination of children. Instead, the competence of the child to testify is located within the system of relationships that includes (a) the child; (b) the parents and their attitudes toward compliance, lying, and so forth; and (c) the legal system, including what procedures are followed by representatives of the legal system in preparation for and during testimony by the child. Assessment of competence to testify, as might be ordered by a judge, is not assessment of something that inheres only within the child; instead, the assessment is of the whole system of relationships. If the conclusion is that there is a lack of competence to testify, then the lack is not the child's alone, but a lack in the system of potential supporting relationships within which the child is embedded. The implication of locating competence not within the child but within the system of relationships is, of course, that a variety of actions might be taken to facilitate the child's competence, actions directed not merely toward the child but more importantly toward the parents and the community. This perspective on the nature and location of competence is most consistent with the image of living with children.

## SUMMARY

I have argued in this chapter that there is a continuity of images among (a) the ways in which we conceive the relationship of humans to the natural environment; (b) the ways in which parents, teachers, and public officials understand the contexts in which children develop; and (c) the various contexts in which children's competence is assessed and the results of those assessments are interpreted. In particular, a continuity exists between the image of the domination of nature by human beings and that of the domination of humans by each other, including the domination of children by their parents, teachers, and public officials. Within the first image of domination, strong intervention into nature by humans is required in order to produce value and profit, just as strong intervention into the lives of children by their parents is required in order to bring about successful development. In both cases, intervention is considered to be primarily a technical matter, free from issues of value and ethics. The interest in assessment is one of determining the extent of the raw capacity for development and evaluating the degree to which interventions in development have been successful. The second major image is that of understanding the ecological system within which humans live and the relationships within which both children and parents are immersed. Both nature and children are assumed to have intrinsic worth apart from any intervention by human adults, and so issues of responsibility and caring are inherent whenever actions toward nature and children are contemplated. The interest in assessment is in ensuring the quality of the communicative relationship between humans and nature and between parents and children, for this relationship is the basis for a sound ecosystem and a sound family system as well as the foundation for future development.

Resolution of controversies in the assessment of children's competence will depend on a closer examination neither of the techniques and tools of assessment nor of an idealized notion of competence. Instead, progress towards resolving these controversies will come through contextualizing the controversy, that is, through examining both the kinds of situations in which the controversy arises and the motivations of the actors in those situations. One must ask whose interests are being served by the process of assessment and by the interpretation given to the assessment of children's competence, as well as what type of assessment is involved: of children and their achievements or of the system of relations in which childen are immersed and the system-wide understanding of the course of development. Finally, one might ask what the type of assessment implies for conceptions of the relationship between parents, teachers, and public officials and the children in their care. The images of nature presented in this chapter do not in themselves provide a simple guide to resolving issues about the competence of young children; instead, the images merely provide a framework within which discussion of the extent of children's abilities might profitably be pursued, as in the case of children's competence at eyewitness testimony. Is circumcision of male children natural or not? The framework provided in this chapter does not directly provide an answer to this question. But events in Bulgaria, from which 320,000 Muslim Turks have recently fled in one of the largest population movements in Europe since World War II, provide evidence of the strong association between implicit images of what is natural and whether and how we can control nature as well as other human beings. The Muslim Turks are fleeing Bulgaria in part because of their perception that their right to circumcise their male children has been denied (Howe, 1989).

## REFERENCES

DeAngelis, T. (1989). Controversy marks child witness meeting. *The APA Monitor, 20*(9), 1, 8–9.

Dent, H. (1988). Children's eye-witness evidence: A brief review. In M. M. Gruneberg, P. E. Morris, & R. N. Sykes (Eds.), *Practical aspects of memory: Current research and issues* (Vol. 1, pp. 101–106). New York: Wiley.

Goodman, G. S., & Hahn, A. (1987). Evaluating eyewitness testimony. In I. B. Weiner & A. K. Hess (Eds.), *Handbook of forensic research* (pp. 258–292). New York: Wiley.

Goodman, G. S., & Reed, R. S. (1986). Age differences in eyewitness testimony. *Law and Human Behavior, 10*(4), 317–332.

Habermas, J. (1982). A reply to my critics. In J. B. Thompson & D. Held (Eds.), *Habermas: Critical debates* (pp. 219–283). Cambridge: MIT Press.

Howe, M. (1989, October 1). Ankara, at U.N., plans to press Bulgaria on the rights of its Turks. *The New York Times*, p. 10.

Joyce, I. (1967). *Never talk to strangers*. Racine, WI: Western Publishing.

Kagan, S. L. (1987). Early schooling: On what grounds? In E. Zigler & S. K. Lynn (Eds.), *Early schooling: The national debate* (pp. 3–23). New Haven: Yale University Press.

Katz, L. G. (1987). Early education: What should young children be doing? In E. Zigler & S. K. Lynn (Eds.), *Early schooling: The national debate* (pp. 151–167). New Haven: Yale University Press.

Langway, L. (1983, March 28). Bringing up superbaby. *Newsweek*, 62–68.

Leiss, W. (1972). *The domination of nature*. Boston: Beacon Press.

Lewis, M., & Freedle, R. (1973). Mother-infant dyad: The cradle of meaning. In P. Pliner, L. Krames, & T. Alloway (Eds.), *Communication and affect: Language and thought* (pp. 127–155). New York: Academic Press.

Meacham, J. A. (1984a). Memory: Developmental changes. In B. B. Wolman (Ed.), *Progress volume: International Encyclopedia of neurology, psychiatry, psychoanalysis, and psychology.* New York: Van Nostrand Reinhold.

Meacham, J. A. (1984b). The social basis of intentional action. *Human Development*, 27, 119–123.

Meacham, J. A. (Ed.). (1985). *Family and individual development.* Basel: Karger.

Meacham, J. A. (Ed.). (1987). *Interpersonal relations: Family peers, friends.* Basel: Karger.

Riegel, K. F. (1979). *Foundations of dialectical psychology.* New York: Academic Press.

Sameroff, A. J. (1975). Transactional models in early social relations. *Human Development*, 18, 65–79.

Sameroff, A. J., & Chandler, M. J. (1975). Reproductive risk and the continuum of caretaking casualty. In F. D. Horowitz (Ed.), *Review of child development research* (Vol. 4, pp. 187–244). Chicago: University of Chicago Press.

Turtle, J. W., & Wells, G. L. (1988). Children versus adults as eyewitnesses: Whose testimony holds up under cross-examination? In M. M. Gruneberg, P. E. Morris, & R. N. Sykes (Eds.), *Practical aspects of memory: Current research and issues* (Vol. 1, pp. 27–33). New York: Wiley.

Vygotsky, L. S. (1978). *Mind in society.* Cambridge, MA: Harvard University Press.

Wertsch, J. V. (1985). *Culture, communication, and cognition: Vygotskian perspectives.* Cambridge, MA: Cambridge University Press.

Yarmey, A. D. (1988). Streetproofing and bystanders' memory for a child abduction. In M. M. Gruneberg, P. E. Morris, & R. N. Sykes (Eds.), *Practical aspects of memory: Current research and issues* (Vol. 1, pp. 112–116). New York: Wiley.

Youniss, J., & Smollar, J. (1985). *Adolescent relations with mothers, fathers, and friends.* Chicago: University of Chicago Press.

Zigler, E. F. (1987). Formal schooling for four-year-olds? No. In E. Zigler & S. K. Lynn (Eds.), *Early schooling: The national debate* (pp. 27–44). New Haven: Yale University Press.

Zigler, E. F., & Lang, M. E. (1985). The emergence of "superbaby": A good thing? *Pediatric Nursing*, *11*(5), 337–341.

Zigler, E. F., & Lang, M. E. (1986, December). The "gourmet baby" and the "little wallflower." *Zero to Three*, 8–12.

# Part II

# Issues in Piagetian Theory

As the preceeding chapters have made clear, questions having to do with the ages at which children first display various cognitive competencies have been debated most often in relation to Piaget's theory and research. Many claims for the early development of competence have been supported with findings from research involving modified versions of the same tasks that Piaget himself pioneered. Such findings were controversial, not only because of the claim that a given ability had been found to develop earlier than Piaget had originally reported, but also because of the stronger implication that the evidence for early competence actually *contradicted* Piagetian theory. Although much of the discussion was focused on issues of assessment and methodology, also at stake were questions about how best to interpret Piagetian theory and what sorts of outcomes reasonably could be predicted from it. Such questions are taken up in the four chapters comprising this second part of the book.

In chapter 4, Leslie Smith argues that, contrary to received interpretations, Piagetian theory was not meant to address the question of the age at which a given competence is first acquired. In his view, age is not a defining criterion of developmental stages, but like social class, an indicator that is empirically associated with them. A further argument is that Piaget's theory is better conceived as a theory about how normatively higher level abilities develop from lower level abilities rather than a theory about how ability develops from the lack of ability. From this perspective, research on early competence in young children appears in a new light; the question is not whether young children do or do not think "logically," but what *sort* of logic is embodied in their thought.

In chapter 5, Anne Dean and James Youniss argue that researchers in North America often assimilated Piagetian theory to categories that were familiar to them without accommodating to the particular issues the theory was intended to address. As a result, a more or less distorted version of Piagetian theory often was made to play the role of a straw man against whom the presumably damaging evidence for early competence could be directed. This thesis is argued in the context of two examples: mental imagery and moral judgment. In each case, evidence for early competence previously believed to be inconsistent with Piagetian theory is judged, upon closer examination, to be either irrelevant to the theory or consistent with it after all. In the case of mental imagery, questions regarding the format of images are said not to be of central importance for Piagetian theory. In the case of intentional moral judgments, Piaget is found to have reported instances of early competence himself. Dean and Youniss' point is not to "defend" the theory against potentially falsifying evidence, but to gain a more differentiated view of it and of the kinds of questions that Piaget sought to address.

A similar concern motivates chapter 6, by Jacques Montangero. The central issue in this chapter is how to explain the fact that children often are able to solve variously modified versions of typical Piagetian tasks at an earlier age than they can solve the original versions. In Montangero's view, such findings do not necessarily imply that the original tasks were faulty assessment instruments, nor that the competence those tasks were intended to assess develops earlier than originally believed. Instead, the use of such modified tasks is said often to result in the assessment of simpler precursor competencies than were targeted with the original tasks. Montangero argues that the problem is one of determining exactly what is assessed in each case and that this end can be accomplished only through a theoretically grounded task analysis in which the successive levels in a common sequence of competencies can be differentiated from each other. This approach is illustrated in the context of research on children's temporal judgments. The basic argument is that some temporal judgment tasks enable children to infer temporal duration from distance or speed alone, whereas other tasks require both speed and distance to be considered. The fact that children are able to solve the first type of task at an earlier age than they can the second does not imply that the latter is a less sensitive measure of the same competence. Instead, different competencies are assessed in each case: inferences from a single antecedent variable as opposed to inferences based on the coordination of two antecedent variables.

A somewhat different approach to problems of competence and task analysis is taken by Eberhard Schröder and Wolfgang Edelstein in chapter 7. Whereas most debates on the timing of cognitive development have involved differences of opinion regarding the earliest manifestations of a particular competence, Schröder and Edelstein argue that the generalization of competence to different problem types is also of interest. Two types of factors are described that constrain the progress of such generalization: intrinsic contraints that include the effects of materials, strategies, and response modalities, and external constraints that involve the opportunities for action and experience available in different sociocultural contexts. The effects of both types of constraints are illustrated in a longitudinal study of children's class inclusion reasoning. Intrinsic constraints were represented by task variations in problem type and response modality, and external contraints by social class and general ability. For present purposes, the major finding was that the generalization of competence across task variations and performance conditions developed relatively late and that this process was affected by interactions involving problem type, social class, and general ability.

In summary, the authors of these chapters are generally skeptical about many claims of early competence or about the relevance of such claims for Piagetian theory. Their skepticism rests on the belief that research findings concerning the development of competence in young children do not necessarily mean what they generally have been interpreted to mean: that a particular competence has been found to develop earlier than previously believed on the basis of some formally equivalent, but procedurally simpler assessment procedure. Instead, these authors claim that such findings often reflect the existence of earlier precursors of later developing competencies and argued that the problem lies in knowing how to conceptualize such precursor abilities in relation to more fully developed competencies.

# Chapter 4

# Age, Ability, and Intellectual Development in Piagetian Theory

Leslie Smith
*Lancaster University*

The main argument of this chapter is that the understanding and assessment of a theory about the development of intellectual competence is dependent on its interpretation. Piaget's theory is a case in point. Developmentalists are not always mindful of the fact that there are several, competing interepretations of this theory. According to one (age-of-acquisition) interpretation, Piaget's theory concerns the ages at which intellectual competence is acquired. According to a second (differentiation-over-time) interpretation, Piaget's theory concerns how new forms of intellectual competence emerge over time. Developmentalists who accept the first interpretation often take Piaget's theory to be misleading or even incorrect. Developmentalists who accept the second interpretation often take questions about the validity and utility of Piaget's theory to be open. Elaboration of this difference with special attention to its implications for resolving currently interesting questions about appropriate criteria for competence will be the central task in this chapter.

The age-of-acquisition interpretation has figured prominently in commentary on Piaget's work for at least 30 years. In his monograph, Braine (1959, p. 1) stated that Piaget's theory has two aspects. First, it is a theory of intelligence: Piaget believed that the development of intelligence consists in the development of an ability to perform logical operations. Second, Piaget made specific statements about the ages at which certain types of reasoning develop and the principal ages of transition are reported to be at 7 and 11 years, approximately.

In this passage, Braine made two points in the interpretation of Piaget's theory. His first point was that, for Piaget, intellectual development is the development of logical abilities. His second point was that this process is age-related and it is on this point that Braine spent most of his discussion. His aim was to show that the ages given by Piaget are wrong. Subsequent commentary has tended to follow suit and the evidence has been generally regarded as running counter to Piaget's position (Gelman, 1978; Gelman & Baillargeon, 1983). A commitment to the same interpretation was given in a discussion of Braine's first point when, some 10 years later, Flavell and Wohlwill (1969, p. 80) took Piaget's theory to raise unanswered questions about the transition from not-in-competence to first-in-competence. The claim made here is that competence which is initially absent is later acquired, leading to the charge that Piaget's theory is conceptually suspicious because development is not an all-or-none process. Indeed, Piaget's theory has been considered problematic just because it seems to lead straight to the learning paradox, that is, that knowledge is somehow made to emerge from ignorance (Bereiter, 1985). The argument used by these developmentalists can be summarized as follows. According to their interpretation, Piaget's theory generates empirical or conceptual problems. Their conclusion is that these problems are so severe that it is better to replace the theory that gave rise to them.

There is, however, an alternative to consider, namely that Piaget's theory can be understood in terms of the differentiation-over-time interpretation. Conflation and attendant inconsistency can only arise if separate interpretations are not kept separate. In this chapter, an argument that shows why the age-of-acquisition interpretation is neither the sole nor the safest way of interpreting Piaget's theory is presented in three parts. The aim in the first part is to show that the ages given in Piaget's theory are indicators, rather than criteria of intellectual development. The aim in the second part is to identify the restricted senses in which the attribution of both ability and inability are central to Piaget's theory. The discussion in these two parts leads away from the interpretation that development is a transition from incompetence to competence. The third part of the argument is a consideration of the differentiation-over-time interpretation and programmatic suggestions are identified for its further investigation.

## The Question of Age

The fact that Piaget attended both to empirical questions related to his theory of stages and to the conceptual question of which criteria should be invoked when the notion of stage is used creates a problem. Although age is not one of his criteria for developmental stages, Piaget nevertheless drew conclusions about the relation of age to developmental change in his empirical accounts. Five criteria for a coherent account of developmental stages are offered by Piaget (1960), namely constant order, integration, consolidation, overarching structure, and equilibration. In commenting on the constant order criterion, Piaget made it clear that age is not a criterion, because the sequence of behavior patterns is "constant, independently of the acceleration or delay which can modify the average chronological age due to acquired experience or social context. . . . In psychology, the distinction is always drawn between chronological and mental age" (Piaget, 1971, p. 17; my amended translation). In this passage, Piaget was making two points. The first is that the appearance of a stage is not age-related, even though the order in which different stages appear is constant. The second point involving the distinction between chronological and mental age reinforces the first. This same denial that age is a criterion of stage is repeated elsewhere by Piaget (1983). Despite these clear theoretical assertions, Piaget nevertheless frequently drew conclusions about children's age in reviewing his own empirical work. In a number of passages, he both reviewed his criteria for the identification of a stage and, in one and the same text, reported the ages at which developmental stages are attained (Piaget, 1960, 1983; Piaget & Inhelder, 1969). In short, Piaget's theoretical account supports the expectation that age is not a criterion of a child's stage of development, but his empirical accounts embody conclusions about the relation of children's age to developmental level. At best, this evident tension merits clarification; at worst, it marks inconsistency.

When problems are found in Piaget's theory, two general lines of response are possible. One is to devise an alternative theory. The other is to devise an alternative interpretation of Piaget's theory (Smith, 1986b, 1986d, 1987a, 1987b). The approach taken here involves the second of these courses and also a reinterpretation of Piaget's empirical claims regarding age. The specific argument is that age is an indicator, not a criterion, of developmental level. This argument has a threefold rationale. First, claims about children's age are theory-laden, whereas claims about children's developmental level are value-laden. This difference renders problematic any explanation of the latter in terms of the former. Second, age is a convenient variable to invoke in the explanation of children's development, but it is not the only, and perhaps not even the main antecedent variable. Social class, for example, is another, significant, antecedent variable, which is typically by-passed in studies of intellectual development. Third, reference to age of success frequently results in age-ranges rather than specific ages. In consequence, age is a poor criterion of developmental level. With these three summaries in mind, discussion can now turn to their more detailed elaboration. A *criterion* of a given concept formulates the properties that must be present or absent for the criterion to be applied to particular case. A criterion is meant to be universally valid, so no exceptions to it should exist. For example, a biological criterion of maleness might specify the chromosomes that a person must possess to be male. Using this criterion, any person who has the stipulated property is and must be male, and any person who does not have this property is not and cannot be male. The biological criterion of maleness is silent about the clothes that people wear, therefore no exception to this criterion arises when a Scotsman wears a kilt or when Margaret Thatcher wears trousers. But the clothes that a person wears provide a convenient *indicator* of a person's gender. An indicator is more or less useful, rather than valid or invalid. Unlike a criterion, an indicator may have exceptions. The utility of an indicator is dependent not on the existence of exceptions, but on their relative frequency. The distinction between a criterion and an indicator is regularly found in philosophical discussions, ranging from Aristotle on essence and accident to Wittgenstein (1958a) on criterion and symptom. Because Piaget (1950) has stressed that his work often has a philosophical dimension, it is reasonable to use this distinction in evaluating his position.

Exceptions to the criteria proposed by Piaget would contradict his account of intellectual stages. The fact that age is not one of these criteria means that some children may succeed on some of his tasks at earlier or at later ages than those stated in his empirical reports without contradicting that account. If the ages stated by Piaget are found to be incorrect because of regular disconfirmation, their utility as an indicator is impaired. But the disconfirmation of an indicator leaves the attendant theory intact. Age is an indicator, but not a criterion of a developmental stage. The three arguments in support of this conclusion follow here.

## FACTS AND NORMS

Piaget took his theory to be explanatory of intellectual development. Demarcating one developmental stage from another is one step toward that end. It is quite a different matter to show how the abilities associated with earlier stages generate those associated with later stages. In the latter case, there may be an implied claim that one stage is more "advanced" than its predecessor. Such a claim is value-laden and normative. A norm is invoked in any claim that one of two abilities is more advanced than another. By contrast, observations are always theory-laden (Popper, 1979) and so observations regarding the ages at which children succeed on certain tasks presuppose some theory that can be used in their interpretation. Nevertheless, observational reports and theoretical statements are intended to be factual descriptions of what is the case. Thus, reports about the ages at which children succeed on developmental tasks, even when interpreted by reference to a theory, are always factual in character. In short, Piaget's theory has a normative component, unlike merely factual reports about the age at which children succeed on developmental tasks. It is widely accepted that a normative conclusion can never be deduced from premises that are exclusively factual. This principle is known as Hume's rule, after the philosopher who is taken to have first stated it (see Smith, 1986c). This philosophical principle is general in its application but it has a special relevance to accounts of children's development. Indeed, there are two ways in which a developmental theory, including Piaget's, is normative. In the first place, a developmental theory is normative when it deals with the development of competences that may be possessed with varying degrees of accomplishment (Wood & Power, 1987). This distinction has a basis in common sense, marked by the difference between the mere possession of a basic competence and the possession of that competence in abundance. The distinction is revealed in practice by contrasting the *successful* display of an ability with a display of *high* (or *expert*) ability. A successful display of an ability is such that the minimum standard for attributing that ability has been met, that a particular ability, and not some other, has been evidenced. A display of high ability requires the display to be successful but also that some further standard has been met as well to indicate that the ability is possessed to some exceptional degree. This distinction has a bearing on familiar discussions about whether a child's possession of an ability requires the production of judgments versus explanations as "response criteria" (Brainerd, 1973), about receptive versus spontaneous understanding (Bryant, 1974), or about the question of transfer (Brown & Desforges, 1979). Many psychological critiques of Piaget's theory have not taken the difference between a successful display of ability versus high ability into account.

In the second place, a developmental theory is normative because it deals with children's acquisition of "better" norms. Two mental activities differ when the (logical) principle used in one is more advanced than that used in the other. This is a normative, and not a factual, difference. In specifying the difference between concrete and formal operational thinking, Piaget (1966) referred to multiplicative classification, which is one manifestation of concrete operations, whereby a child can entertain the four possible ways in which two bi-valent properties can be exemplified. Formal operations is said to be the generalization of these four basic possibilities so as to form a combinatorial system, because there are 16 ways in which this quartet can be realized in specific cases (Byrnes, 1988; Chapman, 1988; Smith, 1987a). Leaving questions about the empirical acceptability of this account to one side, the account clearly addresses the crucial task of clarifying the extent to which one type of thinking might be said to be *better* than another.

Besides such valid reasons why a developmental theory is normative, it is also worth considering some *invalid* reasons why it might be thought to be normative. A developmental theory is not normative merely because the norms used by children are within its domain. As Piaget (1966) noted, the norms used by children can be investigated empirically as "normative facts" in much the same way that an anthropologist can study empirically the (moral, legal, linguistic) norms used in different human cultures. Nor is a developmental theory normative merely because it embodies norm-referenced measurement, such as when a child's performance on a test is related to the performance of peers.

Norm-referenced assessment generally is contrasted with a criterion-referenced assessment, in which a score is interpreted in relation to some external standard (Nitko, 1983). Psychometric tests are norm-referenced and Piagetian tasks are criterion-referenced (Gray, 1978), although some developmentalists have used norm-referenced techniques in relation to such tasks (Kingma & Koops, 1983). In such cases as these, *norm* has a factual and not a value-laden meaning.

Manifestly, a commitment to the general philosophical position that factual premises never have normative conclusions has a clear consequence. Purely factual reports about the ages at which children succeed or fail on Piagetian, or any other, tasks have no explanatory force when normative questions arise. Reports about the ages at which one competence follows an earlier competence cannot by themselves be used to answer the question of which competence is more *advanced*. Such reports may have independent interest, but they could not, in principle, serve as a criterion of developmental level.

## Social Class as an Alternative Antecedent Variable

Age is one of several prospective, antecedent variables that are ignored in Piaget's theory. This proposition may be explained as follows. Charting the course of cognitive growth involves establishing the sequence in which intellectual abilities develop. In this context, reports of children's ages of task mastery have pragmatic value only. Suppose, for example, a developmentalist wished to document examples of IA or IIA or IIIA operational thinking (Inhelder & Piaget, 1958). Which children could be expected to display such thinking? This question has only to be formulated for the utility of age reports to be appreciated in the selection of children to participate in a study. It is plausible to argue that age reports were included by Piaget as an aid to investigators and as an approximate guide to children's abilities in their development over time. This stance is a consequence of an interest in distinctive developmental processes that are taken to be complementary to genetic, environmental, and social processes (Piaget, 1983). Without calling into question the utility of age as an indicator of cognitive development, it is also the case that the average ages given by Piaget in connection with a given developmental level can be increased or decreased by the selection of children on the basis of their social class. In fact, social class has been shown to affect the distribution of performances on Piagetian tasks (Schröder & Edelstein, chapter 7, this volume). Similar marked class differences in successful performance on conservation tasks have been found, in that middle-class children are more likely to be successful than lower class children (Figurelli & Keller, 1972). In other studies of the conservation of liquid quantity, half of the children whose backgrounds were less favorable were found to give nonconserving responses; by contrast, one quarter of the children whose backgrounds were more favorable gave conserving responses (Doise & Mugny, 1984). Sometimes class is invoked to explain un-anticipated findings, such as the lower success rates on some conservation tasks (Light, Buckingham, & Robbins, 1979). Similarly, the incidence of formal oper-ational thinking has been found to be related to schooling in a national study of British children by Shayer and Adey (1981). In their study, three-quarters of the (middle-class) children aged 16 years based in private schools were found to display formal operational thinking, whereas the same proportion of chil-dren in all schools considered together did not. Comparable differences have emerged in American studies of proportional reasoning. In a study by Kar-plus (1981), for example, some two-thirds of the 12th-grade children from middle-class backgrounds in the United States displayed advanced levels of thinking, in contrast to only one sixth of the children in the same grade from poorer backgrounds.

The first conclusion to draw from these several studies is that social class makes a great difference in performances. Consequently, the exclusive pre-occupation with children's age would seem to be misplaced, in so far as the effects of class are at least as strong, and in some cases stronger than those of age. Age is one important variable but certainly not the only one, and it is perhaps not even the major antecedent variable of children's development. This conclusion is compatible with the claim made earlier that the ages given by Piaget are indicators, not criteria of developmental level.

A second conclusion is that the studies just cited are exceptional by their inclusion of information about social class. Most studies are silent about this variable, as are most reviews of intellectual development. Social class is large-ly ignored by many developmentalists, including Piaget. In consequence, the criticism that the ages stated by Piaget are incorrect is premature to the extent that it is based on studies where there is confounding of age and of class. Age claims arising from studies that do not control for social class can be submerged by findings from studies that do. Curiously, experimental studies in which an-tecedent variables are scrupulously manipulated are remiss in failing to con-trol for such an obvious source of variation. At best, critics who contend that age enjoys criterial status present an incomplete case, if no counterpart con-trol for class has been included. At worst, the critics' case is self-refuting, be-cause the failure to control any one major variable, whether criterial or in-fluential, is as damaging as the failure to control any other.

The central conclusion to be drawn from this brief review is not that class should be introduced as a new criterion of development but that neither age nor social class is a criterion of developmental level. The ages given by Piaget can fluctutate, depending on the social class of the children who have been selected for study. Typically, lower class children succeed at a later age than do middle-class children. Although Piaget (1971) acknowledged that both chronological age and social class are variables that can accelerate or delay cog-nitive growth, neither are of criterial importance in his theory, because their presence is always necessary but never fundamental. These two variables are necessary because they *always* affect the actualization of a developmental sequence. They are not fundamental, because they *never* change the sequence itself. Therefore, they do not and cannot function as criteria of developmental level.

## "Age Range" as a Hedge Against the Criteriality of Age

If it were the case that children of *specific* ages either succeed or fail on various measures of concrete or formal operational thinking, then age might have a better claim on being a criterion for, rather than an indicator of, developmental level. Although some (e.g., Neimark, 1985) have claimed that Piaget's findings are "awesomely replicable," it is also true that there are many challenges to such claims about the precision of Piaget's theory. Interestingly, these challenges occur in two ways. On the one hand, various investigators have argued that Piaget overestimated the age at which formal operational (Kuhn, 1979; Neimark, 1975) or concrete operational (Hart, 1981; Winer 1980) thinking is first in place. Others (e.g., Donaldson, Grieve, & Pratt, 1983; Gelman & Baillargeon, 1983) have argued for the contrary position, suggesting that such abilities are in place at a much earlier age than Piaget proposed. These discrepancies have generated disagreement about the extent to which Piaget's theory is vulnerable to their presence.

It is well known that Piaget (1970) accepted the occurrence of certain discrepancies that he baptized as *décalages* or time lags. This notion was invoked by Piaget to mark the variable displays of thinking that is structurally similar, indicated by the different ages at which children succeed on different tasks. Critics have contended that *décalage* is an ad hoc device that has been invoked to insulate a theory from premature falsification (Brown & Desforges, 1979). In this connection, three claims need to be kept distinct. One claim concerns the intellectual structures that are said to underpin operational knowledge, the second the content of such knowledge and the third the tasks to be used in investigating intellectual development. Piaget (1970) could say that his theory embodied the first claim, and competing perspectives exist regarding the second claim, about how development in the content of knowledge occurs (Carey, 1985; Strauss, 1988). Indeed, a case can be made out for claiming that operational thinking is a prerequisite for intellectual progress, including the reorganisation of the content of knowledge (Lawson, 1989; Overton, 1985). With respect to the third claim, a *theory* for the design of tasks is conspicuously absent from developmental psychology. The *practice* of developmentalists is to take one task as a paradigm by reference to which serial modifications can be judged. This practice is rational and defensible, but it does not amount to theory.

Piagetians could at this point say that answers relevant to the third claim are to be judged by appeal to answers to the first, because method is subordinate to theory. Critics could say that their answers to this third question are dependent on an answer to the second. The temptation is to support one side to this dispute, assigning it priority over the other. A better conclusion is that the dispute cannot yet be resolved. A resolution might be possible, if a one-to-one or one-to-many relationship existed between operational knowledge and developmental tasks. This condition has not been met. Developmental tasks vary in unlimited ways, depending on the purposes, beliefs, and values of the investigators who design them. Following Wittgenstein (1958b), their common feature is that they form a family of over-lapping tasks that are *called* developmental. What they have in common is their varying degrees of similarity and difference. But it is not a condition of a task's being a *developmental* task that there should be a set of defining features that all-and-only developmental tasks share.

Operational knowledge, by contrast, is well-defined because there is an explicit account of the defining features whose presence is required in all-and-only operational knowledge (Piaget, 1966). Thus, no one-to-one relation exists between operations and tasks, because by common consent there are variant tasks for each form of operational knowledge (Gelman, 1978). Nor does a one-to-many relationship exist, because the different developmental tasks have not been designed by the use of a common set of principles. There are, of course, methodological techniques and experimental conventions, the use of which typically leads to tasks that are individually designed in a more or less appropriate manner. But there is no common theory whose use underpins those techniques and conventions. An analogous distinction might be made between the ''summer season'' and a ''summer vacation.'' The summer season can be strictly defined by reference to universal astronomical and geographical properties, which all summers and only summers possess. A summer vacation is identified in terms of variable human aspirations and beliefs, bounded by specific circumstances. Summer vacations need have nothing in commmon other than their being called just that. In terms of their defining features, Piagetian structures are like the summer season; in terms of their defining features, developmental tasks are like a summer vacation.

The outcome of this lack of perfect isomorphism between theory and method is variation in the ages at which children succeed or fail on developmental tasks that are *designed* to be used in the diagnostic assessment of operational knowledge. A family of tasks has associated age ranges but not specified ages. The seriation task is exemplary. Piaget (1983) stated that his own version of this concrete operational task would be successfully completed by children aged 7 to 8 years. When this task is redesigned, younger children can succeed at 4 to 5 years (Bryant, 1974), or at 5 to 6 years (Braine, 1959). These discrepancies are a reminder once again that age is an indicator, but not a criterion of developmental level.

Three conclusions can be drawn. First, such studies are often open to the challenge that the younger children's success is attributable to their use of a nonlogical strategy and, in fact, each of the redesigned tasks has been challenged on just these grounds (see Chalmers & McGonigle, 1984; Smedslund, 1963). The fact that such disputes arise is, on the present analysis, only to be expected. Tasks that are designed to be similar may in fact be dissimilar.

Second, there is a reasonable expectation that the redesign of a task can be expected to make a difference to children's performance (Donaldson et al., 1983). The question is not whether differences exist, but how these differences are to be explained. Following Chapman (1988), the redesign of a task frequently embodies a procedural change in the way the task is administered. Procedural changes do, of course, affect the demands made on children's abilities. Such changes are frequently multiple and massive, undertaken in the belief that the task-as-planned corresponds to the task-as-experienced. Developmentalists who attend to the "logic of the task" may fail to ascertain which (logical) ability children actually use when they complete the task. Attention to the *structure* of the task should not be undertaken without equal attention to the *structures* used in children's performances. Referring to children's structures, Piaget (1973) emphasized that it is for developmentalists "to find out whether the structures do exist and to analyse them" (p. 46).

Third, the question arises as to which tasks—Piaget's or his critics'—are the proper tasks to use in the assessment of intellectual development. The assumption ferquently is made that this disjunction is exclusive. On the present analysis, the disjunction is better treated as inclusive. Which member of a family of tasks is to be selected on any occasion will depend on the purpose behind the selection. The effect of this proposal is to shift attention from one question (which age?) to another (which intellectual abilities?).

## THE QUESTION OF ABILITY

The claim that children are incapable or lack competence is ambiguous. It could be a comparative claim that children's abilities are relatively deficient by comparison with those possessed by adults. The suggestion (Gelman, 1978) that developmentalists should focus on the respects in which younger children are both similar to and different from older children makes use of this interpretation. Quite different is an absolute claim about children's lack of competence. This claim is not merely the denial that a mature ability is present, but rather the assertion that an inability is present.

Commentators on Piaget's answer to the age-of-acquisition question often invoke such absolute claims. The implication is that if a new ability is acquired by children at a specified age, then younger children did not have that ability. That is, younger children lack the ability, which will be acquired by a specified later age. Commentators object to this position on two counts. One is that intellectual development becomes, in principle, impossible (Bereiter, 1985). A second is that intellectual development does not, in fact, occur in this way because children have more abilities than are dreamed of in this philosophy (Gelman, 1978).

Piaget apparently made absolute claims about children's incapacity. A Stage I conservation response is styled "absence of conservation" (Piaget, 1952; Piaget & Inhelder, 1974) with the implication that such responses reveal children's lack of intellectual competence. Similarly, Piaget (1952) stated that, at Stage I, children are "incapable of estimating through correspondence" (p. 173) when performing on conservation of number tasks or that children, at Stage I, are "not capable" of making certain types of deductive inferences (p. 150) or show an "incapacity to envisage the part and the whole simultaneously" (p. 173). The implication is that abilities initially absent are later acquired such that intellectual development is a process leading from their absence to their presence.

However, Piaget's position need not be interpreted in this way. The first move in the argument is that absolute claims about lack of competence can be made, provided three distinctions are drawn between: (a) evidence for an inability and lack of evidence for an ability; (b) the absence of a specified ability and the absence of ability; and (c) the absence of an ability and the failure to differentiate distinct abilities. The second move in the argument is the claim that that these distinctions taken together lead away from the view that intellectual development, according to Piaget, procedes from lack of competence to its acquisition, and toward an emphasis on the successive differentiation of abilities through time.

The first move of the argument is the identification of three distinctions on which legitimate claims about children's lack of competence can be based. Each of these distinctions is now discussed in turn.

## Lack of Competence Versus Lack of Evidence for Competence

In research on intellectual development, children are frequently invited to perform a task, and their performance is assessed by the use of operational criteria. When a child's performance satisfies these criteria, the inference to draw is that the child possesses a corresponding ability. The inference to draw when a child's performance does not satisfy the criteria is more difficult to determine. The failure to perform in accordance with the criteria may be due to inability but it may also arise because an ability possessed by the child is not used in performing that task. Thus, there is an asymmetry, in that a successful performance warrants the attribution of some ability, whereas an unsuccessful performance leaves open the question of which abilities a child has.

The logical principle on which this objection is based is unexceptionable. It is colloquially expressed in the dictum that "you cannot prove a negative." The objection itself, however, is based on a false premise about the nature of Piaget's theory. Contrary to common assumptions, Piaget does not argue for evidence of inability but rather for the absence of evidence of an ability.

Piaget's theory is a blend of philosophical epistemology and genetic psychology (Smith, 1986a). He posed epistemological questions, which have previously been subjected to rational (a priori) analysis with a view to reworking them in such a way that empirical investigation can be used in their resolution. His four-step procedure is discussed here:

1. *Select an Epistemological Principle.* The principles that Piaget selected are taken to be constitutive of human understanding in the way in which Kant (1781/1933) took his categories to be the fundamental principles of the mind. On a Kantian view, any person has all of these categories and uses them as a condition of having objective experience at all. The point to notice is that the Kantian categories should be used in all human experience. On this view, we always use these categories as a condition of gaining objective understanding, and necessarily so. Piaget did not raise the question of whether such categories are used but rather whether there is development in their use. Kant's philosophical question has an empirical dimension that Piaget generalized to cover other epistemological principles.

2. *Design a Task That Requires the Use of That Principle.* Piaget's tasks are distinctive in two ways. First, the task is intended to exemplify the selected principle. Second, successful completion of the task requires the use of that principle, and success cannot arise in any other way. Piaget's designs are rarely faulted on this count.

3. *Specify Criteria for the Identification of a Successful Response.* Criteria have to be stated so that a successful performance can be distinguished from one that is not. Further, procedures have to be laid down so that there is an agreed way to ascertain children's responses to the task. Murray (1981) provided such a breakdown of Piaget's procedure.

4. *Use a Method That Shows That a Response is Durable.* Using an early taxonomy (Piaget, 1929), investigators need to find out whether a child's response has been occasioned by the the task and its procedures or whether it is a well-based feature of the child's thinking. The distinction between receptive and spontaneous understanding is implicated here.

The logic of Piaget's position is as follows: The selected principle (Step 1) refers to a fundamental human capacity. From this perspective, the capacity should be used in some degree in all human understanding. When this capacity is present, a child will perform the task (Step 2) in accordance with the specified criteria (Step 3) as shown in the clinical interview (Step 4). The presumption is that Step 1, together with Steps 2, 3 and 4, can be used as the basis for predictions about children's performance. The present problem concerns the conclusion to draw when a performance does not satisfy the criteria, when children make incorrect responses. Piaget's main hypothesis embodies a complex antecedent (Steps 1–4) and a consequent, shown by children's correct responses. A child's failure to perform provides evidence that negates the consequent of this hypothesis. Using *modus tollens*, it is reasonable to deny the antecedent. When the main hypothesis is stated and evidence runs counter to its consequent, the inference to draw is that its antecedent is false. Because the antecedent is a complex conjunction, the question arises as to how many of these conjuncts are false. A conclusion that the child lacks the ability specified in Step 1 is premature because it is at least plausible that the incorrect performance was due to breakdowns arising from any of the other three Steps 2–4. Thus, the objection to a conclusion that children in such cases lack ability is based on the realization that *modus tollens* has a limited use. *Modus tollens* shows that at least one conjunct is false but does not show which one, still less whether more than one conjunct is false. Indeed, this objection gains further support from the fact that psychological criticisms have been independently directed at Piaget's tasks (Step 2), criteria (Step 3), and method (Step 4).

Although this objection is valid, it misses the point. Questions may be raised about the adequacy of Piaget's tasks, criteria and method, but focusing on these alone leaves the main epistemological question untouched. The main question is the extent to which development occurs in the use of Kantian abilities, which are presumed to be present in each-and-every act of understanding. Thus, two levels of analysis must be distinguished. One is psychological and is relevant to the adequacy of Piagetian tasks, criteria, and method (Steps 2–4). Psychological questions legitimately arise at each of these Steps. The point to bear in mind is that whether Piaget's position at each of these Steps is accepted or rejected, his main question concerns epistemological principles (Step 1). According to this interpretation, the aim in an empirical investigation is to use permissible tasks, criteria, and methods with a view to assessing children's use of a selected epistemological principle. When children respond incorrectly, no evidence is available to show that children do use the selected principle at the appropriate standard. In such cases, it is possible to conclude that there is no evidence of competence. (See Smith, 1986a, for an earlier formulation of this argument.)

Using classification as an example, two ways of responding to Piaget's position can be identified. One way is for developmentalists to question Piaget's inclusion task, criteria, and method. These aspects of Piaget's procedure have generated much controversy (Winer, 1980) but it is important to notice whether the controversy turns on Steps 2–4 or on Step 1. Piaget could say that criticism that is not directed on this first step misses the main theoretical point.

A second way of responding is by questioning whether Piaget's theory accords too much importance to Kantian abilities and too little importance to other abilities, such as those used by young children (cf. Gelman, 1978). Evidently, this is the position taken by those who seek to show that there are other types of hierarchical thinking which are by-passed in Piaget's work, but that are central to young children's thinking (Markman, 1985). Piaget could say that his position does not exclude such research but that his position is of equal importance, if only because the use of Kantian principles is one whose use is necessary and universal. In short, the main question to ask is theoretical, concerning the types of thinking that children display. Although this question has a methodological component, the central issue for Piaget is epistemological. So viewed, children who perform unsuccessfully fail to provide evidence of their intellectual competence. In this sense and in this sense only, conclusions can be drawn about young children's lack of competence.

## Absence of Specified Competence Versus Lack of Competence

Some developmentalists argue that Piaget's theory is negative in that young children are presented as illogical and devoid of ability (Donaldson et al., 1983; Gelman, 1978). Alternative perspectives of children's development are commended because they offer a more optimistic account of early childhood development. The objection, in short, is that an account that gives prominence to the abilities that children lack is misleading in failing to do justice to the intellectual strengths that children do possess.

This objection conflates the lack of an ability with the lack of ability as such. To see this, consider the transition from concrete to formal operations. Concrete operations is not merely weaker than formal operations. Rather, certain forms of understanding are lacking in the former yet present in the latter. Manifestly, the suggestion is not that concrete operational thinking is illogical but only that it is weaker than formal operational thinking. Similarly, when Piaget and Inhelder (1974) referred to the "absence of conservation" they had in mind young children's lack of one logical ability (conservation), not the lack of all logical ability. In general, if all thinking is structured and all structures are logical in a general sense (Piaget, 1977), then pre-operational thinking is logical by virtue of its underlying structure. The question raised by Piaget is not whether thinking is logical, because it always has some logical basis, but rather what sort of logical thinking young children display.

A second reply leads to the same conclusion. Piaget was careful to specify some of the abilities that younger children use. Logicians are careful to contrast different principles of classification based on class membership and on class inclusion (Lemmon, 1966). Piaget's claim was that there is serial, rather than simultaneous use of these principles by developing children. Older children are able to use a more complex principle of class inclusion. Further, classification by inclusion is itself open to development because the classification based on the inclusion of complementary classes is posterior to that based on the inclusion of classes (Inhelder & Piaget, 1964). A classification based on a principle of class membership is a classification, and it does have a logical basis.

The interpretation that young children are totally lacking in logical ability and then develop some logical ability in middle childhood runs counter to Piaget's (1971, 1985) basic constructivist position: that a fundamental continuity exists both between biological and psychological functioning and within psychological functioning itself. On this view, structures, which are logical in form, underpin all organic life. Children lack the logical abilities of adolescents, but they have logical abilities of their own. Similarly, young children lack the logical abilities of older children, even though they have specific logical abilities of their own.

## Absence of a Competence Versus Failure to Differentiate Distinct Competences

Piaget's position is interpreted by many commentators to be one that draws attention to children's lack of competence, either because Piaget literally has no positive account of competence or because his account is overly general and underdeveloped. According to this view, Piagetian intellectual development is a process leading from absence to presence of ability. Not surprisingly, such commentators then propose to look at children's development using an alternative perspective altogether. The conclusion is frequently announced, with some claim for novelty, that young children are not as incompetent as Piaget's account suggests (Donaldson et al., 1983; Gelman, 1978).

New perspectives are always welcome. Less welcome is the premature dismissal of Piaget's account of young children's abilities. This premature rejection is probably based both on a preoccupation with Piaget's structuralist account and on a disregard for his constructivist account of how the use of initial abilities develop into more advanced counterparts. Piaget's theory presents intellectual development not so much as a process from absence-to-presence of ability but rather as one of the progressive differentiation of abilities. This position has been formulated by Piaget for 50 years and is evident in the full range of his writings from infancy (Smith, 1987b) to adolescence (Smith, 1987a). A typical expression of this view is in a discussion of conservation, in which young children's understanding is marked by "relative nondifferentiation between the quantity of matter, weight and volume and this is why the child's justifications are circular" (Piaget & Inhelder, 1974, p. 8). Another is in the discussion of formal operations, requiring both the multiplication of possibilities into a closed system of thinking that presupposes "differentiation and coordination of the points of view" (Inhelder & Piaget, 1958, p. 345). Differentiation of abilities starts from their initial nondifferentiation and leads to their later integration or coordination (Piaget, 1987, p. 3).

What is the difference, then, between the lack of an ability and the non-differentiation of abilities? A misleading parallel would be to pose the question about children's abilities as being analogous to a question about responses. Presented with a task to perform, children either display an appropriate response, or they do not. In a literal sense, the response is either present or absent. The difference between the absence-versus- presence of a response is exhaustive and exclusive. A given response is either absent or present and must be one or the other. Further, no response can be both absent and present at once. The temptation is to view an ability in the same way. So construed, an ability is either absent or present and must be one or the other and no ability can be both at once. As Flavell and Wohlwill (1969) put it, development occurs when there is a transition from "not-in-competence to first-in-competence" (p. 80).

There are two reasons for denying that abilities develop from absence-to-presence. One concerns the occurrence of intermediate abilities. The second concerns their distinguising characteristics.

*Intermediate Abilities.*   In Piaget's theory, an ability may be intermediate in one of two ways, one specific and the other general. The specific sense is manifest as a Stage II response. There is a temptation to devalue such responses just because they are taken to be less advanced than Stage III responses. This temptation should be resisted on two counts. First, Stage II responses have independent value, which is lost if prior importance is attached merely to Stage I (incorrect) and to Stage III (correct) responses. This is obvious in the case of Stage II responses on formal operational tasks, because such responses exemplify concrete operational thinking. Similarly, Stage II responses on concrete operational tasks have their own specific character. Second, Stage II responses are intermediate responses. In contrast to experimental investigations, in which two types of response (correct-vs.-incorrect) are distinguished, Piaget's practice is to invoke three. In conservation tasks, this trio would correspond to nonconservation, empirical conservation, and necessary conservation. Empirical conservation represents an advance over nonconservation, because correct judgments can sometimes be given. But it is not as advanced as necessary conservation both because incorrect judgments are still possible and because the judgment is based on its truth value, rather than on its modal status (empirical or necessary). Following modal logicians (Hughes & Cresswell, 1972), modality presupposes truth value and it is for this reason that Stage II thinking could not precede Stage III thinking. The question of whether Stage II thinking and Stage III thinking, so defined, occur simultaneously or successively is an empirical issue (Smith, 1982). It is fair to say that this issue is rarely discussed (Murray, 1981).

There is also a general sense in which an ability is intermediate. This is due to Piaget's constructivist commitments. These commitments are evident in Piaget's stage criteria, according to which earlier stages are precursors of later stages. They are evident in the denial that there is an absolute beginning (Piaget, 1968) or an absolute end (Piaget, 1986) to development. They are also evident in the dialectical nature of equilibration by which new understanding emerges from present understanding (Piaget, 1985). A Stage III concrete operational response becomes in time—*tôt ou tard*, sooner or later (Smith, 1987c)—a Stage III formal operational response. That is, understanding at any level is always an intermediary for understanding at the next level.

*Distinguishing Characteristics.*   A second reason for denying that abililies develop from-absence-to-presence is because intermediate abilities have two distinguishing features. One feature is due to circular reasoning, which may arise when children fail to *maintain* the difference between distinct notions. Consider the serial conservation of quantity, weight, and volume. The suggestion is not that young children lack these notions altogether. Rather, these separate notions are merged in a gross notion of size. For example, *Chev* says that one ball of clay is bigger than another because it is heavier and that it is heavier because it is bigger. *Chev* also says that one ball of clay is bigger because it has more clay and that it has more clay because it is bigger (Piaget & Inhelder, 1974, p. 6). Two separate notions (quantity, weight) are merged in one notion (size) and this is shown by *Chev's* circular reasoning about each. A second feature is inconsistency, shown by the use of independent criteria whose implications are incompatible. For example, *Blas* says both that the higher level of one of two equivalent quantities of liquid results in there being *more liquid* and that there is *less liquid* in that container by comparison with an equivalent amount distributed in three separate containers (Piaget, 1952, p. 6). The inconsistency arises not because the criteria invoked by *Blas* are formally incompatible. Rather, the implications arising from the use of two separate criteria (level-in- container/number-of-containers) are contradictory. One and the same quantity of liquid increases or decreases relative to the criterion used. These two features have been invoked by Piaget in many studies. In his recent work, Piaget (1986, 1987) has provided a modal model of growth in understanding (Smith, 1987c, 1989, in press). Circular reasoning and inconsistency are two manifestations of modal error, reduction in which is an invariant aspect of intellectual growth. On this interpretation, modal notions (possibility and necessity) are viewed as Kantian, epistemological principles that are used in some form at all intellectual levels from infancy to adulthood. Development in their use takes place, and this is shown by the occurrence modal error or the mistaken use of a modal notion. Piaget's position can be outlined by analogy with his view of hierarchical classification. All children have superordinate concepts at their disposal but development takes place in their coordination of the in-

tensional and extensional elements in such concepts. Intensional changes lead
to extensional changes, and vice versa (Inhelder & Piaget, 1964). Similarly,
all children use modal notions and precocious examples of their use are given
(Piaget & Garcia, 1987; see Smith, 1989, in press). Modal errors are also prevalent. The previous example of inconsistency is an example of false–positive modal error in that children are committed to the belief that something is possible, when it is not. It is not possible for the same quantity of liquid to increase
and decrease simultaneously. The previous example of circularity is an example of false–negative modal error in that children are committed to the belief
that something is not necessary, when it is. It is necessary for different properties (quantity/weight) to be distinguished from each other.

From this perspective, intellectual development is marked by the invariant
use of fundamental notions, which have a variable deployment through time.
This is exactly the position that is central to Piaget's genetic epistemology, concerning the growth of knowledge both in the history of science and in individual
children (Kitchener, 1986). Development leads to new understanding based
upon concepts and knowledge that are *already* available to individuals, await-
ing progressive reorganization. The first step in the argument is now complete
and leads to the conclusion that absolute claims can be made about children's
inability, provided the three crucial distinctions described here are drawn. The
second move in the argument is that when these distinctions are drawn, viewing intellectual development as a process starting with initial absence of ability
and ending with full presence of ability is unrealistic. An interpretation based
on the three distinctions states that intellectual development is a process in which
the use of available (less developed) abilities make possible the emergence of
better (more developed) abilities. Central to this interpretation is a focus on
the sequence of intellectual patterns that emerge over time. Children who fail
to display a specified ability (e.g., hierarchical classification) always have some
classificatory abilities, the further differentiation of which is desirable from a
developmental point of view. Development is desirable because available abilities are marked by characteristics, such as circularity and inconsistency, which
constrain the growth of human knowledge. The aim in empirical investigation
is to gain confirming, or disconfirming evidence of the serial differentiation
of intellectual competence through time.

In short, the second step of the argument leads from Piaget's structuralism
to his constructivism. The demarcation of differing developmental levels generates a static account of developmental outcomes. The specification of dynamic
processes that make intellectual growth possible requires abandonment of the
rigid distinction between complete absence and full presence of an ability. Instead, the distinction to draw is always between an ability, characterised in
terms of a weaker normative (logical, linguistic, moral) principle, and an ability which is characterised by a richer counterpart. Thus, the question to ask
concerns how the development of more advanced from less advanced abilities

takes place. This question is notoriously complex. Piaget's account of equilibration is centrally concerned with just this question, but it has not always been well received. It was regarded by Bruner (1959) as a superfluous aspect of Piaget's theory. Less dismissive is the reminder that, from 1918, Piaget invoked some account of equilibration for more than sixty years on the assumption that oversimplified notions about learning have little purchase on complex phenomena.

## DEVELOPMENT AS DIFFERENTIATION OVER TIME

The argument has been that developmentalists have been more concerned with empirical than with theoretical aspects of Piaget's work. They have taken their task to be one of finding an interpretation of Piaget's theory that can be put to empirical test, aided by some seemingly clear claims made by Piaget about his own work. The weakness of this stance is the neglect of alternative interpretations. The remedy for this neglect arises not from further empirical work, but rather from the reconsideration of the *object* of Piaget's theory.

In general, the evaluation of Piaget's theory is dependent on its interpretation. Some caution is necessary, in part because Piaget sometimes wrote as if he committed himself to one (age-of-acquisition) interpretation of his theory, and in part because he also endorsed alternative interpretations. The temptation to take Piaget's theory to be a theory about the ages at which new abilities are acquired by children who previously lacked them has been rejected in this chapter. His theory is normative and deals with children's development of better norms. An incremental increase in knowledge is different from the restructuration of knowledge (Piaget, 1985; cf. Bereiter, 1985; Carey, 1985). An incremental increase in knowledge leads to a larger understanding of the world. The restructuration of knowledge leads to a better understanding of the world. Age is one of several antecedent variables that neither in principle nor in fact could explain how better abilities, marked by better norms, are developed.

A second interpretation, and the one adopted here, is to take Piaget's theory to be a theory about how abilities develop over time. This interpretation is distinctive on the following grounds. First, the main focus of Piaget's theory is understood to be the identification and characterization of successive levels of ability that emerge through time. Questions about the age(s) at which any specific ability develops are dependent on prior agreement about the sequential patterning of ability. That is, questions about age and acquisition presuppose some view of relative ordering of developing competence. Piaget's theory provides one such view, although it is doubtless not the only one. Second, empirical investigation is undertaken to establish the range of confirming and disconfirming instances to that pattern. The research question is directed toward showing the extent to which the available evidence fits the hypothesized pattern, rather than on filling out an inventory of other abilities that are not included in that pattern. This requires use of the hypothesized pattern to find out which abilities children do or do not display under specified conditions. Third, although questions can be raised about which conditions are or are not likely to lead to relevant displays of ability, the substantive question concerns the nature of the fundamental abilities that are taken to be central to human understanding. The question to ask is not whether children have fundamental abilities (because they always do) but rather which particular type they have. This question has normative and empirical components. A set of hierarchically ordered principles must be used to demarcate one type of ability from another, leading to the use of tasks, criteria, and methods in their empirical deployment. Fourth, progress in the use of these norms can be explained by the use of models that embody both invariant functional and variable structural elements. Piaget's modal model is one such model, in that all children have some form of modal understanding, which develops over time in specifiable ways. Finally, children's abilities at any age, have both a positive and a negative aspect. The extent to which later abilities in a sequence are more developed than their predecessors is determined by the normative principles that they exemplify.

Developmentalists can make up their own minds on how to treat Piaget's theory critically. Some take the theory to be of historical interest and look elsewhere for alternative perspectives (Johnson-Laird, 1983). Some take the theory to require complementation because of theoretical or empirical omission (Sternberg, 1987). Some take the theory to be open to several interpretations, leading to further empirical and theoretical evaluation. This last stance is available and productive (Chapman, 1988).

Alternative *theories* (in Popper's, 1979, sense) of intellectual development are not in abundance. Alternative interpretations of existing theories are available. Developmentalists have two routes open to them: to devise new theories, or to derive new interpretations from existing theories. Developmentalists who want to take this second route might want to move back a decade, from Braine's (1959) interpretation, to the differentiation-over-time interpretation that Piaget (1950) stated was a constitutive feature of his theory.

> From a methodological point of view, all knowledge is always taken to be relative to a given earlier state of lesser knowledge and to be capable of itself constituting just such an earlier state in relation to more advanced knowledge (p. 18, my translation).

This is a case of *reculer pour mieux sauter*.

## REFERENCES

Bereiter, C. (1985). Toward a solution of the learning paradox. *Review of Educational Research, 55*, 201-226.

Braine, M. D. S. (1959). The ontogeny of certain logical operations: Piaget's formulation examined by non-verbal methods. *Psychological Monographs: General and Applied, 73*, 475.

Brainerd, C. J. (1973). Judgments and explanations as criteria for the presence of cognitive structures. *Psychological Bulletin, 79*, 172-179.

Brown, G., & Desforges, C. (1979). *Piaget's theory: A psychological critique.* London: Routledge & Kegan Paul.

Bruner, J. (1959). Inhelder and Piaget's *The growth of logical thinking.* I. A psychologist's viewpoint. *British Journal of Psychology, 50*, 363-370.

Bryant, P. (1974). *Perception and understanding in young children.* London: Methuen.

Byrnes, J. P. (1988). Formal operations: A systematic reformulation. *Developmental Review, 8*, 66-87.

Carey, S. (1985). *Conceptual change in childhood.* Cambridge, MA: MIT Press.

Chalmers, M., & McGonigle, B. (1984). Are children any more logical than monkeys on the five term series problem? *Journal of Experimental Child Psychology, 37*, 355-377.

Chapman, M. (1988). *Constructive evolution.* Cambridge: Cambridge University Press.

Doise, W., & Mugny, G. (1984). *The social development of the intellect.* Oxford: Pergamon.

Donaldson, M., Grieve, R., & Pratt, C. (1983). *Early childhood development and education.* Oxford: Blackwell.

Figurelli, J., & Keller, H. (1972). The effects of training and socio-economic class upon the acquisition of conservation concepts. *Child Development, 43*, 293-332.

Flavell, J., & Wohlwill, J. (1969). Formal and functional aspects of cognitive development. In D. Elkind & J. Flavell (Eds.), *Studies in cognitive development* (pp. 67-120). Oxford: Oxford University Press.

Gelman, R. (1978). Cognitive development. *Annual Review of Psychology, 29*, 297-332.

Gelman, R., & Baillargeon, R. (1983). A review of some Piagetian concepts. In P. Mussen (Ed.), *Handbook of child psychology* (Vol. 3, pp. 167-230). New York: Wiley.

Gray, W. M. (1978). A comparison of Piaget's theory and criterion-referenced measurement. *Review of Educational Research, 48*, 223-249.

Hart, K. (1981). *Children's understanding mathematics: 11-16.* London: Murray.

Hughes, G., & Cresswell, M. (1972). *Introduction to modal logic.* London: Methuen.

Inhelder, B., & Piaget, J. (1958). *The growth of logical thinking.* London: Routledge & Kegan Paul.

Inhelder, B., & Piaget, J. (1964). *The early growth of logic in the child.* London: Routledge & Kegan Paul.

Johnson-Laird, P. (1983). *Mental models.* Cambridge, MA: Harvard University Press.

Kant, I. (1933). *Critique of pure reason.* London: Macmillan. (Original work published 1781)

Karplus, R. (1981). Education and formal thought—a modest proposal. In I. Sigel, D. Brodzinsky, & R. Golinkoff (Eds.), *New directions in Piagetian theory and practice* (pp. 285-314). Hillsdale, NJ: Lawrence Erlbaum Associates.

Kingma, J., & Koops, W. (1983). Piagetian tasks, traditional intelligence and achievement tests. *British Journal of Educational Psychology, 53*, 278-290.

Kitchener, R. F. (1986). *Piaget's theory of knowledge.* New Haven: Yale University Press.

Kuhn, D. (1979). The application of Piaget's theory of cognitive development to education. *Harvard Educational Review, 49*, 340-360.

Lawson, A. (1989). Research on advanced reasoning, concept acquisition and a theory of science instruction. In P. Adey (Ed.), *Adolescent development and school science* (pp. 143-75). London: Falmer.

Lemmon, E. J. (1966). *Beginning logic.* London: Nelson.

Light, P., Buckingham, N., & Robbins, A. (1979). The conservation task as an interactional setting. *British Journal of Educational Psychology, 49*, 304-310.

Markman, E. (1985). Why superordinate category terms can be mass nouns. *Cognition, 19*, 131-153.

Murray, F. B. (1981). The conservation paradigm: The conservation of conservation research. In I. Sigel, D. Brodzinsky, & R. Golinkoff (Eds.), *New directions in Piagetian theory and practice* (pp. 143-175). Hillsdale, NJ: Lawrence Erlbaum Associates.

Neimark, E. D. (1985). Moderators of competence: Challenges to the universality of Piaget's theory. In E. D. Neimark, R. DeLisi, & J. Newman (Eds.), *Moderators of competence* (pp. 1-14). Hillsdale, NJ: Lawrence Erlbaum Associates.

Nitko, A. J. (1983). *Educational tests and measurement.* New York: Harcourt.

Overton, W. F. (1985). Scientific methodologies and the competence-moderator-performance issue. In E. Neimark, R. DeLisi, & J. Newman (Eds.), *Moderators of competence* (pp. 15-41). Hillsdale, NJ: Lawrence Erlbaum Associates.

Piaget, J. (1929). *The child's conception of the world.* London: Routledge & Kegan Paul.

Piaget, J. (1950). *Introduction à l'epistémologie génétique [Introduction to genetic epistemology]* (Vol. I). Paris: Presses Universitaires de France.

Piaget, J. (1952). *The child's conception of number.* London: Routledge & Kegan Paul.

Piaget, J. (1960). The general problem of the psychobiological development of the child. In J. M. Tanner & B. Inhelder (Eds.), *Discussions on child development* (Vol. 4, pp. 3-27). London: Tavistock.

Piaget, J. (1966). *Mathematical epistemology and psychology.* Dordrecht: Reidel.

Piaget, J. (1968). *Six psychological studies.* New York: Random House.

Piaget, J. (1970). Introduction. In M. Laurendeau & A. Pinard (Eds.), *The development of the concept of space in the child* (pp. 5-10). New York: International Universities Press.

Piaget, J. (1971). *Biology and knowledge.* Edinburgh: Edinburgh University Press.

Piaget, J. (1973). *Main trends in psychology.* London: Allen & Unwin.

Piaget, J. (1977). *Recherches sur l'abstraction réfléchissante [Research on reflective abstraction]* (Vol. 2). Paris: Presses Universitaires de France.

Piaget, J. (1983). Piaget's theory. In P. Mussen & W. Kessen (Eds.), *Handbook of child psychology* (Vol. 1, pp. 103-128). New York: Wiley.

Piaget, J. (1985). *Equilibration of cognitive structures.* Chicago: University of Chicago Press.

Piaget, J. (1986). Essay on necessity. *Human Development, 29,* 301-314.

Piaget, J. (1987). *Possibility and necessity* (2 Vols.). Minneapolis: University of Minnesota Press.

Piaget, J., & Garcia, R. (1987). *Vers une logique des significations* [Toward a logic of meaning]. Geneva: Murionde.

Piaget, J., & Inhelder, B. (1969). *The psychology of the child.* London: Routledge & Kegan Paul.

Piaget, J., & Inhelder, B. (1974). *The child's conception of quantities.* London: Routledge & Kegan Paul.

Popper, K. R. (1979). *Objective knowledge.* Oxford: Oxford University Press.

Shayer, M., & Adey, P. (1981). *Towards a science of science teaching.* London: Heinemann.

Smedslund, J. (1963). Development of concrete transitivity of length in children. *Child Development, 34,* 389-406.

Smith, L. (1982). Class inclusion and conclusions about Piaget's theory. *British Journal of Psychology, 73,* 767-776.

Smith, L. (1986a). Children's knowledge: A meta-analysis of Piaget's theory. *Human Development, 29,* 195-208.

Smith, L. (1986b). Common core curriculum: A Piagetian conceptualization. *British Educational Research Journal, 12,* 55-71.

Smith, L. (1986c). From psychology to instruction. In J. Harris (Ed.), *Child psychology in action* (pp. 103-26). London: Croom Helm.

Smith, L. (1986d). General transferable ability: An interpretation of formal operational thinking. *British Journal of Developmental Psychology, 4,* 377-387.

Smith, L. (1987a). A constructivist interpretation of formal operations. *Human Development, 30,* 341-354.

Smith, L. (1987b). The infant's Copernican revolution. *Human Development, 30,* 210-224.

Smith, L. (1987c). On Piaget on necessity. In J. Russell (Ed.), *Philosophical perspectives on developmental psychology* (pp. 191-219). Oxford: Blackwell.

Smith, L. (1989). Constructing formal operations. In P. Adey (Ed.), *Adolescent development and school science* (pp. 329–332). London: Falmer.

Smith, L. (in press). The development of modal understanding: Piaget's possibility and necessity. *New Ideas in Psychology*.

Sternberg, R. (1987). A day at developmental downs: Sportscast for race #3 - neo-Piagetian theories of cognitive development. *International Journal of Psychology, 22*, 507–529.

Strauss, S. (1988). *Ontogeny phylogeny and historical development*. Norwood, NJ: Ablex.

Winer, G. (1980). Class inclusion reasoning in children. *Child Development, 34*, 389–405.

Wittgenstein, L. (1958a). *The blue and brown books*. Oxford: Blackwell.

Wittgenstein, L. (1958b). *Philosophical investigations*. Oxford: Blackwell.

Wood, R., & Power, C. (1987). Aspects of the competence-performance distinction: Educational, psychological and measurement issues. *Journal of Curriculum Studies, 19*, 409–424.

# Chapter 5

# The Transformation of Piagetian Theory by American Psychology: The Early Competence Issue

Anne L. Dean
*University of New Orleans*

James Youniss
*The Catholic University of America*

In this chapter, we discuss assessment of cognitive competence in terms of issues that were engendered by the meeting of Piaget's theory with American developmental psychologists. In the first part, we suggest that Piaget's theory did not fare well with North American researchers because they assimilated it to categories familiar to them without accommodating to issues he addressed. Piaget's theory emanated from a biological perspective, in which the subject-object relationship was conceptualized as reciprocal. In contrast, American psychology was dominated by prevailing views of standard science and behavioral science, which sought explanations for psychological phenomena within a stimulus–response frame of reference. The result was a transformation in which issues Piaget thought were important were converted to questions that were more relevant to the American perspective than to Piaget's theory. In particular, Piaget's interest in the structure of actions and interactions, which for him was the foremost criterion for the assessment of competence, was lost when American psychologists redefined competence on Piagetian tasks in terms of performance criteria.

In this chapter, we illustrate this transformation with a discussion of two cases, one pertaining to his work on moral judgment (Piaget, 1932/1965) and the other to his work on mental imagery (Piaget, 1962, 1963; Piaget & Inhelder, 1971). We propose that Piaget's primary interest in the moral judgment domain was in the structure of social interactions from which he argued that children construct moral universals. He took issue with Kant, who contended that moral imperatives could not be reached through empirical exper-

ience, and with Durkheim, who believed that moral principles were transmit-
ted via unilateral authority. Focus on Piaget's interest in structural issues was
lost when American psychologists challenged him on such matters as whether
preschool children reason on the basis of intentionality, or whether they can
be trained to do so.

Piaget's primary interest in mental imagery was, likewise, in structure. He
thought of the mental image as consisting of two aspects; a figurative component that essentially copies particular figural aspects of reality, and an operative component that organizes or structures figural aspects of reality. Piaget's
central hypothesis was that the second, organizational component of images
is contributed by coordinations inherent in thought. Piaget's interests got lost,
however, when his research was assimilated to contemporary cognitive psychology's conceptualization of the mental image as an internal representation
characterized by a particular code or format, which can be transformed via
the processes of mental rotation, translation, scanning, and the like. Rather
than focusing on developments in how children structure figural components
of movements and transformations, cognitive researchers asked whether young
children can code information in an imagery format, and whether they can
use the same processes to transform images as older children and adults.

These examples both help to recall Piaget's original interests and to show
the differences between his interests and those imposed by contemporary
researchers. It is now apparent that in shifting focus from the original issues,
researchers effectively created new phenomena that differed from those that
Piaget had engendered. The field is at least two generations deep into this
process of transformation and it appears that the original issues either have
been rendered irrelevant or have been forgotten. In this chapter, we attempt
to recapture the original framework in which Piaget was operating in order
to offer a new generation of researchers a view of issues that have disappeared
through successive transformations of Piaget's original project (Chapman, 1988;
Gold, 1987). We try to do this by going back to Piaget's writings to reset the
phenomena within his starting framework. Further, we attempt to show the
productiveness of the line of questioning that Piaget opened but others altered
as they brought parts of his work into the American context.

## HISTORICAL BACKGROUND

Piaget's theory was fairly well known to pre-World War II psychologists in
North America. His initial studies on language, thought, and morality were
recognized as important and merited him an honorary degree from Harvard
University at its 300th anniversary in 1937. Thereafter, however, the theory
went into eclipse until the late 1950s, when the reigning behavior paradigm
came under serious questioning and alternatives were sought to its main focus

in "learning theory." One option that emerged conceptualized individuals as cognizing agents who operated on and transformed data from the external world, and created conclusions by utilizing reasoning. Now seen as the "cognitive revolution," this view opened the field to new questions and, in a search for new grounding, Piaget's writings were resurrected as a potentially productive avenue for studying cognition (Kessen & Kuhlman, 1962).

Almost from the outset, however, optimism turned to doubt as American psychology and Piaget's theory clashed more than meshed. North American psychology had established ways of viewing reality and itself that contrasted markedly from Piaget's outlook. Although American psychologists had granted the stimulus power to force reactions in the "subject" or person, Piaget had reversed the relation and made it symmetrical by granting the person power to construct meaning for objects (Piaget & Inhelder, 1969). Further, American psychologists, concerned that they be included within the disciplinary boundaries of American science, disassociated themselves from the methods of literary scholarship and philosophical issues that they deemed unresolvable. Piaget, in contrast, consciously set out to pursue these issues with the novel approach of discovering how children constructed knowledge. He viewed this project as having the potential of helping to resolve classic controversies regarding rationality, authority, autonomy, the relationship between image and thought, and the like. He sought methods that permitted insight into children's constructions and chose open-ended procedures such as the clinical interview as a suitable entry point.

In a prophetic mode, John Flavell (1962) anticipated some of the problems that would arise when Piaget's writings were formally brought into American psychology:

> Piaget generally makes difficult reading, in either French or English, for several reasons. There are unfamiliar and poorly-defined concepts in the system which interlock into a very complex, hard-to-grasp theoretical matrix. The research methods and manner of reporting data are also unfamiliar. Much of the work is saturated with mathematical-logical and epistemological concerns foreign to the experience of the average American psychologist. These difficulties all arise from the fact that Piaget does not approach psychological subject matter in ways familiar to most of us. He sees problems we would not be likely to see, he attacks these problems with methods different from those we would espouse, and he often theorizes about his results in ways which seem esoteric and even incomprehensible to us. For better or worse, it seems to be true that anything like an adequate understanding of Piaget's system demands a certain reorientation and acclimatizing—a certain holding in abeyance of habitual ways of looking at things, at least until it all starts to come clear. (p. 16)

Flavell's fears proved, unfortunately, to be warranted. The meeting of Piaget with American psychology resulted in repeated clashes on concepts,

methods, and more deeply, purposes. The issue of competence and its measurement is a complicated case in point. For many contemporary investigators,
competence is defined solely in performance terms. This entails designating
a standard against which noncompetence is compared; hence, competence is
manifested when a subject evinces a certain act or judgment. This formulation has the advantage that performance can be studied as a function of independent factors, or conditions. Any number of independent variables, for
example, have been shown to affect the manifestation of conservation. They
include how "stimuli" are presented, the grammatical phrasing of questions
to the child, and the sequence of questions in relation to the changing stimulus
array. Piaget (1937), however, had originally generated conservation as a
phenomenon for study in order to demonstrate that a gain in reasoning was
made when mental actions became reversible in a system of actions. Of course,
he needed real performance from children for the demonstration. But the vehicle for the demonstration was less important than what it was meant to signify about the status of interior organization (structure) of mental actions (operations). Performance, in this scheme, was not to be confounded with the structural organization that conservation indicated. Although elements that might
mediate performance were affected by experience and could be learned, the
basis of conservation was children's concern for coherence among their interactions with physical objects and persons.

In what follows, we trace the transformation of Piaget's ideas about two
disparate domains of inquiry—mental imagery and moral judgment. The goals
are to recapture Piaget's original interests and to point to research that can
productively advance these interests. This is not to deny the value of alternative views. Rather, it is to give focus to issues that Piaget identified that many
of the alternatives ignore. Although Piaget collected an enormous amount of
data, his conclusions regarding the issues may be incorrect or incomplete. Openness to other solutions is a given. However, the requisite is that the issues be
recognized as important and be the objects of study for researchers. Hence,
the purpose of attempting to re-establish the original questions.


## EXAMPLE FROM MENTAL IMAGERY

### The Piagetian Perspective

Piaget and Inhelder's (1971) primary interest in mental imagery was in how
children mentally structure figural aspects of reality, in particular, spatial transformations and movements. They hypothesized, first, that developmental
changes occur in the structure of children's images, and second, that these
changes are contingent on developments in children's operative thought. Piaget's early work on infancy, described in *Play, Dreams and Imitation in Child-*

*hood* (1962) and in *Origins of Intelligence in Children* (1963), laid the groundwork for these interests. In these two books, Piaget defined the mental image as a symbol with two components, a signifier and a signified, both products of developments in sensorimotor schemes. The signified, or that to which the image refers, was termed the *conceptual object*, and was theorized to result from the process of reciprocal assimilation of schemes:

> In order that two schemata, until then detached, may be coordinated with one another in a single act, the subject must aim to attain an end which is not directly within reach and to put to work, with this intention, the schemata hitherto related to other situations. Thereafter the action no longer functions by simple repetition but by subsuming under the principal schema a more or less long series of transitional schemata. . . . In effect, the concrete connections uniting objects of the external world are constructed at the same time as the formal interrelations of schemata, since the latter represent actions capable of being brought to bear on objects. . . . During the first stages, it is very difficult to dissociate action from object. . . . In proportion as the action becomes complicated through coordination of schemata, the universe becomes objectified and is detached from the self. (Piaget, 1963, p. 211)

The signifier, or mental image proper, was theorized to result from the accommodative imitation of particular figural aspects of reality by sensorimotor schemes. For instance, when the scheme of looking is applied to the contour of an object, the scheme essentially imitates the object's figural properties. Piaget proposed that as sensorimotor schemes develop by becoming more differentiated and coordinated, more precise accommodations to figural aspects of objects and events are possible. By the time infants can combine schemes mentally before putting them into action—by the time the conceptual object develops—they can perform imitative accommodations of sensory or motor actions internally, without the support of physically present objects or events. Imitative accommodations that occur internally are manifested in the form of deferred imitation or a mental image:

> It thus becomes possible to view the image, even at the highest levels of representation, as interior imitation resulting from the ever-present sensory-motor schemas. . . . What is the process which takes place when we form a mental image of a visual scene perceived earlier? We analyze, compare and transform, using an activity which starts in perceptive regulation and comparison, but is integrated in a system of concepts enabling us to give meanings to the elements and relationships thus analyzed. Now it is this perceptive activity, and not perception as such, which produces the image, which is a kind of schema or summary of the perceived object. Moreover, the image is immediately integrated in conceptual intelligence as a "signifier," in the same way as the perceptive activity was integrated earlier at the very moment of perception, since perception may involve an intellectual as well as a sensory-motor significance. (Piaget, 1962, p. 77)

For Piaget, the mental image proper and the conceptual object were inextricably linked. He proposed that the mental image proper derives from the accommodative function of sensorimotor schemes, whereas the conceptual object derives from reciprocal assimilation of schemes. He argued that it is not possible for the infant to have a mental image of something that psychologically does not exist, nor is it possible to consciously conceive of something in its absence without some form of symbolic representation.

Piaget's later work on mental imagery with Inhelder (1971) traced developments in how children structure the components of the symbol. Piaget had already granted infants the capacity to construct the figurative component of the symbol via accommodative imitation of sensorimotor schemes. His later work focused on further developments in structural organization. Specifically, Piaget and Inhelder's (1971) experiments examined children's images of spatial movements and transformations. The component parts of these spatial events are the separate states that objects assume when they are moved or transformed. For example, when objects rotate from upright to horizontal, the beginning state is the vertical orientation, intervening states are progressively more tilted from upright, and the end-state is the horizontal orientation. Piaget and Inhelder observed that preschool-aged children can often imagine beginning and end states correctly, but distort the sequences of orientations and the positions traversed in intermediate states. To Piaget and Inhelder, the significance of this finding was not in what it implied for task performance, but in what it implied for the status of developing structures of thought and the relationship between the latter and the mental image proper.

## The Cognitive-Psychological Transformation of Piagetian Imagery Theory

When Piaget and Inhelder's mental imagery research was discovered by contemporary cognitive psychology, the performance issue was made paramount. Two studies by Marmor (1975, 1977) illustrate the challenge to Piaget and Inhelder's claim that kinetic and transformational imagery is not demonstrated before concrete operative attainment, at about the ages of 7 or 8. She tested preschool-aged and older individuals on an adapted version of a mental rotation task originally used by Shepard and Metzler (1971) in research with adults. Preschoolers essentially performed like older children and adults, leading Marmor to conclude that preschoolers use the same kinetic imagery processes as older persons. Marmor's two studies have continued to be cited by developmental cognitive psychologists (e.g. Gelman, 1978; Mandler, 1983) as evidence that no qualitative change occurs in mental imagery with development. Since Marmor's studies, little research has been conducted on this issue from the cognitive psychological perspective. In effect, the issue appears to have been closed.

To understand this turn of events and the apparent discrepancy between Piaget and Inhelder's (1971) and Marmor's (1975, 1977) findings, it is necessary to examine the cognitive psychological perspective on mental imagery, as expressed most clearly in the adult cognition literature. In considering this perspective, we emphasize the views of researchers who hold that mental imagery is an analog process (Kosslyn, 1980, 1981; Shepard & Cooper, 1982), because this view has most influenced developmental research.

Coincidentally, Shepard and Metzler's (1971) landmark study of adult mental rotation appeared the same year as the English translation of Piaget and Inhelder's (1971) *Mental Imagery in the Child*. Relying on the computer metaphor to describe the functioning of the mind, Shepard and his colleagues (e.g., Shepard & Cooper, 1982) identified the goals of their research on mental imagery as twofold: to describe the nature of the mental image, and to describe the nature of the internal transformations that are performed on the mental image. The method used in Shepard and Metzler's (1971) study was to measure times required for adult subjects to compare the identities of two differently oriented objects. Their primary finding was that comparison times increased linearly as a function of the angular difference between objects. These and subsequent findings from Shepard and his colleagues have led to two main conclusions: (a) that mental rotation is "an analog process with a serial structure bearing a one-to-one relationship to the corresponding physical rotation," and (b) the mental image "possesses an internal structure that is at least abstractly isomorphic to the structure of (the) external visual stimulus" (Shepard & Cooper, 1982, pp. 118-119). In a somewhat similar vein, Kosslyn (1981) has developed an explicit theory of mental imagery based on the computer metaphor in which mental images are conceived as "data structures" in the mind with a specific "depictive" or spatial format. Images are generated from long-term memory, and then inspected, compared, or transformed by means of imaging processes that are part of the functional capacity of the mind.

The underlying implication for Kosslyn and Shepard is that mental images have definite reality status in the mind. This leads to several implications that differentiate the cognitive psychological and Piagetian perspectives, two of which are relevant for this discussion. One is that mental images are internal representations that encode information in a definable format, which both Kosslyn and Shepard argued is depictive or spatial. The focus in their schemes is, thus, on the properties of the image. In contrast, Piaget conceptualized imaging as a mental activity that "evokes" and organizes figural properties of objects and events in a more or less coherent structural framework. Thus, focus is not on the properties of the image per se, but on how the properties of objects or events are organized in the image. In Kosslyn's and Shepard's schemes, the term *properties* applies to the image itself; in Piaget's theory, the term *properties* applies to the movements and transformations that are imagined (cf. Pylyshyn, 1981, p. 18, for a similar distinction between his and Kosslyn's theories of mental imagery).

A second implication of the notion that mental images are "things" with a definite reality status is that the image itself is distinct from the processes that operate on and transform it. This distinction raises the possibility endorsed by both Shepard and Kosslyn that image representations and processes may have different genetic origins; the former may originate in perceptual experience during ontogeny, whereas the latter may be innate (Kosslyn, 1981; Shepard & Cooper, 1982). Developments, therefore, might be expected in the contents of images, in the efficiency and automaticity with which imaging processes are carried out, or in the ways in which imagery processes operate on image representations, but not in the structure of imagery processes themselves. This view clearly differs from Piaget and Inhelder's in which images undergo structural changes from early childhood to adolescence.

The cognitive psychological perspective, when applied to research with children, leads to the following kinds of questions. Do children represent information in an imagery or spatial format? Do they use the same imagery processes to transform images as older children and adults? Further, the definition of mental imagery as a format with a particular code restricts the kinds of procedures that researchers consider valid measures of mental imagery. As for adults, only tasks that employ measures that reveal the nature of the underlying format are considered valid assessments of children's imagery. The *pièce de résistance* in cognitive psychology's armamentarium of methods is the measurement of real time required to generate, inspect, or transform an image. The rationale is that mental activity of any sort takes time, and the time taken should be a function both of the properties of the activity itself and the format of the information on which the activity is performed.

From this point of view, the usefulness of Piaget and Inhelder's findings is suspect, because their assessment of imagery via drawings leads to indefinite conclusions regarding real-time processing. To quote Kosslyn (1980):

> Some researchers have been tempted to treat children's drawings as data about their imagery. Piaget and Inhelder (1971), for example, asked children to draw a falling stick, and noted that they failed to represent continuity or a proper trajectory. This property was taken to indicate that the child's imagery also fails to preserve these qualities (see also Dean, 1976). Unfortunately, this might simply say something about the child's conventions in drawing, about how the child externalizes internal events onto two-dimensional surfaces. The child's imagery could be perfect but his or her drawing skills limited. Similarly, if a child is able to draw something but is not able to describe it, this does not necessarily show that his or her internal representations are in terms of images, but may only indicate that one response mode is more advanced than another. . . . No matter what the children's drawings look like, we probably can posit an interpretive process that will convert practically any internal representation into that drawing. (pp. 420-421)

One can readily see why Marmor's (1975, 1977) findings take on importance for this approach. Because preschoolers generate linear reaction-time trends on a mental rotation task, they manifest use of an imagery format to encode the object and use of the "rotate" process to transform the image. Because, from the perspective of the computer metaphor, imagery processes in themselves are not expected to undergo structural change in development, Marmor's results suggest no reason to question whether the "rotate" process used by preschoolers is structurally equivalent to the "rotate" process used by older individuals.

## The Piagetian Perspective Re-Visited

Because Piaget does not define mental imagery according to particular formats, reaction-time measures lose their privileged status. Piaget conceived of mental images as the product of the combined accommodative and assimilatory functions of operative schemes. Methods best suited for externalizing how states are organized in children's image are open-ended production measures such as drawings, other types of constructions, and manipulations of objects. As Dean (1991) has commented in a review of mental imagery research, neither reaction-time nor production measures can escape the criticism of ambiguity, and therefore efforts to pre-empt one method in favor of the other seem unwarranted.

From the Piagetian perspective, Marmor's findings may tell us more about ways preschoolers structure figural aspects of rotation movements than about the availability or accessibility of imagery processes. The structural side is what seems to have been lost in the assimilation of Piaget and Inhelder's (1971) theory to the cognitive psychological perspective. In this regard, it is noteworthy that in Mandler's (1983) review chapter on representation in the *Handbook of Child Psychology*, mental imagery is defined as a format for representing information internally, whereas all other categories are defined according to the content of what is represented (e.g., event representations, representations of taxonomies, and story schemas). Claims about format with respect to these latter categories are neutral. This content-based way of thinking about representational categories is consistent with Piaget and Inhelder's definition of mental imagery as the evocation and structuring of figural aspects of external reality. Indeed, when descriptions by cognitive psychologists of developments in children's event representations (Nelson, 1983) or count word sequences (Fuson, Richards, & Briars, 1982) are compared with descriptions by Piagetians of developments in children's mental images of spatial movements and transformations (Dean, 1991), a common trend emerges. Younger children's representations are held to have a global, undifferentiated quality, whereas older children's representations consist of differentiated and logically organized components. The former quality of representation may be sufficient to mentally rotate a visually present starting state into congruence with a visually present end state, as in Marmor's studies, but the latter quality may be necessary to construct a series of ordered intervening and end states, as on Piagetian drawing and other production measures. From the Piagetian perspective, then, Marmor's findings are viewed as but one data point among many in the effort to trace developments in the structure of children's mental imagery.

## EXAMPLE OF MORAL JUDGMENT

### Modeling and Moral Judgments

Piaget's book, *The Moral Judgment of the Child*, was originally published in England in 1932. It was reissued in 1965 in the United States and controversy was immediately sparked as to the age at which children understood "intention" and whether they could be trained to focus on it rather than material consequence in judging moral acts. With rhetorical flair, Bandura and McDonald (1963) showed that children who judged good and bad children in terms of intention, could be made to switch to the criterion of consequence after exposure to adult models who identified consequence as the proper criterion. The authors claimed they had demonstrated that children could be made to change behavior through modeling even when the behavior constituted a developmental "regression" from an advanced to a more primitive stage.

Specifically, children were presented with moral dilemmas similar to those used by Piaget to study "lying" (Piaget, 1932/1965, pp. 109-196). If on a pretest, a child had judged badness according to intention, the child was exposed to an adult model who made judgments in terms of consequence. If the child had judged according to consequence, the model judged dilemmas in terms of intention. Posttest data showed that children changed their judgments so as to be in accord with the models to whom they were exposed. Bandura and McDonald concluded that moral judgment could be accounted for by learning theory and the specific process of modeling. By implication, Piaget's "developmental" explanation was superfluous. The construct of stages was not needed if stage-based behavior could be evoked through brief exposure to modeling. If recognition of intention was the product of long-term development, why was it so easily modifiable?

Ahr (1971); Cowan, Langer, Heavenrich, and Nathanson (1969); and Sternlieb and Youniss (1975) have reported results that counter the modeling study. They showed that modeling is a contingent process, depending on the states children bring to the study. For the present, however, we want to go back to Piaget's analysis to see how he approached the problem and try to figure out how his stated interest and his findings came to be embroiled in a controversy about intention and consequence, stages and learning, and modeling and development.

## The Data

The material regarding intention and consequence is found on pages 109 to 196 in the chapter on "Moral Realism." Let us begin with pages 124 to 131, where Piaget reported the first 16 cases of children's judgments of good and bad with regard to consequences and intentions. The 16 excerpts are taken from nine different children, as some are cited two or more times to make separate points. Although about half of these protocols are presented to show that children judged badness according to material consequences, all nine children, in fact, explicitly recognized the intentions of the actors in the stories. The identification of intention typically occurred in the part of the method when children were to repeat the stories to demonstrate that they had grasped the facts that set up the dilemmas. Although intention was not stated in the stories, children spontaneously introduced it by imputing it to an actor. They said: ". . . he didn't do it on purpose"; "The first one wanted to help her mother"; or "He wanted to please his daddy."

Although each child recognized intention, many of them also judged that badness ensued from the material damage that some actor had caused. It is important to recognize, however, that children's focus on material consequence invariably occurred in response to the interviewer's question: "Which one is naughtiest?" or "Which one would you punish most?" Often the interviewer purposely focused on consequence by asking: "Which would you punish most, the one who broke 1 cup or the one who broke 15 cups?"

It is not surprising that within the same protocol individual children based their judgments sometimes on intentions and at other times on consequences. Piaget noted this fact explicitly: "Thus these answers present us with two distinct moral attitudes—one that judges actions according to their material consequences and one that only takes intentions into account. These two attitudes may co-exist at the same age in the same child" (p. 133).

Piaget expressed no doubt that very young children understand and use intention as a criterion of morality. "The idea of intention (not just the intentional act but the idea of the intentional act . . .) appears roughly at the same time as the first 'whys', that is at about the age of three" (p. 144, p. 179). He recognized that, nevertheless, children would often select consequence as the criterion. We can ask why children chose one criterion over another. Piaget's answer is that children focused on consequence because of the nature of the relationship between children and adults that is marked by unilateral respect and constraint. "The rules imposed by the adults, whether verbally (not to steal, not to handle breakable objects carelessly, etc.) or materially (anger, punishments) constitute categorical obligations for the child . . . Moral realism would thus seem to be the fruit of constraint and the primitive form of unilateral respect" (p. 135). And: "The objective conception of responsibility arises, without any doubt, as a result of the constraint exercised by the adult" (p. 133).

What then of intention? Piaget proposed that intention is likely to be cultivated within symmetrical relationships (cf. Chapman, 1986). "It is when the child is accustomed to act from the point of view of those around him, when he tries to please rather than to obey, that he will judge in terms of intentions. So that taking intentions into account presupposes cooperation and mutual respect . . ." (Piaget, 1932/1965, p. 137). And: "It is always cooperation that gives intention precedence over literalism, just as it was unilateral respect that inevitably provoked moral realism . . ." (p. 138).

It is clear that Piaget believed children understood both intention and consequence as criteria for moral judgment. The roots of each were to be found in forms of relationship children had with other persons, with unilateral constraint and cooperation engendering different focuses. In describing these roots, Piaget carefully avoided a rigid "stage" explanation. Indeed, throughout the book, Piaget used the term *stage* cautiously (e.g., p. 317). In the case of intention and consequence, he was definitely not arguing for stage sequence: "Objective responsibility diminishes on the average as the child grows older, and subjective responsibility gains correlatively in importance" (p. 133). And "A given child who pays no attention to intentions involved in the story of the dog, will on the contrary, judge the stories of the drawing and scissors in accordance with the psychological context . . . There can therefore be no question of two real stages. All we can say is that objective responsibility is a phenomenon frequently to be found among the younger children but subsequently diminishing in importance" (p. 156). The main reason why one waxes and the other wanes is that children's early relationships are mainly with adults whereas, later, they enter new relationships with peers, in which cooperation develops (Chapman, 1986; Youniss, 1980).

Despite what came to be the received interpretation, Piaget stated that young children understood and dealt with intention and it does not seem reasonable to assert that intention came into being because of some late stage attainment: "These answers show what fine shades even some of the youngest children we questioned could distinguish and how well able they were to take intentions into account" (Piaget, 1932/1965, pp. 130-131). And: "It is 'naughtier' to make a big spot on your coat than a small one, and this in spite of the fact that the child knows perfectly well that the intentions involved may have been good" (p. 134)

Intention is considered further in the next section of the chapter that deals with lying. The first five protocols indicate that young children construe lying as "being naughty." This would concur with the general argument regarding the force of adult constraint on children's judgment. Lying is wrong because it displeases adults who let children know that they have done something naughty. Of the next 12 protocols and children, 10 designate some form of intention in their retelling of the original dilemmas. They used phrases like: "he made a mistake," "she didn't know," "he doesn't want to say it," and "she didn't do it on purpose." The point becomes even clearer in the next section (pp. 150-154) when children show the power of the constraining relation on lying. Here are two cases in which children try to explain why lying is wrong. "MAE (6) because he had been naughty and didn't dare say so." And "KE (7) So that his mother should buy him something." It seems evident that children are telling Piaget about their own relationships with parents. They may be saying that if you tell them something nice about yourself, they are likely to give you a reward. If, on the other hand, you tell them something you did wrong, you will likely be punished. Hence, in a relationship of constraint, it pays to tell the adult what he or she wants to hear. This is evident in those protocols in which children expressed avoidance of punishment as the intention behind lying; for instance, "DEPR (7) So that his mother should not punish him." As in the prior section, Piaget concluded by identifying relationships as the source of moral attitude. Adults' rights to reward and punish engender an occasion for lying, whereas, at the same time, adults assert the rule that one should not lie. A change occurs with the development of symmetry: "In so far as habits of cooperation will have convinced the child of the necessity of not lying, rules will become comprehensible [and lead to] subjective responsibility" (p. 163).

Piaget continued his argument in the remainder of the chapter by elaborating on the role of relationship to moral judgment. He used a "James-Lange" type argument in that children view lying as naughty because adults punish lies and if they would not punish lying, children would not feel guilty or naughty. He proposed that truthfulness acquires value when the children feel part "of a society founded on reciprocity and mutual respect . . ." (p. 164). This is because telling the truth is essential to preserving that form of relationship. Cooperation forces focus on intentions because the persons must attend to their respective viewpoints and compare them. Truth is compelled by the terms of relationship in which the individuals have agreed to cooperate for mutual interest.

The last section of the chapter links moral realism to the remainder of the book and Piaget's larger point regarding moral autonomy. It is interesting to note that the concept of autonomy has been tracked back to Piaget by many contemporary moral theorists. They tend to use Piaget's ideas as follows. Autonomy is contrasted with heteronomy and the issue becomes how can the individual have a valid moral position that is not dependent on an outside authority. The supposed answer that is attributed to Piaget is that individuals take recourse to reasoning that is grounded in logicalness. One can readily see why this interpretation is tied to the well-known achievement of formal operative thinking.

Consider, however, Piaget's own definition of autonomy and his description of how it is developed. He defines autonomy in nearly opposite terms from the formula of self-reliance and recourse to logic (pp. 98, 196). Autonomy entails turning to another person in a cooperative relationship and being ready to explain your views clearly to that person while, in turn, listening to the other's views. This form of autonomy is developed within the context of cooperative relationship which entail norms of "sympathy" and "mutual respect." Hence, for Piaget:

> apart from our relations to other people, there can be no moral necessity. The individual as such knows only anomy and not autonomy. Conversely, any relation with other persons, in which unilateral respect takes place, leads to heteronomy. Autonomy therefore appears only with reciprocity, when mutual respect is strong enough to make the individual feel from within the desire to treat others as he himself would wish to be treated. (p. 196)

## CONCLUSION

We tried to make two general points with these examples. The first is that issues Piaget thought were important about development have been reinterpreted by some American psychologists to reflect their concerns and objectives. Throughout his career, Piaget focused his work on the organization of intelligence as it evolves via the functioning of adaptational processes of assimilation, accommodation, and equilibration. Using biology as a model, Piaget assessed competence of the human organism from the beginnings of the sensorimotor period to higher levels of reflective formal thought. He proposed that as coordinations increased, qualitatively new forms of behavior and thought were made possible. Although children's performance was studied on specific tasks, interest was not in the tasks themselves, but in what performance revealed about the underlying organization of thought.

American psychologists took a contrasting route by picking up on Piaget's tasks and seeking the earliest ages at which competencies might be manifested. Often tasks were modified so that they could be presented to very young children. The result was a discovery that children could generate sophisticated appearing performances that preceded in age what Piaget's would have predicted. Ignoring possible nonequivalence across tasks, and discounting the wide age ranges that Piaget consistently reported for phenomena, many researchers concluded that Piaget's theory was so much water under the bridge.

Ironically, claims that Piaget's theory precludes the possibility of so-called precocious performance by young children, show lack of familiarity with Piaget's writings. Piaget's discussion of intentionality is a case in point. Another example is found in Piaget's (1963) discussion of sensorimotor development in which he proposed that behavior patterns typical of a certain substage may be found in identical form at earlier substages. But he emphasized differences between the earlier and later manifestations. First, the behavior is not typical for the earlier period. Second, the manifestation is less systematized and consolidated. And third, it is less accessible to consciousness (Piaget, 1963). What at earlier substages infants do fortuitously and try to rediscover after the event, older children do intentionally and efficiently a few years later.

In the same work, Piaget characterized cognitive development in general as a process of becoming increasingly aware of the coordinations inherent in the organizing activity of previous levels and in life itself (Piaget, 1963). As the example of mental imagery suggests, Marmor's findings may reflect coordinations of earlier, less conscious quality than the explicit renderings of sequential states on a Piaget and Inhelder task.

The second point made with our two examples is that the assimilation of Piaget's theory to American psychology resulted in a closing off of potentially profitable avenues of research. It is interesting that recent thinking about moral reasoning and mental representation has begun to address issues with which Piaget was originally concerned. For instance, many researchers in the field of moral development are now studying the interactive and relationship bases of moral judgment (e.g., Damon, 1988; Kurtines & Gewirtz, 1987). Also, recent work on mental representations of events and other kinds of sequential information is being conceptualized in much the same manner as Piaget's previous formulations (Dean, 1991).

What is partially missing from the new literature is acknowledgment and perhaps awareness of the relevance of Piaget's work to these concerns. Acknowledgment is important not only for historical reasons, but because Piaget's writings contain a mine of ideas and observations that remain to be explored. So as not to be misunderstood, we are neither devaluing multiple approaches to the study of intellectual development nor denying the insights that have been gained from contemporary cognitive approaches. Rather, we are pointing out that one generation of researchers exploited Piagetian phenomena without coming to grips with the issues and solutions which Piaget's scholarship offered. Flavell (1962) anticipated a possible misunderstanding; it is not so clear that he or anyone could have predicted the transformation and eventual nonreading of the theory. Our hope is that another generation of developmental psychologists might be able to approach Piaget's writings with more openness to what he thought and why he saw certain issues as worth studying. Perhaps this chapter will encourage more researchers to read Piaget carefully and to try to build on insights he provided.

## REFERENCES

Ahr, P. R. (1971). *Moral development and social learning: Modeling effects on children's concepts of intentionality.* Unpublished doctoral dissertation, The Catholic University of America, Washington, DC.

Bandura, A., & McDonald, F. J. (1963). Influence of social reinforcement and the behavior of models in shaping children's moral judgments. *Journal of Abnormal and Social Psychology, 67,* 274–281.

Chapman, M. (1986). The structure of social exchange: Piaget's sociological theory. *Human Development, 29,* 181–194.

Chapman, M. (1988). *Constructive evolution: origins and development of Piaget's thought.* New York: Cambridge University Press.

Cowan, P. A., Langer, J., Heavenrich, J., & Nathanson, M. (1969). Social learning and Piaget's cognitive theory of moral development. *Journal of Personality and Social Psychology, 11,* 261–274.

Damon, W. (1988). *The moral child: nurturing children's natural moral growth.* New York: The Free Press.

Dean, A. L. (1976). The structure of imagery. *Child Development, 47,* 949–958.

Dean, A. L. (1991). The development of mental imagery: A comparison of Piagetian and cognitive psychological perspectives. In R.Vasta (Ed.), *Annals of child development* (Vol. 7, pp. 105–144). London: Jessica Kingsley Publishers Ltd.

Flavell, J. H. (1962). Historical and bibliographic note. In W.Kessen & C. Kuhlman (Eds.), *Thought in the young child* (Vol. 27). Monographs of the Society for Research in Child Development, Serial No. 83.

Fuson, K. C., Richards, J., & Briar, D. J. (1982). The acquisition and elaboration of the number word sequence. In C. Brainerd (Ed.), *Progress in cognitive development, Vol. 1: Children's logical and mathematical cognition* (pp. 33–92). New York: Springer-Verlag.

Gelman, R. (1978). Cognitive development. *Annual Review of Psychology, 29,* 297–332.

Gold, R. (1987). *The description of cognitive development.* Oxford: Oxford University Press.

Kessen, W., & Kuhlman, C. (Eds.). (1962). *Thought in the young child.* Monograph of the Society for Research in Child Development, Serial No. 83, Vol. 27.

Kosslyn, S.M. (1980). *Image and mind.* Cambridge, MA: Harvard University Press.

Kosslyn, S. M. (1981). The medium and the message in mental imagery. *Psychological Review, 88,* 46–66.

Kurtines, W., & Gewirtz, J. (Eds.). (1987). *Social interaction and sociomoral development.* New York: Wiley.

Mandler, J. M. (1983). Representation. In J. Flavell & E. Markman (Eds.), *Handbook of child psychology* (Vol. 3, pp. 420–495). New York: Wiley.

Marmor, G. S. (1975). Development of kinetic images: When does the child represent movement in mental images? *Cognitive Psychology, 7,* 548–559.

Marmor, G. S. (1977). Mental rotation and number conservation: Are they related? *Developmental Psychology, 13,* 320–325.

Nelson, K. (1983). The derivation of concepts and categories from event representations. In E. Scholnick (Ed.), *New trends in conceptual representation: Challenges to Piaget's theory?* (pp. 129–146). Hillsdale, NJ: Lawrence Erlbaum Associates.

Piaget, J. (1937). Principle factors determining intellectual evolution from childhood to adult life. In E. D. Adrian (Ed.), *Factors determining human behavior* (pp. 32–48). Cambridge, MA: Harvard University Press.

Piaget, J. (1962). *Play, dreams, and imitation in childhood.* New York: Norton.

Piaget, J. (1963). *The origins of intelligence in children.* New York: Norton.

Piaget, J. (1965). *The moral judgment of the child.* New York: The Free Press. (Original work published 1932)

Piaget, J., & Inhelder, B. (1969). The gaps in empiricism. In A.Koestler & J. R. Smithies (Eds.), *Beyond reductionism* (pp. 118–160). Boston: Beacon.

Piaget, J., & Inhelder, B. (1971). *Mental imagery in the child.* New York: Basic Books.

Pylyshyn, Z. W. (1981). The imagery debate: Analogue media versus tacit knowledge. *Psychological Review, 88,* 16–45.

Shepard, R., & Cooper, L. (1982). *Mental images and their transformations.* Cambridge, MA: MIT Press.
Shepard, R., & Metzler, J. (1971). Mental rotation of three-dimensional objects. *Science, 171,* 701–703.
Sternlieb, J., & Youniss, J. (1975). Moral judgments one year after intentional or consequent modeling. *Journal of Personality and Social Psychology, 31,* 895–897.
Youniss, J. (1980). *Parents and peers in social development.* Chicago: University of Chicago Press.

# Chapter 6

# A Constructivist Framework for Understanding Early and Late-Developing Psychological Competencies

Jacques Montangero
*University of Geneva*

Consistent with psychologists' historical understanding of their discipline as a scientific enterprise, the question of when and at what ages different psychological competencies develop has generally been considered an empirical problem to be decided through an appeal to the results of systematic observation. In this view, the recurring controversies that have accompanied this problem from its inception can be resolved only through methodological refinements leading to more precise and interpretable observational data. However, the fact that several decades of such methodological refinements have not succeeded in resolving such controversies raises doubts about the likelihood of ever doing so through any simple appeal to "the facts."

This chapter is premised on the assumption that the question of early competence is at present more of a theoretical problem than an empirical one. In order to interpret the diversity of empirical findings and to propose methods for assessing levels of competence, several theoretical questions concerning conceptions of development and definitions of competence must be clarified. The major argument is that a constructivist approach to these questions is more adequate to the task than are its competing nativist and empiricist alternatives. This argument is illustrated in the context of issues raised by the occurence of so-called "decalages" in the competencies tapped by Piagetian tasks, especially within the domain of reasoning about time. Before these issues are discussed, it is useful to summarize research findings involving three general sources of variation in the ages at which psychological competencies have been found to develop.

One obvious entry on any list of the ways in which competence can be said to vary is the fact that marked interindividual differences exist in the chronology by which a given competence appears in development. For example, in Piaget's classic studies of concrete operations a wide range of ages are reported at which particular tasks are first successfully passed. The work of Schröder and Edelstein (chapter 7, this volume) further documents the extremely broad "interindividual range" within which the mastery of such competence is achieved. Although interindividual variability of this sort is of considerable practical relevance, it is not especially problematic for a theory in which the sequence of development is more central than its timing. Therefore, the question of interindividual variability is not pursued in the discussion that follows.

A second source of variation in competence is also evident from the most cursory review of the relevant research literature: When assessed repeatedly on the same measure of competence, individual subjects sometimes succeed and sometimes fail. Although such evidence can pose serious interpretive problems, it is wholly consistent with the constructivistic theory developed here. Examples of such intraindividual variation occur whenever subjects are provided with more or less help in their problem-solving efforts (Vygotsky, 1962), or when other contextual or situational matters intrude to alter an individual's level of demonstrated competence. Because such "moderators of competence" (Overton, 1985) are always present, one is always obliged to speak of a "developmental range," rather than a precise level of competence (Fischer & Elmendorf, 1986). But unless such proposed bandwidths of competence are excessive in their scope, they also are not especially problematic.

In contrast, a third class of evidence, also involving intraindividual variations in competence, is much more problematic theoretically. This class of evidence, which frames most of the problems discussed in this chapter, involves the claim that children can be shown to perform successfully at a much younger age than ordinarily supposed if some presumably minor methodological changes are made in tasks commonly recognized as "classic" markers of a given competence. For example, various investigators (e.g., Baillargeon, 1987; Bower, 1974), employing simplified measures of the object concept, have reported that 3- to 6-month-old infants already possess a kind of object permanence that Piaget (1937/1954) and others (e.g., Gratch, 1982) claimed is not in evidence until several months later. Similarly, other investigators have provided putative evidence for the conclusion that 5-year-olds reason as logically as do school-age children (Levin, 1982), or that 2- and 3-year-olds possess concepts of number (Gelman & Gallistel, 1978) or causality (Bullock, Gelman, & Baillargeon, 1982) similar to that of older children and adults. In contrast to the sorts of inter- and intraindividual differences referenced earlier, such claims appear to call into question the concept of competence as such and have led to alternative interpretations of the same evidence (e.g., Montangero, 1985a).

The balance of this chapter is devoted to identifying new and more coherent ways of arbitrating between such competing claims. First, an attempt is made to press the argument stated earlier that any attempt to resolve such disagreements must take place within a theoretical context rich enough to permit some account of the forms and processes that underlie manifest performances. Then, the theoretical importance of a hierarchy of potential levels of knowledge sufficiently complex to allow for the possibility that the same content can be known differently by persons of different levels of cognitive maturity is illustrated.

## CONCEPTIONS OF DEVELOPMENT
## AND THE ASSESSMENT OF COMPETENCE

All assertions about cognitive functioning necessarily rest on implicit or explicit epistemological assumptions about the origins of knowledge and the nature of developmental change. An important element in the confusion that currently attends the notion of cognitive competence results from a failure to make such assumptions explicit. In the following section, an attempt is made to bring these assumptions to light.

At a first approximation, perspectives on the origins of knowledge and the nature of development commonly are described in terms of a continuum ranging from nativism to empiricism. At one extreme, *nativism* is the view that complex cognitive abilities are "wired in" or exist in some potential form from the outset of development, and development is consequently understood as merely a process of actualization and generalization of such pre-existing potentialities. A central task of researchers committed to such a nativistic orientation is the search for early expressions of competence as evidence of its innate potential. For this reason, nativists play the useful role of identifying abilities that may be overlooked by researchers of a more empiricist or constructivist orientation. From a constructivist perspective, however, such nativists often err by assuming that the full task of tracing out the developmental course of that competence is complete once an early instance of some ability is found. Consequently they do not care to give any precise explanation of development, which they often view as the modification of cognitive aspects extraneous to the competence studied.

At the other end of the continuum, *empiricism* involves the assumption that the source of all emerging cognitive abilities is to be found in experience. Although associationism—a rather extreme form of empiricism— has not been prevalent in psychology for two decades, numerous studies continue to be conducted that implicitly take an empiricist perspective insofar as development is described as the product of external factors such as cultural and/or situational influences. As described in the following sections, what is often lacking in research conducted from this perspective is a concern for the subject's own contribution to the development of new abilities. If nativism results in a disregard for the external conditions of development, empiricism leads to a disregard for its internal conditions.

The fact that psychologists do not always examine their epistemological presuppositions frequently allows them to assume different, but equally onesided views on different occasions without being aware of the limitations of each view in turn. For example, an early arriving ability may be described as innate, and a late appearing one as the product of external influences. In each case, something is arguably missing from these accounts in terms of either the external or internal conditions of the developmental process. A central premise of the constructivist position developed here is that both the role of experiential factors and the importance of the subject's structures should be taken into account, allowing a more balanced explanation of the process of development. According to such a genetic epistemology, cognitive development produces qualitative changes—that is, real novelty—but such new forms of knowledge are always understood to be based on and prepared by previously existing competencies. From this perspective, it is neither surprising to find late appearing abilities nor unexpected to observe earlier manifestations of these same competencies.

Before discussing this point in detail, a note of caution is in order regarding a common error of interpretation that the constructivist perspective is meant to avoid: the tendency to describe early maturing competencies in adult terms. Although such adultocentric interpretations might be understandable in research programs designed to detect early emerging competencies that had been overlooked previously, they have the serious disadvantage in ruling out the possibility of structurally simpler forms of the same later developing competency. The research of Baillargeon (1987) on object permanence provides an interesting case in point. In this study, Baillargeon observed infants as young as 3 1/2 to 4 1/2 months to look longer at a perceptual event that violated adult expectations about the physical properties of solid objects. Within the experimental situation, a rotating screen sometimes was made to appear to pass through the space occupied by a solid yellow box standing behind the screen. Young infants found nothing especially noteworthy when the moving screen was blocked by this solid object (possible event), but looked for a measurably longer time when objects that they could no longer see failed to perform their "expected" function of blocking the rotating screen (impossible event). Given a nativist's expectation of finding early manifestations of competence, it is perhaps not surprising that Baillargeon interpreted such results as indicating that an understanding of object permanence was already in place in these infant subjects. More specifically, the author concluded that infants looked longer at the impossible event for two reasons: Because they understood that (a) the box continued to exist after it was occluded by the screen, (b) and the screen could not move through the space occupied by the occluded box. These are the very reasons for which Baillargeon herself or any other adult would pay more attention to the impossible event. However, such an adultocentric explanation is not to be recommended to child psychologists, because the purpose of such studies should be to grasp children's specific way of knowing.

From a more constructivistic perspective, the range of possible interpretations is considerably more extensive. For example, the infants may have looked longer at the impossible event simply because it offered a greater number of interesting visual opportunities (i.e., successively: yellow box, rotating screen, striped back wall, rotating screen, and eventually yellow box again). The order effect reported by the author (when shown the possible event first, infants tended to look equally at both events) is consistent with such an explanation, based on habituation. Alternatively, the young subjects in Baillargeon's study may have evidenced an early form of object-related expectancy, equivalent perhaps to a kind of perceptual persistence. They might expect objects that are momentarily hidden by a moving screen (much like one's own hand or a passing person) to reappear after some specifiable duration. If such a process could be demonstrated, it would not necessarily imply that infants possess the concept of "permanent objects" in the belief that such objects continue to exist when they are occluded, nor would it necessarily imply an understanding of the spatial relations of "in front of" or "behind," nor even the existence of possible causal relations between the relevant objects. From a constructivistic orientation, the fact that some of the criteria for object permanence were in place would not imply that all other criteria commonly associated with such competence in adults naturally cohered in infant children.

## On the Necessity of Defining Competence in Terms of Underlying Forms or Processes

One legacy of psychology's earlier domination by behaviorism is that for many developmentalists, competence is equated with the act of providing correct answers to specific problems. Consequently, correct judgments on tasks representative of a given domain are commonly imagined to reveal the same competence, irrespective of the complexity of the tasks in question. However, even psychologists willing to accept specific behaviors as a proxy for competence recognize that competence is not wholly reducible to an action or a verbal response, but represents instead the ability or abilities by which those actions or responses are generated. In the constructivist perspective represented in this chapter, competence is further distinguished from overt responses in terms of underlying processes or structures that permit the subject to deal efficiently with a range of comparable situations. One possible way of accomplishing this task is to describe such competencies as relations that the subject introduces between meanings corresponding to the cues attended to in the situation presented.

In an effort to exemplify such an account of competence and to demonstrate how it permits similar responses to reference dissimilar competencies, attention is focused in the paragraph that follows on several studies of children's time judgments. In the "canonical" situations first devised by Piaget and his collaborators (Piaget, 1946/1969) and subsequently used by many others researchers (Levin, 1982; Montangero, 1977; Siegler & Richards, 1979; etc.), children were asked to judge the relative time or velocity of simultaneous or partly simultaneous displacements. In order to make correct temporal judgments in such situations, three different parameters of the events must be set in relation to one another: the relative *distance* covered ($d$), the relative *velocity* ($v$), and the relative *time* ($t$) (or more precisely duration) of the displacements. For example, if one considers the synchronous displacement of two toy cars (see Fig. 6.1), one of which overtakes the other, an 8-year-old child usually judges that "they took the same time ($t =$) because one went further ($d +$) but drove faster ($v +$)." Accounts of this sort, commonplace among children of 8 or older, are expressive of their ability to coordinate simultaneously these three separate "meanings." What is related is not the external, "objective" cues, but their mental representations.

In previous studies (Montangero, 1985b), however, still younger children were found to relate certain of these meanings in a simpler way, one that involved the establishment of dyadic and unidirectional relations among two of these cues. In these studies, subjects were presented, for example, with a strip of cardboard that represented a road between two cities (toy houses). Two toy cars were shown to the children: One was a sports car, the other a small ordinary car. Questions of the following sort were asked: "One day at 8:00 a.m. I took the sports car and drove at full speed from City A (start) to City B (end). It took me half a day to arrive at city B (arrival at noon). On another day I took the small car and drove slowly from A to B. Do you think it took more time, less time or the same time (arrival before noon, after noon, or at noon) than with the sports car?" Before asking for the judgment, we made sure subjects had understood and memorized the information. Results showed first that 4- to 5-year-old children could relate the two "meanings" associated with speed and time correctly. In contrast to Piaget's earlier findings (called into question by Fraisse, 1957) that preoperational children tend to conceive of a direct relationship between velocity and time (i.e., more speed entails more time), chil-

FIG. 6.1.   Displacements in parallel paths for which relative durations have to be evaluated. Situation A (passing): duration a = duration b; Situation B (catching up) = duration b > duration a.

dren as young as 4 or 5 answered such questions correctly by successfully relating the "meanings" of these variables (i.e., "The small car took more time, it arrived later"). These findings clearly demonstrate the capacity of such children to form inverse relationships (less speed entails more time or: $v - \rightarrow t +$) providing they can deal with two variables at a time.

Although such performances might seem to imply that the third variable (equal distance covered) also had been taken into account, further questioning showed that young children did not do so. When asked to make a judgment about distance, they tended to produce a new dyadic relation: The faster car covered a longer distance ($v + \rightarrow d +$). Another characteristic of the reasoning of these 4- and 5-year-olds is that their understanding of such relationships is unidirectional. That is, those children who think that less speed implies more time, do not automatically also assume that more time entails less speed.

Utilizing other related procedures involving comparisons of dolls jumping in place or tokens being dropped into a glass, 4- and 5-year-olds were again found able to coordinate two, but not three variables. Here the meanings involved were somewhat different in that the judgments related time ($t$), frequency ($fr$) and number of things done ($n$), but these substitutions had no apparent bearing on children's performance. Similar experiments were also conducted with static events (e.g., comparison of the time two lights were lit or of the time it took to cook pancakes). In these situations, children focused on either "starting orders" (e.g., a boy switched on a light before a girl did, or put his pancake in the pan first), or "ending orders" in making judgments of duration. In all these cases, children under 7 simply inferred one of these variables from a second, without taking into consideration anything about the value of the third. For example, such children reasoned that "ended after" entails "lasted longer" ($t2$ after $\rightarrow t +$) in the absence of any knowledge of starting orders.

A striking characteristic of the dyadic relations envisioned by these young subjects is that some of them were assumed to have more importance than others. For example the assumed covariation between ending orders and duration ($t2 \rightarrow t$) is "stronger" (more evident, more rapidly established) than the covariation between starting orders and duration ($t1 \rightarrow t$). When such young children were asked to consider several such dyadic relations they tended to center on the "strongest" of those relations. Thus if Lamp A is both lighted and switched off before Lamp B, the relation "$t2$ before $\rightarrow t -$" tended to take precedence over "$t1$ before $\rightarrow t +$".

To summarize, the results of the preceding studies make clear that in testing situations in which one variable of a three variables problem is held constant, the judgments of 4- and 5-year-olds correspond with that of adults. When examined more closely, however, it becomes apparent that the thinking of these young subjects is restricted to a consideration of the covariations of only two variables, is unidirectional rather than symmetrical, and involves arbitrary implicit assumptions about the "weight" or "strength" of these variables. These characteristics (with the exception of the last) correspond to the main features of what Piaget (1968/1977b) referred to as the "constituting function," a construct used by him to explain certain preoperational abilities. Unfortunately this useful construct received little attention in subsequent research (but see Chapman & Lindenberger, 1988).

Having defined children's competence in making time judgments in terms of their grasp of multiple relationships of meanings, it is possible to reconcile some of the differences between the earlier findings reported by Piaget (1946/1969) and by others (Lovell & Slater, 1960; Montangero, 1977) and the more recent results that appear to support contrary claims. By the present account, the earlier claims of Piaget that children did not have a working conception of time relations until 8 to 9 years of age can be seen to imply an ability to coordinate three variables at a time and to treat those relations as reversible and independent of order. A representation of relationships of this sort is portrayed in Fig. 6.2b, where it is contrasted to a representation of the diverse possible dyadic relations evident in the thinking of still younger children (Fig. 6.2a).

The foregoing analysis permits a reconsideration of the more recent claims of Levin (1982) who asserted that, when presented with a problem involving lamps lighted for various durations, even 4- and 5-year-olds could reason logically about time. The alternative reading of these results advocated here is that, in her attempt to minimize what were characterized as "misleading cues," Levin succeeded in converting a standard three-variable problem into one in which correct judgments could be achieved by a simpler consideration of the dyadic relations between only two variables. By contrast, if you present such young children with a problem that necessitates the coordination of three variables (even when cues such as speed and distance are absent), they fail to give correct judgments. For example, when presented with an arrangement in which Lamp A is lit 3 seconds after, and switched off 3 seconds after Lamp B, then 5-year-olds infer duration from one of the orders of succession, failing to take into consideration both starting and ending orders (Montangero, 1977). Seven-year-olds, on the contrary, base their judgment on the comparison of starting orders with ending orders. They do reason logically about time.

The preceding examples are intended as a demonstration that defining a competence in terms of underlying processes or structures permits one to distinguish early abilities from later, more complex ones. A second example is provided by the two temporal judgment situations described previously. In the experimental situation involving the "synchronous passing" of two cars (see Fig. 6.1), 5- and 6-year-olds do not understand the equality of duration of the two displacements. Instead they conclude that the car that went further took more time. If such children's attention is drawn to the fact that this car was also moving faster, they still do not change their judgments. In short, they seem incapable of taking into consideration the inverse relationship between

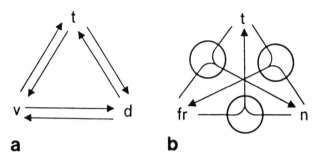

FIG. 6.2.    Forms of relations within subsystems.

velocity and time. Actually some children do say that "this one took more time because it drove faster" (corresponding to Piaget's claim of a direct relationship between speed and time). Yet, when presented with other situations as described earlier (i.e., going from one city to the other with a fast, then a slow car), the majority of the same subjects assert that "the one that goes faster takes less time." In the first situation they neither establish an inverse relationship nor evaluate duration correctly. In the second they do establish an inverse relationship between velocity and duration and correctly anticipate duration. Do such children demonstrate through their correct judgments an early competence? The answer proposed here is that such successes are based only on mastering dyadic relationships that, although representing a positive and important piece of knowledge, is not a competence of the same order as that involved in the solution of problems requiring the symmetrical coordination of three variables (see Fig. 6.2).

Naturally the fact that "correct" answers to seemingly analogous situations may actually reflect very different levels of competence needs to be demonstrated outside the domain of time judgments and at other stages of development than the ones involved in the preceding examples. One further example, already noted in this chapter, is provided by the earlier demonstration that Baillargeon's (1987) procedure meant to reveal object permanence in 3- and 4-month-olds actually might assess another level of object permanence than that measured through the use of more standard Piagetian tasks.

At the other end of childhood, comparable examples exist in which "slightly" modified formal operational tasks are sometimes passed long before the usual age at which more standard problems are mastered (because simpler forms of reasoning are involved). One such example concerns problems of probability quantification (Piaget & Inhelder, 1951/1975). In the usual measure of this ability, two collections of white tokens are presented. Some tokens have a cross on their reverse side, and subjects are shown how many tokens do and do not have a cross in each of the two collections. Following this demonstration, subjects are asked in which collection they would have a better chance of drawing a token with a cross when they see only the white sides of the tokens. Compare two seemingly similar versions of this task: In Situation 1, Collection A consists of one token with a cross and one without (1:2 ratio), and Collection B consists of one token with cross and two without (1:3). According to Longeot (1978), in this situation, 88% of 10- and 11-year-olds understand that there are more chances to draw a token with cross in Collection A. Is this an early demonstration of a competence believed by some to be mastered later, at the formal level? Certainly not, if the competence assessed is the understanding of proportionality as defined by Piaget. In effect, a mere "intercollection" comparison of the subsets without cross produces a "correct" answer: There are more "bad" tokens in Collection B than in Collection A.

Consider, by comparison, a second and in some sense similar situation in which only 37% of 10- and 11-year-olds succeed. In this situation, Collection A is similar to collection A of the situation considered previously (1:2 ratio), whereas Collection B has two tokens with cross and two without (2:4). The correct answer is that there is the same chance to draw a token with cross in either collection. In order to answer this, subjects have to establish an "intracollection" ratio for each collection, and then compare these ratios. In doing so they establish relations on relations, a typical formal competence that is implied in the understanding of proportionality. Thus, "correct" answers in Situations 1 and 2 reflect two different levels of competence.

*Acknowledging and Defining a Hierarchy of Levels of Knowledge.* Levels of competence can be defined with reference to several criteria. Within a theory that distinguishes various levels of knowledge, one criterion of competence is the location of that competence in the hierarchy of the cognitive ability considered. Some such distinction of levels of cognition is necessary if there is to be any hope of sorting out claims regarding early and late appearing competence.

In nonconstructivist theories, development is most often understood as a cumulative phenomenon (enlarging knowledge contents or generalizing cognitive processes). Consequently the very first manifestations of a cognitive content (e.g., an idea of time or of quantity) or strategy (e.g., a detour or the inversion of an action) are automatically deemed to be similar to later occurring analogous contents or strategies. From within such theories, the possibility of hierarchies of knowledge and consequently hierarchies of competencies is completely overlooked.

As an example, consider the possibility that each of the five cases listed here actually represents a coordination of the three variables time, velocity and distance:

1. A 2-year-old child can accelerate his or her pace, when walking, in order to reach a goal as soon as possible. This implies the coordination: $v+$ and $d = \rightarrow t-$.

2. A 5-year-old child can take into account both time and velocity in infer-

ring the relative distance covered, in the following situation (Wilkening, 1981): The subject hears the sound of a dog barking and must determine how far a second animal could travel, on a rectilinear path, during the barking sound. In this procedure, subjects were required to make several judgments in situations in which the duration of the barking sound was sometimes shorter and sometimes longer and the supposed speed of the animal that runs away was either slow (turtle) or fast (cat, rabbit). In this context, it is possible to see whether subjects' responses take into account both the dimensions duration and velocity. A correct answer implies, for example: $t +$ and $v- \rightarrow d =$ . In these situations an imaged representation of the displacements, accompanied with corresponding eye movements, could be involved in the production of answers.

3. A 9-year-old child shown the situation of "synchronous passing" (see Fig. 6.1), judges correctly that both cars drove for the same length of time, because the one that went further drove faster. In this judgment velocity, distance covered and duration are related ($v +$ and $d + \rightarrow t =$ ). Note that in this situation, the coordination is made on a purely inferential level, without the potential help of eye movements.

4. Adolescents can compute the exact value of speed or time in kinematic problems. This computation clearly involves the understanding of proportionality.

5. Adults can define and symbolize how they reason regarding problems of duration. Newton could thus define time by the equation $t = d/v$.

In these five examples, a related capacity is involved: that of coordinating time, velocity, and distance. Why do the five abilities described appear at such different times in development? A constructivist theory that distinguishes levels of knowledge can provide an answer to this question. According to Piaget (1967/1971, etc.) development consists, among other things, in reconstructing previously acquired knowledge at higher levels of cognitive organization. For example, the infants' practical understanding of spatial rotation on a sensorimotor level must be reconstructed on the level of representation. Such a reconstruction implies a process of reflexive abstraction (Piaget, 1977a) through which some aspects of the organization of previous cognitive activities is projected and reorganized on a superior level. This process of reconstructing some knowledge on a higher level therefore entails an enrichment of this knowledge.

To return to the five cases just outlined, it is meant to be clear that in the first, the coordination is on a sensorimotor level (actual actions coordinated with perceptions); in the second, time, velocity, and distance are related on a mixed inferential level partially supported by perceptual movements. In the third example, the coordination is on a purely inferential level, with each of the connected meanings corresponding to some aspect of concrete reality; in the fourth, some relations on relations (proportionality, time metrics) are involved; and finally at the last of these levels, the coordination concerns symbols that represent a metareflexion on the subject's own knowledge.

From any theoretical perspective that is insensitive to such a hierarchy of levels of knowledge, the competence involved in relating simultaneously distance, velocity, and duration could be assumed to emerge at age 2, or at age 5, or at some other age, depending on the particular findings available. Within such a view, the order and interval of acquisition of the five abilities mentioned above cannot be explained. However, within a constructivist theory that distinguishes among various knowledge levels, the developmental sequence observed could be shown to make sense. The conclusion to be drawn from this illustrative example is that any coherent effort to assess competencies necessarily requires some account of the levels of knowledge on which such competencies rest.

One possible way of discussing such levels of knowledge is in terms of the concepts of vertical and horizontal decalages. According to Piaget (1941), vertical decalage refers to the time lag between the appearance of a cognitive ability and the recontruction of a related ability on a superior level of knowledge, as in the example of spatial rotation given previously. In the case of vertical decalage, not only is the level of knowledge different (in our example, inferential representation opposed to sensorimotor cognition), but so is the complexity of mental structuration of the content. By contrast, the concept of horizontal decalage refers to the time lag between the appearance of cognitive abilities situated by Piaget on the same level of knowledge. The best known example is that of the invariance of quantity, which is typically mastered around the age of 7 when substance is concerned, 1 or 2 years later when weight is concerned, and still later when the invariant is volume. The striking point is that, when all of these tasks eventually are mastered, they seem completely isomorphic, and the answers to each are justified by the same arguments (e.g., "There is the same amount (or weight or space occupied) because you did not add nor take away anything").

I would suggest that the term *early competence* be used only when an early appearing cognitive ability bears a horizontal decalage relationship with some second ability appearing later in development. Such a designation would then clearly imply that both abilities have some common underlying process and that both are situated on the same level of knowledge. If the competence is based on simpler processes or structures (as in the examples described in the preceding section), or if it is situated on a lower level of knowledge (as in the five examples described in this section), then the earlier ability is better viewed as a distinct competence that prepares the way for, but cannot be equated with the later appearing ability. In such cases, the performance gap between the two behaviors is better thought as a "pseudo-horizontal" decalage, one that is actually a vertical decalage.

In Piaget's theory, the existence of horizontal decalages is somewhat embarrassing, because the observed time lag cannot be explained in terms of the main constructs of the theory that specify the structure of the ability involved.

Both the grouping model and the INRC group fail to provide explanations for such time lags in the appearance of what are assumed to be isomorphic forms of reasoning. Weight conservation, for instance, is mastered thanks to the same type of mental structure as substance conservation, which appears earlier. That is why Piaget tended to consider horizontal decalages in negative terms as "obstacles," "resistance," or "friction" preventing the cognitive coherence that might otherwise be expected from exerting itself. In his first attempts at explaining these decalages, Piaget (1941) did refer to the subject's actions or inferences. Decalages were discussed in terms of the actions of which the concept is a representation (e.g., retrieving an object, which corresponds to substance conservation, necessarily precedes weighing that object, which corresponds to weight conservation). The importance of nonoperational factors (figural aspects) and of the construction of relations between concepts was also acknowledged. However, later in the development of his theory, Piaget (1968) undertook to explain horizontal decalage in terms of resistance of the object, with the double meaning of the figurative aspects of the situations presented and of the physical laws inherent in objects.

Piaget's explanations of horizontal decalage in terms of resistance of the object of knowledge (as well as explanations of other authors that rely on distinctions between "epistemic" and real subjects, or between competence and performance) do not seem wholly satisfactory. Even in the case of horizontal decalages, there must be some difference in complexity of mental activity necessary to master the two tasks or situations compared. When the general structure of reasoning applied is identical, the difference must concern the understanding of the precise content to be structured. Explanations of horizontal decalage must therefore take account of the various aspects of the experimental situation as well as of the ways in which the child connects them. This requires a more precise descriptive language than that of Piaget's mental operations. For this reason, it is indispensable to specify more precisely the nature of the subject's inferences that deal with the significant aspects involved (i.e., inferences at the "infraoperatory" level). Such a specification should allow us to see that decalages involve differences at the level of the meanings processed with similar logical tools. This type of analysis will be sketched out for a decalage (of about 1 year) between the mastery of judgments of duration for two problems of displacements in parallel paths at different speeds (Montangero, 1977).

By way of example, consider the following situations. In Situation A (synchronous passing), a moving object a covers more distance than another moving object b during the same time interval (see Fig. 6.1). At 8 years, 85% of subjects' judgments are correct. By contrast, in Situation B (catching up) Object b starts first and a catches up at the moment both stop (see Fig. 6.1). Of the judgments of 8-year-olds, 55% are correct in this situation.

From one perspective, Problems A and B appear to be identical, because

TABLE 6.1
Inferences Involved in Duration Judgments of Operatory Level for the
Displacement of Moving Object (a) in Situations A and B

| Situation Presented | Subsystem | Cues related | Results of relation |
|---|---|---|---|
| A | 1 | t1 = and t2 = → | t = |
|   | 2 | d + and v + → | t2 = |
| B | 1 | t1≠ and t2 = → | t≠ |
|   | 2 | d + and v + → | t2 = |

they consist of the evaluation of relative durations using spatial and kinematic data for situations with two variable parameters. The mental activities involved in resolving the problems can also seem identical if judged by the justifications given by children or if we refer to a general logic (grouping of mental operations). This apparent equivalence breaks down, however, if we consider the "infraoperatory" inferences on meanings involved. Two subsystems of these inferences are at work in the understanding of such problems. The first subsystem relates initial orders of succession, final orders of succession, and duration, and it makes possible a deduction of the relative value of duration. The second subsystem relates velocity, distance, and time, and provides a means of explaining the possible changes of final spatial or temporal orders. Let us consider, for Situation A and B, the various inferences related to one of the moving objects (a).

*Situation A*

*Subsystem 1*: a starts together with b and stops simultaneously, implying the same duration as b.

*Subsystem 2*: a moves faster and covers more distance than b implying equal times, by compensation, in spite of the noncongruent spatial orders.

*Situation B*

*Subsystem 1*: a starts after b and stops at the same time as b, implying a shorter duration.

*Subsystem 2*: From the moment it starts, a covers a longer distance and moves faster, implying equal times by compensation. The initial difference in spatial order is nullified.

The inferences that connect the cues taken into consideration are shown in Table 6.1. For Situation A, the conclusion drawn from the inferences in Subsystem 1 is that duration is *the same*, and the inferences of Subsystem 2 explain why the stopping times are *the same*, despite the difference in distance covered. For Situation B, the conclusion drawn from the inferences of Subsystem 1 is that durations are *not the same*, and inferences of Subsystem 2 explain why the stopping times are *the same*. Thus, a conflict can occur between the two types of inferences if the correspondences between the two subsystems are not clearly understood. Experiments on time concepts (Montangero, 1985b) reveal that correct correspondences between subsystems are constructed somewhat later than within subsystem relations. In Situation B, the idea of equality that concerns the spatiotemporal data may unduly extend to the judgment of duration, if between-subsystem correspondences are not mastered. In short, the number of equal or unequal cues does not differentiate Situations A and B, but the presence or absence of agreement between the results of the two types of evaluation does differentiate them. At a later stage in development, inferences of the second subsystem are used by the child to explain the changes that happen between initial and ending orders (i.e., between cues connected within the first subsystem). This integration or correspondence of the two subsystems, which is necessary in order to judge correctly Situation B, explains the lower percentage of correct judgments for Situation B in 8-year-olds.

The fact that the situation mastered later in development requires a greater cognitive differentiation must not be used as an excuse for ignoring the real similarity of the main operations involved. Undoubtedly Situations A and B are on the same level of knowledge and the later mastery of the second situation reveals a phenomenon of horizontal decalage. If a situation involving the same basic coordinations were mastered by 4-or 5-year-olds, one could acknowledge a case of early competence. But, as has already been shown in the second section of this chapter, tasks like the one described previously (anticipation of the duration of successive journeys, on the same road, of a fast and a slow car) require a simpler form of inference existing at a lower level of development. There is no horizontal decalage between tasks situated on this level and Situations A and B, but a vertical decalage (restructuration on an upper level involving more complex forms of reasoning).

## CONCLUSIONS

A constructivist perspective on cognitive development greatly facilitates our efforts to come to grips with the problem of assessing competence, because it can give account both of early abilities and late achievements. In effect, constructivism implies that development permits the appearance of real novelty in cognition: new levels of knowledge, new structures of reasoning, new concepts of understanding. In this perspective, knowledge is conceived of as a process of constant restructuration and "openings" onto new possibilities. On the other hand, a constructivist viewpoint implies that new forms of knowledge are constructed on the basis of earlier forms. For example, acts of sensorimotor intelligence, appearing toward the end of the first year of life, are special forms of coordination of previously existing "schemas." Similarly, categorization of things, or conceptualizations of time in young children can be seen as rooted in previous sensorimotor knowledge (the recognition of things as related to a given action schema, and the temporal order of actions and perceptions). Another example is the fact that logical classification in the 8-year-old child is prepared by categorization and early attempts at classifying.

Compared to constructivism, other epistemological perspectives such as nativism or empiricism make it very difficult to define and assess competencies. Although any contemporary account of the oppositions between nativism and empiricism may seem outdated, it can be argued that tacit allegiance to one or the other of those two positions is at the root of much of the ongoing confusion about the concept of competence. Such misunderstandings are further amplified whenever authors fail to adopt a precise position concerning the origin and causes of cognitive development. The consequence is that they may make inconsistant assertions or simply ignore the question of the processes of development. As was shown in previous sections of this chapter, two aspects of a constructivist theory like that of Piaget are indispensable to any serious attempt to deal with the problem of assessing competence. The first such aspect is the definition of competence in terms of underlying structures or processes. The functionalist perspective prevailing in current cognitive psychology fails to address this issue by seemingly exempting researchers from the necessity of defining forms of knowledge (and particularly knowledge forms of a certain generality). It is anticipated that in the more or less distant future, psychologists will rediscover the importance of some variation of structuralism. At the present moment developmentalists should find a way to define competence, if not in terms of systems or structures, at least in terms of general programs or specific processes. This is the necessary condition for assessing competence and distinguishing abilities of different levels, as was attempted in this chapter.

The second aspect of a developmental theory necessary for any coherent account of competencies is the establishment of a hierarchy of knowledge levels. Abilities that seem identical in terms of the complexity of inferences they reflect and the number and nature of meanings related are not similar if situated at different levels of knowledge. The absence of any such distinction between these levels completely blurs the picture of cognitive development. In addition, criteria for defining a hierarchy of levels may be diverse. I propose the following sequence of plans of knowledge, inspired by Piaget's works and more recent research:

1. *A level of sensorimotor activity* (actual actions guided by or coordinated with perceptions). Several sublevels could be distinguished within this sensorimotor level.

2. *A first level of symbolic cognition* (capable of solving problems involving re-

lations between mental images, or concepts, etc). Such cognitive activities would bear on concrete entities or their predicates, and consist of step-by-step dyadic unidirectional relations.

3. *A second level of symbolic cognition* in which dyadic relations are grouped together. At this level subjects simultaneously process more than two elements. This level corresponds to Piaget's concrete operational stage.

4. *A third level of symbolic cognition* in which the content of the inferences or operations is constituted by relations of the second level. For instance, the act of grasping proportional relations consists of establishing a relation between numerical relations such as "4 is the double of 2." Such cognitive activities do not necessarily process existing entities or their predicates. This level corresponds to Piaget's formal operational stage.

5. *Subsequent levels* in which concepts or reasoning consist of establishing a relation whose content is a relation of the preceding level.

Note that especially in Levels 2 and 3, sublevels must be distinguished when there is either a strong perceptual processing component or the possibility of relying on mental images in finding problems solutions. For instance within Level 3, a mixed level of inferences and perceptual activities (see the preceding discussion of Wilkening's findings) precedes the level where the processing is purely inferential.

More concretely, what advice can be given regarding the assessment of cognitive competence? My first suggestion would be to consider carefully what competence is at stake. This can be accomplished by conducting a careful task analysis and by studying the variations in observed responses as a function of task modifications. Competence can then be defined in terms of the meanings that are related and the type or complexity of the relations involved. Such a study should permit us to determine the level of knowledge implied by the mastery of any given task. In the process of developing such a definition of competence, one should avoid adultocentric perspectives such as those pointed out in the first part of this chapter. When simple processes known to exist in young subjects suffice to produce a correct answer, it is not necessary to postulate more elaborate forms of knowledge.

For assessing a competence, the methodology of data collection is naturally very important. An individual interview based on a clinical method provides the possibility of finding the optimal level that subjects can reach without help and of testing the stability of their answer. In order to take account of intraindividual variations, providing some kind of help, or learning opportunity should also be attempted. Each subject would thus be characterized by a level of success at certain tasks and the possibility of learning within a short time interval.

The question of competence is not only a question of finding suitable theoretical and methodological tools in order to assess the mastery of certain abilities. It is also a question of the value attached to these abilities. The determination of values is perhaps more subjective, ideological, and therefore controversial than the determination of the nature and complexity of cognitive activities. Nevertheless, it would be a valuable exercise for developmentalists to attempt at defining criteria for valuing forms of knowledge and establishing—or refusing to establish—degrees of improvement of cognition during development. As far as intrinsic criteria are concerned, the ideas of differentiations of global abilities or contents of knowledge and of coordination of otherwise dissociated elements may be helpful as a means of distinguishing levels of competence. The open question that remains is how much more valuable are the complex competencies that result from such a process of differentiation and coordination.

An answer to this question in terms of adaptation (Piaget, 1936/1952, 1967/1971) may seem too vague, because early forms of behaviors are adaptive within the usual life context in which they appear (see, e.g., Butterworth, 1987, as regards infants). However, adaptation may be understood as something more than the mere possibility of surviving and achieving a well-balanced relation with the environment. One important criterion for biological as well as cognitive adaptation is the possibility of solving a maximum number of the problems raised in the environment. Such a definition may prove useful in future efforts to define a hierarchy of competencies.

This is not the place to develop such considerations at length. I only suggest in conclusion that a higher level competence should not be defined only in terms of its complexity, but also in terms of the range of new problems it is likely to solve and the possibilities for new cognitive constructions it permits.

# REFERENCES

Baillargeon, R. (1987). Object permanence in three and a half- and four and a half-month-old infants. *Developmental Psychology, 23*(5), 655–664.

Bower, T. G. R. (1974). *Development in infancy.* San Francisco: Freeman.

Bullock, M., Gelman, R., & Baillargeon, R. (1982). The development of causal reasoning. In W. J. Friedman (Ed.), *The developmental psychology of time* (pp. 209–254). New York: Academic Press.

Butterworth, G. (1987). Some benefits of egocentrism. In J. Bruner & H. Haste (Eds.), *Making sense: The child's construction of the world* (pp. 62–80). London & New York: Methuen.

Chapman, M., & Lindenberger, U. (1988). Functions, operations, and decalage in the development of transitivity. *Developmental Psychology, 24*, 542–551.

Fischer, K. W., & Elmendorf, S. (1986). Becoming a different person: Transformations in personality and social behavior. In M. Perlmutter (Ed.), *Minnesota Symposium on Child Psychology* (Vol. 18, pp. 137–178). Hillsdale, NJ: Lawrence Erlbaum Associates.

Fraisse, P. (1957). *Psychologie du temps [Psychology of time].* Paris: Presses Universitaires de France.

Gelman, R., & Gallistel, C. R. (1978). *The child's understanding of number.* Cambridge, MA: Harvard University Press.

Gratch, G. (1982). Responses to hidden persons and things by 5-, 9-, and 16-month-old infants in a visual tracking situation. *Developmental Psychology, 18*(2), 232–237.

Levin, I. (1982). The nature and development of time concepts in children: The effects of interfering cues. In W. J. Friedman (Ed.), *The developmental psychology of time* (pp. 47–85). New York: Academic Press.

Longeot, F. (1978). *Les stades opératoires de Piaget et les facteurs de l'intelligence* [*Piaget's operatory stages and factors of intelligence*]. Grenoble: Presses Universitaires de Grenoble.

Lovell, K., & Slater, A. (1960). The growth of the concept of time: A comparative study. *Journal of Child Psychology and Psychiatry and Allied Disciplines, 1*, 179–190.

Montangero, J. (1977). *La notion de durée chez l'enfant de 5 à 9 ans* [*The concept of duration in 5- to 9-year-olds*]. Paris: Presses Universitaires de France.

Montangero, J. (1985a). *Genetic epistemology: Yesterday and today.* New York: The Graduate School and University Center, City University of New York.

Montangero, J. (1985b). The development of temporal inferences and meanings in 5- to 8-year-old children. In J. A. Michon & J. L. Jackson (Eds.), *Time, mind, and behavior* (pp. 279–287). Berlin: Springer.

Overton, W. F. (1985). Scientific methodologies and the competence-moderator-performance issue. In E. D. Neimark, R. De Lisi, & J. L. Newman (Eds.), *Moderators of competence* (pp. 15–42). Hillsdale, NJ: Lawrence Erlbaum Associates.

Piaget, J. (1941). *Le mécanisme du développement mental et les lois du groupement des opération: Esquisse d'une théorie opératoire de l'intelligence* [The mechanism of mental development and the laws of grouping of operations: Sketch of an operatory theory of intelligence]. *Archives de Psychologie, 28*, 215–285.

Piaget, J. (1952). *The origins of intelligence in children.* New York: International University Press. (Original work published 1936)

Piaget, J. (1954). *The construction of reality in the child.* New York: Basic Books. (Original work published 1937)

Piaget, J. (1968). Introduction. In M. Laurendeau & A. Pinard (Eds.), *Les premières notions spatiales de l'enfant* [*The child's first conceptions of space*] (pp. 5–10). Neuchâtel: Delachaux et Niestlé.

Piaget, J. (1969). *The child's conception of time.* London: Routledge & Kegan Paul. (Original work published 1946)

Piaget, J. (1971). *Biology and knowledge.* Chicago: The University of Chicago Press. (Original work published 1967)

Piaget, J. (1977a). *Recherches sur l'abstraction réfléchissante* [*Research on reflective abstraction*]. Paris: Presses Universitaires de France.

Piaget, J. (1977b). General conclusions. In J. Piaget, J.-B. Grize, A. Szeminska, & Vinh Bang (Eds.), *Epistemology and psychology of functions* (pp.167–196). Dordrecht, Boston: D. Reidel. (Original work published 1968)

Piaget, J., & Inhelder, B. (1975). *The origin of the idea of chance in children.* London: Routledge & Kegan Paul. (Original work published 1951)

Siegler, R. S., & Richards, D. D. (1979). Development of time, speed, and distance concepts. *Developmental Psychology, 15*(3), 288–298.

Vygotsky, L. S. (1962). *Thought and language.* Cambridge, MA: MIT Press.

Wilkening, F. (1981). Intergrating velocity, time and distance information: A developmental study. *Cognitive Psychology, 13*, 231–247.

# Chapter 7

# Intrinsic and External Constraints on the Development of Cognitive Competence

Eberhard Schröder
Wolfgang Edelstein
*Max-Planck-Institute for Human Development and Education*

The recent cognitive developmental literature has been marked by a rush of studies in which one or another of a range of cognitive competencies have been reported to emerge much earlier in development than Piaget's structural theory appears to warrant. One result of these controversial research reports has been to provoke a debate as to whether responsibility for such findings is to be assigned to the presence of spurious methodological artifacts, or whether they actually signal some more fundamental flaw in the theories they are meant to evaluate. This chapter explores this issue of ''early'' versus ''late'' emergence by (a) analyzing the particular criteria for competence employed in one of these controversial areas, the study of class inclusion; and (b) reporting the results of a longitudinal study in which the potential effects of a series of possible constraints on the acquisition of class inclusion were examined.

An assumption that has guided the work reported here is that more customary accounts of structural development have tended to ignore a number of potential sources of variation and individual differences in the process of cognitive development. In the language employed throughout this chapter, these differences are said to represent both the effects of *intrinsic task constraints*, such as those imposed by the particular stimulus materials, procedural strategies and response modalities employed, and the effects of *external constraints* or influences on children's actual developmental rate, such as those introduced by variations in the social life worlds of the subjects tested, or other unspecified psychological characteristics that might influence their performance, or more generally, their cognitive developmental status. Not accounting for intrinsic

131

constraints has led researchers systematically to overestimate children's test abilities. Similarly, failure to pay adequate attention to the external constraints has led other researchers to observe especially advantaged subpopulations and thus to conclude that various cognitive competencies are consolidated at a much earlier age than is the case in the population as a whole.

Informed by our interest in these two likely sources of measurement difficulty, we have organized the materials presented in this chapter around two issues. The first of these issues concerns the general problem of establishing the age at which subjects can be said to possess specific cognitive competencies, and leads to a general discussion of problems associated with identifying those cognitive competencies to begin with. The second is the issue of how best to account for the range of individual differences commonly observed in the measurement of these same competencies, and leads to a more systematic examination of the interaction between the development of cognitive structures and various measurement and sociocultural constraints. Our plan is to begin with a general conceptual account of these issues and their interrelations, then to illustrate these matters by presenting data from our own longitudinal study. These empirical data, which concern the development of hierarchical classification abilities, clearly demonstrate the slow and uneven developmental course that we argue is the general rule in the ontogenesis of such operatory systems. In particular, these data describe a 5-year longitudinal course during which first 7- and eventually 12-year-olds work out their understanding of matters having to do with hierarchical classification. These data offer an opportunity to monitor the same individuals as they progress (a) from their first insights about classification matters, (b) through an interim period in which these early marks of potential competency actually unfold, and (c) into a final period of consolidation in which these abilities are broadly generalizable and can be explained or justified. As we make clear in the course of this chapter, we believe that this consolidated ability to generalize and to explain one's judgments is the only defensible criterion of competence for such structurally based cognitive abilities.

## GENERAL PROBLEMS ASSOCIATED WITH THE MEASUREMENT OF COGNITIVE COMPETENCY

The concept of "competence," in its dictionary definition, means fit and fully capable of meeting the requirements of some task. In developmental psychology and especially in the framework of structural theories of development the concept of competence is used quite differently. In this framework it is assumed that competence is available to the subject when one certain step in the acquisition sequence of a cognitive structure is performed. We think that developmental psychologists would be advised to hold more closely to the standard definition in their discussions of children's emerging cognitive competence. Notwithstanding the obvious problem that any concrete way of measuring general fitness may be somehow flawed, we argue that the child's earliest sign of skill in a particular area of intellectual functioning should not be mistaken for evidence for the possession of some real but largely hidden structural competence. Instead, it is better read as evidence only of the first steps taken in the direction of a more fully consolidated and later developing set of abilities that deserve to be characterized as "full" cognitive competencies (Chapman, 1987a; Piaget, 1977; Pinard & Laurendeau, 1969). This view grows out of our understanding of the notion of cognitive structures, according to which we see certain performances on the part of children as necessary prerequisites for the acquisition of cognitive abilities. The emergence of cognitive structures, especially of concrete operations, is highly dependent on the performance because cognitive structures will be consolidated by generalized application to different domains (Piaget, 1971). According to this conception, the development of cognitive competence can only be analyzed adequately if structural development is related to concrete performance conditions and to contexts of development and if their specific interaction is taken into account.

One example of the confusion that has characterized psychologists' attempts to understand the ways in which specific skills or abilities are eventually consolidated by overarching cognitive structures is found in the competing accounts of children's hierarchical classification abilities. For example, Gelman (1978), and more recently, Gelman and Baillargeon (1983) characterized children as regularly evidencing what they call cognitive competencies at a considerably earlier age than that commonly reported by investigators more closely associated with the traditions of Piagetian research. However, many of the empirical studies on which they based these generalizations employed "simplified" versions of standard Piagetian tasks or included training procedures specifically intended to demonstrate that subjects could acquire particular skills (and the cognitive competencies with which such skills are associated) at an earlier age than had been typically observed by Piaget and his co-workers. For example, Markman (1981) and Markman and Hutchinson (1984) studied a modified version of Inhelder and Piaget's (1964) classic version of the class inclusion problem in such a way as to show that young children's difficulties with the traditional task do not reflect true deficits in logical reasoning, but merely various processing or performance problems. The task modifications introduced new figural and semantic features to the measure originally developed by Piaget, which were intended to facilitate the same process of reasoning that was the target of Inhelder and Piaget's original studies. Markman found that preschool children achieved significantly higher levels of success on the modified than on the standard task.

Whereas both Gelman and Baillargeon (1983) and Markman (1981) interpreted these different results as evidence that children acquire the competence to solve class inclusion problems at an earlier age than previously reported and thus concluded that Piaget and his colleagues had systematically overestimated the age at which children typically acquire particular cognitive competencies, other authors (e.g., Brainerd, 1978; Chapman, 1987a; Hofman, 1982; Keating, 1980; Larsen, 1977; Schröder, 1989) read the same findings as artifacts of various methodological and measurement problems. Such critiques stem from the fact that even investigators closely affiliated with the tradition of Genevan research often disagree on how to assess cognitive structures and how to operationalize cognitive competence. In particular it is argued that (a) the status of Piaget's so-called "critical method" or quasi-clinical interview for the assessment of cognitive structures is not clear; (b) even when his research was most experimental and laboratory oriented, he failed to develop standardized instruments and procedures; and (c) there is a lack of agreement as to whether actual judgments or explanations (justifications of these judgments) stand as a proper criterion for the cognitive structures in question (see Chapman, 1987a). The consequence of these sources of confusion and disagreements is that the results of various studies available in the literature are not comparable because the data are derived on the basis of different assessment and scoring procedures and measurements are grounded in different rationales. In discussing the adequacy of various measures of cognitive competence by analyzing the potential sources of errors that possibly are introduced into measurement Brainerd (1973) adopted the position that especially explanations or justifications of judgments are subject to various sources of systematic error and, thus, are biased measures of cognitive competence.

In our view these supposedly empirical debates are better understood as stemming from an unvoiced theoretical difference of opinion as to how the competencies in question are best understood. There may be some merit in the methodological arguments of these authors to the effect of biased measurement, but any such appeals to measurement error presuppose the unsettled question of what the competence to be measured should be taken to *mean*.

In the work presented here, we argue that what is most coherently regarded as full, or consolidated cognitive competence not only requires that subjects should be able to justify or give reasons for their judgments, but that they also should be able to generalize such solutions across a variety of problem types. This is the case, we argue, because such generalizations and explanations stand as a mark of the epistemic interaction that must obtain between the subject and the object of any real knowledge. Only by both justifying their judgment and generalizing, do children make clear whether their actions are based on the figural components of particular tasks or whether they actually reflect some true interiorization of the logical structures.

However important it may be to clarify the definition of cognitive competence, added conceptual clarity cannot actually solve the general problem created by the range of competing measurement strategies currently loose in the field. As both Keating (1980) and Schröder (1989) have pointed out, few empirical studies in cognitive development rely on the same operationalizations, and most fail to specify sufficiently the details of their measurement efforts. As a consequence, the results of different studies can only rarely be directly compared. Keating (1980) summarized this confusing state of affairs by commenting that:

> Since performance features have typically been unsystematically added or subtracted relative to the original construct, there is as yet no conceivable overall integration (at least not by me). It is something like a merry-go-round, where each horse is a performance factor-rising here to discount discrepant evidence, rising there to discount supportive evidence; and since each researcher chooses which horse to ride and for how long, no comprehensive picture of the construct or its range is obtained ... In other words, we need to examine how general a model of cognitive development should be. (p. 235)

In response to this same state of affairs Brainerd (1978) reversed his own earlier commitment to the notion that only judgments had a place in the measurement of cognitive competence (Brainerd, 1973). Instead, he came to the conclusion that essentially none of the "measurement sequences," which supposedly reflected the order in which various structural competencies are acquired, could be evaluated empirically, so there is little reason to consider them further. In response to the same dilemma, Keating (1980) reached a different, but no more satisfactory solution. Rather than simply abandoning the entire enterprise, he called for an attempt to standardize the various assessment measures in current use. In one sense, Keating's seemingly reasonable proposal could be seen as an attempt to legislate a problem out of existence rather than attempting to meet it more directly. Depending on how such attempts at standardization were carried out, the special interests and concerns of whole branches of cognitive psychology (e.g., structural theories) could be discarded.

## INTRINSIC AND EXTERNAL CONSTRAINTS ON COGNITIVE DEVELOPMENT

In our own approach to this measurement problem we attempt to avoid these difficulties. First, we formulate a model of the intrinsic constraints on the display of cognitive competence, then consider the effects of external constraints on their development.

Hofman (1982), with reference to an S–R model, has proposed a taxonomy of potential sources of structural invalidity in Piagetian and neo-Piagetian assessment. Hofman distinguished between potential sources of invalidity that belong to (a) the presentation of the task (stimulus), (b) the procedural schemes

TABLE 7.1
Model of Sources of Variation in the Measurement of
Cognitive Competencies

| Task | Organism |
|------|----------|
| *Presentation (Stimulus)* | *Representation* |
| • Media of presentation<br>  • objective<br>  • pictorial<br>  • symbolic-verbal<br>  • phonetic | • Sensory perception<br>  • visual<br>  • tactile<br>  • kinesthetic<br>  • auditory |
| • Modes of presentation<br>  • covered vs. uncovered | • Mental representation<br>  • encoding<br>  • chunking |
| • Constellation of variable<br>  systems (complexity) |   • capacity for processing<br>  • attentional capacity |
| • Attributes of reference systems<br>  • open vs. closed gestalt<br>  • defined vs. undefined | *Conceptualization (Contexts)* |
| *Procedure* | • Dimensions and domains<br>  • attribute of objects<br>  • attribute of signified |
| • Reproductive interiorized<br>  (S→O→R) | • Contextualization in the lifeworld<br>  • experiential-counterintuitive<br>    abstract |
| • Exploratory/manipulative/constructive<br>  (S→(O⟷S′)→R) |   • experiential knowledge<br>  • Subculture, Culture, Society |
| *Performance (Type of Response)* | • Reference-affiliation<br>  • self-referential<br>  • distinction subject-object |
| • Recognition<br>• Pictorial reproduction<br>• Construction |   • interest-motivation<br>  • emotion |
| • Behavior and explanation<br>  (judgment and justification) | • Structure of knowledge<br>  • expertise |

and performance of the subjects (response), and (c) the content of the tasks. Although Hofman constructed his taxonomy with the intention to criticize the assessment model of Piagetian theory, the model can be used to distinguish performance factors that are relevant, or contribute, to the acquisition of cognitive operations. On the basis of Hofman's taxonomy, Schröder (1989) proposed a model of potential sources of variations necessary for analyzing structural development (see Table 7.1).

This model distinguishes two major factors. The first factor relates to matters that have to do with the presentation of a task. This includes differences in the stimulus (material setting of the task, mode of presentation, complexity of the system of variables), the procedural scheme of task administration, and the response modalities employed (judgment vs. explanation). The second factor involves effects due to the mental representation (sensory perception and mental space) and the conceptualization of the content of a task (dimensions or domains of application, the context of the tasks and the knowledge systems to which such operations refer). If cognitive development and the onset of a given operatory competence is to be adequately assessed, these sources of variation must be distinguished and the interaction between them systematically observed. In what follows, we attempt to show that both of these factors have massive effects on the time of acquisition of hierarchical classification abilities. In the empirical study presented here, alternative sets of tasks are used to separate different intrinsic factors that influence the acquisition of competence including: (a) mode of task presentation (experimental setting vs. verbal categories), (b) performance conditions (judgment vs. explanation), and (c) content of verbal task (experiential context).

Whereas such *intrinsic constraints* on performance are located in the interface between the epistemic subject and the object of knowledge, *external constraints* are conceptualized as "sociocultural" modifiers of these epistemic interactions. These constraints or conditions determine the availability of knowledge-related experience and of objects of knowledge, and thus may promote or delay the acquisition of cognitive structures. By the present account, however, they do not lead to different forms of cognitive competence.

Whereas intrinsic constraints are acknowledged within psychometric discourse as legitimate sources of measurement differences, external constraints on development are typically understood as belonging to a different tradition— the tradition of individual differences and socialization research. This artificial separation is characteristic of Piaget's developmental theory, which is notorious for its lack of attention to socialization effects on development (Broughton, 1981; Buck-Morss, 1975): The psychological subject, according to Piaget's own testimony (Inhelder & Piaget, 1971) was not of major interest to this epistemological psychology (see also Bullinger & Chatillon, 1983; and Chapman, 1988).

Many serious misunderstandings as well as real weaknesses and contradictions of Piagetian theory can be traced to the fact that it has ignored the impact of interindividual differences on development. Such an approach unnecessarily precludes the analysis of the impact of culture, class, and gender on individual development, thereby preventing Piagetian psychology from making contributions to our understanding of the interface of the macrostructures and microprocesses of development (see Broughton, 1981; Buck-Morss, 1975; Edelstein, 1983; Edelstein, Keller, & Schröder, 1989). Moreover, a potentially important theme of Piagetian psychology itself is ruled out when individual differences in development are ignored. For Piaget, social interaction provides the basic mechanism responsible for the activities of the internal adaptation processes that themselves lead to structural development. For example, Piaget assumed that interaction with nonauthoritative others or basically equal peers (Youniss, 1980) serves as a lever for inducing structural change. Interaction, as a means of exploration, negotiation, and verification is therefore an experiential and epistemic process, and the opportunity structure that distributes epistemic experiences is highly relevant to the course of cognitive growth and to the individual differences found in development. In summary, external conditions such as those afforded in the form of economic or ecological opportunity, of enrichment or handicap, and perhaps more basic still, in the form of opportunities for interaction, represent the opportunity structure of epistemic experience that differentially enhances or impedes epistemic growth. In the empirical study reported here, social class and gender may be taken to reflect such opportunity structures directly and "ability" may represent such structures indirectly by mediating the selection of epistemic experiences in the socialization context of the home and, even more tangibly, of the school.

What are the consequences of these theoretical considerations for the analysis of cognitive development? The analysis of internal constraints on cognitive development, we argue, leads to a more differentiated picture of structural development. By this account, the operation of such constraints can serve to prevent various operational structures from reaching consolidation, with the effect that such structures cannot be applied successfully to certain domains of performance or experience (see Piaget, 1977). On this reading, intraindividual differences in children's test performance can be interpreted as an expression of the fact that such subjects are blocked from applying otherwise available cognitive structures to particular content domains. In other words, some subjects have failed to adequately generalize the application of cognitive structures. By contrast, as such structures become more broadly generalized and consolidated there are fewer restrictions on their domain of application. Thus, the consolidation of the cognitive structure leads to a decrease in the intraindividual variability of children's test performances (see Schröder, 1989). In short, the development of cognitive competence is considered here to correspond to the progress that has been made in the consolidation of the structure. Mature, consolidated competencies will be acquired relatively late in development, because such generalized structures require that a series of constraints be overcome. In contrast, particular domain-specific abilities can be expressed earlier, as they represent only one developmental step in the acquisition sequence leading to a consolidated structure.

It follows from the preceding argument that, whereas intrinsic constraints will affect *intraindividual differences* between tasks, external conditions will affect *interindividual differences* in the onset of competence. In other words, the structure of opportunities will provide individuals with different amounts and qualities of epistemic experience, thereby either advancing or delaying consolidation. Thus, the timing of consolidation will vary as a function of sociocultural factors, a fact that Piaget himself has acknowledged, referring to his somewhat underdeveloped notion of décalage (Piaget, 1972). Within limits, longitudinal studies can contribute to the separation of these effects. Nevertheless, the effects of the opportunity structure will interact with the effects of intrinsic constraints in various systematic ways that still remain opaque in longitudinal research. Specific cultures will provide differential exposure to different tasks. Such differences are especially likely in view of the different levels of opportunity different cultures provide for its members to acquire practice in providing explanations or conceptual reasons for their actions. It nevertheless remains important to separate as much as possible the effects of intrinsic and external constraints on development.

In the longitudinal study reported here, the influence of intrinsic constraints was represented by mode of task presentation, performance conditions, and content of verbal task, whereas the external opportunity structures were represented by the factors of social class, gender, and ability that specify the quasi-experimental designs of the study as described in the next section.


## DESIGN, SUBJECTS, AND METHOD

In an effort to demonstrate the slow and uneven development of competence toward the consolidation of operatory structure, the development of classification was chosen as an example. More specifically, the acquisition of the concept of hierarchical classification was investigated longitudinally from childhood into early adolescence (see Edelstein et al., 1989). In this study, two different types of class inclusion tasks were presented to an initial sample of 121 seven-year-old urban children in Iceland. These same children were reassessed at ages 9 and 12 (see Fig. 7.1).

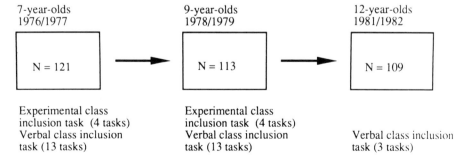

FIG. 7.1.   Longitudinal measurement design of the study.

The two class inclusion tasks differed with respect to the content, the context, and the specific reality systems to which they refer. The variations were introduced in order to maximize the effects of *intrinsic* constraints on performance. The "experimental task" developed by Smedslund (1964) is administered in an experimental setting and makes use of a set of plastic chips of different forms and colors. The "verbal" task calls for class inclusion of semantic categories. Both sets of tasks involve the typical class inclusion question comparing subordinate and superordinate classes. (For example, in the experimental task the following question was asked "Are there more red ones, or are there more round ones?" and in the verbal task "Are there more oranges, or are there more fruits?") Both tasks were varied with regard to performance type (judgment vs. justification). Two modes of presentation were chosen for the experimental task: a covered versus an uncovered condition. In the verbal task, semantic meaning was varied across 13 concepts specifically chosen for their validity in the particular cultural context studied. In addition to maximizing individual differences due to intrinsic constraints on performance, content variations in verbal classification can also be taken to reflect variable opportunities for epistemic experience available in a subculture. The two tasks are described in Table 7.2.

Both judgments and explanations were scored dichotomously as pass and fail. A judgment was scored as an adequate answer to the test question, if the

TABLE 7.2
Description of the Hierarchical Classification Tasks

*Class Inclusion—Experimental Version (CI)*

| | | |
|---|---|---|
| CI01: | Red rounds and red squares: | Uncovered presentation |
| CI02: | Red rounds and red squares: | Covered presentation |
| CI03: | White squares and white rounds: | Uncovered presentation |
| CI04: | White squares and white rounds: | Covered presentation |

*Class Inclusion With Verbal Categories (CV)*

| | | |
|---|---|---|
| CV01: | Cats/animals | Experiential |
| CV02: | Ducks/birds | Experiential |
| CV03: | Buttercups/flowers | Experiential |
| CV04: | Oranges/fruits | Experiential |
| CV05: | Volkswagens/cars | Experiential |
| CV06: | Boys or girls/children | Experiential–self-referential |
| CV07: | Trawlers/ships | Experiential |
| CV08: | Lego blocks/toys | Experiential |
| CV09: | White sheep/sheep | Experiential |
| CV10: | Black sheep/sheep | Experiential |
| CV11: | Pants or dresses/clothes | Experiential–self-referential |
| CV12: | Sweets/candy | Experiential |
| CV13: | Reykjavik citizens/Icelanders | Experiential–self-referential |

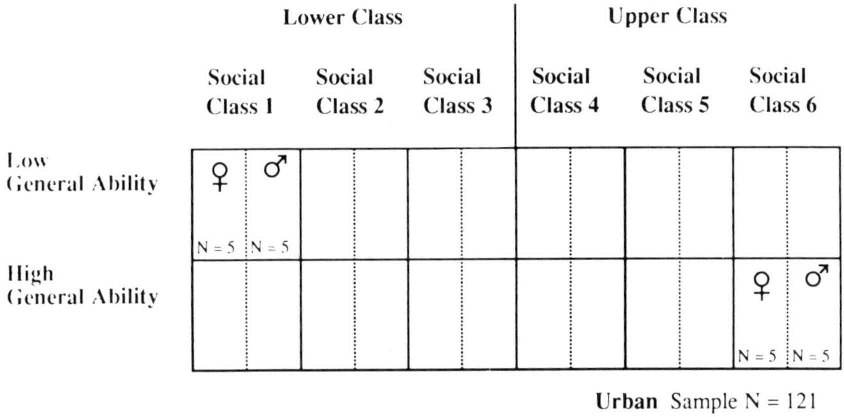

|  | Lower Class | | | Upper Class | | |
|---|---|---|---|---|---|---|
|  | Social Class 1 | Social Class 2 | Social Class 3 | Social Class 4 | Social Class 5 | Social Class 6 |
| Low General Ability | ♀  ♂<br>N = 5  N = 5 |  |  |  |  |  |
| High General Ability |  |  |  |  |  | ♀  ♂<br>N = 5  N = 5 |

Urban Sample N = 121

FIG. 7.2.   Sampling design of the study.

child was able to assign the superordinate attribute. An explanation was scored as an adequate answer if the child was able to compare quantitatively the extensions of the superordinate and the subordinate classes (e.g., "There are more fruits than oranges, since there are still other fruits than oranges").

The sampling design of the study was chosen to maximize individual differences due to *external* constraints on development, with variations in ability, social class, and gender representing what were hypothesized to be major determinants of the experiential input relevant to development (see Fig. 7.2).

"Ability level" was determined as follows: In the absence of other relevant information about school entrants, teachers of all first grades in the city were asked, during the first weeks of school, to nominate three children in the upper third and three children in the lower third of the general ability distribution of their particular classes. In a second step, approximately 20 subjects from each of six social classes were drawn from that pool, 5 male and 5 female from each social class from the high ability group and similar numbers from the low ability group. The final sample ($N$ = 121) thus represents as nearly a balanced design as could be achieved, and the selective procedure was as nearly random as could be accomplished once the ability levels had been defined.

In what follows, the rationale for the sampling design is briefly explained.

*Ability Level.* On the assumption that essentially all children eventually acquire those abilities relevant to first-grade children, teacher's judgments of initial ability can be understood to have distinguished between early and late developers. Such differences in rate of development or developmental status of a given age group will also likely capture differences between types of socialization and thus opportunities and experiences that are relevant for development. The selection of low and high ability children will also enable the investigators to observe the natural spread of developmental attainments within these opportunity groups. Further, differences between low and high ability children also throw light on the functioning of certain internal constraints, such as information processing capacity, mental space or attentional capacity, which can have large impact on developmental change (see Chapman, 1987b).

*Social Class.* Social class was taken in this study to represent quasi-independent "treatments," reflective of different exposure to relevant experience that may trigger potentially differing developmental trajectories (see Björnsson, Edelstein, & Kreppner, 1977). The patterns of data characterizing these trajectories may then be analyzed longitudinally and compared across relevant cells of the design. For the present analyses a dichotomous measure of socioeconomic status is used, summarizing the social class distribution in terms of "low" and "high" social class.

*Gender.* Björnsson et al.'s (1977) data had revealed that social class effects were importantly and differentially mediated through gender. Lower class girls were generally and substantively higher both in verbal IQ and grades than lower class boys, whereas conversely upper class boys had higher IQs than upper class girls. In view of the controversial literature on gender effects in structural development (see, for instance, the controversy between Walker, 1984, and Baumrind, 1986), it appeared important to analyze the present longitudinal data set with regard to potential differences between developmental trajectories of boys and girls.

Intrinsic constraints and external conditions that impact on the development of hierarchical classification as investigated in the present study are summarized in Table 7.3.

In an attempt to analyze the effects of internal constraints (response modality, task content, and task form) the empirical investigation focused on the following questions: Do different response modalities, task forms, and task con-

TABLE 7.3
Intrinsic Constraints and External Conditions in the
Development of Hierarchical Classification

| | |
|---|---|
| *Intrinsic Constraints* | |
| Task (presentation): | Experimental setting versus verbal concepts |
| Performance: | Judgment versus explanation |
| Content: | Different experiential referents |
| | (for verbal class inclusion only) |
| *External Conditions* | |
| Gender: | Girls versus boys |
| General ability: | Low versus high |
| Social class: | Low versus high |

tents represent relevant sources of developmental variation (i.e., produce relevant differences in individual development), and do such differences decrease over time?

To analyze the effects of external conditions of development, the influence of gender, socioeconomic status, and initial ability on acquisition rate were investigated. It is of special relevance to developmental accounts of change whether these conditions affect developmental processes directly, or whether they contribute to development through the mechanism of specific internal constraints.

## EMPIRICAL ILLUSTRATIONS

In exploring the available data set having to do with hierarchical classification abilities it became clear that some instances of ''early'' competence emerged only in certain specific combinations of task variations, performance conditions and modes of presentation. Figure 7.3 shows the developmental courses of hierarchical classification from age 7 through 12. Differences between items are indicated by the range of clustered items for each measurement occasion and performance type (judgment and justification). For each from of task (experimental vs. semantic categories) the developmental courses of both judgment and explanation are shown.

More specifically, although there were large differences between judgment and justification in verbal reasoning at ages 7 and 9, only small differences were found for the experimental version of the class inclusion task by age 7. Moreover, differences between performance types decrease over time for both forms of task. This result—decreasing intraindividual variability—can be interpreted as indicating ongoing consolidation of the cognitive structure. Although at the onset of the study (at age 7) there were substantive intraindividual differences between children in judgment and explanation, at the end of the time span under study both processes of performance were more or less integrated. The same process of consolidation was found to obtain in the verbal task. From age 9 to 12 there was a sizeable decrease in intraindividual variability between different verbal classification items (content). Again this can be taken as an indication of ongoing consolidation of the cognitive structure.

Differences between the developmental courses of the two forms of task (both concerning performance type and general development) can be traced back either to the *extension* of the reality systems to which they refer or to the *type* of reference system. The former specifies the difference between a finite and limited material setting in the case of the experimental Smedslund task, and an open and essentially infinite system of reference in the verbal tasks. The latter opposes materials that are meaningful only within the context of the experiment to semantic categories that refer to experiential knowledge. Although in the experimental task the system of reference is limited to a certain perceiv-

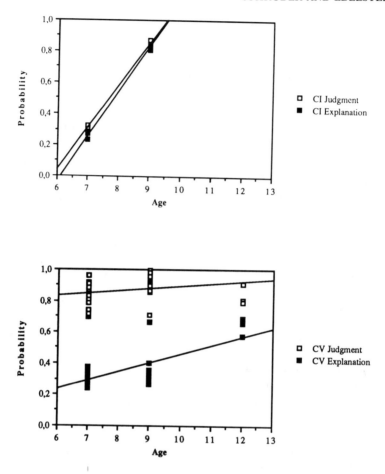

FIG. 7.3.   Developmental courses of experimental class inclusion (CI) and verbal class inclusion (CV) at ages 7 through 12.

able number of objects to be classified, verbal classification refers to semantic categories where the extension of reference objects is potentially unlimited. Moreover, the application of semantic categories depends on the elaboration of the language system, as the outcome of the inference, in each case, must relate meaningfully to the experience of the subjects. When class inclusion was tested in an experimental setting with a limited number of objects, no relevant differences were found between types of performance. Judgment and explanation thus appear to belong to the same inferential process. One reason for this conclusion is that the reference objects in the experimental setting (plastic chips) derive their meaning from the experimental setting itself. The plastic chips do not refer to anything outside the framework of the experiment. Therefore previous knowledge or experience does not interfere with the process of logical inference in class inclusion. In contrast, previous knowledge of semantic categories interferes heavily with the process of verbal classification. At age 7, most children can give adequate judgments of the relationship between subordinate and superordinate verbal categories but they are rarely able to explain the assumed inclusive relationship correctly.

Let us now look at interindividual differences in performance as represented by the external conditions exemplified by the factors of the sampling design. Different patterns of developmental progression were obtained for hierarchical classification as measured by the two sets of tasks—experimental and verbal. External conditions and intrinsic constraints also interacted systematically. Gender, contrary to some expectations, did not influence the pattern of cognitive development. However, both ability and social class do. Ability

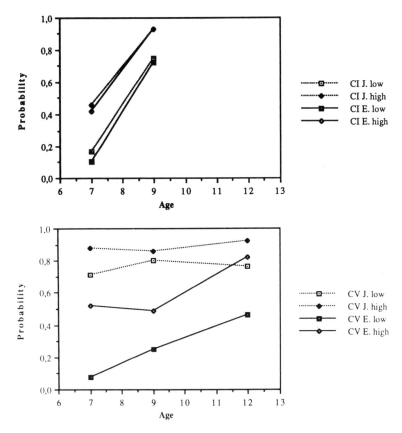

FIG. 7.4. Developmental courses of experimental class inclusion (CI) and verbal class inclusion (CV) at ages 7 through 12 by ability (low vs. high). J = Judgment; E = Explanation.

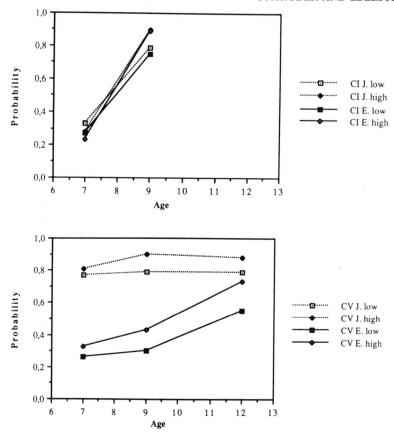

FIG. 7.5.  Developmental courses of experimental class inclusion (CI) and verbal class inclusion (CV) at ages 7 through 12 by social class (low vs. high). J = Judgment; E = Explanation.

influences developmental change in both the experimental and the verbal classification tasks. Social class influences verbal classification, but not the Smedslund task (see Fig. 7.4 and 7.5).

In the verbal classification task, explanations are much more affected by general ability than are judgments. Thus, differences in general ability appear to specifically influence the inferential process of verbal reasoning.

In Fig. 7.5 the developmental courses of hierarchical classification abilities are depicted for children from lower and upper social classes at ages 7 through 12. As the figure shows, social class only affects the development of verbal classification. The influence of social class increases over time: At age 12 the differences between social classes are considerably larger than at age 7. This finding can be interpreted as follows. Social class membership represents cumulative experience in different social lifeworlds and opportunity structures. This will affect the development of abilities in tasks that tap children's experience of the world and may either interfere with or reinforce knowledge previously held. Thus, children from the higher social classes on the average achieve higher developmental status because, presumably, both their experience of objects and their experience with verbal interaction about objects is richer than that of lower class children. In contrast, tasks that use materials that are meaningful only within the framework of the experiment will not be affected by experience derived from the social lifeworlds of the children, as the available knowledge system and previous structural development will interfere less, or not at all, with the achievement on such a task. Thus, somewhat unexpectedly, but still in agreement with theory, the "more abstract" experimental task is both less difficult and more amenable to earlier consolidation than the verbal task because the latter refers to everyday figural experience that is nested within subcultural traditions of knowledge exchange in everyday experience, whereas the former does not.

When analyzing the interaction of general ability and social class in the development of explanations of verbal classification increasing differentiation of the developmental trajectories of low ability children was found (see Fig. 7.6). Although at ages 7 and 9 low ability children from both low and high social class show similar developmental status with regard to the explanation of verbal classification judgments, at age 12 only the low ability children from upper class origins made progress. Low ability children from the lower social class, by contrast, stagnated. Very few children from this social group succeeded in mastering the class inclusion task by age 12. Although the development of low ability children is heavily affected by social class, the developmental trajectories of high ability children do not differ at all by social class. Children from both lower and higher social class achieve the same developmental status at

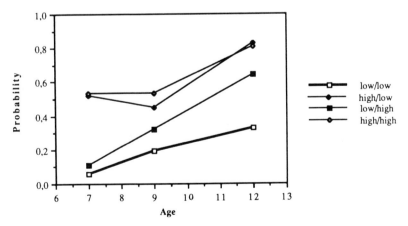

FIG. 7.6.   Developmental courses of explanations in verbal class inclusion at ages 7 through 12 by ability (low vs. high) and social class (low vs. high).

ages 7, 9, and 12. Thus, the influence of social class is mediated by general ability.


## CONCLUSIONS

Although intraindividual differences due to intrinsic constraints (content and performance type) decreased over time, interindividual differences in performance either persisted or increased across the 5-year period of this study. Thus, even at age 12 (or older), many subjects experienced difficulties in justifying (explaining) the inclusion relation between superordinate and subordinate classes represented by various common verbal concepts. This was the case, in particular, for subjects of low initial ability and from low socioeconomic backgrounds.

Initial ability level had a significant effect on the development of both the experimental and the verbal class inclusion task. Children of high initial ability achieved mastery on these tasks much earlier than did children of low initial ability. Gender did not affect this aspect of structural development at all. Thus, no support was found for the assumption that gender-specific experiences in the lifeworlds of children influence the acquisition of class inclusion ability. Social class selectively affected tasks that refer to everyday experience. Children from the higher social classes performed better only on verbal tasks, presumably because both their experience of objects, and their experience with verbal interaction about objects is richer than that of lower class children. Inversely, children of lower class origin performed as well as upper class children in the experimental task. This may indicate that the performance on this task is not affected by class-specific privileges or experience.

Although the process of decreasing intraindividual variability and instability and increasing intraindividual consistency can be interpreted as the consolidation of the operatory structure of hierarchical classification, this process is certainly a very slow and gradual one. Moreover, it is still incomplete at the end of the period under observation (age 12). Other tasks investigated in the present study (see Edelstein et al., 1989) also provide evidence that the consolidation of other concrete operations similarly remains incomplete, even in adolescence.

Another major finding emerging from the analysis was that the inferential process operating in solving class inclusion tasks differs as a function of specific intrinsic constraints introduced into the assessment. Tasks that relied only on subjects' judgments differed systematically from those requiring verbal explanations. For the judgments-only criterion, children were able to master inclusive relationships adequately at age 7, or perhaps even earlier, presumably on the basis of figural knowledge about the categories required. When asked to explain these hierarchical relationships, however, these same children do not refer to the quantitative relationship that exists between superordinate and subordinate classes. However, some quantitative comparison of superordinate and subordinate classes is a logically necessary criterion of classificatory competence. Therefore we conclude—contrary to Brainerd's argumentation, but in agreement with Chapman's thesis in this volume—that the measurement of competence must be based on explanations of judgments because only explanations demonstrate the full inferential and epistemic logic applied to the task.

Regarding the onset of a given competence in the course of cognitive development, instances of what might be called "early" competence certainly can be found whenever certain configurations of task variations and performance conditions happen to elicit conditions of optimal performance. However, when competence is defined in terms of the consolidation of operatory ability across multiple tasks and procedures, then its acquisition is a long and arduous process. In fact, this process is far from complete, even for concrete operational abilities, well into early or even middle adolescence. As defined here, the concept of competence requires generalized application of an underlying cognitive structure. By this standard, evidence of *early competence* of the sort so frequently cited in the literature is likely to reflect limited or restricted competence at best. Instead, such instances of early task mastery can be viewed as representing domain-specific precursors of full, or consolidated, competence, the supporting structures for which may not develop for many years. From the viewpoint of equilibration theory, the acquisition of particular domain-specific abilities is a necessary prerequisite, but not a sufficient realization of the consolidation of a domain-general structure of the whole. It follows that much of what passes as evidence for early mastery on specific tasks remains of doubtful relevance to any account of competence in which this term is treated in the ordinary sense of full fitness or ability.

## REFERENCES

Baumrind, D. (1986). Sex differences in moral reasoning: Response to Walker's (1984) conclusion that there are none. *Child Development, 57,* 511–521.

Björnsson, S., Edelstein, W., & Kreppner, K. (1977). *Explorations in social inequality: Stratification dynamics in social and individual development in Iceland (Studien and Berichte,* Nr. 38). Berlin: Max Planck Institute for Human Development and Education.

Brainerd, C.J. (1973). Judgments and explanations as criteria for the presence of cognitive structures. *Psychological Bulletin, 79,* 172–179.

Brainerd, C.J. (1978). The stage question in cognitive-developmental theory. *The Behavioral and Brain Sciences, 2,* 173–213.

Broughton, J.M. (1981). Piaget's structural developmental psychology: IV. Knowledge without a self and history. *Human Development, 24,* 320–346.

Buck-Morss, S. (1975). Socio-economic bias in Piaget's theory and its implications for cross-cultural studies. *Human Development, 18,* 35–49.

Bullinger, A. & Chatillon, J.-F. (1983). Recent theory and research of the Genevan school. In P. H. Mussen (Ed.), *Handbook of child psychology. Vol. 3: Cognitive development* (pp. 231-262). New York: Wiley.

Chapman, M. (1987a). Inner processes and outward criteria: Wittgenstein's importance for psychology. In M. Chapman & R. A. Dixon (Eds.) *Meaning and the growth of understanding* (pp. 103-127). Berlin: Springer Verlag.

Chapman, M. (1987b). Piaget, attention capacity, and the functional implications of formal structure. In H.W. Reese (Ed.), *Advances in child development and behaviour* (Vol. 20, pp.289-334). Orlando, FL: Academic Press.

Chapman, M. (1988). *Constructive evolution: Origins and development of Piaget's thought.* Cambridge: Cambridge University Press.

Edelstein, W. (1983). Cultural constraints on development and the vicissitudes of progress. In. F.S. Kessel & A.W. Siegel (Eds.), *The child and other cultural inventions* (pp. 48-81). New York: Praeger.

Edelstein, W., Keller, M., & Schröder, E. (1989). Child development and social structure: Individual differences in development. In P.B. Baltes, D.L. Featherman, & R.M. Lerner (Eds.), *Life-span development and behaviour* (Vol. 10, pp. 151-185). Hillsdale, NJ: Lawrence Erlbaum Associates.

Gelman, R. (1978). Cognitive development. *Annual Review of Psychology, 29,* 297-332.

Gelman, R. & Baillargeon, R. (1983). A review of some Piagetian concepts. P.H. Mussen (Ed.), *Handbook of child psychology* (Vol. 3, pp. 167-230). New York:Wiley.

Hofman, R.J. (1982). Potential sources of structural invalidity in Piagetian and Neo-Piagetian assessment. In S. Modgil & C. Modgil (Eds.): *Jean Piaget: Consensus and controversy* (pp.233-239). London: Holt, Rinehart & Winston.

Inhelder, B., & Piaget, J. (1964). *The early growth of logic in the child.* New York: Norton.

Inhelder, B., & Piaget, J. (1971). Closing remarks. In D. R. Green, M. P. Ford, & G. B. Flamer (Eds.), *Measurement and Piaget* (pp. 210-213). New York: McGraw Hill.

Keating, D.P. (1980). Thinking processes in adolescence. In J. Adelson (Eds.), *Handbook of adolescent psychology* (pp. 211-246). New York: Wiley.

Larsen, G.Y. (1977). Methodology in developmental psychology: An examination of research in Piagetian theory. *Child Development, 48,* 1160-1166.

Markman, E.M. (1981). Two different principles of conceptual organization. In M.E. Lamb & A.L. Brown (Eds.), *Advances in developmental psychology* (Vol. 1, pp. 199-236). Hillsdale, NJ: Lawrence Erlbaum Associates.

Markman, E.M. & Hutchinson, J.E. (1984). Children's sensitivity to constraints on word meaning: Taxonomic versus thematic relations. *Cognitive Psychology, 16,* 1-27.

Piaget, J. (1971). The theory of stages in child development. In D. R. Green, M. P. Ford, & G. B. Flamer (Eds.), *Measurement and Piaget* (pp. 1-11). New York: McGraw-Hill.

Piaget, J. (1972). Intellectual evolution from adolescence to adulthood. *Human Development, 15,* 1-12.

Piaget, J. (1977). *The development of thought: Equilibration of cognitive structures.* New York: Viking Press.

Pinard, A., & Laurendeau, M. (1969). "Stage" in Piaget's cognitive developmental theory: Exegesis of a concept. In D. Elkind & J. H. Flavell (Eds.), *Studies in cognitive development: Essays in honor of Jean Piaget* (pp. 121-170). New York: Oxford University Press.

Schröder, E. (1989). *Vom konkreten zum formalen Denken: Individuelle Entwicklungsverläufe von der Kindheit bis zum Jugendalter [From concrete to formal thinking: Individual developmental processes from childhood to adolescence].* Bern: Huber.

Smedslund, J. (1964). Concrete reasoning: A study in intellectual development. *Monographs of the Society for the Research in Child Development, 29*(2), 1-39.

Walker, L.J. (1984). Sex differences in the development of moral reasoning: A critical review. *Child Development, 20,* 353-376.

Youniss, J. (1980). *Parents and peers in social development: A Sullivan-Piaget perspective.* Chicago: University of Chicago Press.

# Part III

# Beyond Piaget

Whereas the authors of the immediately preceding chapters chose to discuss issues of early competence from viewpoints within the broad horizon of Piagetian theory, the chapters in this section each go beyond Piagetian theory in some significant way. In chapter 8, for example, Juan Pascual-Leone and Janice Johnson argue that Piagetian (or neo-Piagetian) structuralism can at best be considered a first approximation toward a deeper underlying causal analysis. Like Montangero, they believe that debates regarding early competence are likely to remain inconclusive without an effective method of task analysis to differentiate the distinct demands of superficially similar tasks. However, they doubt that purely *structuralist* task analysis is sufficient to this end. Instead, they argue that such analyses must be based on what they call a causal theory of "dialectical equilibration." The first step toward the application of such a theory to the analysis of specific tasks is the definition of *schemes* as the functional units of mental processing. The bulk of the chapter is devoted to the articulation of such a definition and to principles of task analysis construed in this way. These principles are then applied to the specific case of Piaget's object permanence problem in order to explain why different versions of this task vary in difficulty and are solved at different ages during the sensorimotor period.

According to Piaget, sensorimotor development culminates in the development of what he variously called "cognitive representation" or "the semiotic function." Although he believed this capacity played an essential role in all subsequent cognitive development, he did not devote as much attention to it as he did, for example, to the development of operations. In chapter 9, Irving

Sigel proposes that cognitive representation is a competence that involves the "conservation of meaning": the understanding that the referential meaning of a sign or symbol is conserved across instances that may be phenomenally quite dissimilar. He argues that such "representational competence" is prerequisite for many forms of cognitive functioning and provides examples from his own research in which apparent failures of cognitive competence were found to result from a noncomprehension of meaning. One implication of this view is that cognitive competence is firmly embedded in the social contexts in which symbols are interpreted and exchanged. Sigel illustrates the importance of family interaction, culture, and social class as interpretative contexts affecting cognitive development, implying that cognitive competence cannot be considered totally in isolation from such contexts. Significantly, the research on "cognitive distancing" that Sigel reviews in this chapter had its origins in a problem also raised in the chapters by Smith and by Schröder and Edelstein: the attempt to understand typical social class differences in cognitive performance.

But the role of symbol interpretation in cognition is potentially ambiguous. On the one hand, interpretation is an inherent part of interpersonal communicative exchange. On the other hand, the interpretation and manipulation of symbols often has been considered an essential characteristic of intrapsychic cognitive processes. In chapter 10, Michael Chapman considers the relation between these two aspects of symbol use in rejecting the prevailing methodological skepticism toward children's verbal justifications as a marker of cognitive competence. In his view, the rejection of such justifications as data is based on three misconceptions: (a) that intrapsychic inference is the only competence of interest to cognitive psychologists, (b) that verbal justifications are of interest only as a potential indicator of intrapsychic inference, and (c) that the relation between the two is primarily a methodological question. Against these common assumptions, Chapman argues that children's understanding of how their conclusions can be justified is a competence of interest in its own right and that such understanding may be developmentally related to intrapsychic inference. The relation between competence in intrapsychic inference and competence in verbal justification is thus an empirical question. This argument is based on a theoretical model of the *epistemic triangle*, consisting of the active subject, the object of knowledge, and a real or implicit interlocutor, together with their mutual interactions. The major implication of this view is that conceptual knowledge is based, not only on the operative interaction between subject and object, but also on communicative interaction among subjects. From this perspective, the elimination of children's verbal justifications as data in studies of concrete operations has led, not merely to purer measures of intrapsychic inference, but also to the neglect of the understanding of justification, particularly of justification by necessity, as a competence worthy of study for its own sake.

# Chapter 8

# The Psychological Unit and its Role in Task Analysis: A Reinterpretation of Object Permanence

Juan Pascual-Leone
Janice Johnson
*York University*

There are two major problems that Piaget's work poses for modern psychology: the problem of discontinuous development via *qualitative stages*, and that of learning and stage transitions via *equilibration* (see Pascual-Leone, 1980). Only the first problem is fully recognized. Most developmentalists accept that some form of qualitative stages/levels of processing exists. These stages emerge in spurts in correlation with age, but are not bound to age in any simple manner— at least when stages are formulated as general structures (i.e., defined across types of situations for a type of subject). The hierarchy of stages is often expressed by means of a psychological series of models, Piagetian or neo-Piagetian, each describing the competence of one stage and, indirectly, showing the processing complexity that the child of this stage can handle.

Piaget called the psychogenetic ordering of qualitative stage models a *vertical decalage*—a concept often interpreted as chronological time needed to acquire the corresponding *competence*, perhaps in interaction with maturation. He called a *horizontal decalage* the reliable empirical ordering of tasks in terms of their passing age, when the tasks in question fall under the same *psycho-logical stage model*. Horizontal decalages are often attributed to "performance" factors and, thus, are seen as less interesting from the viewpoint of competence. The presumption is that horizontal decalages are due largely to limitations of mental attention or working memory; or, as Piaget (1941) would have it, due to the need to develop an interface between "abstract" structures, which define the stage in question, and concrete situation-specific processes responsible for the actual performance.

**153**

Montangero (chapter 6, this volume) offers a clear defense of structuralism against neo-empiricist opponents (cf. Johnson & Pascual-Leone, 1989b). A similar structuralist stand has been adopted by many neo-Piagetians, who tacitly maintain the same categorical distinction between vertical and horizontal decalages, albeit in a modified form (where "horizontal" levels seem to serve to separate into substages the main "vertical" stage levels—e.g., Case, 1985; Fischer, 1980). The tacit presupposition in all these cases is that mechanisms causing vertical decalages are intrinsically different from those that cause horizontal decalages. Yet, somewhat mysteriously, the assumption is also made that some equilibration or regulatory mechanisms could, when properly explicated, account for both kinds of decalage.

We want to challenge this view by asserting that structuralist models, with their intrinsic categorical distinction between "vertical" competence and "horizontal" performance, should be accepted only as first descriptive approximations (or initial necessary "moments") of a deeper causal analysis, based on an explicated theory of dialectical equilibration (Pascual-Leone, 1983, 1984, 1987, 1988, 1990, 1991). This new dialectical equilibration theory is constituted by a two-level organization of *causal mechanisms*: the level of *organismic schemes* (information-carrying—informational—processes) and the level of *organismic hardware operators* (i.e., endogenous mental attention, structural- and content-learning operators, Gestaltist internal Field factors, etc.—constraints that express the brain's "functional architecture"). We suggest here that this dialectical constructivist alternative to structuralism leads to more refined methods of task analysis.

A key to this new approach is the proper definition of organismic schemes as psychological units. We elaborate this definition, using as counterpoint the concept of hardware operators—which we introduce less directly and as needed. We illustrate our analytical methods in the context of Piaget's object permanence paradigm. This paradigm shows well the achievements, and also the problems, of structuralism. It also enables us to show how our methods, by taking structuralism as a necessary but not sufficient "moment," can obtain deeper analytical results that complement methods and theories of Piagetians and neo-Piagetians, by providing a causal account.

We reject the dichotomy "vertical" competence versus "horizontal" performance, and reject also the dichotomy of logical/psychological versus physiological/neuropsychological levels of reality. Our schemes are both psychological-structural *and* neuropsychological–functional. Somewhat like the later Piaget (Piaget IV—Pascual-Leone, 1988, 1989b), we define schemes/schemas as informational *functional systems* that can be demarcated in abstract functional terms. Consistent with neurologists, neuropsychologists, and connectionist researchers (e.g., Smolensky, 1988), we define schemes/schemas as manifold collections of neurons (nodes), distributed over the brain, that are co-functional and often co-activated (or activated in lawful sequences) because they together

generate *situation-specific components of praxis*—that is, minute or large functional systems that the subject uses.

## SCHEMES AS DIALECTICAL EMBODIMENTS
## OF INFRASTRUCTURE

A scheme is a functional unit or component of mental processing *that is necessary for praxis* (i.e., goal-directed activity, ultimately addressed to the environment to satisfy some needs). The goal of this praxis is a given outcome and/or
the representation of a given, simple or complex, distal object (i.e., representation of a "real" object or state of affairs as a manifold of constraints the subject
experiences or must obey). The subject's praxis is an experiential totality that
he or she internalizes by means of a multiplicity of schemes, each *epistemologically reflecting* a certain "functional system" or component of this praxis totality. If the *infrastructure* of praxis is defined as the real, necessary and sufficient
constraints ("perceptions," "actions," "motor movements," "representations," etc.) that make praxis possible in performance, then a scheme is an
internal model of that infrastructure of praxis—that component—which it
intends.[1]

Any scheme can be demarcated by means of a pair of components: a releasing component and an effecting component (Pascual-Leone, 1969, 1976a, 1983,
1984; Pascual-Leone & Goodman, 1979; Pascual-Leone, Goodman, Ammon,
& Subelman, 1978). The *releasing component* (*rc*) is constituted by *conditions*, which
can be matched to features of the external or internal state (the input to the
scheme in question), thereby creating a *cue* for the scheme when one such match
has occurred. When this state of affairs occurs, the scheme is said to have been
*activated*. Activation leads to the scheme's *application*. The *effecting component* (*ec*)
is constituted by *effects*, whose application in praxis serves to constrain and
produce (overt or mental) performance. The ordered pair *rc:ec* suffices to demarcate (but just demarcate!) any scheme. Schemes are recursive units: Any scheme
can in turn appear (be copied) as a condition or effect within other schemes.
Complex nested scheme-structures, which serialize or coordinate ("chunk")
simpler schemes, can be generated in this manner.

Piaget attempted to capture the meaning of what we here call functional
systems with the notion of *structure*. For Piaget, structures are constituted by
dynamic, performatory, complex figurative *invariants* that are always coupled
to *the related systems of operative schemes* (operations, preoperations, or proto-

---

[1]*Intend* refers to the phenomenological concept of *intentionality*. The intentionality of schemes
can be of two kinds (Pascual-Leone, 1990, 1991). It can be *referential*, in the sense of present-
ing/representing a referent—as in perception and imagery—or it might be *conative*, in the sense
of giving operative direction to acts like mentations or motor movements.

operations) *that generate these invariants psychogenetically*. Perceptual constancies, object permanence, and the various sorts of conceptual conservations are good examples of structures (complex systems of schemes). Note that simple schemes (e.g., touching an object, producing a certain sound) are already functional systems. Functionally speaking, the *rc/ec* components of simple schemes play the role that figurative/operative aspects take in complex structures.

A given kind of praxis may contain many different schemes (such as the praxis of "driving to the University in the morning"), or it may have as few as one (such as the praxis of "listening to a noise," or of "moving a finger towards the doorbell"). But the number of schemes a theoretician recognizes in any activity in part depends on the adopted level of analysis. This limitation, found in any sort of psychological unit, imposes a *hermeneutics*—such as *rational task analysis*—to demarcate schemes and other mechanisms involved in a task. This demarcation requires that we assume the *causal mechanisms* (Piaget's regulations) of the subject, as well as the scheme *repertoires* available to him or her. Task analysis must epistemologically reflect strategies actually used by subjects. Because these strategies are relative to both the subject (maturation, past experience) and the "nature" of the task, schemes and other mechanisms should be defined contextually in reference to both.

## SCHEMES AS NEUROPSYCHOLOGICAL FUNCTIONAL ABSTRACTIONS

From a neuropsychological perspective, a scheme is a collection of neurons, often distributed over the brain, that are cofunctional (i.e., together they can bring about certain results, which are the referent and/or goal(s) of the scheme in question) and are often coactivated (i.e., activated simultaneously or in a lawful sequence). Thus schemes are *neuronal networks* that, albeit defined functionally, have neurophysiological representation; and the nature of their content (e.g., whether they are cognitive—verbal, logical-conceptual, spatial—or affective) entirely depends on where in the brain they are located (prefrontal, frontal, parietal, temporal, limbic regions, etc.).

There are two principles that formulate how the brain adapts/relates to psychological experience: the principle of *plasticity at the service of praxis* and that of *psycho-physiological correspondence*. The first (i.e., plasticity at the service of praxis) posits that the cortex tends to internalize the infrastructure of functional systems that recur in praxis, and it does so in the form of neuronal collections that are coactivated frequently (NB, this is our definition of organismic schemes!). Any given instance of praxis (e.g., driving a car through the city) can be decomposed into functional systems (i.e., "jobs" or qualitatively different activities) that are jointly necessary for the praxis to take place. For instance, driving a car through the city demands coordination of five functional system categories: monitoring of mechanical controls (e.g., gear shift), steering the car, management of speed and car stability, road negotiation (e.g., avoiding obstacles, cars, keeping to the road, etc.), and route planning (e.g., generating an efficient course).

Because performances are repeated only when they either satisfy affective goals or are imposed by environmental resistances, repeated patterns of cofunctional and coactivated collections of neurons become consolidated, thereby giving origin to schemes. Organismic schemes, therefore, necessarily embody infrastructure of functional systems, where the goals are set by affects (the brain's limbic system), and the prefrontal lobes interpret these goals in terms of plans (these are the executive schemes mentioned later).

On first approximation, we consider the cortex to be a vast manifold repertoire of schemes; each scheme is relatively autonomous because it possesses its own set of releasing conditions. Because they are collections of neurons in a neuronal network, all schemes exhibit "spreading of activation." They, thus, pass their activation *down* to other related schemes that may have a better chance to determine performance, because the latter schemes risk less to be inhibited (lateral inhibition) by yet other strongly activated and incompatible schemes. This dynamic spreading of activation is ensured by a functional principle of neuronal transmission: the principle of summation (Sherrington, 1947). This principle says that synaptic sources of activation impinging upon a neuron summate algebraically (positive activation facilitating, negative activation inhibiting) to determine the final activation strength of the neuron. A neuron will fire as soon as this activation strength is higher than its own current firing threshold.

Because schemes are dynamic collections of interconnected neurons, this principle of neuronal firing in some sense transfers to the functioning of schemes, and through them affects performance. This is why performance is, at any moment, *overdetermined* by *that cluster of compatible schemes* (collection of collections of neurons) that momentarily is dominant (i.e., most highly activated).[2] This is the *principle of schematic overdetermination of performance*, pioneered by Freud (Rapaport, 1960), which we have formulated as *SOP principle* and interpreted neuropsychologically (Pascual-Leone, 1989a).

Finally there is the *principle of psycho-physiological correspondence*. Under the assumption that both subjective and objective content/structure of human performance—psychological reality—emerge from brain activity (e.g., Sperry, 1985), modern neuroscience tacitly accepts that distinguishable differences in human performance must have corresponding processing differences in the brain substratum (Pascual-Leone, 1989a). But this informational correspon-

---

[2]If schemes are compatible and apply together to produce performance, their neurons in the brain substatum become interconnected with activatory/positive (rather than inhibitory/negative) links.

dence need not involve a configural correspondence (i.e., no "pictures" or simple one-to-one mappings are being assumed). Because human performance is purposeful and constrained by infrastructure, acquired collections of cortical neurons should conform to information-processing analyses in terms of a valid theory of subjective action/praxis (goals, objects, mental states, actions, figurative encodings, operative transformations, etc.). But the reader must then think of the subject as being no more than a manifold repertoire of schemes (collections of collections of neurons) organized in flexible context-sensitive hierarchies (heterarchies), from which performances are *synthesized by over-determination*.

The brain's principles of functioning that synthesize adapted performance out of collections of schemes, and *modify these collections in conformity with experience*, must then be recognized as different from the schemes themselves (the collections of neurons or "software" of the brain). Pylyshyn (1984) has referred to these principles as the brain's "functional architecture." Our theory describes this "functional architecture" in terms of a set of *hardware operators and principles* (Pascual-Leone & Goodman, 1979; Pascual-Leone et al., 1978). We call *metasubjective* (Pascual-Leone, 1976a, 1987) a psychological theory defined in this manner: where there is *"subject-generating" hardware*, and the "subject" is construed in terms of processes that contain no ego/homunculus (Sartre, 1957; Schrag, 1989).

## GENERAL POSTULATES OF SCHEMES

We present here postulates that apply to *every kind* of organismic scheme and that should help in demarcating schemes empirically.

***SC1.*** For Piaget (1958), a scheme is the common structure of all the actions that a subject takes as interchangeable vis-à-vis a goal. It is also "an organized set of reactions that can be transferred from one situation to another by assimilation of the second to the first" (Piaget & Morf, 1958, p. 86). The first definition emphasizes the effecting component of schemes, that is, schemes as infrastructure of informational functional systems (or action "games"). The second definition obliquely refers to the schemes' releasing component, and the situations to which they apply. More abstractly, we can state that a scheme is a unitized system of processing that (a) is constituted by a hierarchy of informational functional systems (*one or more*) at the direct or indirect service of potential affective goals; and (b) is regulated by two sorts of components: releasing component(s) (*rc*), which stipulate conditions of activation, and effecting component(s) (*ec*), which give effects of application.

A scheme is not well defined until its components and functional system are stipulated. But the informational functional system might be no more than application of the *ec* (e.g., the encoding of an aspect of the input/output in the case of simple perceptual/motor schemes); or it may be different, often involving the anticipation (Tolman's expectancy) of one or more resulting effects or outcomes. (This anticipation constitutes another possible component of schemes, a *tc* or *terminal/temporary component.*) These more complex functional systems are *temporally organized* into interactivation or coactivation patterns. To emphasize that the *flow* of time-ordered events, and perhaps time itself, are represented in the organism by these means, we have proposed to call this type of scheme a *fluent*—a term coined by the computer scientist McCarthy (McCarthy & Hayes, 1969) for a somewhat similar unit (Johnson, Fabian, & Pascual-Leone, 1989; Pascual-Leone, 1976a; Pascual-Leone et al., 1978). A fluent is a scheme structure that includes in the essence of its *rc* or *ec* a temporally *ordered set* of schemes. (The modern cognitive-science notion of a "script" corresponds to what we might call a complex intellective or intellectual fluent.)

**SC2.** The form of informational functional systems is relative to the total praxis that employs them as modules, and so *schemes must be defined relative to the praxic totality that prompts their emergence.* The definition of a given scheme is relative to all other schemes that make up the total infrastructure of the task's strategy. The task-analytical implication is that good analysts *begin* by looking at the intended task as a whole, and then at the subconstituents, often working backwards from target results.

**SC3.** Because every scheme emerges from the *invariant* infrastructure of an informational functional system, *the scheme must be internally consistent*; otherwise, the invariant would not materialize, and the scheme could not be learned or abstracted. Consequently, *misleading factors (dialectical contradictions) elicited by situations*—for example, interference among schemes, S–R incompatibility, and/or Gestaltist field misleadingness—*become hard dividers that demarcate different schemes and prevent them from coordinating into superordinate scheme structures* (or schemas), until the misleadingness is eliminated. It follows that in task analysis, *misleading factors are "golden threads"* that help us to demarcate the different discrete schemes that the organism has retained and used to synthesize the task performance.

**SC4.** Functionally, a scheme is an indivisible *unit*. This implies that whenever two objects or two aspects of the environment, or two operative moves, are reliably different or reliably play different functions (even if they look alike), they will have to be represented *separately*, in two different schemes, if the organism is to perceive, treat, or use them differently (Pascual-Leone et al., 1978). This postulate follows from the principle of psychophysiological correspondence.

*SC5.* A scheme is a sort of *recursive function*: The conditions and/or effects of *any* scheme could in turn be constituted by schemes or scheme structures. Thus two separate schemes, such as those mentioned in Postulate SC4, could with practice become schematized (learned) into a structure that includes them both. In this case, if the task does not require the use of one of the schemes to the exclusion of the other, this superordinate structure (schema) might be applied instead of the two original schemes—thus providing a saving in mental demand (see later).

*SC6.* In neuropsychological terms, a scheme *h* is a collection of neurons that are co-functional and co-activated vis-à-vis a certain praxis. The scheme's *releasing component*(s) correspond(s) to the information-processing characteristics of any other neuronal collection that is (functionally speaking and in the present context) "upstream" (i.e., sends local activatory cortical connections to *h*). The *effecting component*(s) of *h* correspond(s) to information-processing consequences (local activatory or inhibitory effects) produced by *h* when its neurons fire "downstream" to connections with other collections of neurons (i.e., other schemes and schemas). Note that connections are "downstream" if they are closer to those neurons that will finally produce an overt or covert performance.

By virtue of their having the two components *rc* and *ec*, schemes can be in three different states: *inactive, activated,* or *applied.* The *activation* of a scheme *h* results from the proper match of its *rc* conditions to features of the input and/or of the internal field of activation; in neuropsychological terms it is the actual activation of the collection of neurons *h* by the firing of its "upstream" connections. The *application* of a scheme *h* is the concrete implementation in overt or covert performance of its *ec* effects. Neuropsychologically, application corresponds to the firing of connections that activate other informational processes (neuronal-scheme collections) that are found "downstream" and that succeed in co-determining performance. These final downstream neuronal connections are often called, following Sherrington (1947), the *final common path* of a given neurophysiological performance.

*SC7.* By virtue of the dynamic interaction between the principle of schematic overdetermination of performance (SOP principle) and various hidden-hardware operators, the overt or covert performance can exhibit structure that does not come from schemes, but rather from *dynamic syntheses.* These dynamic syntheses can be influenced by conscious mental processes via the conscious control of *M-operator, I-operator, L-operator,* and so on (see later). The causal determination of these syntheses is, however, unconscious and "automatic": It results from the dynamic processes of the brain's functional architecture. In task analysis, the existence of dynamic syntheses makes it necessary to assume dynamic interactions among hidden-hardware operators, if performance is to be derived from the inferred repertoire of schemes in the subject, and from the nature of the task.

*SC8.*   Piaget repeatedly emphasized that any scheme is analogous to the *intensional*, that is, purely semantic and nonextensional, definition of a concept. The *extension* of a scheme/concept would be constituted by all the things on which the scheme can lawfully apply. A scheme is thus an intensional entity that has no here-and-now extension—the extension, or rather part of it, appears only when the scheme applies to co-produce a performance. The logico-mathematical notion of *function*, including predicate function and operator, is biologically prefigured in the functional characteristics of schemes. Schemes are the organism's "psycho-functions." In contrast, the notion of a here-and-now extension, as illustrated by the logico-mathematical notion of a *set*, is not originally prefigured by a scheme but rather by a *dynamic synthesis*. This dynamic synthesis is often attained with the help of mental attentional energy (the *M*-operator mentioned later), which is applied to a small collection of schemes, thus constituting the subject's focus of attention or *field of centration*. This field of centration (a "psycho-set") constitutes the intuitive basis of a small set. This intuitive notion results from bringing together into synthesized unity (i.e., mental *centration*) a small collection of schemes, each with its own intension or content-value. The experience of numerosity, well studied in developmental psychology (e.g., Gelman & Gallistel, 1986; Klahr, 1984), is one manifestation of "reading" the synthetic unity of attended-to schemes.

## MODALITIES AND MODES OF SCHEMES

*Modalities* are natural kinds of schemes defined in terms of the *content* they bear. They are natural kinds because they are prefigured in the brain by way of distinct areas where the modalities have their exclusive cortical projections: visual, auditory, somatosensory, affective, linguistic, and so forth. *Modes* are natural kinds of schemes defined in terms of their *processing structure* and independently of the content—in the sense that the same structural characteristics (the same mode of processing) can be found in many different modalities. *Natural-kind modes* (i.e., modes with a separate projection on the cortex) are those recognized by neo-Piagetian theory (e.g., Case, 1985; Pascual-Leone et al., 1978). We discuss here three examples of natural kind modes: executive, figurative, and operative schemes.

*Executives* are schemes that embody "plans" and "control structures" of the psychological organism. They can best be defined as the internal structures that functionally interrelate three essential and distinct kinds of processes that intervene in purposeful performance. The first of these are the subject's *affects* and affective goals. Second are the subject's *action schemes* (whether operative or figurative), which are informational processes directly responsible for concrete, behavioral or mental performances that implement plans. Third are the *hidden-hardware operators*, such as *M*-operator (central activatory processes monitored by the dominant Executive), $I$-operator (central active inhibitory processes monitored by the dominant Executive), $F$-operator (Gestaltist internal field processes), $L$-operator (logical-structural learning), etc. By dynamically coordinating these three kinds of processes, executive schemes (the Executive, see later) produce their hidden interaction, which causes the emergence of complex organismic functions such as mental attention (Pascual-Leone, 1983, 1984, 1987), intelligence (Pascual-Leone & Goodman, 1979), memory, and so on.

Executives are fluents (i.e., temporally organized informational structures of the brain) that are usually first activated/inhibited by their connections with affects. This activation of executive schemes by affects leads to an internal "executive choice point," where executive schemes that are incompatible compete for dominance. The most highly activated cluster of compatible executives becomes the *current* dominant executive "center" (*the Executive*) of the subject in the situation.

To ensure implementation of its plans, this Executive often mobilizes and allocates the brain's attentional resources. Our neo-Piagetian theory (Pascual-Leone, 1984, 1987; Pascual-Leone et al., 1978) describes the attentional resources directly controlled by the Executive: the $I$-operator (used to actively inhibit competing schemes) and the $M$-operator (used to boost with activation the relevant action schemes). When these *hardware operators* (described later) have been applied, the dominant cluster of compatible schemes in the subject's field of activated schemes (also called working memory), is constituted by only relevant schemes—and is largely restricted to the field of mental centration. These attentionally centrated schemes implement the Executive plans. At this point the principle of schematic overdetermination of performance (SOP principle), as well as the $F$-operator (see later, this is the local lateral inhibition in the cortex) intervene to produce a *dynamic synthesis* of this predominantly relevant field of activated schemes. This may result in the desired performance, if the available action and executive schemes are in fact suitable for the intended results. A detailed account of these processes has been presented elsewhere (Pascual-Leone, 1984, 1987; Pascual-Leone et al., 1978; Pascual-Leone, Johnson, Goodman, Hameluck, & Theodor, 1981).

*Operative schemes* or *operatives* embody transformations or procedures that, if applied in the current mental state and situation, produce predictable results. When these results are represented as terminal/temporary components within the same scheme, the operative is said to be a kind of fluent—the kind that, after Tolman (1959), we call *operative expectancy* (scripts—Nelson, 1986; Schank & Abelson, 1977—are instances of complex operative expectancies).

*Figurative schemes* or *figuratives* are the only vehicles for "presentation" or "representation" of mental states, distal objects, and objectified concepts. Figuratives constitute the "mental objects" on which mental computation is carried out: Such computation involves application of operatives on figuratives, as prescribed by executives. Complex figuratives often result from the coordination of simple figuratives (*facets* or manifestations of objects) along with the temporal organization of operatives that can change a given facet into another facet of the same object. The fluent schemes that embody this distal-object information are *figurative expectancies* (Pascual-Leone et al., 1978).

In the cortex, executive schemes are found in the prefrontal lobes (Pascual-Leone, 1974, 1984, 1989a), operative schemes in the frontal lobe (pre-central regions), and figurative schemes in the parietal, occipital, and temporal lobes (post-central regions). *Thus the anterior brain is operative (when executive is regarded as a specialized kind of operative), and the posterior brain is figurative.*

## THE DIAGNOSIS OF SCHEMES AND SCHEMAS IN THE CONTEXT OF TASKS

Let us call *metasubjective* a theory that is capable of describing processes from the perspective of a subject's organism and in addition can (a) model these processes in "real time," so that sequences of steps prescribed by its analyses can be shown (or are intended) to reflect sequences of real processes in the organism; (b) model causally the processes of organismic change, that is, development and learning, including change in hidden-hardware operators or organismic capacities; (c) model the causal "formulas" of organismic individual differences, including differences in hidden-hardware operators and principles; and (d) have a proper (i.e., experimentally testable in terms of causal predictions) interpretation within neuropsychological theory. With this definition, *metasubjective analysis* is a method of process/task analysis guided by a metasubjective theory. Metasubjective analysis, and task analysis in general, is a collection of heuristic methods capable of assigning to any task a specific model of the *processes in the subject* that intervene in the production of a *task performance*; these models are always relative to a chosen *strategy* and a stipulated *situation*.

In order to do task analysis one has to make definite theoretical commitments regarding the functional characteristics of the psychological organism. We assume here the metasubjective theory that was intimated above and has been presented elsewhere (i.e., the theory of constructive operators—Johnson et al., 1989; Pascual-Leone, 1984, 1987, 1989a; Pascual-Leone & Goodman, 1979; Pascual-Leone et al., 1978).

There are four dialectical "moments" or phases in task analysis, the last one being exclusive to metasubjective analysis. These moments/phases are: *objective* analysis, *subjective* analysis, *ultrasubjective* or real-time mental computational analysis, and *metasubjective* or subject-organismic analysis.

*Objective analysis* consists in the structural and substantive description of all the externally objective aspects of the situation in which the to-be-produced performance will take place; this includes explicit task instructions. When the subject's performance is already known (in postdictive, as opposed to predictive, task analysis), detailed description of this performance from an ideal observer's perspective is a part of objective analysis. In this phase of analysis the choice of psychological unit is arbitrary, and researchers often choose the most obvious one from an observer's perspective. The methods of task analysis currently available in Cognitive Science are customarily instances of objective analysis, or include this phase and go beyond it; we assume that readers are familiar with this method.

*Subjective analysis* consists in the formulation of the to-be-produced performance from the perspective of the subject's organism. Some ontological commitment regarding organismic processes is now necessary, along with the tacit or explicit formulation of a psychological unit. The assumed unit can no longer be arbitrary, for it must reflect functional information-processing invariants that in some sense correspond to those of the brain. In addition to objective analysis, introspection and phenomenological analyses are commonly used for subjective analysis. In introspection one asks: "If I were this subject in this particular task/situation what would I do?" In phenomenology, one raises a generalized version of this question: "If I were *any subject whatsoever*—or any subject of type $j$, an ideal subject of type $j$—in this *type $i$ of situation*, what would I do?"

The mental attitudes that allow an analyst to move from the particular analyses of introspection to the general analyses of phenomenology involve mental techniques that Husserl (1970) called *phenomenological reduction* (and other kinds of reduction). That is, the analyst must intentionally disregard ("bracket") his or her own conceptual preconceptions and "knowledge" of the external/internal experience, and must pay attention to the subject's mental operations. Only the actual structure of the here-and-now experience of subject $j$ in situation $i$, as described by an open-minded and affectively detached "ideal observer," is retained (e.g., Husserl, 1970; Van Peursen, 1972). Descendants of phenomenology, such as *existential phenomenology, hermeneutics*, and *deconstruction analysis*, have relativized the basic phenomenological method vis-à-vis the empirical realities of subject and object, and anchored it better in empirical verifiability.

From the perspective of Psychology a second level of subjective analysis is found in *structuralism*—provided we use "structuralism" to refer to *any method that aims to generate explicit generic models* of the experienced objective-and-subjective (i.e., *phenomenological*) realities, and/or their generating processes; *but which so doing disregards the real-time, step-by-step temporal aspect of the evolving realities being modeled.* In developmental psychology, classic structuralism is represented, for instance, by Piaget's and by most neo-Piagetian theories and methods (Case, 1985; Case & Griffin, 1990; Fischer, 1980; Halford, 1982), as well as by much of psycholinguistics.

The basic mental method of structuralist analysis is the *constructive abstrac-*

*tion* of functional-invariant categories (or *structures*) that correspond to sequences of (one or more) informational functional systems. These structures correspond to relational systems of overt or covert performance patterns, characteristic of some type of subject in a type of performance. As a method, phenomenology is tacitly or explicitly included into structuralism as a moment; but structuralism adds to it the explicit formulation of process models, and a terminology and notation for representing psychological units and their functional interrelations.

The temporal representation of change in time—modeling in real time—is not done well within classic structuralist methods. As a result, psychological units—for example, the schemes of Piaget as they appear in his logistic models (and related models of neo-Piagetians)—are only categorical descriptions of the subject's performatory capabilities in a type of task (i.e., are categorical descriptors of performatory competence), and they are not properly defined organismic schemes. An obvious consequence of this limitation is that structuralist models cannot show the process of transition for passing from one developmental stage to the next, even though the existence of stages can be discovered by means of structuralist methods.

*Ultrasubjective or mental-computational analysis* adds, to objective and subjective methods of process analysis, techniques for modeling process in real time—that is, in some idealized molar version of the real-time evolution of processes. Examples of these methods are found in computer-simulation approaches to information-processing psychology, although these approaches tend to define their units arbitrarily (i.e., without sufficient regard for either empirical descriptive-structural constraints—e.g., the constraints of developmental structuralism—or organismic/metasubjective constraints as formulated in neuroscience and above). These information-processing approaches use computational methods inspired by the current computer.

Ultrasubjective considerations, that is, real-time analysis of process, make explicit the need to distinguish the different modes of schemes that we distinguished above. For instance, the distinction between executive and action schemes becomes very apparent, because real-time intentional processes are goal-directed, and thus generic or quasi-generic schemes (the executive) must be posited to explain this purposeful direction.

*Metasubjective or organismic-computational analysis* adds, to the methods already mentioned, organismic constraints that have been inferred from psychological research across specialties, including neuropsychology. We intimated some of these constraints earlier and have formulated them within the theory of constructive operators. The mark of metasubjective analysis is the incorporation, into the analysis, of theoretical constructs that represent a modular decomposition of the brain's functional architecture—the *hidden hardware operators and principles*—which constrain the subject's performance and therefore are needed in task analysis.

We believe that in developmental processes, metasubjective analysis must give special consideration to sequences of *mental attentional centrations (M-centrations* in our theory's terminology), because these serve to model developmental—as distinct from learning—aspects of performance. Nowadays this sort of analysis is often carried out in a purely mental-computational (i.e., ultrasubjective) manner, by appealing to the construct of a "working memory" that is said to grow in capacity with age in normal children. Performances that are constrained by development are then described as resulting from syntheses (although this term is often not employed) of schemes that are being concurrently held inside "working memory" (e.g., Anderson, 1983; Case, 1985; Fischer & Pipp, 1984; Halford, 1982; Klahr, 1984).

Such a formulation is problematic, however, because it makes difficult empirical estimation of the size of working memory as invariant across tasks for a type of subject. This is because the number of schemes contributing to a synthesis is a function of *all* the highly activated schemes in the subject's repertoire (i.e., in the cortex); and these schemes can be activated by a number of different factors that the descriptive concept of working memory does not clarify. More explicitly, at the time when the response is produced, the cluster of most highly activated compatible schemes within the subject can be determined by experiential learning factors and affective factors, as much as by mental capacity. Thus, unless a whole system of organismic hardware operators is formulated and assumed (corresponding to the learning, affective, perceptual saliency, etc. determinants of working memory), the true developmental growth of the subject's mental ($M$) capacity—the developmental determinant of working memory—cannot be assessed. This is implicit in the principle of schematic overdetermination of performance (SOP principle), which is consistent with neuropsychology (i.e., with Sherrington's, 1947, principles of summation and of final common path).

## HIDDEN OBJECTS AND THE EMERGENCE OF MENTAL PROCESSING

To illustrate the role of psychological units in task analysis we consider the case of searching for an object that has been hidden successively under various screens—Piaget's canonical paradigm for testing object permanence with location (Piaget, 1954).

Piaget's paradigm can serve to illustrate the limitations of both subjective/structuralist analysis and ultrasubjective or mental-computational analysis. With its help we show that it is impossible to explain this paradigm without contradiction unless one appeals to the existence in the child's brain of *hidden hardware operators*, in addition to software units (i.e., schemes and structures). Hidden hardware operators are content-free functional systems of the brain (cf. Luria, 1973); in their dynamic interaction, they constitute the mechanism for a kind of *mental attention (mental effort) that is ontologically* (i.e, inside the real brain) *independent from the software units on which it applies to bring about a heightened level of activation.* Piaget's paradigm affords an elegant task analytical (and neuropsychological) proof of the existence of hidden hardware operators (e.g., mental capacity, mental interruption), although neither Piaget nor others using this paradigm (fixated into a subjective/structuralist analysis) have fully appreciated this point.

Lack of space prevents us from showing in detail the four "moments" or phases of a metasubjective analysis outlined earlier. Instead we present a summary that collapses across the four "moments" and reduces the step-by-step (ultrasubjective or mental computation) analysis to an *idealized critical step*—a step that shows the dimensionality of the strategy being modeled. By *dimensionality* we mean the set of *separate units of the strategy's infrastructure* that are not perceptually salient, but must be part of the performance to make the result possible *for the first time.* This is what we have called a *metasubjective dimensional analysis* (Johnson & Pascual-Leone, 1989a; Pascual-Leone, 1980; Pascual-Leone et al., 1978).

A *metasubjective analysis* (whether it is *dimensional* or is a real-time mental reconstruction—which we call an *M-construction*) is a generic summary representation of the real-time process responsible for the subject's performance. A step in this analysis need not correspond to an unit of time, but may represent a segment that could in turn be unfolded into a sequence. In this regard, the steps of a metasubjective analysis are like the block units of a detailed flowchart.

When a component of the strategy being modeled is represented by a scheme, the assumption is being made that the scheme is sufficiently well learned (or overlearned) to function as a unit with regard to its activation either by the input or by other schemes. The plausibility of this assumption can be evaluated rationally by means of the method of *genetic reconstructions.* This method has four analytical phases (cf. de Ribaupierre & Pascual-Leone, 1979).

The first analytical phase, *scheme definition*, consists in hypothesizing the functional (semantic-pragmatic) structure of the scheme in question: the informational functional system, and releasing and effecting components for which the scheme stands. The second phase, *ecological evaluation*, consists in evaluating whether the subject's usual expectable environment (his or her ecological niche) offers sufficiently frequent opportunities for practicing, and thus learning, this scheme so as to warrant the assumption of its being part of the subject's current repertoire. The third phase, *motivational/operative evaluation*, involves determining whether the subject's interest will lead him or her repeatedly to the circumstances where the ecology can foster the learning of that scheme, perhaps because the subject's own actions generate the scheme as a performatory invariant (an incidental component of praxis). The fourth phase, *psychogenetic evaluation*, can add credence to the conclusions from the other three. It consists in evaluating whether younger children from the same population, on the basis of the first three analytical moments and in view of their actual performance on suitable tasks (*or of their theoretically known mental attentional and learning capacities*), may have acquired the scheme in question. This fourth phase explicates Piaget's tacit *psychogenetic assumption*: If younger (or peer age) children can be said to have acquired a certain scheme, then older (or peer-age) children of the same sociocultural background should also have it. A scheme that has passed these four evaluations is an *acceptable scheme* for the task analysis in question.

Tolman and Brunswik (1935) called *causal texture of the environment* the causally relevant relations that hold among distal objects of the ecology. Piaget and others described them as (positive or negative) *resistances*. Intelligence solves tasks by recognizing resistances that are favorable to a certain praxis (these are positive resistances—i.e., what Gibson, 1982, called *affordances*), and by integrating these resistances into a strategy. Affordances are so called precisely because they serve to overcome obstacles—negative resistances—that oppose the desired praxis.[3] Negative resistances often appear as misleading factors, conflicts, or contradictions; and the errors they induce are used by organisms to demarcate affordances. For this reason attention to errors and their causes (e.g., misleading factors) is important in task analysis.

In metasubjective dimensional analysis the *mental* (developmental) *demand* of a task's strategy is obtained by enumerating *acceptable schemes* that meet the following conditions. They (a) reflect essential task-relevant affordances; (b) are not already highly activated by perception or by learning/automatization— and thus still require mental attention (*M-capacity*) in order to be activated; and (c) must simultaneously be "coordinated" in a *dynamic synthesis* to produce the desired results. The concept of an *acceptable scheme*, as defined earlier, implies that scheme constituents of a metasubjective task analysis *must not* necessitate, for their own construction/synthesis, a *mental (M) capacity* higher than the one of the task analysis in which they are used. If the required *M*-capacity (i.e., the *M-demand*) of any constituent scheme is in fact greater than that of the strategy being modeled, then the *M*-demand of this constituent scheme will be taken as *M*-demand of the task strategy as a whole.


## PIAGET'S OBJECT PERMANENCE PARADIGM


In the most difficult of this family of tasks, the child has to get the toy *t* she wants, which has been hidden behind one of the three screens—*A*, *B*, or *C*— that are accessible to her. First, the toy *t* is hidden only behind *A*, and the child

---

[3]Very often, negative resistances or obstacles that impede solution of a task are constituted by misleading schemes that are activated within the subject and applied to the situation.

must reach for $t$ by removing $A$. This is done one or more times. The practice of this action "game" (a dynamic functional system of percepts, images, actions, and intentions) leads the baby to develop a mental habit or belief—the scheme $OPa1$ "($t$ is behind $A$; to get it remove $A$)."[4] At this point the experimenter takes the toy again, hides it inside his hand, and brings the toy behind $A$ while saying: "The toy! The toy!". But now, instead of leaving $t$ behind $A$, he keeps the toy hidden and moves the hand behind screen $B$, repeating the same routine. Then, without interruption, he moves his hand with the hidden toy behind screen $C$ where, while repeating aloud "The toy! The toy!", he drops the toy. The experimenter then shows his opened hand to the child to demonstrate that it is empty.[5]

The aforementioned is a description of the subparadigm called *successive invisible displacement* of $t$. An alterative subparadigm involves *successive visible displacement*; here the hand does not conceal the toy, but moves it visible from screen to screen. It is intuitively clear that the *visible displacements* subparadigm is easier than the *invisible displacements* one. Here we show task analytically why this must be so. But there are even easier subparadigms. We can eliminate successive displacements, and make the task one of simply searching for an object that has been visibly hidden behind one of two or more screens. We call this paradigm *single visible displacement*; this task often elicits the much researched "A-not-B error" (for reviews see Bremner, 1985; Gratch, 1975; Harris, 1987; Wellman, Cross, & Bartsch, 1986). This error occurs when, for example, after finding the toy behind screen $A$ on the first trial, the child returns to search behind $A$ after having seen the toy hidden behind screen $B$ (or $C$) on the next trial. Finally, another important simplification occurs when the number of screens is reduced to one, and the object is hidden visibly and, of course, without displacement.

In this final *single screen* case, the task is *motivationally* (i.e., affectively) *immediate* (Pascual-Leone et al., 1978), because the baby wants the toy $t$ that has just disappeared behind screen $A$. The affect itself boosts the child's cognitive schemes for $t$ and for the screen $A$, evoking the action of grasping and removing $A$. Provided that, at the point when she is looking at $A$, the child can evoke and coordinate within mental attention the schemes of $t$ and of the grasping

---

[4]The reader should observe that we name a scheme by giving its mode, followed by letters indicative of its function, and an ordinal number indicating its relative order of appearance in the task. For instance, $OPa1$ stands for "operative or strategy a, number 1." We then explain the function of the scheme in an observer's language by giving an English description inside quoted parentheses.

[5]As becomes clear later, our model proposes that scheme $OPa1$ becomes a misleading factor that forces the child to use an effortful mental-analytical strategy to solve the task. In the *successive invisible displacement* task we are describing here, initial trials in which the toy is hidden behind screen $A$ are not, in fact, needed for the misleading scheme to be constructed. In this task, the role of screen $A$, in scheme $OPa1$, can be taken by the hand in which the toy is hidden or by the screen that the hand initially moves behind.

action (i.e., two schemes), the action of removing $A$ to get $t$ will occur immediately. This is the origin of scheme $OPa1$ mentioned previously.

Contrast this with a task in which displacement is used. Now, whereas the initial search behind $A$ is motivationally immediate and is solved by means of a scheme such as $OPa1$, the subsequent search behind screens $B$, $C$, and so on, is *motivationally (affectively) mediated* (Pascual-Leone et al., 1978). This is because after successfully searching behind $A$, the affective disposition (affective schemes), which is (are) cognitively global and "egocentric" (cf. Bryant, 1989), should induce the infant to go back to $A$ (i.e., commit the A-not-B error) before attempting to find $t$ behind $B$, or $C$, etc. Given this "egocentricity" of affect (i.e., this tendency of affect to *repeat* blindly the acts that succeeded in the past), the solution of a task involving single or successive displacements becomes motivationally mediated. This means that initial search behind the correct screen, without going to $A$, must be induced not by affect, but by a mental synthesis that coordinates cognitive schemes boosted by mental attention. We might safely say that *mental processing*, as contrasted with *impulse or affective/emotional processing*, begins at this point. Because mental processing necessitates both the inhibition of impulses and the use of attentional effort to coordinate cognitive schemes (cf. Rapaport, 1960), the displacement paradigms are more difficult than the single screen (i.e., no displacement) one.

A typical 13- to 16-month-old child reacts to the *successive invisible displacement* situation by first removing screen $A$, looking for the toy. When she does so the habit-scheme $OPa1$ "($t$ is behind $A$; to get it remove $A$)" controls her performance. In contrast, a child over 18 months of age is likely directly to search behind $C$ for the toy, without first searching behind $A$ or $B$. The *successive visible displacement* subparadigm might be solved correctly at 13 months, but is failed by 9- or 10-month-olds—these younger children can succeed, however, with the easier *single visible displacement* task. Finally, the *single screen* (no displacement) subparadigm, being motivationally immediate, is solved at 6 to 8 months; but it is failed at the point when visual-motor coordinations have just been established (i.e., about 4 months)—at this point only partially hidden objects are retrieved.

Piaget (1954), using a brilliant structuralist analysis, interpreted these results, at each level, as showing the conflict between two contradictory strategies, which we call strategies $a$ and $b$; but his emphasis and main interest was with the "intelligent" strategy $b$. Strategy $a$ is the scheme $OPa1$ mentioned earlier, which leads to the A-not-B error; that is, it compels the baby to search for the toy behind $A$, even though the toy has now been hidden under another screen.

For Piaget, as for many later researchers (Diamond, 1985, 1988; Diamond & Goldman-Rakic, 1983; Harris, 1986; Wellman et al., 1986), the origin of scheme $OPa1$ is obvious: It is an example of associative memory (connecting $t$ with grasping and removing $A$), and the import of its manifestation (e.g., the A-not-B error) is to show that strategy $b$ is not yet in place. According to

Piaget, strategy *b* consists in the application of an organized system of schemes (a proto-operational structure) that he called "group of displacement" and interpreted as a mental organization of the possible displacements of objects in space—the objects now having acquired some substantive permanence. Note that Piaget's "group of displacement" structure encompasses information from the present situation as whole, as well as all other possible situations of object displacement in space. It is a *very abstract* structure and cannot be expected to account by itself for specific unique details of the family of object permanence subparadigms. Piaget explained the disappearance of Λ-not-B errors as showing that strategy *b*, interpreted as using the "group of displacement" structure, was fully formed, and dialectically superseded strategy *a* (reducing it to be just one of the *b* alternatives).

The Piagetian structuralist account fails, however, because it is internally inconsistent; *and this failure is caused by the structuralist unit of analysis adopted by Piaget for strategy b.* Let us explain this failure. In terms of causal mechanisms, Piaget's theory (like other neo-Piagetian and post-Piagetian theories—see Pascual-Leone, 1980, 1987) is in fact a *cognitive-learning theory.* In such a theory, the very active experiencing (assimilation and accommodation) of the praxic possibilities offered by objects is what leads automatically to the emergence of group-like structures. But in the present paradigm, in particular when *invisible displacement* of the toy is used, this explanation encounters a contradiction, which Pascual-Leone (1980, 1987) has called the *learning paradox.* This paradox stems from the fact that learning a group-like structure by means of experience requires an exhaustive, complete experiencing of all *different possible* empirical cases. In the case of *strong* (i.e., with invisible displacement) *object permanence,* however, the A-not-B error caused by strategy *a* should always prevent the experience of going directly to *B* (or *C*), because strategy *b* will not emerge until the "group of displacement" structure is fully operative. This structure cannot be operative, however, until the subject has experienced *all different empirical cases,* including of course the one that (according to Piaget's model) only strategy *b* can afford in the present situation.

We see that Piaget's theoretical position contains the tacit assumption that a "group of displacement" structure can be completed without sufficient experience. Thus, a learning paradox shows his model to be contradictory. The model's durability can only be explained by the fact, implicitly established by Wellman et al.'s (1986) monograph on the single displacement subparadigm, that no better model for the *b* strategy has yet appeared in the literature.

## AN ULTRASUBJECTIVE MODEL
## OF OBJECT PERMANENCE

To construct a better model we must do two things. First, we must change the psychological unit to bring it down to the step-by-step details of the task (as done in ultrasubjective or mental-computation analysis), so that real-time processes of task solution are represented explicitly. Second, we must explicitly formulate hardware mechanisms, hidden-hardware operators and principles of the brain's "functional architecture," that can explicate the mysterious *regulations* that in Piaget's theory could, without contradiction, make possible the strategies needed for the task at hand.

We proceed to do this for the *successive invisible displacement* situation described earlier. Consider first the reformulation of the psychological unit. The concrete test situation is that the baby directly searches for *t* behind *C* without first searching behind *A* or *B*, even though she previously found the toy at *A* and should still have the scheme *OPa1* in her repertoire. Thus, schemes must exist that make it "intelligent" for the child not to go to *A*, and mechanisms (hardware operators!) must be available to override and inhibit the strong scheme *OPa1*.

As Piaget (1954) and others (Corrigan & Fischer, 1985; Harris, 1987; Wellman et al., 1986) seem to intimate, a key *infrastructural* component of strategy *b* is the search for *t* behind that screen *where t disappeared last*. Under certain conditions stated here, we find it *acceptable* (using the method of genetic reconstructions) to postulate that babies older than 12 months can acquire in their daily experiences a purely relational scheme or *knowledge figurative structure* (a declarative, as opposed to procedural, piece of knowledge) that, in practical terms, corresponds to the expression "(any object *x* is always found behind the obstacle-screen *z* where it disappeared *last*)". The condition for this purely relational learning is that the baby recognize the same patterns of experience across different concrete objects and concrete obstacles. This demands that the baby keep in mind simultaneously the essential parameters of the pattern in question: knowledge relation *K*, object *X*, obstacle *Z*, and time of disappearance *T*-last. We believe (see later) that a 14- or 15-month-old can spontaneously "keep in mind" all these parameters, and thus we find it acceptable that the knowledge scheme *KXZT* should be in the repertoire of a child of at least 18 months, when she enters the task (cf. Haake & Somerville, 1985; Halford, 1989). Other schemes activated by the task, such as schemes *FIGthand2*, *FIGhandC3*, and *FIGnotthand4*, described later, should cue *KXZT* into activation. To indicate the likely temporal order of activation of this scheme in the task, we henceforth write it with its ordinal number: *KXZT5*.

But scheme *KXZT5*, as tacitly defined earlier, is an *abstract* and *generic structure*. It is an early exemplar of what Piaget called "logical" as contrasted with "infralogical" structures (we prefer to talk of *logological*/conceptual versus *infralogical/merelogical*/experiential structures, but essentially adopt Piaget's distinction—Johnson, 1991; Johnson & Pascual-Leone, 1989a; Pascual-Leone, 1976a, 1984; Pascual-Leone & Goodman, 1979). Because scheme *KXZT5* is a logological structure (a generic figurative/declarative rule) its application to performance in context requires concrete implementation by means of some other infralogical schemes. Namely:

1. *EXt1* "(search for and find *t*)", an executive scheme (i.e., a logological or infralogical fluent). The affix digit *1* symbolizes that this scheme was *differentiated* (i.e., *instantiated* from general schemes already available in the repertoire) at the ordinal time moment 1 within the task.
2. *FIGthand2* "(*t* is hidden inside the hand)", an infralogical relational figurative scheme (a fluent) differentiated in the course of the task as the child, aroused by the affective desire to have the toy, observes the experimenter. The affix *2* indicates that this scheme was created at ordinal moment 2, within the task (all numbers affixed to scheme names have a similar meaning).
3. *FIGhandC3* "(hand last disappeared behind C)", an infralogical relational figurative (a fluent) differentiated in the course of the task.
4. *FIGnotthand4* "(hand is opened showing that *t* is *not* in it)", an infralogical figurative scheme differentiated when the experimenter opened his hand at the end of the item sequence.

Thus, it appears that in order to implement strategy *b*, no fewer than five schemes must be "coordinated" by means of a dynamic synthesis. These five schemes cannot be directly boosted in their activation by perception, because at the point when the child has to produce a response, no perceptual processes—but only memory—can activate them. Nor can these schemes be activated by automatized learning because the schemes were differentiated (instantiated) just for the task, and the task is new. Nor can they be activated by affect because in a displacement subparadigm the *b* strategy is not motivationally immediate, but rather motivationally mediated (i.e., executive schemes are needed to monitor activation of the action schemes). Thus, within the limits of *ultrasubjective* (mental computational) *analysis* we cannot settle the issue of what cause maintains the schemes' activation, unless we appeal to a purely descriptive notion such as working memory.[6]

Let us summarize the structure of the *successive invisible displacement* task as it appears to us after the *objective, subjective,* and *ultrasubjective analyses* condensed here.[7] The task exhibits a conflict (dialectical contradiction) between two strate-

---

[6]The notion of working memory is purely descriptive (if not too global) because the causes or determinants that "place a scheme inside working memory" are not explicated, although they may be very diverse: perceptual (e.g., Gestaltist Field factors), learning/automatization (either simple Content learning or Logical-structural learning), affective/emotional factors (affective schemes boosting the activation of the cognitive schemes in question), endogenous mental attentional capacity (i.e., a mental capacity which would be different from all other factors causing working memory), language rehearsal, etc.

[7]Explicit ultrasubjective analyses (i.e., real-time, step-by-step) have been conducted but are omitted here. The interested reader can find examples of our type of real-time analyses in two doctoral theses completed in Pascual-Leone's laboratory (Benson, 1989; Holloway, 1986). Small substantive differences that do not affect the evaluation of complexity can be found between these analyses and our own that we have summarized here. Metasubjective task analysis is the construction of refined theoretical process models, and as such it is subject to improvement.

gies, $a$ and $b$. These strategies share a number of perceptual and context-defining schemes (e.g., the three screens, the toy, the operative movements of reaching, etc.). We have omitted these, and in formulas F1 and F2 we represent them as suspension points. The strategies also contain important differential schemes that we represent in the formulas.

$$a\text{``}\{. \ . \ . \ OPa1\}\text{''} \tag{F1}$$

$$b\text{``}\{. \ . \ . \ Ext1, \ FIGthand2, \ FIGhandC3, \ FIGnotthand4, \ KXZT5\}\text{''} \tag{F2}$$

Formula F1 contains the set of schemes (the *endogenous mental centration* or contents of *mental attention*) that enables strategy $a$. Formula F2 does the same for strategy $b$. It is apparent that more working memory is involved in strategy $b$. But working memory by itself cannot explain the actual eventual implementation of strategy $b$ when the child is of the appropriate age (cf. Diamond, 1985, 1988; Goldman-Rakic, 1987; Wellman et al., 1986). For this explanation we need also mechanisms producing *dynamic syntheses* that "coordinate" the information that these centrated schemes carry. Furthermore, as Harris (1987) and Wellman et al. (1986) clearly emphasized, one also must explain why strategy $a$ is so preeminent over strategy $b$—even in the visible-displacement subparadigms in which the child sees the toy actually disappearing under $C$. As Wellman et al. demonstrated, just saying that strategy $a$ is driven by habit (overlearning or automatization), whereas strategy $b$ under visible displacement has no habit supporting it, goes counter to available empirical data.

But before addressing these difficulties we should point out why the different subparadigms discussed above have different developmental difficulty. In *successive visible displacement* the strategy is simpler: Schemes *FIGthand2*, *FIGhand C3*, and *KXZT5* are not needed, because toy $t$ is visible in its displacement. Instead in this subparadigm, strategy $b$ requires a figurative fluent scheme *FIGtC3* "(toy $t$ has just disappeared behind screen $C$)", which substitutes for *FIGhandC3*. It also requires a much cruder (simpler and more concrete) replacement for *KXZT5*, a figurative fluent scheme *FIGtABC2* "(toy $t$ has moved from $A$ to $B$ to $C$)". Note that scheme *FIGtABC2* is needed because the strong, affectively boosted, misleading scheme *OPa1* (of strategy $a$) would otherwise contradict and override scheme *FIGtC3*, inducing the equivalent of an A-not-B error. Thus, whereas the endogenous mental centration of the *successive invisible displacement* subparadigm contains five schemes in need of attentional effort, the *successive visible displacement* subparadigm contains only four schemes using mental centration.

Consider now the subparadigm of *single visible displacement*. In this task the toy $t$ is not moved across screens, and therefore, relative to the task analysis of successive visible displacement, the scheme *FIGtABC2* is not needed. Thus, in single visible displacement, the endogenous mental centration of strategy $b$ contains only three schemes: *EXt1*, *FIGtC3*, and *FIGnotthand4*.

Finally, consider the *single screen* (no displacement) subparadigm. Because in this paradigm affect directly boosts the correct response (i.e., the task is motivationally immediate), the executive scheme *EXt1* is not needed, and thus the mental centration required for this subparadigm is two schemes (*FIGtA3* and *FIGnotthand4*). The subsequent implementation of this *a* strategy also requires that two schemes be maintained with endogenous mental centration: the scheme of *t* just disappearing behind *A* (*FIGtA3*) and the operative scheme of grasping and removing *A*. The structuring of these two schemes produces the scheme *OPa1* "(*t* is behind *A*; to get it remove *A*)", discussed earlier as responsible for the *a* strategy.

## METASUBJECTIVE ANALYSIS
## OF OBJECT PERMANENCE

To proceed further in task analysis we need a stronger organismic theory; that is, we must make deeper ontological commitments regarding the processes involved. At least three *Controversial Issues* are left unexplained by theories of schemes—in general, by theories that model only software informational processes.

**CI1.** Which are the causal determinants of *endogenous mental centrations*? What is the causal theory of *endogenous mental attention*?

**CI2.** What are the mechanisms that generate *dynamic syntheses* responsible for the final *truly novel performance* (Pascual-Leone, 1980), when a child solves the object permanence problems for the very first time?

**CI3.** Why is it, because it cannot be just habit strength, that strategy *a* is so much stronger than strategy *b*, even in visible-displacement subparadigms?
These are not idle questions, as shown by the fact, well argued by Wellman et al. (1986), that after 25 years of research the object permanence literature still lacks a fully satisfactory theoretical model for even the single displacement task.
The answer to the questions posed in CI1 was historically at the origin of Pascual-Leone's (1969, 1970, 1976a; Pascual-Leone & Goodman, 1979) theory of constructive operators, which is an organismic general model of dialectical equilibration. The theory's novel idea is to model the "functional architecture" of the brain's hardware as a dialectical organization (a heterarchy) of functional modules—*hidden hardware operators* and *principles*. Together these content-free operators and principles begin to explain, in their dynamic interactions and effects on the schemes, not only question CI1 but questions CI2 and CI3 as well. (For more detail on this theory see, e.g., Chapman, 1981; Johnson et al., 1989; Pascual-Leone, 1980, 1983, 1984, 1987, 1989a; Pascual-Leone & Goodman, 1979; de Ribaupierre, 1983; Vuyk, 1981.)
We restrict ourselves to discussing briefly two aspects of the theory: its model

of *endogenous mental attention* and its *principle of schematic overdetermination of performance*. We consider the mechanisms of *endogenous mental attention* to be a dynamic system constituted by four different functional constructs or *operators* in dialectical interaction. We denote each of these constructs with a capital letter that stands for the construct's function.

The first operator of endogenous attention is $E$. This is the software repertoire of *executive* schemes of the subject, in particular the dominant set of compatible executive schemes here-and-now directing the mental process. We call this dominant set of executive schemes *the Executive* (i.e., the $E$-operator). This Executive is activated initially by the dominant affective schemes, or goals, of the subject; and in turn it can mobilize and allocate the $M$- and $I$-operators to change and adapt the state of working memory, in accordance with the Executive plan. It is generally believed in neuropsychology that executive schemes—plans and planning—are located in the dorsolateral parts of the prefrontal lobes (e.g., Goldman-Rakic, 1987).

$M$ is the hardware operator that serves to boost endogenously the activation of task-relevant schemes. It is a limited-capacity and general purpose resource—a kind of *Mental energy*. The capacity of the $M$-operator increases endogenously with development. Its measure—given by the number of schemes that it can boost simultaneously—is a quantitative characteristic of Piagetian and neo-Piagetian qualitative stages (for empirical validation of this claim see, e.g., Johnson & Pascual-Leone, 1989a; Johnson et al., 1989; Pascual-Leone, 1970, 1976b, 1980, 1987, plus references cited in these papers). We think, consistent with Luria (1973) and others (Fuster, 1985), that this mental energizing function (which is driven by dominant executive schemes—the current $E$-operator) is also connected with the prefrontal lobes.

The hardware operator $I$ serves centrally to inhibit software processes (schemes and structures) that are not relevant to the current task of the Executive. $I$ is a central organismic function not unlike the computer-science concept of an *Interrupt*, and so we call it an *Interruption* mechanism. It works, and develops with maturation, in tandem with the $M$-operator, which it complements (Pascual-Leone, 1984, 1987, 1989a; Pascual-Leone et al., 1978). Consistent with Luria (1973) and many others, we think that this *central* (as opposed to local or peripheral) *inhibitory mechanism* is also controlled from the prefrontal lobes.

The hardware operator $F$ serves to ensure that the performance being produced (perception, imagery, thinking, language, motor activity, etc.) is *minimally complex* and *maximally informed*. A performance is maximally informed when it accounts for or embodies all the information encoded in schemes that are directly activated by the context (input) and/or the organism (physiological state). In other words, the $F$-operator maximizes the number of activated low-level schemes that co-determine the overall integrated (high-level) performance, while at the same time minimizing the complexity of the integration.

The *F*-operator is akin to the Gestaltist internal/authoctonous *Field* processes (the "Minimum Principle" of perception, the "S–R compatibility" of performance, etc.); it is a sort of *minimax function* that operates in the neuronal *final common path* and is generated by neuronal "lateral inhibition" mechanisms. In process-analytical terms this minimax function can be formulated as follows: The performance produced will tend to be such that it minimizes the number of (high-level) schemes that directly apply to inform (i.e., "inject form into") the performance; while simultaneously maximizing the set of distinct aspects/features of experience (i.e., activated low-level schemes) that actually informs this performance. Pascual-Leone and Goodman (1979) discussed this mechanism (see also, Pascual-Leone, 1976b, 1980, 1989a).

The *SOP principle* (schematic overdetermination of performance) was described earlier (section on Schemes as Neuropsychological Functional Abstractions), and we ask the reader to review this description.

As a result of dynamic interaction among these mechanisms, a heuristic and nonsymbolic "choice" takes place subconsciously. The mechanisms that transform this "choice" into a performance are the *F*-operator and *SOP principle*. This *F-SOP* mechanism brings about a *dynamic synthesis* of activated schemes in the currently dominant cluster of schemes in the field of activation, and in so doing, it generates the performance (cf. Pascual-Leone, 1976b, 1983, 1984, 1987, 1989a; Pascual-Leone & Goodman, 1979). This conception of a subconscious "choice" that generates performance was inspired by Freud's principle of overdetermination, but it is congenial also with modern computational theories of induction (e.g., Holland, Holyoak, Nisbett, & Thagard, 1986; Thagard, 1989), and with aspects of neuronal/connectionist/parallel distributed processing models (Rumelhart, McClelland, & the PDP Research Group, 1986). For instance, the effects of the *F-SOP* mechanism are analogous epistemologically to those of mathematical "relaxation methods," which are used in neuronal/connectionist modeling to reach "choices" of performance that resolve conflicts among competing processes. To emphasize this similarity we talk about a *subconscious "relaxation choice"* under these circumstances.

In the concrete case of object permanence paradigms we can formulate this subconscious "choice," and the production of a dynamic synthesis, by means of the following *Mental Process* sequence. Again, we focus initially on the successive invisible displacement task, but the same sequence, suitably modified, applies to the other subparadigms.

***MP1.*** If formulas F1 and F2 are taken to represent the field of activated schemes of a child, then it must be the case that the child can use her *M-operator* to boost into high activation five non-salient schemes—those explicitly written in F2 as constituents of strategy *b*. These schemes require *M*-boosting because they are *not being boosted* in their activation either by the input or by other hardware operators. That is, they are *not* being boosted by Content acquired via the $C$-learning operator, nor by Logical—in the broad sense of structural and relational—learning (this is the $L$-operator), nor by strong Affective schemes (this is the $A$-operator), nor by Gestaltist Field factors (this is the $F$-operator), etc.

In contrast, the scheme *OPa1* of strategy *a* does not need to be boosted with $M$-capacity because when it emerged, at the point when *t* was being hidden under $A$ (i.e., at this point when strategy *b* had not yet been synthesized!), *affective desire to get t had strongly boosted and become associated (via C- and L-learning)* with scheme *OPa1*. Thus *OPa1* is boosted affectively by the conative impulse of emotion—the initial desire to get the toy (we refer to this Affective boosting as the *A-operator*; Pascual-Leone, 1991). This affective boosting of *OPa1* begins to answer the question of why strategy *a* is strong, relative to strategy *b* (CI3).

To see why affective boosting ($A$-operator) suffices to cause $C$-learning (i.e., conditioning or simple associative learning) with little repetition, consider the following. First, affects and emotions are cued by $C$- and $LC$- structures—that is, by already automatized associative structures. Second, affects ensure that the to-be-associated schemes are repeatedly activated together (i.e., coactivated) and are cofunctional (i.e., together produce the affectively rewarding result) (cf. Pascual-Leone & Goodman, 1979).

**MP2.** After the hiding of hand/toy behind $C$ the dynamic state of equilibration within the child's current *field of activation* changes. Now a conflict, or dialectical contradiction, appears between strategy *a*, which is boosted by affect ($A$-operator), and strategy *b*. Assuming that the child has generated all the schemes listed in F2, in the temporal order indicated by the affixed digits, and that all are being retained in the field of activation, the *SOP* principle in combination with the $F$-operator should induce a "relaxation choice" favoring $C$ as the screen where *t* is hidden. This is because strategy *b*, as suggested by formulas F1 and F2, contains more schemes that are *highly activated and compatible* than does strategy *a*; and, last but not least, these schemes contain more compatible distinct information about the situation than do the schemes of strategy *a* (for this reason, they are made dominant, as "relaxation choice," by the $F$-operator/*SOP* mechanism).

**MP3.** If the "relaxation choice" favoring $C$ has been reached, the *Executive* directs the I-operator to interrupt the schemes of strategy *a* that, in their application, are incompatible with strategy *b* (see Pascual-Leone, 1984, 1987, for more detail on this mechanism). This *I-interruption* explains an empirically well established but perplexing paradox (Wellman et al., 1986). Namely, although the scheme *OPa1* is emotionally boosted, and it quickly becomes a habit ($C$- and $L$-learning) in the prior trials, the number and kind of these search-behind-$A$ practice trials do not seem to affect the results. That is, the child's disposition to produce strategy *b*, once the "relaxation choice" for $C$ has taken place, is unaffected by the number of practice trials. This is paradoxical (cf. Wellman et al., 1986), because practice should increase the habit-strength of *OPa1* (the search-behind-A scheme). The solution to this paradox is the *I*-interruption of strategy *a*, because *active interruption renders the habit-strength effect ineffective*. Consistent with this interpretation, Benson (1989) found that exposure to "misleading" trials, designed to strengthen strategy *a*, had little effect on children's (10- to 35-month-olds) use of strategy *b* in single visible displacement and successive (visible and invisible) displacement tasks. This completes our explanation of research results connected with question CI3.

***MP4.*** Now the application to performance of the "relaxation choice" described in MP2 is assured. This is because the brain's "spreading of activation" network must yield as *final common path* (by virtue of the *F-operator* and *SOP*) the path that is semantically primed by the *dominant* (i.e., most strongly activated) cluster of interconnected schemes in the current field of activation. The common semantic-pragmatic path of strategy *b* is "(reaching towards *C*)", because this response is consistent with every scheme in strategy *b*. This response, therefore, becomes the "relaxation" solution in the brain network (other competing clusters of schemes—such as those of strategy *a*—have been *I*-interrupted!). This completes our response to question CI2.

***MP2*.*** Let us now consider possible effects of situational variables. One well-studied variable in the case of the *single visible displacement* task is the time *delay* between the moment when baby sees the hand/toy go behind *C* (or *B*, if only two screens are used) and the moment when she is allowed to respond (e.g., Bell, 1989; Diamond, 1985; Diamond & Goldman-Rakic, 1983; Fox, Kagan, & Weiskopf, 1979; Harris, 1987; Wellman et al., 1986). An increase in this time interval (*the interval AFTER the elicitation of strategy b*) seems to affect the child's disposition to produce a "relaxation choice" *against* strategy *b*. That is, correct responding decreases as delay increases. Increasing this time interval should not affect much the strength of scheme *OPa1*, because this scheme is habit-like and *A*-boosted, but it *should erode the activation strength of the schemes in strategy b* (formula F2) for two reasons. First, if these schemes are not yet being *M-centrated* (are not yet in the focus of the child's mental attention) *any* event that attracts the child's attention during this interval might generate a different irrelevant Executive that could *I*-interrupt the schemes of strategy *b* (cf. Burtis, 1982; Pascual-Leone, 1984); further, the schemes might slowly decay in their activation if they are not used. Second, if the schemes were already in the focus of mental attention (*M-centration*), the longer the delay, the more sophisticated must be the attentional Executives of the child that protect her from distraction (otherwise the first case will apply). Whether under the first or second alternative, the only remedy to this negative effect of delay is a greater sophistication of the child's executive repertoire. This sophistication of the executive repertoire should increase with experience and, therefore, the older a child is the more resistant she should be to delays in this task.

This explanation is consistent with the empirical results. For example, in a longitudinal study, spanning the age range 8–12 months, Diamond (1985) found that the duration of delay necessary to maintain the A-not-B error increased continuously at the rate of about 2 seconds per month; Bell (1989) reported similar results. Fox et al. (1979) examined performance on the A-not-B task longitudinally over the same age range. They reported that as the children got older, they tolerated longer delays *and* other sources of potential interference with the *b* strategy (e.g., a screen lowered between the child and the task materials during the delay period).

Further, the work of Diamond (1988; Diamond & Goldman-Rakic, 1983), Goldman-Rakic (1987), and Bell (1989) shows that the ability to withstand delay in object permanence tasks is directly related to the amount of activity in the baby's prefrontal lobes. Because the prefrontal lobes are informationally nonspecific, this finding adds credence to our claim: A *nonspecific activatory function*—the *M-operator*—*is boosting with mental energy the schemes of strategy b*. In fact Pascual-Leone made the prediction that the *M*-operator would be localized in the prefrontal lobe, before the current consensus about prefrontal functions existed (Pascual-Leone, 1974, 1984, 1987, 1989a).

A situational variable that empirically appears to favor strategy *b* is the number of screens (locations) behind which *t* might be hidden. Wellman et al. (1986), in a careful meta-analysis of the literature on the *single visible displacement* subparadigm (i.e., A-not-B task), showed the importance of this variable. In brief, lower error rates were found for multiscreen versus two-screen versions of the task. How is this finding consistent with our model? Our model should predict that two locations (screens *A* and *B*) will be hardest, for two reasons. First, prior to the disappearance of *t* behind *B* (i.e., *PRIOR to the elicitation of strategy b*), the strength of strategy *a* could be eroded by the presence of situational distractors (e.g., instances of the gaze exploring one more screen). This is because strategy *a* is being directly boosted by affective desire and by the (perhaps weak) habit *OPa1* (boosters are *A*-, *C*-, and *L*-operators); and alternative *M*-centrations, driven by the distractors, could *I*-interrupt scheme *OPa1*. Second, the presence of more screens could make it harder for scheme *OPa1* to be cued (activated) during step MP2, if the child is looking at other screens. This is because the scheme *OPa1* is not necessarily developed under high attentional arousal (a low *M*-operator power is used in developing it—see above and below); and therefore it is like an egocentric global template, cued only by the original field of activation (cf. Bryant, 1989). As the two factors just cited should increase in potency with the number of screens (up to some asymptote), our model predicts that, other things being equal, strategy *b* will be relatively more potent, whenever the number of screens is increased in the single visible displacement task.

TABLE 8.1

Predicted $M_e$ Capacity Corresponding to Average Chronological Age
and Piagetian Substage in the Sensorimotor Period

| Predicted Maximal Power of $M_e$ | Sensorimotor Substage | Average Age in Months |
|:---:|:---|:---:|
| 0 | Local perceptual & motor coordinations | 0–1 |
| 1 | Beginning of primary circular reactions | 1–4 |
| 2 | Beginning of secondary circular reactions | 4–8 |
| 3 | Coordination of secondary circular reactions | 8–12 |
| 4 | Beginning of tertiary circular reactions | 12–18 |
| 5 | Coordination of tertiary circular reactions | 18–26 |
| 6 | Transition to mental processing | 26–34 |
| 7 | $M = e + 1$ | 34–59 |

*MP4*\*.   Consider finally how this model accounts for effects of development—*age* in the "normal" child. It was suggested earlier that all the schemes
in formula F2—strategy *b*—in the successive invisible displacement task, could
be highly activated *only if* the child possessed an *M*-operator with a *power of
centration* of at least *M-power* = 5. The power of mental centration is measured
in terms of the number of schemes that *M* can simultaneously boost.[8] Three
extensive doctoral theses from the first author's laboratory (Alp, 1988; Benson, 1989; Holloway, 1986; see also Holloway, Blake, Pascual-Leone, & Middaugh, 1987; Pascual-Leone, Johnson, & Benson, 1989) provide strong evidence in support of Pascual-Leone's model of *M*-power growth, as shown in
Table 8.1. According to this model, the *M-capacity* of infants measured in terms
of their *M-power* (i.e., the number of separate schemes *M*-capacity can simultaneously centrate), grows with the Piagetian sensorimotor stages.

This model explains why a child older than 18 or 19 months should be able
to generate strategy *b*, even in the *successive invisible displacement* subparadigm
(which requires *M*-centration of all the schemes in formula F2). A child of 12
months should fail successive invisible displacement, but pass the *successive visible
displacement subparadigm*. This is because successive visible displacement does
not require *M*-centration of scheme *FIGhand2* "(*t* is hidden inside the hand)",
but only variants of the remaining four schemes in F2. Children younger than
12 months will tend to fail both successive displacement subparadigms, but
will pass the single visible displacement task if they are older than 8 months
of age (i.e., are in Stage 4 of the sensorimotor period) because, as discussed
earlier, this subparadigm requires only three schemes to be endogenously cen-

---

[8]Readers familiar with our developmental work might notice that the units of mental capacity
we are counting in infancy are those that we call *e*-units (e.g., Johnson et al., 1989; Pascual-Leone,
1987; Pascual-Leone & Goodman, 1979). Our behavioral measurement of mental attentional capacity (*M*-power) is said to be equal to *e* + *k* where both *e* and *k* stand for scales of *M*-power.
The *e*-scale is used to boost sensorimotor schemes, whereas the *k*-scale serves to boost the more
complex symbolic schemes. The *e*-units are much smaller than the *k*-units available beyond infancy.

trated with $M$-capacity (i.e., has an $M$-demand of 3). Finally because, as discussed previously, the task of simply finding an object that has been visibly hidden behind a single screen (i.e., the search-behind-$A$ task) requires only two schemes to be $M$-centrated (has an $M$-demand of 2), it can be passed by children older than 4 months who have had sufficient visual-motor experience (e.g., 6- to 8-month-olds). If a subparadigm has an $M$-*demand* greater than the age group's $M$-power, then the children's $M$-centration capacity will be inadequate for dynamically synthesizing strategy $b$. In these children strategy $a$ will be dominant, causing A-not-B (or equivalent) errors as a norm. These results are well established in the literature (e.g., Benson, 1989; Fox et al., 1979; Harris, 1983; Uzgiris & Hunt, 1975; Wellman, 1985).

We have mentioned that our interpretation of $M$ and $I$ as being two nonspecific, general-purpose hardware operators of the brain, is consistent with findings regarding activity in the prefrontal lobe during success in object permanence tasks. Our interpretation is also consistent with results from Pascual-Leone's laboratory (Alp, 1988; Benson, 1989; Holloway, 1986). Benson, for example, found a very close quantitative relation among empirically estimated $M$-power scores obtained by babies in object permanence tasks and in other types of task, such as: (a) theoretically constructed new $M$-capacity measures (i.e., a *semantic complexity* task—language comprehension—and an *imitation sorting* task—non-verbal imitation); (b) an adaptation of Case's (1985) *Balance Beam* task; and (c) the semantic complexity of babies' *spontaneous utterances* to their mothers, in seven different semi-structured situations, which were scored (via metasubjective analysis) to estimate the $M$-demand of the utterances.

## CONCLUDING REMARKS

These data of Benson, Alp, and Holloway, together with the results analyzed here, and the prefrontal-activity experiments related to object permanence (e.g., Bell, 1989; Diamond & Goldman-Rakic, 1983; Goldman-Rakic, 1987) suggest that *metasubjective analysis* (a method of task analysis using assumptions about the hardware mechanisms of subjective/objective performance) can reach a power of prediction that the usual *objective, subjective,* and real-time mental computational (i.e., *ultrasubjective*) analyses of tasks cannot yield. As our careful analysis of object permanence paradigms should suggest, this power of prediction in metasubjective analysis is largely due to two epistemological/theoretical innovations. First is a stricter and narrower definition of the psychological unit—the organismic scheme and its kinds—than is found in the Piagetian and neo-Piagetian structuralist, or the experimental information-processing, traditions. Second is the explicit positing, and use in a strong hypothetical-deductive manner, of an organismic theory of universal hidden hardware operators and principles. This organismic theory attempts to model the "functional architecture'' (Pylyshyn, 1984) of the organism. And it does so in terms of relatively autonomous, but dynamically interacting, functional modules, which have been empirically inferred across types of situations and types of subjects.

As discussed in the Introduction, this theory does not distinguish between ''vertical-decalage'' or competence factors and ''horizontal-decalage'' or performance/individual difference factors in development. These factors all can be explained by the same causal theory. Perhaps for this reason our method of metasubjective analysis can be used, at any age, to model and predict age-linked mental-processing characteristics that account for vertical decalages (such as that found between successive visible- vs. successive invisible displacement subparadigms). But the same organismic process models predict horizontal decalages in tasks (such as the effect of increased delay in the single displacement task), as well as ''individual decalages'' (de Ribaupierre, in press; Longeot, 1978) in types of subjects.

Another advantage of metasubjective analysis over structuralist analysis is that it suggests how *dynamic syntheses*—the hidden heart of Piagetian equilibration—actually may take place in the organism. The analysis of dynamic syntheses led Pascual-Leone (1969) independently to postulate views that resemble *some* key functional-architectural assumptions of current neuropsychology and neuronal/connectionist computational models. This resemblance illustrates the heuristic value of these methods.

## ACKNOWLEDGMENTS

Preparation of this chapter was facilitated by a Social Sciences and Humanities Research Council of Canada research grant to the first author. We are grateful to Suzanne Prior for valuable comments on the manuscript.

## REFERENCES

Alp, I. (1988). *Mental capacity and working memory in 1- to 3-year-olds.* Unpublished doctoral dissertation, York University, Toronto.

Anderson, J. (1983). *The architecture of cognition.* Cambridge, MA: Harvard University Press.

Bell, M. (1989). *Changes in frontal EEG in relation to cognitive and affective development between 7 and 12 months of age.* Paper presented at the meeting of the Society for Research in Child Development, Kansas City, MO.

Benson, N. (1989). *Mental capacity constraints on early symbolic processing: The origin of language from a cognitive perspective.* Unpublished doctoral dissertation, York University, Toronto.

Bremner, J. (1985). Object tracking and search in infancy: A review of data and a theoretical evaluation. *Developmental Review, 5,* 371–396.

Bryant, P. (1989). Commentary on Halford (1989). *Human Development, 32,* 369–374.

Burtis, P. J. (1982). Capacity increase and chunking in the development of short-term memory. *Journal of Experimental Child Psychology, 34,* 387–413.

Case, R. (1985). *Intellectual development: Birth to adulthood.* New York: Academic Press.

Case, R., & Griffin, S. (1990). Child cognitive development: the role of central conceptual structures in the development of children's scientific and social thought. In C.-A. Hauert (Ed.), *Advances in psychology—Developmental psychology: Cognitive, perceptuo-motor, and neurological perspectives* (pp. 193-230). The Netherlands: Elsevier.

Chapman, M. (1981). Pascual-Leone's theory of constructive operators: An introduction. *Human Development, 24,* 144-155.

Corrigan, R., & Fischer, K. (1985). Controlling sources of variation in search tasks: A skill theory approach. In H. M. Wellman (Ed.), *Children's searching* (pp. 287-318). Hillsdale, NJ: Lawrence Erlbaum Associates.

Diamond, A. (1985). Development of the ability to use recall to guide action, as indicated by infants' performance on AB̄. *Child Development, 56,* 868-883.

Diamond, A. (1988). Abilities and neural mechanisms underlying AB̄ performance. *Child Development, 59,* 523-527.

Diamond, A., & Goldman-Rakic, P. (1983). Comparison of performance on a Piagetian object permanence task in human infants and rhesus monkeys: Evidence for involvement of prefrontal cortex. *Neuroscience Abstracts, 9,* 641.

Fischer, K. (1980). A theory of cognitive development: The control and construction of hierarchies of skills. *Psychological Review, 87,* 477-531.

Fischer, K., & Pipp, S. (1984). Processes of cognitive development: Optimal level and skill acquisition. In R. Sternberg (Ed.), *Mechanisms of cognitive development* (pp. 45-80). New York: Freeman.

Fox, N., Kagan, N., & Weiskopf, S. (1979). The growth of memory during infancy. *Genetic Psychology Monographs, 99,* 91-130.

Fuster, J. (1985). The prefrontal cortex and temporal integration. In A. Peters & E. G. Jones (Eds.), *Cerebral cortex, Vol. 4: Association and auditory cortices* (pp. 151-177). New York: Plenum.

Gelman, R., & Gallistel, C. (1986). *The child's understanding of number.* Cambridge, MA: Harvard University Press.

Gibson, E. (1982). The concept of affordances in development: The renascence of functionalism. In W. Collins (Ed.), *Minnesota symposia on child psychology* (Vol. 15, pp. 55-81). Hillsdale, NJ: Lawrence Erlbaum Associates.

Goldman-Rakic, P. (1987). Development of cortical circuitry and cognitive function. *Child Development, 58,* 601-622.

Gratch, G. (1975). Recent studies based on Piaget's view of object concept development. In L. B. Cohen & P. Salapatek (Eds.), *Infant perception: From sensation to cognition* (Vol. 2, pp. 51-99). New York: Academic Press.

Haake, R., & Somerville, S. (1985). Development of logical search skills in infancy. *Developmental Psychology, 21,* 176-186.

Halford, G. (1982). *Development of thought.* Hillsdale, NJ: Lawrence Erlbaum Associates.

Halford, G. (1989). Reflections on 25 years of Piagetian cognitive developmental psychology, 1963-1988. *Human Development, 32,* 325-357.

Harris, P. (1983). Infant cognition. In M. M. Haith & J. J. Campos (Eds.), *Handbook of child psychology: Vol. 2. Infancy and developmental psychobiology* (pp. 689-782). New York: Wiley.

Harris, P. (1986). Bringing order to the A-not-B error. *Monographs of the Society for Research in Child Development, 51*(3, Serial No. 214), 52-61.

Harris, P. (1987). The development of search. In P. Salapatek & L. B. Cohen (Eds.), *Handbook of infant perception (Vol. 2): From perception to cognition* (pp. 155-207). New York: Academic Press.

Holland, J., Holyoak, K., Nisbett, R., & Thagard, P. (1986). *Induction: Processes of inference, learning, and discovery.* Cambridge, MA: MIT Press.

Holloway, R. (1986). *Mental capacity, language, and play: A neo-Piagetian study of aspects of cognitive development from 6 to 20 months.* Unpublished doctoral dissertation, York University, Toronto.

Holloway, R., Blake, J., Pascual-Leone, J., & Middaugh, L. (1987). *Are there common mental-capacity constraints in infant cognition, communication, and play abilities?* Paper presented at the meeting of the Society for Research in Child Development, Baltimore, MD.

Husserl, E. (1970). *The crisis of European sciences and transcendental phenomenology* (D. Carr, Trans.). Evanston, IL: Northwestern University Press.

Johnson, J. (1991). Constructive processes in bilingualism and their cognitive growth effects. In E. Bialystok (Ed.), *Language processing in bilingual children* (pp. 193–221). Cambridge: Cambridge University Press.

Johnson, J., Fabian, V., & Pascual-Leone, J. (1989). Quantitative hardware-stages that constrain language development. *Human Development, 32,* 245–271.

Johnson, J., & Pascual-Leone, J. (1989a). Developmental levels of processing in metaphor interpretation. *Journal of Experimental Child Psychology, 48,* 1–31.

Johnson, J., & Pascual-Leone, J. (1989b). Reply to A. Karmiloff-Smith. *Human Development, 32,* 276–278.

Klahr, D. (1984). Transition processes in quantitative development. In R. Sternberg (Ed.), *Mechanisms of cognitive development* (pp. 101–139). New York: Freeman.

Longeot, F. (1978). *Les stades opératoires de Piaget et les facteurs de l'intelligence [Piaget's operatory stages and the factors of intelligence].* Grenoble: Presses Universitaires de Grenoble.

Luria, A. (1973). *The working brain.* Middlesex, England: Penguin Books.

McCarthy, J., & Hayes, P. J. (1969). Some philosophical problems from the standpoint of artificial intelligence. In B. Meltzer & D. Michie (Eds.), *Machine intelligence* (Vol. 4, pp. 463–502). New York: American Elsevier.

Nelson, K. (Ed.). (1986). *Children's event knowledge: Structure and function in development.* Hillsdale, NJ: Lawrence Erlbaum Associates.

Pascual-Leone, J. (1969). *Cognitive development and cognitive style: A general psychological integration.* Unpublished doctoral dissertation, University of Geneva.

Pascual-Leone, J. (1970). A mathematical model for the transition rule in Piaget's developmental stages. *Acta Psychologica, 32,* 301–345.

Pascual-Leone, J. (1974). *A neo-Piagetian process-structural model of Witkin's psychological differentiation.* Paper presented at the meeting of the International Association for Cross-Cultural Psychology, Kingston, Ontario.

Pascual-Leone, J. (1976a). Metasubjective problems of constructive cognition: Forms of knowing and their psychological mechanism. *Canadian Psychological Review, 17,* 110–125.

Pascual-Leone, J. (1976b). On learning and development Piagetian style: I. A reply to Lefebvre-Pinard. *Canadian Psychological Review, 17,* 270–280.

Pascual-Leone, J. (1980). Constructive problems for constructive theories: The current relevance of Piaget's work and a critique of information-processing simulation psychology. In R. Kluwe & H. Spada (Eds.), *Developmental models of thinking* (pp. 263–296). New York: Academic Press.

Pascual-Leone, J. (1983). Growing into human maturity: Towards a metasubjective theory of adulthood stages. In P. Baltes & O. Brim (Eds.), *Life-span development and behavior* (Vol. 5, pp. 117–156). New York: Academic Press.

Pascual-Leone, J. (1984). Attention, dialectic, and mental effort: Towards an organismic theory of life stages. In M. Commons, F. Richards, & C. Armon (Eds.), *Beyond formal operations: Late adolescent and adult cognitive development* (pp. 182–215). New York: Praeger.

Pascual-Leone, J. (1987). Organismic processes for neo-Piagetian theories: A dialectical causal account of cognitive development. *International Journal of Psychology, 22,* 531–570.

Pascual-Leone, J. (1988). Affirmations and negations, disturbances and contradictions, in understanding Piaget: Is his later theory causal? [Review of *Equilibration of cognitive structures*]. *Contemporary Psychologist, 33,* 420–421.

Pascual-Leone, J. (1989a). An organismic process model of Witkin's field-dependence-independence. In T. Globerson & T. Zelniker (Eds.), *Cognitive style and cognitive development* (pp. 36–70). Norwood, NJ: Ablex.

Pascual-Leone, J. (1989b). Commentary on Halford (1989). *Human Development. 32,* 375–378.

Pascual-Leone, J. (1990). Intension, intention, and early precursors of will: Constructive epistemological remarks on Lewis' research programme. *Psychological Inquiry, 1,* 258–260.

Pascual-Leone, J. (1991). Emotions, development, and psychotherapy: A dialectical constructivist perspective. In J. Safran & L. Greenberg (Eds.), *Affective change events in psychotherapy* (pp. 302–335). New York: Academic Press.

Pascual-Leone, J., & Goodman, D. (1979). Intelligence and experience: A neo-Piagetian approach. *Instructional Science, 8,* 301–367.

Pascual-Leone, J., Goodman, D., Ammon, P., & Subelman, I. (1978). Piagetian theory and neo-Piagetian analysis as psychological guides in education. In J. Gallagher & J. Easley (Eds.), *Knowledge and development* (Vol. 2, pp. 243–289). New York: Plenum Press.

Pascual-Leone, J., Johnson, J., & Benson, N. (1989, July). Mental-capacity constraints on symbolic processing: The onset of human language. In J. Johnson (Chair), *Mental capacity constraints on cognition: Studies from the Theory of Constructive Operators.* Symposium conducted at the meeting of the International Society for the Study of Behavioural Development, Jyvaskyla, Finland.

Pascual-Leone, J., Johnson, J., Goodman, D., Hameluck, D., & Theodor, L. (1981). *I*-interuption effects in backward pattern masking: The neglected role of fixation stimuli. In *Proceedings of the third Annual Conference of the Cognitive Science Society* (pp. 310–322). Berkeley, CA.

Piaget, J. (1941). Le mécanisme du développement mental et les lois du groupement des opérations [The mechanism of mental development and the laws of the grouping of operations]. *Archives de Psychologie, 28,* 215–285.

Piaget, J. (1954). *The construction of reality in the child.* New York: Ballantine.

Piaget, J. (1958). Assimilation et connaissance [Assimilation and knowledge]. In A. Jonckheere, B. Mandelbrot, & J. Piaget (Eds.), *La lecture de l'experience* (pp. 49–108). Paris: Presses Universitaires de France.

Piaget, J., & Morf, A. (1958). Les isomorphismes partiels entre les structures logiques et les structures perceptives [The partial isomorphisms between logical and perceptual structures]. In J. Bruner, F. Bresson, A. Morf, & J. Piaget (Eds.), *Logique et perception* (pp. 49–116). Paris: Presses Universitaires de France.

Pylyshyn, Z. (1984). *Computation and cognition.* Cambridge, MA: MIT Press.

Rapaport, D. (1960). *The structure of psychoanalytical theory: A systematizing attempt.* New York: International Universities Press.

de Ribaupierre, A. (1983). Un modèle neo-Piagetien du développement: La theorie des opérateurs constructifs de Pascual-Leone [A neo-Piagetian model of development: Pascual-Leone's theory of constructive operators]. *Cahiers de Psychologie, 3,* 327–356.

de Ribaupierre, A. (in press). Cognitive style research and developmental psychology. In J. Berry & P. Schmitz (Eds.), *Psychological differentiation: An appreciation of Witkin's contribution to psychology.* Hillsdale, NJ: Lawrence Erlbaum Associates.

de Ribaupierre, A., & Pascual-Leone, J. (1979). Formal operations and M power: A neo-Piagetian investigation. In D. Kuhn (Ed.), *Intellectual development beyond childhood (Sourcebooks on new directions in child development)* (pp. 1–43). San Francisco: Jossey-Bass.

Rumelhart, D., McClelland, J., & the PDP Research Group. (1986). *Parallel distributed processing* (2 Vols). Cambridge, MA: MIT Press.

Sartre, J-P. (1957). *The transcendence of the ego: An existentialist theory of consciousness.* New York: Noonday Press.

Schank, R., & Abelson, R. (1977). *Scripts, plans, goals, and understanding.* Hillsdale, NJ: Lawrence Erlbaum Associates.

Schrag, C. (1989). *Communicative praxis and the space of subjectivity.* Bloomington: Indiana University Press.

Sherrington, C. (1947). *The integrative action of the nervous system* (2nd ed.). New Haven: Yale University Press.

Smolensky, P. (1988). On the proper treatment of connectionism. *Behavioral and Brain Sciences, 11,* 1–74.

Sperry, R. (1985). Consciousness, personal identity, and the divided self. In D. Benson & N. Zaidel (Eds.), *The dual brain* (pp. 36-70). New York: Guilford.

Thagard, P. (1989). Explanatory coherence. *Brain and Behavioral Sciences, 12*, 435-502.

Tolman, E. (1959). Principles of purposive behavior. In S. Koch (Ed.), *Psychology: A study of a science* (Vol. 2, pp. 92-157). New York: McGraw-Hill.

Tolman, E., & Brunswik, E. (1935). The organism and the causal texture of the environment. *Psychological Review, 42*, 43-77.

Uzgiris, I., & Hunt, J. McV. (1975). *Assessment in infancy: Ordinal scales of psychological development.* Chicago: University of Illinois Press.

Van Peursen, C. (1972). *Phenomenology and reality.* Pittsburgh: Duquesne University Press.

Vuyk, R. (1981). *Overview and critique of Piaget's genetic epistemology 1965-1980* (Vol. 2). New York: Academic Press.

Wellman, H. (1985). *Children's searching: The development of search skill and spatial representation.* Hillsdale, NJ: Lawrence Erlbaum Associates.

Wellman, H., Cross, D., & Bartsch, K. (1986). Infant search and object permanence: A meta-analysis of the A-not-B error. *Monographs of the Society for Research in Child Development, 51*(3, Serial No. 214).

# Chapter 9

# Representational Competence: Another Type?

Irving Sigel
*Educational Testing Service*

> . . . . *as human beings, we must inevitably see the universe from a centre lying within ourselves and speak about it in terms of a human language shaped by the exigencies of human intercourse. Any attempt rigorously to eliminate our human perspective from our picture of the world must lead to absurdity.*
>
> —Polanyi (1958)

The purpose of this chapter is to focus attention on what is termed *representational competence* and to argue that such competence is necessary, but not sufficient, for effective cognitive functioning. To foreshadow the discussion, I provide a brief definition of *representational competence*. It refers to the *understanding and utilization* of a fundamental rule to the effect that knowledge presented in various forms (e.g., pictures, words, signs) still retains its intrinsic meaning in spite of variations in form of presentation. For example a *cup*, whether presented in pictorial form or as a three-dimensional item, still retains its intrinsic identity as a "cup." A picture of a person retains the intrinsic identity of the person even if the person is presented only in the picture. Representational competence is a form of conservation, in which the meaning of an instance is retained in spite of change in form or symbolic level. I offer the term *conservation of meaning* to be added to the lexicon of conservation types.

I argue here that this representational competence is necessary to perform any psychological task beyond the level of sensorimotor functioning.[1] It is rare-

---

[1]It may be obvious that no action, activity, or task is unidimensional. However, for the sake of discourse and methodological analysis, the singularity of a particular act is assumed. We are all aware of the artificiality of such assumptions, but at the moment have little recourse but to follow this type of approach.

**189**

ly, if ever, conceptualized or assessed in the course of evaluating an individual's test performance as a factor affecting how the task is executed. Overlook-
ing representational competence as an intimate ingredient of all assessments
compromises validity of psychological assessments in general, and cognitive
evaluations in particular, simply because all tests employ some type of
representation.

My interest in, and conceptualization of the problem of representational
competence had its roots in experiences I had while working with under-
privileged Black and White preschool children. I discovered that these children had more difficulty generating classes when presented with pictures
of familiar objects then when engaging in the same type of classification task
when presented with three-dimensional objects. Middle-class Black and/or
White preschool children did not have such a difficulty (Sigel, Anderson,
& Shapiro, 1966; Sigel & McBane 1967; Sigel & Olmsted 1970a, 1970b).
Results from these studies led me to ask fundamental developmental questions such as: "Why is it the case the impoverished children had difficulty
realizing the equivalence of the three-dimensional object and its pictured
counterpart? Is this problem one of understanding the representational rule—
that is, of understanding that the object and the picture share some common
meaning in spite of differences in symbolic representation? If so, then the first
order of business is to determine if this finding is an instance of a general case
of representational competence. Replications of these studies have led to the
conclusion that the discrepancy in classification of photographs of objects, as
compared to the three-dimensional objects, does index a low level of representational competence. If such competence is deemed significant for cognitive
functioning, then it is important to seek understanding of what accounts for
differences in the child's and in the adult's understanding of the representational rule.

Searches for answers to this question led to the investigations of bio-
sociocultural factors as antecedents for representational competence, because
my basic theoretical bias is that all phases of cognitive development evolve as
a function of biological force interacting with sociocultural experience. As part
of a research program intended to address the question, I developed a conceptualization of the problem and placed it in a developmental framework. The
question then became transformed into more general ones, such as: How is
experience transformed into mental products? What systems do children use
to encode and decode these experiences? How do the encoding/decoding
processes change with increased maturity?

In this chapter, I first define the concepts of representation and representational competence. Then I proceed to consider the development of representational competence, using it as a background for discussing issues and problems
in the assessment of such competence.

## DEFINITION OF REPRESENTATION

*Representation* as a psychological construct has had a long and varied history. In an extensive review of representation, Mandler (1983) stated that the term has been used in two ways:

> The first of these. . . refers to knowledge in the way in which it is organized. . . . The second . . . refers to words, artifacts, or other symbolic productions that people use to represent (to stand for, to refer to) some aspect of the world or some aspect of their knowledge of the world. (p. 420)

Piaget (1962), on the other hand, has offered a more inclusive definition where he wrote:

> Representation is characterized by the fact that it goes beyond the present, extending the field of adaptation both in space and time. In other words, it evokes what lies outside the immediate perceptual and active field. (p. 273)

He also added:

> We use the word "representation" in two different senses. In its broad sense, representation is identical with thought, *i.e.*, with all intelligence which is based on a system of concepts or mental schemas and not merely on perceptions and actions. In its narrow sense, representation is restricted to the mental memory image, *i.e.*, the symbolic evocation of absent realities. (p. 67)

This concept of representation, according to Piaget, involves understanding the principle of transformation of symbols and also the understanding of relationships among nonobservable events. This notion of representation for Piaget can be integrated into the concepts of sign and symbol understanding from Werner and Kaplan (1963), who wrote about representation in the context of symbols and symbol formation. They use the term *symbol* in two senses: "In one, it is employed . . . to emphasize a fusion or indissolubility of form and meaning; in the order it serves to designate a pattern or configuration in some medium (sounds, lines, body movements)" (p. 15). Symbols are "entities which subserve a novel and unique function, the function of *representation*. The function of representation is a constitutive mark of a symbol; it distinguishes anything qua symbol from anything *qua sign, signal, or thing*" (pp. 13-14).

For the purpose of this chapter, I work closely with the Piagetian definition, integrating the notion of sign and symbol as Werner and Kaplan describe it.[2]

---

[2]Signs and symbols have been used in many different ways (e.g., Pribram, 1971, used signs as universal representations and symbols as context defined). Others such as Morris (1946), Piaget (1962), and Wertsch (1985) used other definitions. For my purposes here, the differences are less important than the concept of a sign or symbol serving a similar function of representing some other external or internal event.

## KNOWLEDGE IS REPRESENTATIONAL

The potential for *knowledge* exists in the "outer world," and is available for whomever wishes to partake. The world is saturated with potential knowledge, which is available in many forms and many places. Knowledge is a *state of knowing*, that is, familiarity, awareness, understanding of information about something(s) gained through experience (including the sensorial system). In general, knowledge is "the sum or range of what has been perceived, described or learned" (*American Heritage dictionary*, 1982). Knowledge is mentally represented in some semiotic or figurative form.

Knowledge can be categorized in three broad categories: *physical knowledge, social knowledge*, and *logico-mathematical knowledge*. Knowledge from each of these categories is represented in forms particular to its type or semiotic forms. For example, mathematics is usually learned with a particular notational system representing mathematical operations, whereas social knowledge is probably acquired in the context of oral or written language. The knowledge may be stored in the form initially experienced. With increasing maturity, knowledge forms can be generalized. For example, mathematical notations can be transliterated to a comparable meaning in words.

Languages are expressions of the culture; therefore, knowledge acquired and stored in verbal forms is culture bound. Thus, the meanings of particular phenomena may differ as a result of linguistic differences. In other words, the semiotic codes may differ for various language groups. This suggests that even similar contents expressed in different semiotic codes could lead to differences in meaning. If an English person points to his car and says, "The boot is full" (meaning the trunk), an American would wonder what he was referring to since *boot* to an American refers to something one wears on one's feet—not part of a car.

Knowledge systems may be represented by different orthographic or notational systems. For example, social knowledge is usually represented in written form in the orthography of the culture in which the knowledge is generated. It is obvious that translations of material in one orthographic form entails two types of transformation, one the language form and the other the orthography. For example, writing a Russian message in Cyrillic adds a double burden to the reader because neither the language nor the orthography is widely shared. On the other hand mathematic notations or music notations require fewer transformations to evoke shared meanings. Chances are there might be greater sharing of meaning in music or mathematics than in verbal forms. For example, the violin player in the Tokyo quartet will understand the notational system of a Beethoven String Quartet similarly to an American musician. The notational systems are more precise. Differences in interpretation are due to factors other than the mode of representation.

If one takes this principle a bit further, one comes to the realization that culture permeates semiotic forms, hence any conceptualization of representational thought (signs and symbols) must take cultural contents into account in order to understand the meaning and the origins of representational thinking. Knowledge is then acquired and used in cultural contexts.

Before going on, I wish to make clear that in this context culture broadly refers to lifestyles, language (dialects), religion, ethnicity, and social structure. Incorporating sociocultural factors into our conceptualization highlights the point that any investigation of cognitive development and representational thought must be sensitive to cultural differences among groups. Further, within-group differences must also be considered because life experiences will vary as a function of social status and idiosyncratic social and family variables. In other words, culture differentiates groups on the basis of their language or language heritage, religion, social status, and so on. It is in the family, however structured, that the culture is initially expressed, especially in values and beliefs about child rearing, communication, and world views (Sigel, 1985).

Knowledge is stored on two levels: a shared meaning level and an idiosyncratic level. *Shared meaning* refers to congruence in understanding and it is a function of socialization at home, at school, and in the larger environments. *Idiosyncratic meaning* is derived from unique and personal feelings and experiences engendered in the course of knowledge acquisition. Thus, I assume that shared knowledge equals shared meaning, but the significance of unique experiences that influence the way knowledge is organized and used should not be overlooked. Individuals differ in the way knowledge is organized. Individuals may organize their knowledge on the basis of some metaphor. For example, Pepper (1942) showed how scientists rely on various metaphors as a way to organize their knowledge systems. Some view their world in a mechanistic fashion, whereas others view their world as one in which everything is connected to everything else and events are influenced by the context in which they function. These two views coexist in our modern scientific society. Applying this analogue to the everyday world, is there any reason to expect individuals to organize their world views in a uniform way? We know that this is not the case. The good folks to the fundamentalists are not the good folks to the liberals. The implication of this perspective is that although knowledge on one level is acquired and stored, it does not mean that the level of meaning in shared. As we see here, this has implication for assessment of a child's knowledge.

Knowledge is represented and knowledge is used. The *how* of knowledge acquisition and its utilization depends on biological, sociocultural, intellectual forces in conjunction with a particular family history. Ultimately these factors influence the individual's developing representational competence.

## Acquisition of Knowledge

The child acquires knowledge within the semiotic codes. The question of interest is whether the initial assimilation of the knowledge in a particular code is the form in which the knowledge is stored. This is essentially the hypothesis

I am working with: Knowledge is not only stored, but also initially minimally encoded. The encoding process is a subsequent cognitive skill that evolves along with an increase in mental operational skills. In essence, younger children are more likely than older children to assimilate new knowledge passively, and with increasing maturity they begin to engage the new knowledge by employing mental operational skills, such as transformation, categorization, and integration. For example, young children may assimilate color names in a rote manner and evidence recognition of the colors when asked to do so. The colors are passively assimilated and repeated as such on demand. There is minimal encoding in this example. Instead, the child assimilates the knowledge as presented. Later, colors can be coded into a system because the child develops a color schema and so encodes the colors irrespective of the symbolic representational system in which the knowledge is encountered. I argue that "outer" knowledge is assimilative through activity that varies from a relatively passive assimilatory experience such a viewing a scene in a relaxed state, to actively encoding a complex passage of text that entails active and conscious construction. Further, knowledge is not a copy of the experience, but is constructed and mapped on previous existing internal schema. The construction of the new knowledge and the mapping on previous schemas will vary with the experience of the individual. For example, Piaget contended that a child of about 2 years of age will map experiences via images on biologically established internal schema. The opening example describing the difficulty impoverished children had classifying photographs of familiar objects as compared to the three-dimensional object illustrates the issue. Somehow these children had not acquired the principle that I refer to as the *representational rule* (i.e., an object, an event, or a person can be presented in different symbols or signals and still retain its meaning). As previously described, this capability can be considered as a *conservation of meaning*. That is, meaning is conserved irrespective of its semiotic, figurative, or significant form. If the children are working with this rule, and accordingly are conservers of meaning, they have considerable overlap in developing their classifications of pictures and objects. An example might help sharpen the point. A person sees a sunset and stores this percept. Is that percept stored purely as a figurative representation of the scene? It is clear that the content of the experience is not stored in a manner isomorphic to the scene itself because there are mental processes that are at work influencing the internalization of the experience (Mandler, 1983).

In summary, representational competence refers to the understanding of the representational rule: Instances can be represented by signs or symbols, and the instance does not lose its generic identity in the representation. The competence to employ the representational rule is needed in daily life. For example, the signal for stopping in traffic can be a red light, a stop sign, the international symbol of a hand, or the word "STOP." Each calls for the same action. The principle also holds for activities involving higher mental processes and complex content, for example, using mathematical symbols or symbols in symbolic logic, or words as representations of meaning. The fundamental principle here is that a sign or a symbol does represent and does convey similar meaning. The skill in using signs and symbols in the course of solving a problem, communicating an idea, or engaging in a conversation will vary, reflecting differential ability to engage in such activities. This indicates that individual differences in representational competence are reflected in the quality of performance, because competence is an attribute of performance.[3] It reflects skill level. The children who realized that the three-dimensional objects and their photographic representations could be conceptualized as members of the same class, reflected representational competence. They could understand that the picture and its three-dimensional counterpart are members of the same class. Postulating skill differences leads to a conceptualization of individual differences in performance. Individual differences exist in part because individuals vary in their developmental histories relevant to the acquisition of representational competence.

Although this is not the place to detail the developmental history of representational competence, the general idea can be placed into a broader context by describing the developmental process and theory guiding our effort. In brief, representational competence is a product of socialization, initially experienced in the context of the family. As children engage with parents and peers in the family context, they encounter a variety of opportunities to become involved in language and sharing space and objects. In the course of such encounters, they also begin to develop a sense of self. All of these experiences form the knowledge base that is assimilated and organized in schematic ways. In effect, all of this experience is stored in representational formats. The initial and primary set of interactions occur with the parents, because the parents function as both an active teacher–socializer and as role models. How parents communicate with their children and how they enable the children to engage with them and the larger culture into the broader culture, influences the way children will come to represent their experiences (Sigel & Cocking, 1977). We do know that different competencies emerge as a result of early experience that continues on through middle childhood and preadolescence (Sigel, 1982; Sigel & Cocking, 1977; Sigel, Stinson, & Flaugher, in press).

---

[3]A number of theorists have differentiated between competence and performance. I do not wish to engage in that debate at this time, but present my own working definition that is used in my work. The interested reader can review the work of Chomsky (1965), Davidson and Sternberg (1985), Flavell and Wohlwill (1969), and Overton and Newman (1982). The others who were influential in elaborating on the competence-performance distinction are members of the University of Minnesota Center for Research in Human Learning whose members at the time of the Flavell-Wohlwill (1969) article were: Foss, Halwes, Jenkins, and Shaw.

## CONCEPTUALIZATION OF
## REPRESENTATIONAL COMPETENCE

On the basis of this research, the concept of representational competence was integrated with Piaget's (1962) notion of representational thinking and further elaborated leading to the following basic definition of *representational competence*: "the ability . . . to represent an object which is absent or an event which is not perceived, by means of symbols or signs, that is, of signifiers differentiated from their significants" (Piaget, 1970, p. 717). Indications of representational competence are reflected not only in the reconstruction of previous experiences, but also in employing previous experience in the service of planning or predicting outcomes. To predict or to plan, or in Piaget's terms, to employ anticipatory imagery, involves emancipation from the ongoing present, projecting oneself into the unknown future. To be able to do that is another manifestation of representational competence.

A related aspect of representational competence is the ability to transcend the ongoing present and transform the here and now into some signal or symbolic system. These conceptions lead to the idea that if one is thinking of the object in its absence (and I use *object* as a generic term referring to instances of any kind), then one's thoughts about it are not time bound. Therefore, one can think in terms of the future or the ongoing present or re-present the past in the service of either the ongoing present and/or the future. Representational thinking and the competence to engage in such thought is involved in each of these temporal contexts when there is no ostensive object present. Essentially in each case re-presentation is necessary for action. The mental activity involved in these engagements are intrinsic to my conceptualization of representational competence. Finally, representational competence can vary in quality as a function of many of the factors enumerated earlier (McGillicuddy-DeLisi, DeLisi, Flaugher, & Sigel, 1987).

The understanding of symbolic representations may be domain specific, because knowledge systems have their own symbolic representational form (Halford, 1982). Competence to understand orthographic symbols does not mean that one understands mathematical notation, nor that one can transform mathematical notions into English (Cocking & Chipman 1988). Spatial knowledge is learned through visual experience. Individuals born blind learn about space tactility, and if their sight is restored they need to relearn by integrating their knowledge from a tactile system to a visual system (Senden, 1932/1960). I believe that there is no psychological reason to assume that competence in one domain will perforce relate to competence in others. Thus, there is no reason to assume that representational competence is a generalized competence.

Increasing support for this point of view has become available in reports on studies of visual thinking, visual literacy, and understanding diagrams and charts (examples of external representation, but requiring representational competence to comprehend). As individuals develop in a society, there may be emphasis in educational circles on particular semiotic codes. It may well be that overemphasizing a particular semiotic mode, from being able to acquire new knowledge efficiently. The limited ability of adults to engage in visual thinking as reported by Arnheim (1969) and Sigel (1978) is illustrative of this phenomenon.

Working with this hypothesis requires not only postulating the set of processes involved in the transportation of outer experience to the inner world, stored and organized, but also constructing a method for assessing the semiotic priorities that individuals have for acquiring and using new information. These days, for example, we have semiotics of films, semiotics of verbal languages, and we can ask whether knowledge can be transformed from one of these semiotic codes to another and what the consequences are of such transformations. My contention is that the greater the possibility for individuals to encode and decode knowledge systems into other systems, the greater the communication potential will be. Thus, the ability to transform pictures into words, numbers into words, words into numbers, exemplifies a level of representational competence that will maximize intellectual functioning and enhance the breadth of knowledge acquisition (Sigel, 1978). This claim is open to question and I discuss it later.

Now that I have clarified the definition of representational competence, I spell out the mental model of cognitive functioning in which representational competence is embedded, with particular focus on representational competence processes. As I indicated earlier, young children assimilate knowledge from the environment in the form in which it is presented. They may not be aware that what they are experiencing is symbolic. Rather, they think it is reality. They see a picture, not as a representation of a particular event, but the event in and of itself. Such knowledge is initially coded as a visual percept, a mental picture—an image. I have referred to this process as the *primary process*. However, during this time children are having many experiences, and the next phase in the process of knowledge acquisition and utilization involves the following kinds of mental work: The initial assimilation of encoded knowledge, its transformation into other codes, reorganizing the knowledge into schemas different from the initial one, and recognizing that the process of mental transformation and organization of that knowledge does not change the intrinsic meaning of equivalent information in spite of symbolic representational differences. To be sure, there may be additional mental processing which meaning may attenuate the basic meaning in some way—but the core meaning is conserved.

An example may help instantiate my perspective, because it involves every aspect of representational thinking discussed. In this way, the example ipso facto expresses the significance of representational competence in the service of acquisition and utilization of knowledge.

A young boy learns that whenever he sees two numbers connected by a " + " a mental operation may be activated. Such an identification may not be made if he sees the " + " by itself for then it can index a cross, a plus meaning, or more than, or an arithmetic operation addition. So, the first step in the process of understanding is to identify just what the context is for the " + ." In this way, the context clarifies the meaning. If he has learned to act on this knowledge, then he can go through the specific operation that is also labeled *addition*. However, if he has not learned to index this " + ," then he may well associate it with a previous experience, such as being told it is a "cross." Indexing it as a proxy for an operation is the product of another knowledge experience that enables him to exclude the notion of "cross" and to build the notion of "add." Now the " + " has two meanings, and being aware of them, while differentiating them, is an example of representational competence. Having achieved this state relative to these concepts the child is able to carry out further mental actions with " + " and addition, as well as contextually to differentiate when the " + " means "add" from when it means "cross." Later, the boy learns that the word "addition" is another word meaning of " + ." Now he has more information which leads to the notion that the same sign or signifier has more than one referent. So in arithmetic he is now ready to deal with an addition problem in words, still retaining the meaning of the " + " as a cross. Now he has learned that the same sign can have multiple meanings—the " + " is a sign with shared meanings. This is the building of a schema of " + ." If presented with a word problem such as, "If you add two apples to your package of 5 apples, how many apples do you have?", is an equivalent problem to "How much is 5 + 2?" He can also answer the question of "What else can a + mean?" The awareness that the sign can have two referents and also have a different word signifying that the same sign and the word are equivalent, indexes representation competence.

Implied in the aforementioned comments is the understanding that the assimilated knowledge is retained in memory and can be retrieved when needed, and further, it may be retrieved in forms not initially experienced. Knowledge, as all experience, may be retained on a conscious awareness level or on a tacit level (Polanyi, 1958). Conscious knowledge may be retrieved as needed, usually under the control of the individual; whereas tacit knowledge is not in awareness, although it may be brought into awareness. This is not the place to develop these concepts, but to acknowledge that executive mental functions come into play during the processes of transformation and reconstruction of experience.

In summary, representational competence, as I indicated, is fundamentally the competence to understand that objects, events, and persons can be represented in modalities other than those which were involved in the initial experience of experiences with the aforementioned instances, or in Ortony's (1979) words:

The central idea of this approach is that cognition is the result of mental construction. Knowledge of reality, whether it is occasioned by perception, language, memory, or anything else, is a result of going beyond the information given. It arises through the interaction of that information with the context in which it is presented, and with the knower's pre-existing knowledge. (p. 1)

Empirical evidence for competence to employ representations in humans is reported as early as infancy. In fact, an early type of representational competence is evident in the newborn who has learned very quickly to search for a nipple. The fact that she can search by groping with her mouth suggests that there is some internal sense that there is something desirable out there (Bower, 1989; Cohen & Gelber, 1975; Mandler, 1983; Piaget, 1970).[4]

These early competencies foreshadow the potential for the development of an increase in skill and competence. I turn now to the assessment of representational competence.

## ASSESSMENT CONSIDERATION

Most psychological test or task procedures are polydimensional in some representational form. As I point out later, children need to have the competence or the skill in order to understand the representational form of the problem before they can proceed to solve it. It is this competence that determines their entry into a problem-solving attitude that is consistent with that of the examiner, that is, their knowledge of what problem is to be solved. To be sure, there are moderators of task performance, such as attention, motivation, and knowledge level, that also underlie the primary prerequisite for problem solving—the competence to engage in representational thinking.

### Instructions as a Source of Influence in Performance

In a conservation training study my colleagues and I discovered that children had difficulty in conserving mass, weight, and volume (Griffiths, Shantz, & Sigel, 1967). After each transformation of the materials, we always asked whether there was now more, less, or the same mass, weight, or volume as in the pretransformation situation. Many of the children failed and hence were classified as "nonconservers." Because this result was consistent with the literature, we accepted our findings and proceeded to assign the children to the various training groups in the experiment. In pretesting our training sessions,

---

[4]Recent studies have found, contrary to previous perspectives, that young infants at birth show individual differences in competencies that form the bases for subsequent representational thinking. The interested reader is referred to the summary in Pribram (1971), Bever (1982), and Trevarthen (1982).

we discovered serendipitously that a few did not understand the term *less*, but they all understood terms such as *not as much*, or *more*, or some common synonym for less. We then proceeded to replicate the experiment with the new, revised questions and discovered that most children could solve the problem. The nonconservers immediately manifested conservation and became conservers—and with no training. However, we discovered that the reason those children had difficulty to begin with was because they did not understand some of the terms in the questions we asked.

Instructions also play an important role when working with free sorting tasks in which children are asked to classify items. When children were given an array of familiar materials and asked to group them on the basis of things that are alike or almost alike, many groupings were made on the basis of some aspect of the objects that were identical, such as color or shape. However, when the instructions were modified and the children were asked to group on the basis of things that belonged together, or went together in some way, more grouping were constructed on the basis of relationships. Thus, the type of classifications made was not independent of the instructions. Yet, in common parlance we often use *go together* as equivalent to *the same*, or *similar to*, or *alike*. These terms are used interchangeably although we know that each of these terms does have a different meaning. Asking children to sort items on the basis of similarity yields different results than when they are asked to sort on the basis of belongingness.

## The Role of Materials

The primary experience that initiated the study of representational competence was the observation that impoverished children created different groupings when employing three-dimensional materials than when employing two-dimensional pictures of these same materials. Interestingly enough, the children did not have difficulty labeling the pictures, but they did have difficulty treating them as representative of the same class of instances as the three-dimensional objects.

Some years ago, Patricia Olmsted and I (Olmsted & Sigel, 1970) set out to study whether materials and format influenced classification behavior among young preschool children. We used the problem of determining the generality of color–form preferences as a prototype problem to test the generality of the preference. We administered several color–form tasks to the same group of Black, low-income boys and girls ranging in age from 61 to 76 months. The tasks included one using geometric forms and another using familiar objects. Using a match to standard procedure we discovered that the mode of response varied with the task. It was concluded that generalization for color–form dominance varied with task.

David Bearison and I (Bearison & Sigel, 1968) did a similar study varying the materials in a more controlled way. We also included "representational meaning'' in addition to color and form. We found that there was a hierarchy of choices, with meaning or familiarity being the most preferred, then form, and then color. No significant findings were found for age or grade.

Not only did we do performance differences for tasks of individual performance, but we also found that strategies parents use in teaching their children vary with the task. For example, when parents teach their preschool children a structured task they use different strategies than when they teach an unstructured task. The strategies are applicable to either task—for example, asking questions, giving directions, telling the child what to do. It became clear that different tasks require different cognitive functions to complete. Thus, generalizations of parental teaching strategies are constrained by the types of tasks used in elicit such behaviors.

Another illustration of format effects is evidenced in a study of classification (Sigel, 1953): In one condition, classes were constructed by the examiner, and children were asked to label the classes in question; in the other condition, the free sort condition, the children themselves determined the classes. It was found consistently that children did less well when the examiner made the sort than when the child did. The issue is one of knowing the implications of these differences in performance. The children's responses in this study were consistent with what Bearison and I had found (Bearison & Sigel, 1968); when color or form is pitted against meaningfulness or familiarity, meaningful and familiar items win out. In essence, the content of the item defines the type of response in classification tasks.

## The Role of Context in Assessment

An example that takes the context into account is provided in Sigel (1974). Preschool children were administered items from the *Bailey Test* by a familiar examiner in a quiet, familiar room. One item involved number concepts 2, 3, and 4, understanding of propositions, and remembering commands. The children did very poorly. The teachers claimed that these results were invalid. To check this out we tested the children in the classroom, sitting around a table with a basket of crackers in the center. Each child was asked, one at a time, to pass one, two, or three crackers to the child next to him or her. The number game was played until every child had a chance to demonstrate at least one problem in each of these categories. In this context, children did not fail any of the items. One might argue that they copied from each other, but because they were given different problems, they had nothing to "copy." If anything, they simply figured out what was required when asked to pass or take back some crackers. My point is that the results from this group-type assessment yield far different results form the standardized test procedures. Why? In part, the notational system and the actions asked for resembled each other more.

One implication of these observations is that performance may be influenced by the representational form of these tasks. For example, verbal analogies might have different cognitive demand qualities than nonverbal analogies and so performance on one might be influenced because of an ability problem. Usually in the assessment tasks responses are either right or wrong with no allowance for interpretation of the item. This is especially the case in multiple-choice tests. When used with children, the items assess the adult's conception of the right answer and do not reflect the possibility that the child may work with a different logic. Thus, the test is assessing the degree to which the child's logic conforms to the adult logic rather than the child's way of thinking. If this is the case, the meaning of the response has to be reconsidered. A correct answer is an index to the child's conformity to adult standards and does not reveal the process of the child's thought, whereas a wrong answer has a more ambiguous meaning, because it may reflect a lack of knowledge, a lack of understanding of the question or an instance of a child's logic. Is this not the issue that Piaget initially confronted when he worked in the laboratory of Simon and Binet? (See Chapman, 1988.)

## ALTERNATIVE ASSESSMENT PROCEDURES
## FOR REPRESENTATIONAL COMPETENCE

Assuming that assessment procedures generally tap into a relatively narrow band of competence, it behooves us to create tasks that evaluate the individual's performance more broadly, thus controlling for the bias created by the choice of representational mode of the test. Oltman (1983) addressed the issue succinctly when he wrote:

> Symbol systems differ in the kinds of mental skills they invoke in translation. To the extent that symbol systems require more or less mental translation, and to the extent that the skills invoked during the translation to an internal representation differ qualitatively, the knowledge acquisition outcomes can be expected to vary as well. (p. 1)

Applying Oltman's assertion to the test batteries such as the *Wechsler–Bellvue* or the *Stanford–Binet*, it becomes clear that performance on these tasks reflects not only content performance, but also comprehension of the representational semiotic system, along with the operations required. For example, solving an arithmetic problem requires mental operations different from performance. If Oltman is correct, different notational systems require different mental transformations to convert an external depiction or presentation of a problem into an internal representation. It follows that the individual has to proceed to execute relevant mental operations on the representations. For example, students in algebra classes are often asked to translate verbal problems into algebraic equations. It has been reported that the students find it easier to use algebraic notations in solving problems than in solving word problems requiring identical operations (Lochhead, 1980). Why the difficulty? One reason is that the different notational systems place different operational demands on the cognitive system. The encoding process, coupled with the internal representational process, is not equal for each of the two notational systems.

To assess representational competence would require extending the number of tasks and varying the test format. An example might be one suggested by my colleague, Richard Lesh, when he offered an example wherein an individual was asked, "Show me how many ways you can depict one-third." Each depiction is a transformation, and converting one notational system from another reveals a *conservation of meaning* that reflects a true understanding of the idea and notational systems as representations (Lesh & Hamilton, 1983).

The assessment of representational competence requires the construction of a mental model that takes into account the following features: the type of notational system in which the knowledge to be assimilated is presented, the developmental level of the subject involved, the available knowledge or the cognitive structure operating at the time of the presentation, and the rate and quality of knowledge assimilation. The level of representational competence is revealed to the degree the respondent shows an understanding that the meaning of the instance of the concept in question is conserved in spite of different notational presentations.

Two bodies of knowledge are relevant for our discussions of the assessment of representational competence. One is the literature on problem solving and the other is on communication. In the case of problem solving, assessment involves presenting the individual with a specific "problem" to be solved. The problem presented is in some representational, notational system.[5] So, the immediate task for the subject is to encode the problem.

*Alternatives for Children.*   The usual assessment situation with young children is a one-on-one setting with an adult examiner and a child. In most of the tasks employed the examiner asked questions and the child was expected to produce a response. To do this the child has to share the semantic system of the examiner. As implied earlier, the degree to which the meaning of the instructions is shared by the examiner and the child poses a persistent problem; whether the child's response is an indicator of competence in solving the problem

---

[5]The particular notational system as used in the arts or music is conceptualized in the same genre as language, but is not addressed in detail here, because it is beyond the scope of this chapter. However, it should be made clear that notational systems in these areas follow the same principles of shared meaning and of the awareness that the notational form can represent experience. The degree to which the experience is shared is another issue, because different types of art and music are more or less abstract and probably more or less subject to idiosyncratic representation.

in general or in solving the problem when structured in this particular way. In addition, the tasks may have been sufficiently different in spite of our definition that there was little consistency among them. Perhaps instead of using a question-and-answer format, alternatives could be constructed enabling the child to employ different symbol systems. For example, to apply Lesh's example to children, instead of asking children how much is "one half," they might be asked to produce as many ways as they can to illustrate "one half." This strategy empowers them to produce their own ranges of meanings for the same concept. Of course, the issue of comprehending the instructions still exists, but this is an intrinsic problem that is always with us and the challenge is to minimize its potential confounding effect. As the children proceed to demonstrate the different ways of expressing one half, they are presenting different symbols or signs. In tasks proposed, the more extensive the list of options is, the more children would seem to be able to understand the meaning of "one half." The number of alternatives produced may be an indicator of the degree to which the individual understands the representational rule. The number of options produced may be an index of representational competence.

To check for the degree children can transcend the concrete and passive presentation of such a problem, it might be possible to give them a set of items in which "one half" is presented in different representational modes. If the children are able to perform equally well on both sets of materials, there is good reason to believe that they are operating on a notion of "one half," independent of the format, the instructions, or the context of the problem. In this way, an index of understanding can be established.

I believe that the challenge is to construct tests or tasks in which the same basic problem is presented in different symbol systems, but with increasing difficulty. In this fashion, the basic competence can be assessed taking into account the influence of representational elements. The category breadth in this instance may also be a good index of representational competence, because the child is doing a number of mental transformations, demonstrating general cognitive competence.

One contribution of this approach to the understanding of cognitive development is that children's understanding of the representational systems can be an index of cognitive maturity. The assumption is that a greater awareness of the representational rule will make children more effective problem solvers. However, they have to acquire more experience and more knowledge in order to perform competently. That is, children may be unable to solve problems because of either a lack of knowledge or of operational skill. In either case, a lack of representational competence will result. In summary, assessments of representational competence are possible if we create a conceptual structure from which to derive our formats, materials, constructions, and categories representing processes employed in problem solving.

## CONCLUSIONS

The basic argument in this chapter is that representational competence undergirds cognitive functioning in a complex technological-industrial society. The mission of research into cognitive development and cognitive function is to understand the basic proposition that to be representationally competent is to be a human symbol-using organism, and by virtue of that competence, to acquire knowledge. However, the question of what knowledge is acquired and how it is used and organized leads to another critical set of dimensions— value and affect. Discussion of the role of these two dimensions is beyond the scope of this chapter, but it is assumed that they are subject to many of the same rules described in relation to *representational competence*. If this be reductio ad absurdum, so be it.

## ACKNOWLEDGMENTS

I would like to acknowledge the thoughtful, constructive comments of Henry Braun, Drew Gitomer, Richard Lesh, Brian Vandenberg, and James Wertsch. Thanks to the editors for thoughtful reactions. My gratitude to Linda Kozelski for her careful work in preparing this manuscript.

## REFERENCES

*American Heritage dictionary of the English Language* (2nd college ed.). (1982). Boston: Houghton-Mifflin.

Arnheim, R. (1969). *Visual thinking*. London: Farber & Farber.

Bearison, D. J., & Sigel, I. E. (1968). Hierarchical attributes for categorization. *Perceptual and Motor Skills, 27*, 147–153.

Bever, T. G. (Ed.). (1982). *Regressions in mental development: Basic phenomena and theories*. Hillsdale: NJ: Lawrence Erlbaum Associates.

Bower, T. G. R. (1989). *The rational infant: Learning in infancy*. New York: Freeman.

Chapman, M. (1988). *Constructive evolution: Origins and development of Piaget's thought*. Cambridge, England: Cambridge University Press.

Chomsky, N. (1965). *Aspects of the theory of syntax*. Cambridge, MA: MIT Press.

Cocking, R. R., & Chipman, S. (1988). Conceptual issues related to mathematics achievement of language minority children. In R. R. Cocking & J. P. Mestre (Eds.), *Linguistic and cultural influences on learning mathematics* (pp. 17–46). Hillsdale, NJ: Lawrence Erlbaum Associates.

Cohen, L. B., & Gelber, E. R. (1975). Infant visual memory. In L. B. Cohen & P. Salapatek (Eds.), *Infant perception: From sensation to cognition, Vol. 1: Basic visual processes* (pp. 347–403). New York: Academic Press.

Davidson, J. E., & Sternberg, R. J. (1985). Competence and performance in intellectual development. In E. D. Neimark, R. De Lisi, & J. L. Newman (Eds.), *Moderators of competence* (pp. 43–76). Hillsdale, NJ: Lawrence Erlbaum Associates.

Flavell, J. H., & Wohlwill, J. F. (1969). Formal and functional aspects of cognitive development. In D. Elkind & J. H. Flavell (Eds.), *Studies in cognitive development* (pp. 67–120). New York: Oxford University Press.

Griffiths, J. A., Shantz, C. U., & Sigel, I. E. (1967). A methodological problem in conservation studies: The use of relational terms. *Child Development, 38,* 841–848.

Halford, G. S. (1982). *The development of thought.* Hillsdale, NJ: Lawrence Erlbaum Associates.

Lesh, R., & Hamilton, E. (1983). Conceptual models and applied mathematical problem-solving research. In R. Lesh & M. Landau (Eds.), *Acquisition of mathematics concepts and processes* (pp. 263–343). New York: Academic Press.

Lochhead, J. (1980). Faculty interpretations of simple algebraic statements: The professor's side of the equation. *Journal of Mathematical Behavior, 3,* 29–37.

Mandler, J. M. (1983). Representation. In P. H. Mussen (Ed.), *Handbook of child psychology* (4th ed., pp. 420–494). New York: Wiley.

McGillicuddy-DeLisi, A. V., DeLisi, R., Flaugher, J., & Sigel, I. E. (1987). Familial influences on planning. In S. L. Friedman, E. K. Scholnick, & R. R. Cocking (Eds.), *Blueprints for thinking: The role of planning in cognitive development* (pp. 395–427). New York: Cambridge University Press.

Morris, C. (1946). *Signs, language and behavior.* New York: Braziller.

Olmsted, P., & Sigel, I. E. (1970). The generality of color-form preference as a function of materials and task requirements among lower-class Negro children. *Child Development, 41*(4), 1025–1032.

Oltman, P. K. (1983). *Cognitive assessment and the media.* (College Board Rep. No. 83–1). New York: College Entrance Examination Board.

Ortony, A. (Ed.). (1979). *Metaphor and thought.* Cambridge: Cambridge University Press.

Overton, W. F., & Newman, J. L. (1982). Cognitive development: A competence-activation/utilization approach. In T. Field, A. Houston, H. Quay, L. Troll, & G. Findley (Eds.), *Review of human development* (pp. 217–241). New York: Wiley.

Pepper, S. C. (1942). *World hypotheses: A study in evidence.* Berkeley, CA: University of California Press.

Piaget, J. (1962). *Play, dreams and imitation in childhood.* New York: Norton.

Piaget, J. (1970). Piaget's theory. In P. H. Mussen (Ed.), *Manual of child psychology* (Vol. 1, 3rd ed., pp. 703–732). New York: Wiley.

Polanyi, M. (1958). *Personal knowledge.* Chicago: The University of Chicago Press.

Pribram, K. H. (1971). *Language of the brain: Experimental paradoxes and principles in neuropsychology.* Englewood Cliffs, NJ: Prentice-Hall.

Senden, M. von. (1960). *Space and sight: The perception of space and shape in the congenitally blind before and after operation* (P. Heath, Trans.). Glencoe, IL: The Free Press. (Original work published 1932)

Sigel, I. E. (1953). Developmental trends in the abstraction ability of children. *Child Development, 24*(2), 131–144.

Sigel, I. E. (1974). When do we know what a child knows? *Human Development, 17,* 201–217.

Sigel, I. E. (1978). The development of pictorial comprehension. In B. S. Randhawa & W. E. Coffman (Ed.), *Visual learning, thinking, and communication* (pp. 93–111). New York: Academic Press.

Sigel, I. E. (1982). The relationship between parental distancing strategies and the child's cognitive behavior. In L. M. Laosa & I. E. Sigel (Eds.), *Families as learning environments for children* (pp. 47–86). New York: Plenum.

Sigel, I. E. (Ed.). (1985). *Parental belief systems: The psychological consequences for children.* Hillsdale, NJ: Lawrence Erlbaum Associates.

Sigel, I. E., Anderson, L. M., & Shapiro, H. (1966). Categorization behavior of lower and middle class Negro preschool children: Differences in dealing with representation of familiar objects. *Journal of Negro Education, 35,* 218–229.

Sigel, I. E., & Cocking, R. R. (1977). Cognition and communication: A dialectic paradigm for development. In M. Lewis & L. A. Rosenblum (Eds.), *The origins of behavior: Vol. 5. Interaction conversation, and the development of language* (pp. 207–226). New York: Wiley.

Sigel, I. E., & McBane, B. (1967). Cognitive competence and level of symbolization among five-year-old children. In J. Hellmuth (Ed.), *The disadvantaged child* (Vol. 1, pp. 433–453). Seattle, WA: Special Child Publications of the Seattle Sequin School.

Sigel, I. E., & Olmsted, P. (1970a). The development of classification and representational competence. In A. J. Biemiller (Ed.), *Problems in the teaching of young children* (pp. 49–67). Ontario, Canada: The Ontario Institute for Studies in Education.

Sigel, I. E., & Olmsted, P. (1970b). Modification of cognitive skills among lower-class black children. In J. Hellmuth (Ed.), *The disadvantaged child* (Vol. 3, pp. 300–338). New York: Brunner-Mazel.

Sigel, I. E., Stinson, E. T., & Flaugher, J. (in press). the distancing model: A paradigm for studying parental influences on children's cognitive development. In R. J. Sternberg & L. Okagaki (Eds.), *Directors of development: Influences on the development of children's thinking.* Hillsdale, NJ: Lawrence Erlbaum Associates.

Trevarthen, C. (1982). Basic patterns of psychogenetic change in infancy. In T. G. Bever (Ed.), *Regressions in mental development: Basic phenomena and theories* (pp. 7–46). Hillsdale, NJ: Lawrence Erlbaum Associates.

Werner, H., & Kaplan, B. (1963). *Symbol formation: An organismic developmental approach to language and the expression of thought.* New York: Wiley.

Wertsch, J. V. (1985). *Vygotsky and the social formation of mind.* Cambridge, MA: Harvard University Press.

# Chapter 10

# The Epistemic Triangle: Operative and Communicative Components of Cognitive Competence

Michael Chapman
*University of British Columbia*

Determining at what points in development children and other developing organisms acquire particular competencies would appear to be the least of the tasks with which developmental psychologists might be charged (Chandler & Chapman, this volume). In fact, controversies regarding the "true ages" at which various competencies develop have been among the most intractable of disputes in the history of research in child development. Such disputes typically have been debated in terms of measurement issues, beginning with the claim that refined methods enable the investigator to detect the competence in question at an earlier point in development. However, decades of methodological refinements have not succeeded in resolving the issues. Instead, the debate has become stuck on questions of measurement validity: whether successful performance on a given task in fact reflects the intended comeptence or something else entirely. The fact that investigators cannot agree on what is actually measured with different procedures is perhaps an indication that they differ, not merely on questions of appropriate methodology, but in their very conceptualizations of the competencies in question. In this chapter, this argument is pursued in the context of disputes regarding the validity of verbal explanations as criteria for cognitive competence.

Since the publication of Braine's (1959) influential monograph on nonverbal methods in Piagetian research, the predominant view has been that verbal explanations are highly suspect as indicators of children's reasoning abilities and should be replaced whenever possible by procedures involving a minimum of verbal content. Piaget's "clinical method" has been a frequent target of such criticisms because of its reliance on verbal questioning. Typically, researchers using nonverbal or judgments-only response criteria have found children to pass Piagetian reasoning tasks at an earlier age than have researchers using more traditional verbal methods. These results have been interpreted as indicating that verbal methods are a powerful source of false negative measurement error and inevitably result in a significant underestimation of children's true abilities (Brainerd, 1973; Gruen, 1966; Siegel, 1978).

Such claims have not gone unchallenged, but most parties on both sides of the issue have shared the following assumptions: (a) that the competencies of interest in studies of children's reasoning are the cognitive processes by which correct judgments are obtained; (b) that those processes are functionally prior to, and independent of the ability to provide verbal explanations; and (c) that verbal explanations are of value only insofar as they reflect the cognitive processes leading to the original judgments. Thus, verbal explanations are judged to be valid response criteria to the extent that one credits children with the ability to report accurately on their own cognitive processes. Alternative response criteria are favored to the extent that one doubts this ability.

But those assumptions are not self-evident. When we ask someone, "How do you know?", we are typically asking for a *justification* of a particular judgment, not for an introspective report on its psychological antecedents. Against the assumptions stated in the preceding paragraph, the following arguments are advanced: (a) that children's explanations of their judgments on reasoning tasks should be considered as attempts at justification, rather than as introspective reports on their own cognitive processes; (b) that children's justifications are of considerable theoretical interest as such, not merely as clues to the processes by which their judgments were obtained; and (c) that the relation between children's justifications and such prior cognitive processes is an important theoretical and empirical problem, not an a priori given.

In order better to understand the relation between children's verbal justifications and their intrapsychic cognitive processes, the role of communication in cognitive development must be reconsidered. First, the relation between operative and communicative aspects of cognitive competence is discussed with respect to the development of cognitive representation and concrete operations. Then, the argument is advanced that Piaget neglected to specify the relation between language and the development of operational thought. An attempt is made to remedy this neglect with the help of Gal'perin's (1969) theory of mental acts, and an illustrative example of the type of research suggested by the present approach is provided. Finally, the conclusion is drawn that "verbal" and "nonverbal" assessment procedures should not be considered as alternative criteria for the same cognitive competence, but as complementary criteria for different aspects of an expanded notion of cognitive competence.

## PIAGET AND THE EPISTEMIC TRIANGLE

Piaget's use of verbal explanations as criteria for cognitive competence in children has been criticized mainly on the grounds that verbal explanations have no place in his theoretical definitions of the competencies in question (Brainerd, 1973). For example, he defined concrete operations in terms of the grouping structures by which interiorized actions are intercoordinated (Piaget, 1947/1950), but gave no detailed account of how such grouping structures are reflected in the verbal justifications used to identify concrete operational thinking. This gap between the structural theory and verbal method has been labeled a *paradox* in Piagetian theory (Siegel, 1978).

Significantly, Piaget's first two books, *The Language and Thought of the Child* (1923/1955) and *Judgment and Reasoning in the Child* (1924/1928), were devoted in part to the study of children's understanding of justification. Briefly, the development of justification in children's arguments and in their responses to questioning by adults was found to coincide with the decline of egocentric speech around the age of 7–8 years. Both trends were said to result from children's communicative interactions. Justification developed from the desire to convince others of one's own viewpoint, and ''logical'' justification in particular from the attempt to avoid contradiction among opposing views. Following the formulation of the theory of concrete operations, Piaget wrote that he had overestimated the importance of linguistic factors in his early work (e.g., Piaget, 1954/1973). Through his observations of sensorimotor development, he had come to see that the roots of logical thought and the sense of necessity lay deeper than language, in the coordination of interiorized actions. Yet he continued to rely on children's verbal justifications as criteria for concrete operational thought. To some observers, his methods now seemed to be inconsistent with his theory (Braine, 1959; Brainerd, 1973).

However, this anomaly can be resolved through a closer integration of Piaget's early research on children's communication and his later work on concrete operations. In criticizing Piaget's *The Language and Thought of the Child*, Vygotsky (1934/1986) remarked that Piaget derived children's development purely from interpersonal dialogue; what was missing was the relation between the child and reality. In contrast, Piaget's later theory has often been criticized for its emphasis on subject–object interaction to the exclusion of interpersonal interaction (Cohen, 1983; Suarez, 1980; Wallon, 1947). The substance of both criticisms can be addressed simultaneously in the proposal that human knowing involves an irreducible *epistemic triangle*, consisting of an active subject, the object of knowledge, and a (real or implicit) interlocutor, together with their mutual relations (Fig. 10.1). Both the subject and the interlocutor have direct acquaintance with the object by virtue of their respective *operative* interactions with it, and they acquire knowledge of each other (and each other's

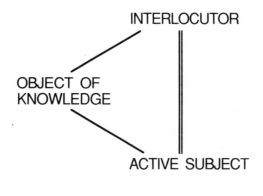

FIG. 10.1.   The epistemic triangle.

experience) through *communicative* interaction (cf. Habermas, 1982). Further, the ability of agents to communicate with each other by means of a semiotic system such as language allows them to exchange knowledge of the object as well as to coordinate their actions in *cooperative* action. In what follows, the argument is advanced that although Piaget recognized the importance of both operative and communicative forms of interaction in various phases of his work, he never integrated those components in a single model. In particular, communicative interaction was addressed in some detail only in his early work in the 1920s and was relatively neglected in his work on operational thought after 1940.

The notion of the epistemic triangle preserves the insight common to Piaget and other pragmatically oriented epistemologists that knowledge is based on action. The further distinction between operative and communicative forms of interaction is intended to illuminate the role of symbolic or semiotic mediation (Mead, 1934/1962; Peirce, 1955; Vygotsky, 1978) alongside object-oriented action, without reducing either one to the other. According to the model, operative and communicative forms of interaction are partially independent and partially interdependent processes. They are independent insofar as a person may have operative understanding without sufficient means for communicating this understanding, or conversely, forms of communication for which one has insufficient operative understanding. But this independence is limited: A certain level of operative understanding might be necessary for, or conducive to a certain level of communicative competence, and vice versa (e.g., see Beilin, 1975, on possible two-way relations between language and operational thought). In short, the epistemic triangle is a total system with interacting operative and communicative subsystems.

In order to gain a better understanding of the relations between operative and communicative forms of interaction, a closer look at the defining concepts is necessary. The term *operative* is taken from the verb "to operate," meaning to exert force or influence, to produce something or to perform some work (L. *operari*). Operative interaction between the subject and the object involves an asymmetric relation between subject and object insofar as their respective contributions are fundamentally different, but complementary. The subject acts on the object with some expectation of the resulting effects. The object's contribution to the interaction is in the extent to which it conforms to the subject's expectations or not. Knowledge of the object is constructed from the pattern of confirmed and discomfirmed expectations.

Operative interaction can be divided into two general subtypes. *Instrumental* interaction (cf. Habermas, 1982) is action undertaken in pursuit of an intended goal. As such, it involves the coordination of means and ends; something is done in order that something else should be achieved. The object enters into the interaction either as part of the means or as part of the goal. In Piagetian terms, instrumental interaction first develops in the interval from sensorimotor Stage 2 to Stage 4, as infants gradually begin to differentiate means and ends in action and, eventually, to coordinate them. Later, instrumental interaction becomes mediated by language and the semiotic function. At every level of development, knowledge of the object is acquired incidentally in the wider context of goal attainment. In contrast, *experimental* interaction is undertaken for the main purpose of discovering something new about the object. This purpose is fulfilled by acting systematically on the object in various ways and observing how the latter reacts in each case. In Piagetian terms, experimental interaction first manifests itself in the tertiary circular reactions of sensorimotor Stage 5, and its scope is vastly extended through the development of language and cognitive representation.

In contrast to the asymmetry of operative interaction, communicative interaction between two subjects or interlocutors is symmetric in the sense that both participants are potentially capable of taking the same active roles in turn. In the terminology of Mead (1934/1962), communication presupposes that the would-be interlocutors share a common repertoire of "significant gestures" capable of evoking the same meanings in both participants. Such gestures are "significant" insofar as they are used to "stand for" things beyond themselves, including objects, situations, other actions, states of mind, or anything else. The purposes served by the exchange of significant gestures are as multifarious of the "language-games" described by Wittgenstein (1958/1968).

The foregoing conceptualization of communicative interaction as an exchange of significant gestures exceeds the ethological conception of "communication" as a form of influence that one organism's behavior has on that of others (Wilson, 1975). In the ethological sense, human infants "communicate" with others in their environments from the moment of birth. However, the

ability to communicate intentionally by means of significant gestures develops
only gradually during the first 2 years of life. The first step in its development
might be called one of *communion*: infants' discovery of what they have in common with other persons. From the beginning, one must assume that interaction with persons represents a very different experience for infants than interaction with physical objects. Not only are persons quite literally "livelier" than
objects, but evidence suggests that infants might be born with some pre-tuned
sensitivities for the particular sights and sounds presented by human interaction partners (Cole & Cole, 1989). However, what interests young infants most
about other human beings, according to Watson (1972), is their ability to play
"the game"—that is, to engage in sustained contingent interaction. Because
of the infants' limited sensorimotor competence, their contributions to such
interactions differ from those of adults. Therefore, what they experience themselves as sharing with their interaction partners is not particular action patterns, but the more general capacity for contingent interaction and the affective accompaniments of such mutually coordinated activity. Such exchanges
of action and affect have been labelled "primary intersubjectivity" by Trevarthen (1989).

In time, the "game" of contingent interaction becomes more symmetrical
as infants acquire the ability to *imitate* the specific actions of their interaction
partners (Piaget, 1945/1962a). To focus on the development of imitation alone,
however, is to obscure other aspects of the context of contingent interaction
in which imitation occurs. Infants' "imitative" actions are not merely attempts
to recreate the actions of others, but also efforts at influencing the others' actions. Thus, they acquire an awareness of sharing, not only the specific actions, but also the intentions of others. In the context of the imitative "game,"
infants perform particular actions as a means of signalling to their partners
that they wish them to act in a similar manner, and their partners' actions
are understood in the same way. A new level of intersubjectivity is reached
in which the communion between infant and adult is extended to include the
mutual recognition of intention. However, the gestures that are exchanged at
this level are still relatively undifferentiated from what they are intended to
signify; the gesture of one partner "refers" only to another gesture of the same
kind, to be enacted by the other partner to the dialogue.

At the next level, gestures are not merely shared with the partner; they also
begin to be used to refer to things beyond themselves. The dialogue of gestures
is no longer as symmetrical as it was in imitation; the significant gesture now
can be used to evoke a response from the partner that is different in kind from
the gesture itself. For example, Vygotsky (1981) believed that *indication* was
the most fundamental function of human semiotic systems. In indicating, or
calling attention to something, one person's gesture (e.g., pointing or showing) is intended to evoke a different kind of response (e.g., looking at the object so indicated). The *referential* character of indication is even more striking

in the case of language. Thus, Piaget (1945/1962a) described Jacqueline at 13 months using the sound "*tch tch*" to indicate a passing train. The onomatopoeic character of this word suggests its transitional character between imitation and referential communication. In such cases, the verbal gesture imitates the *object*, but its intended meaning for the partner is no longer imitative, but indicative.

It should be clear from such examples that in referential communication, all the pieces of the epistemic triangle are in place. As Peirce (1955) pointed out, signification has an irreducible triadic structure involving the sign itself, the object signified, and the effect of the sign for an interpreting consciousness (the interpretant). It follows that the epistemic structure of signification is also irreducibly triadic in form. In order for one person to communicate with another about something else, the partners to the interaction must share a repertoire of significant gestures as well as a minimal acquaintance with the domain of reference. This is not to say that communication is always successful, nor that the knowledge of the two partners regarding the domain of reference is necessarily equal. One of the common goals of communication is the transmission of knowledge from one person to another. To communicate in this sense is to *make common* (L. *communicare*). Such epistemic communication is common between adults and children precisely because their respective knowledge of the world is unequal. But any such communication of knowledge presupposes that the recipient knows at least enough about the domain of reference to understand the other's referential intent. The epistemic triangle is irreducibly triadic, because referential communication between two persons by means of a shared semiotic system depends on some shared acquaintance with the object of reference, but also because each person's acquaintance with the object becomes enriched by the ways in which the object is understood in terms of the semiotic system. The developmental step between sensorimotor intelligence and representational intelligence in the second year of life is precisely of this nature; objects and events previously known only in terms of children's action schemes now become known as the material components of emerging language games.

The purpose of tracing the development of operative and communicative forms of interaction during the sensorimotor period is to point out that, although Piaget studied most of the developmental components of the epistemic triangle (e.g., operative interaction, imitation, the "semiotic function"), he did not see them as integral parts of a total system with an irreducible triadic structure. His account of the semiotic function was essentially dualistic; he described sensorimotor development in terms of a gradual differentiation between the "signifier" and the "signified" (Piaget, 1936/1963). What is missing in his account is a recognition that the "signifier" itself acquires a dyadic relational structure in the process. The fully differentiated signifier is a gesture that possesses a meaning shared both by the actor and the interpreter. What is differentiated during the course of sensorimotor development is not merely the Saus-surean dyad of signifier and signified, but the Peircean triad of sign (signifier), object (signified), and *interpretant* (the "significance" of the signifier *for* the interpreter).

Piaget's neglect of the triadic structure of representational intelligence had important implications for his account of later development. He described knowledge and development solely as products of subject–object interaction without elucidating the intersubjective dimension between subjects. In the fol-lowing section, the significance of this point is pursued in connection with the development of concrete operations.

## FROM COGNITIVE REPRESENTATION
## TO CONCRETE OPERATIONS

According to Piaget (1952), the study of sensorimotor development led him to revise his earlier overemphasis on the role of language in the development of thought and to develop instead the theory of concrete operations as a product of the interiorization and intercoordination of action. Most of Piaget's writ-ings on concrete operations (e.g., Piaget, 1947/1950) lead one to identify oper-ational thought solely with the interiorization and structural coordination of operative (i.e., object-oriented) action. But if both operative and communica-tive action are components of a single system, then one might expect that the development of concrete operations would involve them both in some capaci-ty. In this view, it is significant that the early Piaget found egocentric speech to decline and the understanding of justification to emerge at roughly the same point in development that he later found concrete operations and the sense of necessity to appear. The question is whether the processes presumed to un-derly these two developmental events are in any way related. As previously indicated, Piaget explained the development of concrete operations as a process of interiorization (and intercoordination) of actions. What about the decline of egocentrism?

Taking a cue from Vygotsky (1934/1986), egocentric speech can be inter-preted as an intermediate phase in the interiorization of communicative ac-tion. The original function of language is communicative. The self-directed character of egocentric speech is a reflexive application of the communicative function. According to Vygotsky's account, reflective thought develops from the interiorization of egocentric speech as the phonetic aspect of such speech gradually drops out and leaves a purely semantic component behind. The decline of egocentric speech found by Piaget in the early school-age years thus can be interpreted as an indication that the interiorization of communicative action is more or less complete by that time. Significantly, Piaget (1962b) af-firmed his "complete agreement" with Vygotsky's thesis that reflective thought is the interiorized product of egocentric speech. As pointed out by Wertsch (1985), the apparent differences between Vygotsky and Piaget on this point hinge in large part on their different uses of the terms *social* and *socialized*. Contrary to Vygotsky's (1934/1986) interpretation, Piaget never doubted that language was *social* from the beginning, in the sense that children intended to communicate with others through speech. But he still believed that language and thought became progressively *socialized* during the preschool years, in the sense that children became better able to understand, to represent, and to anticipate other points of view in speaking (see Piaget, 1962b).

So the development of concrete operations and the decline of egocentric speech both result from interiorization: concrete operations from the interiorization of operative interaction and the decline of egocentric speech from the interiorization of communicative interaction (i.e., speech itself). But the question still remains whether these two processes are at all related to each other.

Piaget's occasional writings on the relation between language and thought (e.g., Piaget, 1954/1967, 1954/1973) are suggestive, but hardly definitive. His main point is clear enough: Language is not sufficient for the development of operational thought. As usual, his major concerns were epistemological in nature; he sought to oppose conventionalist interpretations of operational thinking with his own constructivism. Thus, he argued that logical thinking cannot be acquired ready-made by means of language, but is constructed instead by means of the interiorization of actions and their structural intercoordination. A central piece of evidence for this argument was the fact that a "logic of action" can be discerned in the organization of sensorimotor schemes prior to the development of language. The implication is that logical thought develops in a similar manner, through the organization of *interiorized* actions (i.e., operations).

Because this model of the development of operational thinking makes no reference to language, one could interpret it as an argument for the independence of language and logical thought. But Piaget also insisted in these essays that language is *necessary* for operational thinking, even if it is not *sufficient*. Language is necessary for the construction of a logical operations, (a) because without language the operations would not be regulated by interpersonal exchange and cooperation, and (b) because without the semiotic system of language the operations would remain successive actions without being integrated into systems of simultaneous transformations (Piaget, 1954/1967). The first of these reasons is a restatement of Piaget's well-known view that children's thinking becomes decentered in being confronted with other points of view; communication by means of language simply facilitates this process (see also Piaget, 1954/1973). The second reason, however, is somewhat cryptic. For Piaget, operational thinking involves the *simultaneous* coordination of internalized actions, as opposed to the *successive* coordinations of actions characterizing sensorimotor intelligence and "intuitive" thought (see Chapman, 1987,

1988). To affirm the *necessary* role of language in the process by which successive actions become integrated into "systems of simultaneous transformations" (i.e., operational structures) is therefore to accord it considerable importance in the development of operational thought.

Thus, the standard interpretation—that Piaget viewed the relation between thought and language as that between an independent and a dependent variable (Brainerd, 1973; Flavell, 1963)—must be rejected as too simplistic. Piaget granted language in its semiotic function a more important role in cognitive development then is generally realized. The point is easily overlooked, because he was more concerned to point out the insufficiency of language for operational thought than its necessity and because he never explained just *how* language played its essential role in the development of operations.

In this connection, Gal'perin's (1969) theory of the development of "mental acts" is instructive. Reflecting the long-standing interest of Soviet developmental psychologists in the relation between thought and language, Gal'perin argued that speech appeared to function as an "auxilliary means" in the interiorization of action. Although actions may be represented in mental imagery, such dynamic images are not sufficient for transfering actions completely onto the cognitive plane because such imagined actions remain dependent on their concrete, material context. They are freed from the material context only through an intermediate step of being represented in audible, self-directed speech. Only by being so represented in speech do actions acquite abstract contents. As self-directed speech itself becomes internalized, such semiotically represented actions become fully interiorized.

Gal'perin's account suggests that the phenomena of "egocentric" speech and the interiorization of action, considered only separately by Piaget, in fact are intimately connected. The early Piaget found egocentric speech to decline at roughly the same age that he later found concrete operations to develop, because (a) the decline of egocentric speech is indicative of the internalization of speech (cf. Vygotsky, 1934/1986), (b) the internalization of self-directed speech is the means by which actions become fully interiorized, and (c) the interiorization of actions enables them to become integrated in operational structures. Because Piaget apparently considered egocentric speech merely as a manifestation of immature thought, the potentially positive contribution of self-directed speech for cognitive development generally has been ignored in the Piagetian research tradition. Only recently, Schmid-Schönbein (1988) suggested that the "action-accompanying speech" of children engaged in problem-solving tasks serves the structural function of making them simultaneously aware of different aspects of the situation and of the various consequences of their actions.

Gal'perin's theory also might provide an explanation for Piaget's otherwise cryptic statement that language is necessary for integrating actions into systems of simulaneous transformations. The fact that actions are carried out successively in time prevents them from being coordinated directly in systems of simultaneous transformations. Such coordinations become possible only through the medium of inner speech, because the semiotic representations acquired by actions through inner speech lack the temporal character of the actions themselves.

The overall point is that language may not be as unrelated to the development of concrete operations as it has appeared in most interpretations of Piagetian theory. Piaget himself affirmed a necessary role of language in operational thought, but neither explained nor justified it. Gal'perin's theory provides a possible model, insofar as speech is viewed as an essential means in the interiorization of action, one of the major processes involved in the development of concrete operations according to Piaget. In the terminology proposed in this chapter, concrete operations develop not merely through the interiorization of operative interaction, but through the interiorization of the epistemic triangle as a whole, including its communicative aspect. Operative interaction is interiorized in the form of "cognitive operations," and communicative action in the form of "semiotic mediation." Each component of the epistemic triangle acquires an interiorized aspect: The active subject becomes the agent both of cognitive operations directed at the interiorized object of knowledge and of communicative, semiotic exchanges with the interiorized interlocutor. In this view, such interiorized communicative exchange between the subject and the interiorized interlocutor is the origin of reflective awareness. The coordination of cognitive operations by the subject and the interlocutor is the source of the "operational compositions" that characterize concrete operations. Such coordinations are the interiorized counterpart of interpersonal cooperation (cf. Doise & Mugny, 1984).

## NECESSITY AND JUSTIFICATION

In addition to the role of language in the simultaneous coordination of operations, the other reason given by Piaget (1954/1967) for his assertion that language is necessary for operational thought was the fact that, without language, the operations would not be regulated by interpersonal exchange and cooperation. As he wrote elsewhere (Piaget, 1954/1973), the "conditions of communication" extend the process of equilibration and result in the "education" of thought and reasoning. These remarks may sound rather vague and abstract, but they nevertheless contain an elliptical reference to a central phenomenon that his theory was intended to explain: the understanding of logical necessity.

Two general approaches to the problem of logical necessity can be distinguished in Piaget's thinking, corresponding to the periods before and after the development of the theory of concrete operations. In his early work on children's language and reasoning, Piaget believed that the understanding and

use of logical justification (i.e., justification based on a sense of necessity) resulted from the interiorization of interpersonal argumentation (Piaget, 1924/1928).
From the confrontation with other points of view, children acquire the need
for justifying their own assertions. Logical justification based on a sense of necessity develops because it is presumably a form of justification valid for all: It
does not depend on the empirical contingencies of any particular point of view
(Piaget, 1924/1928).

Following the formulation of the theory of concrete operations, Piaget
presented a somewhat different explanation for the development of the sense
of necessity. Now it was seen to result from the "closure," or completion of
an operational structure (Chapman, 1988). Closure results when the set of possibilities engendered by a given system of transformations becomes exhaustive. Under closure, those affirmations are *necessary*, the negation of which are
impossible within the system. In other words, necessity is a function of invariance across the range of possibilities defined by the structure. This operational
theory of necessity appears to have little in common with Piaget's earlier view,
based on social interaction. In fact, an argument can be made for continuity
between the two.

Piaget's later operational theory of necessity can be understood as sup-
plementing rather than replacing his earlier social-interactionist theory. Originally, he had believed that cooperation and the confrontation with other points
of view were both necessary and sufficient for the development of the sense
of necessity. The operational theory was based on his insight that such forms
of social interaction were *not sufficient* (because an operational system was also
required), although he still believed them to be *necessary*. The problem is that
once Piaget developed the theory of concrete operations, he spent most of his
time on describing the development of operational structures and very little
on the relation between operational development and social interaction. The
nature of this relation is a major gap in the theory.

According to the present reconstruction of Piaget's theory, the experience
of interpersonal argumentation provides children with the need and the occasion to justify their assertions, ideally with arguments that have force even for
persons who do not share the same perspectives. The structural coordination
of operations as described by Piaget provides them with the intellectual means
for constructing justifications based on a sense of necessity. However essential
operational structures might be in this process, the construction of such structures would not be completed without the pressure of contact with other minds
and other viewpoints. Without this social-interactive context, there would be
no need nor any occasion for carrying operational construction to the point
of closure.

In other words, there are two ways in which language is necessary for concrete operations. In addition to the role of semiotic mediation in the interiorization of action as described in the previous section, interpersonal communi-

cation by means of language provides children with the motive and the opportunity for coordinating those interiorized actions as a way of generating inter-
personally valid justifications. The broader implication of this argument is that,
if linguistic communication is so intimately implicated in the development of
concrete operations, then it is surely an illusion to believe that one should attempt to eliminate it completely in their assessment. Rather than debate (either
for or against) the validity of verbal justifications as indicators of a purely intrasubjective cognitive competence, what is required is a reconceptualization
of the *various* competencies involved in concrete operations and the assessment
criteria appropriate to each. If one expands the notion of concrete operational
competence to include the whole cycle of (a) conceiving a need to justify one's
assertions in a manner independent of one's particular point of view, and (b)
using the coordination of cognitive concrete operations as a means of understanding the relations of necessity underlying an inference, and (c) constructing a justification on that basis, then the justification so constructed will provide appropriate evidence for the competence so conceived. If instead one wishes
to investigate only one moment in this process (e.g., the coordination of operations), then justifications assess too much, and one needs narrower and more
indirect assessment criteria. Such is the context in which the many ingenious
''nonverbal'' or semiverbal assessment methods developed over the years are
meaningful. What is ruled out by the present approach is considering the coordination of operations (or any other intrasubjective cognitive process involved
in logical reasoning) as *essentially independent* of the communicative context of
such reasoning, whatever assessment criteria are used.

## JUDGMENTS AND JUSTIFICATION
## IN TRANSITIVE REASONING

The significance of the expanded notion of cognitive competence just discussed
lies not merely in its possible value in resolving a recondite methodological
dispute, but also in its potential for suggesting new research questions. In particular, the relation between the intrasubjective coordination of operations and
particular forms of social interaction becomes particularly relevant (e.g., Doise
& Mugny, 1984). A fundamental question in this connection is whether and
to what extent the capacity for constructing logical justifications is related to
the intrasubjective inferential processes that are presumably active in its construction. According to a line of reasoning based on the ubiquitous competence-
performance distinction, the intrasubjective competence develops first and is
reflected in verbal performance only after being matched with verbal skills that
develop independently. In the present view, the relation between intrasubjective cognitive processes and verbal justification should be much closer because
intrasubjective forms of inference develop as a function of the need for justification arising from interpersonal communication.

One way of addressing this question in research is now illustrated with a reanalysis of data from a study of transitive reasoning in 120 first, second, and third graders by Chapman and Lindenberger (1988). In that study, children's justifications were analyzed, and the decalage between the transitivity of length and the transitivity of weight was found to result primarily from children's tendency to infer differences in weight from differences in size. The question considered now is how children's *justifications* were related to the forms of reasoning by which their *judgments* were inferred. For this purpose, some method is required for assessing those forms of reasoning independent of children's verbal justifications.

One way of addressing this question is to observe the contingency between children's judgments and their memory for premise information. If children infer their weight judgments with an *operational* form of reasoning—that is, if they infer that A is heavier than C from an operational composition of the relations "A is heavier than B" and "B is heavier than C"—then their judgments should be related to their memory for premises (cf. Brainerd & Kingma, 1984). More specifically, the predicted distribution shown in Table 10.1 should obtain (Chapman & Lindenberger, in press). First, memory for premises should be accurate, because operational reasoning presupposes the information contained in those premises. Second, judgments should be correct, because operational reasoning "by necessity" leads to a correct judgment. In theory, all observations should be concentrated in the upper left corner of this 2 x 2 table; the other cells in the table are "error cells," in which no observations should occur. In reality, of course, some errors might well be observed, if only because of imperfect measurement. The statistical question of interest is whether the number of observed errors is less than that *expected by chance*.[1] Because Chapman and Lindenberger (1988) included a memory probe as part of their task presentation procedures, their data can be reanalyzed to test this hypothesis.

The actual distribution of judgments by memory-for-premises for children giving justifications of different types on Chapman and Lindenberger's (1988) three-term transitivity of weight task is presented in Table 10.2. As predicted, all 34 children giving *operational* justifications had accurate memory for premises as well as correct judgments. Because prediction was perfect, the PRE-statistic, a measure of Proportion Reduction in Error, was equal to 1.00 (Hildebrand, Laing, & Rosenthal, 1977). This PRE-value is significantly greater than zero ($z = 3.98$, $p < .001$), indicating that the number of obtained errors was sig-

---

[1]Expected frequencies were based on the marginal distributions of the 2 x 2 x 4 (judgments x memory-for-premises x justifications) cross-classification shown in Table 10.2, under the null hypothesis of independence among the three factors. That is, the expected probability of an observation occurring in any cell of Table 10.2 is equal to the product of the respective marginal probabilities.

TABLE 10.1
Predicted Distribution of Transitivity Judgments
by Memory for Premises, Given Operational Reasoning

| Memory for premises | Judgments | |
|---|---|---|
| | Correct | Incorrect |
| Accurate | n | 0 |
| Inaccurate | 0 | 0 |

*Note:* The cells enclosed by the box are "error cells" and should be empty, according to theory.

nificantly fewer than that expected by chance.[2] Thus, the data are consistent with the assumption that children giving operational justifications also inferred their judgments with operational reasoning.

As described in the original study, the most common reason for children's failure on the transitivity of weight task was their tendency to justify judgments of weight as a function of "*bigness.*" As indicated in the table, the 30 children giving "functional" justifications of this kind frequently gave incorrect judgments, and an appreciable number had inaccurate memory for premises. The PRE-value of –1.19 means that there was 119% *more* errors than expected by chance, a result that is significantly different than that obtained for operational justifications ($z = 5.92$, $p < .001$). Because the size and weight of comparison objects were uncorrelated on this task, the high rate of incorrect judgments is consistent with the interpretation that these children inferred their judgments in the same way that they justified them—as a function of "bigness."

Also presented in Table 10.2 is the distribution of judgments by memory for premises is presented for the 23 children who justified their weight judgments as a function of *smallness* or of the *surface texture* ("shininess") of the comparison objects. If children in fact inferred their judgments with operational reasoning and gave these functional justifications only after the fact, then again one would expect the obtained distribution shown in Table 10.2 to approximate the theoretical distribution shown in Table 10.1. In fact, the number of obtained errors was only 5% less than the number expected by chance, as indicated by the PRE-value of 0.05. This value is significantly less than that obtained for operational justifications ($z = 2.95$, $p < .005$). In other words, the data are not consistent with the assumption that these children generally inferred their original judgments with operational reasoning, giving justifications in terms of smallness or surface texture only after the fact.

What about the 30 children who gave *no justifications* at all on this task? The relation between their judgments and memory for premises is also shown in

---

[2]The significance of PRE was tested with the binomial approximation recommended by von Eye and Brandtstädter (1988).

TABLE 10.2
Transitivity Judgments by Memory for Premises,
for Children Giving Justifications of Different Types

| Memory for premises | Judgments | | PRE |
|---|---|---|---|
| | Correct | Incorrect | |
| *Operational justifications* | | | |
| Accurate | 34 | 0 | |
| Inaccurate | 0 | 0 | 1.00 |
| *Weight a function of "bigness"* | | | |
| Accurate | 3 | 18 | |
| Inaccurate | 2 | 7 | – 1.19 |
| *Weight a function of "smallness" or texture* | | | |
| Accurate | 14 | 4 | |
| Inaccurate | 5 | 0 | 0.05 |
| *No justifications* | | | |
| Accurate | 20 | 4 | |
| Inaccurate | 5 | 1 | 0.19 |

*Note:* The cells enclosed in each box are the error cells for the hypothesis that children giving the respective type of justification inferred their judgments through operational reasoning.

Table 10.2. If these children were "false negatives" who in fact inferred their judgments with operational reasoning, then once again one would expect the distribution of their judgments and memory for premises to approximate the theoretical distribution for operational reasoning. As indicated, one third of the observations fell within the error cells, a number 19% less than that expected by chance. The corresponding PRE-value (0.19) is again significantly less than that obtained for operational justifications ($z = 2.41, p < .01$). Therefore, the obtained distribution is not consistent with the assumption that these children generally used operational reasoning in inferring their weight judgments and were simply unable to verbalize their reasoning when asked for a justification.

## CONCLUSION

The foregoing results are consistent with the conclusion that children giving operational justifications also used operational reasoning in inferring their judgments. In contrast, the hypothesis that children giving functional justifications (i.e., justifications in terms of size or surface texture) or no justifications at all might have inferred their judgments with operational reasoning was not supported. This correspondence between operational inferences and operational justifications need not be interpreted as the result of accurate introspective reports on the part of children asked to explain their judgments. Instead, such a correspondence could result from the use of operational reasoning both in deriving a judgment from a given set of premises and in constructing a justification for a particular conclusion. Children capable of operational reasoning might simply use it in both situations.

These findings illustrate the argument that the ability to give a verbal justification of a certain type is a competence of interest in its own right, not merely an imperfect indicator of the ability to infer a correct answer. By itself, the ability to generate correct answers on a particular task could reflect only what Inhelder and Piaget (1980) once called *procedural knowledge*, or "knowing-how." In contrast, the ability to justify one's answer reflects what they called *structural knowledge*, or "knowing-why." The problem was that Piaget explained structural knowledge at the level of concrete operations and beyond solely in terms of the interiorization and intercoordination of actions. Despite his occasional statements regarding the "necessity" of language for operational thought, he did not explain how language was related to the coordination of interiorized actions from which concrete operations were presumably derived. Therefore, his use of verbal explanations as criterion for operational thought appeared highly paradoxical, and the idea that verbal explanations were mere performance factors, extraneous to the cognitive competence being assessed, seemed self-evident.

According to the argument advanced in this chapter, signification has an irreducible triadic structure as reflected in the image of the epistemic triangle. From this it follows that forms of knowing based on signification have a similar triadic structure as well. In this view, concrete operations develop, not merely from the interiorization of operative interaction, but from the interiorization of the epistemic triangle as a whole. Communicative interaction enters into the development of concrete operations in at least three ways: (a) by providing the basis for cognitive representation in general; (b) by mediating the interiorization of (operative) actions as described by Gal'perin; and (c) by provoking children to coordinate those interiorized actions in constructing justifications for their inferences.

One consequence of this view is that children's communicative competence cannot be neatly pared away from their cognitive competence, leaving the latter whole and intact. Instead, cognitive and communicative competencies are closely related in different ways at different levels of development. Thus, the strategy of eliminating children's verbalizations as criteria for concrete operations might have accomplished more than it was intended to do. Rather than peeling the husk of verbal performance from the kernel of cognitive competence, that strategy might have succeeded instead in removing successive layers of cognitive competence as well. As in peeling an onion, one is left not with a purer form of cognitive competence, but simply with a smaller piece. In particular, the rejection of verbal explanations as response criteria has resulted in a narrow focus on children's competence in problem *solving* to the neglect of their competence in understanding the *reasons* for their particular solutions. Paradoxically, Piaget's failure to explain exactly how language was related to concrete operations led, via the arguments of Braine (1959), Brainerd (1973), and others, to all but total neglect of the kind of structural knowledge, or *knowing-why*, in which he was mainly interested.

In itself, nothing is wrong with studying children's ability to solve problems, even without assessing their understanding of the reasons for their answers. The mistake is the belief that, in so doing, one has penetrated more closely to their "true" competence. Instead, one simply has conceptualized the competence of interest in a different way: as successful problem solving rather than as the understanding of reasons. By eliminating children's verbal explanations, one does not succeed merely in measuring children's true competence with less error, but in measuring a competence differently conceived.

This view also has consequences for research. Instead of eliminating children's verbal justifications from consideration, one can make them an object of investigation in their own right. Instead of conceiving nonverbal methods as a better way of measuring children's "true" cognitive competence, such methods can be used to measure the intrapsychic component of children's inferential problem-solving ability, independent of their understanding of reasons. From this perspective, the question of how children's justifications are *related* to their intrapsychic forms of inference also becomes of interest. The research described in this chapter was intended to illustrate this kind of research.

The more general implication of this argument for issues of assessment and developmental timing is that the competence–performance distinction (and the "simplification strategy" based on this distinction) is meaningful only when the competence of interest is substantively independent of the "performance factor" in question. The question of independence in turn will depend on how competence is conceptualized within a particular theoretical perspective. From one perspective, the independence of competence and performance factors may seem self-evident—just as the independence of concrete operational competence and verbal explanations appeared self-evident from the perspective of a theory in which no essential connection between the two was specified. From another theoretical perspective, the same competence and the same "performance factor" may be viewed as nonindependent—as is the case for communicative interaction and concrete operations as conceived from the perspective of the epistemic triangle.

## ACKNOWLEDGMENT

The preparation of this chapter was supported in part by Operating Grant #0GP0037334 from the Natural Sciences and Engineering Research Council of Canada. A preliminary version was presented at the Meeting of the Society for Research in Child Development, Kansas City, April 1989.

## REFERENCES

Beilin, H. (1975). *Studies in the cognitive basis of language development.* New York: Academic Press.

Braine, M. D. S. (1959). The ontogeny of certain logical operations: Piaget's formulation examined by nonverbal methods. *Psychological Monographs: General and Applied, 73*(5, Whole N. 475), 1-43.

Brainerd, C. J. (1973). Judgments and explanations as criteria for the presence of cognitive structures. *Psychological Bulletin, 79*, 172-179.

Brainerd, C. J., & Kingma, J. (1984). Do children have to remember to reason? A fuzzy-trace theory of transitivity development. *Developmental Review, 4*, 311-377.

Chapman, M. (1987). Piaget, attentional capacity, and the functional implications of formal structure. In H. W. Reese (Ed.), *Advances in child development and behavior* (Vol. 20, pp. 299-334). Orlando, FL: Academic Press.

Chapman, M. (1988). *Constructive evolution: Origins, and development of Piaget's thought.* Cambridge: Cambridge University Press.

Chapman, M., & Lindenberger, U. (1988). Functions, operations, and decalage in the development of transitivity. *Developmental Psychology, 24*, 542-551.

Chapman, M., & Lindenberger, U. (in press). Transitivity judgments, memory for premises, and models of children's reasoning. *Developmental Review.*

Cohen, D. (1983). *Piaget: Critique and reassessment.* London: Croom Helm.

Cole, M., & Cole, S. R. (1989). *The development of children.* New York: Scientific American.

Doise, W., & Mugny, G. (1984). *The social development of the intellect.* Oxford: Pergamon.

Flavell, J. H. (1963). *The developmental psychology of Jean Piaget.* Princeton, NJ: Van Nostrand.

Gal'perin, P.Y. (1969). Stages in the development of mental acts. In M. Cole & J. Maltzman (Eds.), *A handbook of contemporary Soviet psychology* (pp. 249-273). New York: Basic Books.

Gruen, G. E. (1966). Note on conservation: Methodological and definitional considerations. *Child Development, 37*, 977-983.

Habermas, J. (1982). *Theorie des kommunikativen Handelns* [*Theory of communicative action*] (2 Vols.). Frankfurt: Suhrkamp.

Hildebrand, D. K., Laing, J. D., & Rosenthal, H. (1977). *Prediction analysis of cross classifications.* New York: Wiley.

Inhelder, B., & Piaget, J. (1980). Procedures and structures. In D. R. Olson (Ed.), *The social foundations of language and thought* (pp. 19-27). New York: Norton.

Mead, G. H. (1962). *Mind, self, and society.* Chicago: University of Chicago Press. (Original work published 1934)

Peirce, C. S. (1955). *The philosophical writings of C.S. Peirce.* New York: Dover.

Piaget, J. (1928). *Judgment and reasoning in the child.* London: Routledge & Kegan Paul. (Original work published 1924)

Piaget, J. (1950). *The psychology of intelligence.* New York: Harcourt, Brace. (Original work published 1947)

Piaget, J. (1952). Jean Piaget. In E. G. Boring (Ed.), *A history of psychology in autobiography* (Vol. 4, pp. 237–256). New York: Russell & Russell.

Piaget J. (1955). *The language and thought of the child.* Cleveland: Meridian. (Original work published 1923)

Piaget, J. (1962a). *Play, dreams and imitation in childhood.* New York: Norton. (Original work published 1945)

Piaget, J. (1962b). *Comments.* (Attachment to the hardcover edition of L.S. Vygotsky, *Thought and language.*) Cambridge, MA: MIT Press.

Piaget, J. (1963). *The origins of intelligence in children.* New York: Norton. (Original work published 1936)

Piaget, J. (1967). Language and thought from the genetic point of view. In J. Piaget (Ed.), *Six psychological studies* (pp. 88–99). New York: Vintage. (Original work published 1954)

Piaget J. (1973). Language and intellectual operations. In J. Piaget (Ed.), *The child and reality* (pp. 109–124). New York: Grossman. (Original work published 1954)

Schmid-Schönbein, C. (1988). Wie entsteht Einsicht in das eigene Handeln? Spontanes handlungsbegleitendes Sprechen als frühe Form reflexiver Erkenntnisaktivität [How does insight into one's own action develop? Spontaneous action-accompanying speech as an early form of reflective knowing]. *Schweizerische Zeitschrift für Psychologie, 47,* 161–170.

Siegel, L. S. (1978). The relationship of language and thought in the preoperational child: A reconsideration of nonverbal alternatives to Piagetian tasks. In L. S. Siegel & C. J. Brainerd (Eds.), *Alternatives to Piaget* (pp. 43–67). New York: Academic Press.

Suarez, A. (1980). Connaissance et action [Knowledge and action]. *Revue Suisse de Psychologie, 39,* 177–199.

Trevarthen, C. (1989, Autumn). Origins and directions for the concept of infant intersubjectivity. *SRCD Newsletter,* pp. 1–4.

von Eye, A., & Brandtstädter, J. (1988). Evaluating developmental hypotheses using statement calculus and nonparametric statistics. In P. B. Baltes, D. Featherman, & R. M. Lerner (Eds.), *Life-span behavior and development* (Vol. 8, pp. 61–97). Hillsdale, NJ: Lawrence Erlbaum Associates.

Vygotsky, L. S. (1978). *Mind in society.* Cambridge, MA: Harvard University Press.

Vygotsky, L. S. (1981). The development of higher forms of attention. In J. V. Wertsch (Ed.), *The concept of activity in Soviet psychology* (pp. 189–240). Armonk, NY: M. E. Sharpe.

Vygotsky, L. (1986). *Thought and language.* Cambridge, MA: MIT Press. (Original work published 1934)

Wallon H. (1947). L'étude psychologique et sociologique de l'enfant [The psychological and sociological study of the child]. *Cahiers Internationaux de Sociologie, 3,* 3–23.

Watson, J. S. (1972). Smiling, cooing, and "the game." *Merrill-Palmer Quarterly, 18,* 323–340.

Wertsch, J. (1985). *Vygotsky and the social formation of mind.* Cambridge, MA: Harvard University Press.

Wilson, E. O. (1975). *Sociobiology.* Cambridge, MA: Belknap Press.

Wittgenstein, L. (1968). *Philosophical investigations* (3rd ed.). New York: MacMillan. (Original work published in 1958)

# Part IV

# Modeling the Development
# of Competence

Factor analytic methods have been used to model cognitive competence ever since Charles Spearman hypothesized at the beginning of this century that intelligence test scores could be accounted for by a single underlying factor of general intelligence. Quite apart from Spearman's particular hypothesis, such methods have found broad application in psychology. Since the 1970s in particular, factor analytic methods have been extended and generalized as a means of testing causal relations among the latent variables underlying observed measurements. The most frequent developmental application of such latent variable analysis probably has been in testing "autoregressive" models of change over time. In such applications, alternative models of the covariation among latent variables from one time of measurement to the next are fit to the data obtained from repeated observations in a latent-variable extension of cross-lagged correlational techniques.

An alternative to autoregressive models of this kind is described by Mark Aber and J. J. McArdle in chapter 11 in the form of *latent growth curve models*. Besides modeling covariation among latent variables from one time or age to the next, latent growth curve techniques allow the researcher to model changes of level (or patterns of change) across time. Such methods have several potential applications that are directly relevant for the kinds of questions regarding the development of competence that have been raised in the preceding chapters of this book. Perhaps the most obvious of such applications is the possibility of testing the hypothesis that scores on measures believed to reflect a single underlying competence should have a common underlying component of growth. If, in addition, one has independent measures of some of the performance factors believed to be necessary in the expression of that competence, then one can test more specific hypotheses as well. For example, one could test the hypothesis of independence between competence and performance factors over time or the expectation that performance factors in some domains should reach a certain degree of proficiency before competence can develop.

One potential difficulty in applying such methods is that they would appear to require longitudinal data, with all the practical and logistic problems that longitudinal methods imply. However, Aber and McArdle describe another use of latent growth curve modeling that provides a potential short-cut to long-term longitudinal designs. If one obtains short-term longitudinal data from overlapping cohorts, one can test whether the growth curves of those cohorts *converge* with each other. If so, then one obtains the functional equivalent of a long-term longitudinal growth curve by piecing together two or more short-term curves. Besides removing one obstacle to the use of latent growth curve modeling for substantive purposes, such tests of convergence have the potential for circumventing some of the practical difficulties in employing longitudinal methods in general.

Chapter *11*

# Latent Growth Curve Approaches
# to Modeling the Development
# of Competence

Mark S. Aber
*University of Illinois*

J. J. McArdle
*University of Virginia*

The central question of this book, "how to decide when, or if, people of certain ages are 'able' to do certain things," prompts consideration of a more general question—"how to characterize growth or developmental change." Certainly many useful data-analytic methods are available to address these fundamental questions. Here, we discuss the fitting and testing of convergence hypotheses using latent growth curve structural models (LGM). We find these methods both powerful and under utilized in the identification and understanding of changes in behavior over time. By fitting these models to data on changes in antisocial behavior during adolescence, we illustrate the potential utility of these methods for structuring questions related to the development of competencies. Throughout this discussion we hope to emphasize the compatibility of these methods with current concerns for establishing "criteria for competence." In particular, we emphasize the utility of these methods in formalizing a variety of testable hypotheses that may be of interest to developmental psychologists whose research addresses questions of competency.

We set the stage for this illustration by examining the question "Why growth curves?" Next we examine the question "Why convergence hypotheses?"

## WHY GROWTH CURVES?

As described elsewhere in this volume, much past research examining the development of competencies sought to document differences, or the lack thereof, in the types or rates of errors made by children and adults on tasks thought to measure the competencies (usually cognitive) under study. This strategy was first employed to document differences in competence in order to debunk the view of children as "unpracticed" adults (Chandler & Chapman, this volume). Much of this research led to conclusions about the relative incompetence of children. These studies were eventually followed by others that sought to separate "performance factors" from other competencies in attempts to demonstrate that children actually do possess many competencies that earlier research had suggested they did not. Underlying both of these trends was a focus on age differences. This general strategy has yielded some interesting and important results, including, in some areas, rather detailed catalogues of specific performance characteristics of various age groups (Perlmutter, 1988). Yet, as the other chapters in this and other volumes illustrate, it has some clear and important limitations.

In 1970, Wohlwill made an observation that is not much less true in the 1990s than it was in 1970. It appears to be an apt description of much of the work in developmental psychology focused on competencies:

> the widespread tendency (is) to consider age as an independent variable, comparable to others employed in differential research, and to study age differences rather than age changes. An alternative view . . . treats developmental questions as analogous to other phenomena involving changes in behavior over time. Age is looked at as a dimension along which behavior changes are to be traced, forming part of the definition of the dependent variable in developmental studies. This dependent variable is to be defined in terms of specified aspects or parameters of the function describing changes which occur with age for a given behavioral variable. . . . (Wohlwill, 1970, p. 49)

Wohlwill appealed to developmental scientists to focus their inquiry on the study of dynamic processes and outcomes. This focus would emphasize analysis of intraindividual change as well as interindividual differences in such change. Unfortunately, his plea has been largely ignored. In a recent review of cognitive development across the life-span Perlmutter (1988) could still maintain:

> Analysis of extant research points to limitations in both the independent and dependent variables. Because most studies of cognitive development involve cross-sectional designs in which cognitive performance serves as the dependent variable and age serves as the main independent variable, only descriptions of age differences, not explanations of ages changes, are available. Longitudinal studies in which indices of cognitive change, rather than simply cognitive performance, serve as the dependent variable would better address the development of cognition. (pp. 212-213)

These concerns point to the analysis of developmental functions which view age as "functional age," or the substantiation of an age related but substantively grounded index.

The concept of a "functional unity" (Horn, 1972) provides one useful way to frame such age-related but substantively grounded indices within the context of a structural equation model. Horn (1972) described a functional unity to be:

> indicated by a configuration—a pattern—of processes which are themselves distinct but are integral parts of a more general process. To distinguish a functional unity from a mere collection of distinct processes it is necessary to show that the processes work together—that they rise together, fall together, appear together, disappear together or, in general covary together. . . . A functional unity is thus a rather high level of abstraction. In operational terms it can be defined in a number of ways. One of the simplest such definitions is that furnished by the methods of factor analysis. According to this definition a functional unity is indicated by the set of variables which go together in the sense of correlating in a way that defines a particular factor. . . . (pp. 161-162)

Following this theme, a common factor of repeated observations over time may be used to represent a developmental function. Although confirmatory factor analysis most often is used to identify latent "psychometric" variables, here we apply the same techniques to examine latent "chronometric" variables. In the latent growth models that follow, we do not pose the longitudinal scores as causes of themselves, as is the case in Markov autoregressive models, nor even as surrogates for other temporal causes. Rather, we view the repeated measures as multiple indicators of latent underlying developmental processes. In some models we estimate aspects of a single process and in others these are compared with other dynamic alternatives. The use of functional ideas in this way has been applied successfully in research on aging (Horn & McArdle, 1980; McArdle & Anderson, 1989), child development (McArdle & Epstein, 1987), and behavior genetics (McArdle, 1986).

## A Latent Growth Curve Model

The latent growth curve concepts employed here were introduced by both Tucker (1958) and Rao (1958) some time ago and have since been discussed by others (e.g., Hultch, Nesselroade, & Plemons, 1976; McArdle 1988a; Rogosa, Brandt, & Zimowski, 1982). Only recently, however, has work by Meredith and his colleagues (McArdle, 1986; McArdle & Aber, 1990; McArdle & Anderson, 1989; McArdle & Epstein, 1987; Meredith & Tisak, 1984) demonstrated how a wide variety of growth curve concepts can be modeled using standard structural equation techniques.

The path diagram of Fig. 11.1 presents a model of longitudinal data termed a *latent growth curve model* (LGM) (after Tucker, 1966; McArdle & Epstein, 1987; Meredith & Tisak, 1984). The mathematical and statistical equations

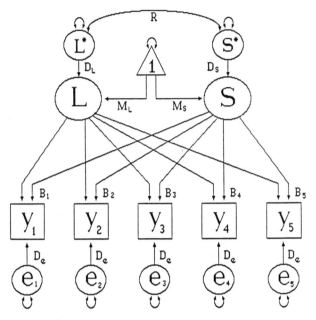

FIG. 11.1.   A latent growth structural model.

for this model are listed in the Appendix. In this path model we assume that $n = 1$ to $N$ individuals have been measured on five occasions, $t = 1$ to $T = 5$, on the variable overt antisocial behavior $Y(t,n)$ (drawn as squares). This model assumes the observed antisocial behavior scores to be a weighted sum of three individual unobserved components:

1. $L(n)$ are Level scores representing individual differences in level of overt antisocial behavior, and can be formulated as an initial level or an average level for each individual's curve. In either case, the $L$ score is constant across all ages $t = 1$ to $T = 5$.

2. $S(n)$ are Slope scores representing individual differences in slope or change in overt antisocial behavior over time. The contribution of the slope to the observed score $Y(t,n)$ is weighted by the basis coefficient $B(t)$.

3. $E(n)$ are Error or residual scores assumed to be random variables with mean zero and zero correlations over time. These scores may be interpreted as disturbance factors or errors of measurement.

Thus, we can write

$$Y(t,n) \; = \; L(n) \; + \; B(t)\,S(n) \; + \; E(t,n). \tag{1}$$

The LGM in Fig. 11.1 is essentially a confirmatory factor analysis model with a few important exceptions. The loadings of the unobserved Level factor,

$L$, are restricted to have a value of 1 at all ages, whereas the loadings of the unobserved Slope factor, $S$, are allowed to change with age. Although the unobserved Slope score is an individual characteristic which remains the same across all times of measurement, the impact of this score changes as a function of age, as it is weighted by the $B(t)$, or basis coefficients for age. Thus, the $B(t)$ coefficients define an overall reference shape or change pattern for the entire group. The latent component $S$ in this LGM represents a "component of time."

In these LGM we assume that the $L(n)$ and $S(n)$ have standard deviations $Dl$ and $Ds$, and optional correlation $Rls$. The error variables $E$ are required to have zero mean, a deviation $De$ that may be constant or variable over time, and zero correlation with all other $E$ terms. Finally, and perhaps the most important departure from the traditional correlation or covariance factor model, the level and slope factors are assumed to have non-zero means $Ml$ and $Ms$ respectively. These means will follow the basic pattern of change seen in the correlations and variances. That is, in our longitudinal data, the means $My(t)$ and covariances $Cy(t, t + d)$ of variable $Y(t)$ over time are proportional.

Note that the LGM requires no particular presumption about the nature of the change pattern represented by the basis coefficients. Rather, the time of measurement is merely used to organize individual differences in change. If the basis coefficients are taken to be the actual age at testing, then the basis is proportional to age or linear, and the shapes are interpreted as slopes. This model is an exact structural equation representation of linear trend analysis or a repeated measures MANOVA. However, this LGM provides the flexibility to move far beyond MANOVA to model a wide variety of developmental conceptions of individual change. For example, the $B(t)$ can be restricted to examine various staggered or nonlinear functions. Moreover, the $B(t)$ may be estimated from the data to provide the reference shape of the optimal developmental function for the organization of individual difference in change patterns (see McArdle 1986, 1988, in press; McArdle, Anderson, & Aber, 1987; McArdle & Epstein, 1987).

The unobserved slope factor scores $S(n)$ in the LGM reflect individual differences in rates of change over the entire age span in the data. We interpret these scores in the same way as factor scores from any factor analysis. Here we take them as a reflection of the most likely shape of a single function organizing all individual curves. Although predictions about individual curves would follow the shape of the average reference curve for the group provided by the basis coefficients, $B(t)$, each will be different by the multiplier or amplitude $S(n)$. Thus, an individual's latent score on the slope factor, $S(n)$, provides information about how similar that individual's curve is to the group average. If the component score is $S(n) = 1$ then the individual's curve equals the group curve. If, however, the score $S(n)$ is low, say .20, then the individual's curve is much lower than the group curve, but still has the same shape.

### Advantages of the Latent Growth Curve Approach to Competence

As can be seen from the preceding discussion, the basic parameters of our LGM describe a systematic pattern of individual difference in change over time, providing an integrated structure for analysis of the correlations, variances, and the means in longitudinal data (McArdle, 1988). These LGM allow for the examination of a number of characteristics of developmental functions relevant to establishing criteria for competence. These include group means and individual differences in rate of change, asymptotic level (i.e., the point at which development stops), and the shape of the developmental function. The focus on individual difference parameters facilitated by our LGM is consistent with much that we know about the considerable individual variation within age in the development of competencies. When these models are expanded from univariate to multivariate forms additional characteristics of the patterning of change can be examined, including the synchronicity and relative sequencing of multiple growth processes.

Our LGM also provide a marked alternative to the use of autoregressive models of change that has characterized much work on the development of competence. There are a variety of well-known limitations of simple autoregressive models in the analysis of behavioral change (see Rogosa & Willett, 1985). At the conceptual level, for example, the characteristic reliance in developmental psychology on autoregressive models to represent developmental change may have slowed progress in defining and distinguishing the concepts of developmental stability and continuity. In this vein Wohlwill (in press) has argued that conceptual confusion in this area has resulted from the identification of stability or continuity with predictability. Instead he called for the examination of continuity as an attribute of developmental processes, with a focus on the degree of intraindividual regularity, consistency, and susceptibility to change of behavior across successive points in time.

At the mathematical level, autoregressive models assume that changes over time are independent of prior changes. One may be unwilling to make this assumption in the case of the development of a variety of competencies, especially complex competencies that require the combination of previously acquired skills and abilities. Our LGM, on the other hand, define changes over time to be *dependent* on the prior changes. Second, simple autoregressive models assume that all individuals change according to the same coefficient, yet many examples can be found in the empirical literature that call this assumption into question. Third, simple autoregressive models assume that the "stable" component is uncorrelated with the "unstable" component. Fourth, simple autoregressive models assume that the raw score means can be removed from the analysis without loss of generality. Our LGM, in contrast, allow one to include the means. This may be particularly important for the analysis of questions of competence as we are interested not only in normative stability (Rutter, 1984) over time as indexed by longitudinal correlations, but also in differences in the mean level of ability at various ages. Thus, limitations of the autoregressive depiction of developmental change suggest that for some analyses of the development of competencies, latent growth curve models may be more appropriate.

Hypotheses related to the explanation of change can also be accommodated in our LGM, which enable examination of the influence exogenous variables on parameters such as interindividual differences in mean level and rates of change. This type of analysis may inform theoretical arguments about the nature and meaning of individual differences. Interindividual differences in cognitive performance are interpreted differently from different theoretical perspectives. For example, from a mechanistic perspective, which posits that cognitive processes are universal across substantive domain and age, interindividual differences typically have been treated as measurement error. Given the measurement of theoretically relevant variables, this a testable assumption in LGM. From a contextual perspective, in contrast, development is assumed to be a reciprocal or bidirectional process between organism and context. From this perspective the development of competencies occurs in an open system and individual differences in the trajectories along which development proceeds are of theoretical interest. The dynamic parameterization of LGM is highly compatible with this perspective.

## WHY CONVERGENCE HYPOTHESES?

One problem with growth curve models is that they usually require information obtained on a single individual measured over a long period of time. Often this is not possible within the constraints of a single longitudinal study. In an effort to deal with these constraints Bell (1953, 1954) proposed a method, which he called "convergence," for piecing together separate longitudinal datasets into a single longitudinal function.

> This method consists of making limited remeasurements of cross-sectional groups so that temporally overlapping measurements of older and younger subjects are provided. The remeasurements may be used as a way of determining whether trends which would otherwise be seen only between different age groups are corroborated within short time periods for each age group. The method may also provide a means of actually linking up individuals or subgroups between adjacent segments of a developmental curve, each segment consisting of a limited longitudinal study on a different age group. (Bell, 1954, p. 281)

Bell (1954) illustrated the efficiency of his convergence method by showing that a 10-year longitudinal span could be approximated with only 3 years of data collection. He linked information from different curve segments by employing a distance index to match different subjects across different curve segments. Similar strategies have since been described or applied by a number of researchers dealing with the analysis of incomplete longitudinal data (Brown, 1983; Bryk & Raudenbush, 1987; Glindmeyer, Diem, Jones, & Weil, 1982; van't Hof, Roede, & Kowalski, 1977; Goldstein, 1987; McArdle & Hamagami, in press; Rao & Rao, 1966).

Here, we combine multiple group structural equation modeling techniques with LGMs to model and test Bell's convergence hypotheses. The statistical basis of the convergence model has been illustrated in previous work (McArdle et al., 1987; McArdle & Hamagami, in press; Meredith & Tisak, 1984; Tisak & Meredith, 1989) and parallels related structural equation modeling approaches to incomplete growth curve analyses (e.g., Horn & McArdle, 1980; Joreskog & Sorbom, 1980). These LGM-convergence methods are consistent with Bell's "accelerated longitudinal approach" but avoid the problem of matching specific individuals across cohorts by treating the problem of linkage as one of missing data. The relevant statistical quantities used to characterize the overlapping data points are estimated from all available data across cohorts at each point of overlap.

A path diagram for this model is depicted in Fig. 11.2. In this figure a latent growth model is presented for each of four independent groups (cohorts) measured on the same variable on two separate occasions. These measured variables are represented by squares in each path diagram. Each group provides a different, measured, short-term longitudinal segment. Group 1 in Fig. 11.2 was measured at $t = 1$ and $t = 2$. Group 2 was measured at $t = 2$ and $t = 3$. But to test the hypothesis of convergence in developmental function across these separate groups, each short-term segment is assumed to come from the same longer term longitudinal curve. Thus, the pattern of correlations, variances, and means in the data of each group are assumed to make the same predictions about the level and shape of that curve across the measurement ages of all four groups. Thus, we first assume that the identical path model, with the same numerical parameters, is invariant over all groups. Next, we assume that the dataset from each group has a slightly different set of latent (missing) variables (represented by circles). The basic data layout for four independent groups is written in matrix form using latent variables as surrogates for the missing data. Use of standard techniques for testing the invariance of factor loadings across groups then provides a test of convergence across separate groups.

Appropriate use of these LGM-convergence techniques requires that the data have the following characteristics:

1. the cohorts need to overlap as much as possible to test the hypothesis of "linkage" or "convergence" of the longitudinal and cross-sectional curves;

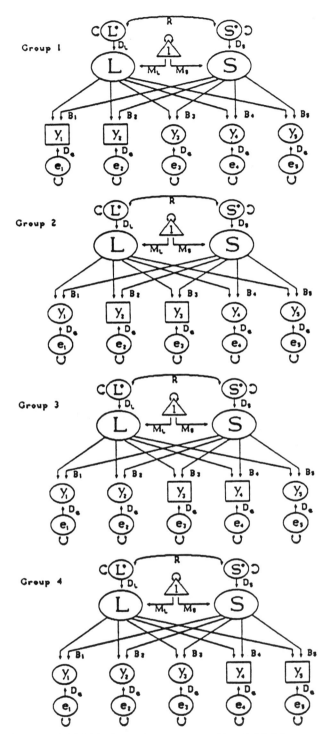

FIG. 11.2.   A Multiple Group Age-convergence Growth Model.

2. the groups need to be independent of one another;

3. the groups should be homogenous within group;

4. the sample size needs to be large enough to effectively test alternative curve forms (simple models with few parameters require fewer subjects, whereas complex models with large numbers of parameters will require more subjects);

5. each group needs to be representatively sampled from a population of interest;

6. each variable should to be scored in the same way over all occasions so that the curve represents interpretable changes over time; and

7. the variables should be normally distributed.

## METHODS

We now illustrate empirical results from analyses using these methods for a sample of adolescents measured on overt and covert antisocial behaviors.

### The Study Design

Data for the present study were provided by Delbert Elliot and his colleagues from their National Youth Survey (NYS). The NYS involved a multicohort panel design with a nationally representative sample of 1,725 U.S. adolescents ages 11–17 in 1976. Data collected on youths' involvement in delinquent behavior during the calendar years 1976 and 1978 are used in the present illustration. (For details of data collection procedures see Elliot, Ageton, Huizinga, Knowles, & Canter, 1983.)

Figure 11.3 presents an overview of the "accelerated" longitudinal data design. All individuals in this study were measured twice over a 2-year period,

| Birth Cohort | Age at Testing | | | | | | | | |
|---|---|---|---|---|---|---|---|---|---|
| 1965 | 11 | | 13 | | | | | | |
| 1964 | | 12 | | 14 | | | | | |
| 1963 | | | 13 | | 15 | | | | |
| 1962 | | | | 14 | | 16 | | | |
| 1961 | | | | | 15 | | 17 | | |
| 1960 | | | | | | 16 | | 18 | |
| 1959 | | | | | | | 17 | | 19 |
| | | | | | | | 1 | | 1 |
| | | | | | | | 9 | | 9 |
| | | | | | | | 7 | | 7 |
| | | | | | | | 6 | | 8 |

FIG. 11.3.   Structure of the NYS dataset

first in 1976 and again in 1978. Each single line spans 2 years and represents two scores for a cohort of individuals born in a particular year. Thus, some individuals were born in 1965 and were measured at ages 11 and 13, others were born in 1964 and were measured at ages 12 and 14, still others were born in 1963 and measured at ages 13 and 15, and so on out to the final cohort that was born in 1959 and measured at ages 17 and 19. This structure is exploited in the testing of the convergence hypotheses as described earlier.

Summary statistics required for our LGM-convergence analyses are presented in Tables 11.1a-11.1e. The summary means, variances, and correlations for each of our seven groups were combined to form the cross products matrices used in the following analyses.

## Sample Selection for the Present Study

Of the 1,725 NYS subjects originally interviewed in 1976, there were 1,626 who participated in the 1978 follow-up interview. A subsample of 510 of these subjects who were actively involved in both some overt and covert antisocial behavior during both 1976 and 1978 are included in the present study. It should be noted that the sample used here is not, as was Elliot's original sample, representative of all American youth, but rather, representative of American youth engaged in both overt and covert antisocial behavior. The distribution of youth across gender and age differs in these two samples. (For more details see Aber, 1989.)

TABLE 11.1A
Overt Scores

| | Means for Seven Groups | | | | | | | | |
|---|---|---|---|---|---|---|---|---|---|
| | Age at Testing | | | | | | | | |
| Birth Cohort | 11 | 12 | 13 | 14 | 15 | 16 | 17 | 18 | 19 |
| 1965 (N = 46) | 19.65 | — | 21.11 | — | — | — | — | — | — |
| 1964 (N = 62) | — | 22.05 | — | 20.03 | — | — | — | — | — |
| 1963 (N = 80) | — | — | 22.44 | — | 20.42 | — | — | — | — |
| 1962 (N = 90) | — | — | — | 21.91 | — | 19.51 | — | — | — |
| 1961 (N = 89) | — | — | — | — | 21.76 | — | 19.39 | — | — |
| 1960 (N = 77) | — | — | — | — | — | 20.23 | — | 18.69 | — |
| 1959 (N = 66) | — | — | — | — | — | — | 20.50 | — | 17.70 |

Note: — denotes data missing by design structure

TABLE 11.1B
Overt Scores

| | | | | | | | | | |
|---|---|---|---|---|---|---|---|---|---|
| | *Standard Deviations for Seven Groups* | | | | | | | | |
| *Birth* | | | | | Age at Testing | | | | |
| *Cohort* | *11* | *12* | *13* | *14* | *15* | *16* | *17* | *18* | *19* |
| 1965 | 5.42 | — | 4.77 | — | — | — | — | — | — |
| (*N* = 46) | | | | | | | | | |
| 1964 | — | 8.33 | — | 5.37 | — | — | — | — | — |
| (*N* = 62) | | | | | | | | | |
| 1963 | — | — | 8.26 | — | 6.90 | — | — | — | — |
| (*N* = 80) | | | | | | | | | |
| 1962 | — | — | — | 6.07 | — | 4.76 | — | — | — |
| (*N* = 90) | | | | | | | | | |
| 1961 | — | — | — | — | 5.33 | — | 5.54 | — | — |
| (*N* = 89) | | | | | | | | | |
| 1960 | — | — | — | — | — | 5.53 | — | 5.44 | — |
| (*N* = 77) | | | | | | | | | |
| 1959 | — | — | — | — | — | — | 5.20 | — | 4.78 |
| (*N* = 66) | | | | | | | | | |

*Note:* — denotes data missing by design structure

TABLE 11.1C
Covert Scores

| | | | | | | | | | |
|---|---|---|---|---|---|---|---|---|---|
| | *Means for Seven Groups* | | | | | | | | |
| *Birth* | | | | | Age at Testing | | | | |
| *Cohort* | *11* | *12* | *13* | *14* | *15* | *16* | *17* | *18* | *19* |
| 1965 | 9.89 | — | 10.59 | — | — | — | — | — | — |
| (*N* = 46) | | | | | | | | | |
| 1964 | — | 10.55 | — | 11.13 | — | — | — | — | — |
| (*N* = 62) | | | | | | | | | |
| 1963 | — | — | 11.11 | — | 11.29 | — | — | — | — |
| (*N* = 80) | | | | | | | | | |
| 1962 | — | — | — | 11.77 | — | 11.79 | — | — | — |
| (*N* = 90) | | | | | | | | | |
| 1961 | — | — | — | — | 11.89 | — | 12.08 | — | — |
| (*N* = 89) | | | | | | | | | |
| 1960 | — | — | — | — | — | 11.54 | — | 12.05 | — |
| (*N* = 77) | | | | | | | | | |
| 1959 | — | — | — | — | — | — | 11.47 | — | 10.92 |
| (*N* = 66) | | | | | | | | | |

*Note:* — denotes data missing by design structure

TABLE 11.1D
Covert Scores

| | | | | | | | | | |
|---|---|---|---|---|---|---|---|---|---|
| | | | | *Standard Deviations for Seven Groups* | | | | | |
| Birth | | | | | Age at Testing | | | | |
| Cohort | 11 | 12 | 13 | 14 | 15 | 16 | 17 | 18 | 19 |
| 1965 | 1.42 | — | 1.37 | — | — | — | — | — | — |
| (N = 46) | | | | | | | | | |
| 1964 | — | 1.65 | — | 2.69 | — | — | — | — | — |
| (N = 62) | | | | | | | | | |
| 1963 | — | — | 3.14 | — | 5.03 | — | — | — | — |
| (N = 80) | | | | | | | | | |
| 1962 | — | — | — | 4.69 | — | 4.37 | — | — | — |
| (N = 90) | | | | | | | | | |
| 1961 | — | — | — | — | 3.79 | — | 3.96 | — | — |
| (N = 89) | | | | | | | | | |
| 1960 | — | — | — | — | — | 3.77 | — | 5.75 | — |
| (N = 77) | | | | | | | | | |
| 1959 | — | — | — | — | — | — | 3.08 | — | 2.35 |
| (N = 66) | | | | | | | | | |

*Note:* — denotes data missing by design structure

TABLE 11.1E
Correlations Between Overt and Covert
Scores for Seven Groups

| | $O_{T1}$ | $O_{T2}$ | $C_{T1}$ | $C_{T2}$ |
|---|---|---|---|---|
| | | *Group 1 (Ages 11 and 13)* *(N = 46)* | | |
| Overt$_{T1}$ | 1.0 | .06 | .6 | − .03 |
| Overt$_{T2}$ | .06 | 1.0 | − .05 | .27 |
| Covert$_{T1}$ | .6 | − .05 | 1.0 | − .09 |
| Covert$_{T2}$ | − .03 | .27 | − .09 | 1.0 |

*Note:* T1 = 1976    T2 = 1978

| | $O_{T1}$ | $O_{T2}$ | $C_{T1}$ | $C_{T2}$ |
|---|---|---|---|---|
| | | *Group 2 (Ages 12 and 14)* *(N = 62)* | | |
| Overt$_{T1}$ | 1.0 | .33 | .39 | − 0.03 |
| Overt$_{T2}$ | .33 | 1.0 | .08 | .52 |
| Covert$_{T1}$ | .39 | .08 | 1.0 | .11 |
| Covert$_{T2}$ | − .03 | .52 | .11 | 1.0 |

*Note:* T1 = 1976    T2 = 1978

*(Continued)*

TABLE 11.1E
*(Continued)*

| | $O_{TI}$ | $O_{T2}$ | $C_{TI}$ | $C_{T2}$ |
|---|---|---|---|---|
| | | *Group 3 (Ages 13 and 15)* | | |
| | | *(N = 80)* | | |
| Overt$_{T1}$ | 1.0 | .28 | .79 | .29 |
| Overt$_{T2}$ | .28 | 1.0 | .25 | .6 |
| Covert$_{T1}$ | .79 | .25 | 1.0 | .3 |
| Covert$_{T2}$ | .29 | .6 | .3 | 1.0 |

*Note:* T1 = 1976   T2 = 1978

| | $O_{TI}$ | $O_{T2}$ | $C_{TI}$ | $C_{T2}$ |
|---|---|---|---|---|
| | | *Group 4 (Ages 14 and 16)* | | |
| | | *(N = 90)* | | |
| Overt$_{T1}$ | 1.0 | .23 | .32 | .13 |
| Overt$_{T2}$ | .23 | 1.0 | .16 | .42 |
| Covert$_{T1}$ | .32 | .16 | 1.0 | .63 |
| Covert$_{T2}$ | .13 | .42 | .63 | 1.0 |

*Note:* T1 = 1976   T2 = 1978

| | $O_{TI}$ | $O_{T2}$ | $C_{TI}$ | $C_{T2}$ |
|---|---|---|---|---|
| | | *Group 5 (Ages 15 and 17)* | | |
| | | *(N = 89)* | | |
| Overt$_{T1}$ | 1.0 | .48 | .55 | .34 |
| Overt$_{T2}$ | .48 | 1.0 | .32 | .7 |
| Covert$_{T1}$ | .55 | .32 | 1.0 | .5 |
| Covert$_{T2}$ | .34 | .7 | .5 | 1.0 |

*Note:* T1 = 1976   T2 = 1978

| | $O_{TI}$ | $O_{T2}$ | $C_{TI}$ | $C_{T2}$ |
|---|---|---|---|---|
| | | *Group 6 (Ages 16 and 18)* | | |
| | | *(N = 77)* | | |
| Overt$_{T1}$ | 1.0 | .18 | .61 | .19 |
| Overt$_{T2}$ | .18 | 1.0 | .2 | .78 |
| Covert$_{T1}$ | .61 | .2 | 1.0 | .43 |
| Covert$_{T2}$ | .19 | .78 | .43 | 1.0 |

*Note:* T1 = 1976   T2 = 1978

| | $O_{TI}$ | $O_{T2}$ | $C_{TI}$ | $C_{T2}$ |
|---|---|---|---|---|
| | | *Group 7 (Ages 17 and 19)* | | |
| | | *(N = 66)* | | |
| Overt$_{T1}$ | 1.0 | .07 | .4 | −.14 |
| Overt$_{T2}$ | .07 | 1.0 | −.08 | .41 |
| Covert$_{T1}$ | .4 | −.08 | 1.0 | −.01 |
| Covert$_{T2}$ | −.14 | .41 | −.01 | 1.0 |

*Note:* T1 = 1976 T2 = 1978

## Measures

The *OVERT antisocial behaviors scale* was created for this study using 14 items from Elliot et al.'s (1983) self-reported delinquency scale. The behaviors represented in this scale were observable, or open to view by others, with presumably little or no effort on the part of the youth to hide the behavior from others. These items were primarily aggressive behaviors displayed across a variety of the youth's social settings including the family, school, and peer contexts, including behaviors such as hitting or threatening to hit teachers or other adults at school, parents, other students at school; strong-arming other students and teachers; throwing of objects at cars or people; involvement in gang fights; assault with intent to seriously hurt or kill; and purposely damaging property belonging to parents, family members, school, or others.

The *COVERT antisocial behaviors scale*, also created for this study, was a nine-item subscale composed of crimes of theft, burglary, breaking and entering, and drug sales. These items reflect behaviors that presumably involved deliberate efforts on the part of the youth to conceal or keep secret their own identity in the commission of the behavior.

Items for both scales were scored from 1 to 9, and items were summed within scale to create composite OVERT and COVERT scores for each testing occasion. The average reliabilities across waves of testing for the OVERT and COVERT scales, as measured by coefficient alpha (Kuder & Richardson, 1937) was .77 and .80, respectively. (See Aber, 1989, for more details.)

## RESULTS

### Alternative Model Estimation

The longitudinal OVERT and COVERT statistics of Tables 11.1a through 11.1e are now used to obtain empirical values for the LGM model parameters of Tables 11.2a and 11.2b. Tables 11.2a and 11.2b present numerical results for each of four models fit to the univariate time series for OVERT and COVERT scores respectively. To simplify this illustration, only the results for the OVERT scores are considered in detail. When we examine a fifth, bivariate model, we examine results for both OVERT and COVERT scores in a single model. Estimation of the following models merely requires the use of available computer programs for structural equation modeling such as CO-SAN II (McDonald, 1978, 1985) or LISREL (Joreskog & Sorbom, 1979, 1985).

Because the LGM techniques used here are not standard or classical structural equation models, a few words of explanation are in order. Some of our LGM place joint constraints on the means, variances, and covariances. Therefore, we must fit these models to average cross products or moment matrices. Cross-products matrices are calculated from the usual sums of squares and cross-

TABLE 11.2A
Overt Scores

| Parameter Estimates | No Growth | Linear | Latent | Dual | |
|---|---|---|---|---|---|
| | | | | *(Sa₁)* $(Sa_1)$ | $(Sa_2)$ |
| | | *Shape Loadings* | | | |
| S - > 11: $B_{11}$ | 0.0 | 1.0 | 0.3 | -0.21 | 0.0 |
| | - | - | (0.13) | (0.4) | - |
| S - > 12: $B_{12}$ | 0.0 | 0.875 | 1.0 | 1.0 | 0.0 |
| | - | - | - | - | - |
| S - > 13: $B_{13}$ | 0.0 | 0.75 | 0.77 | 0.0 | 0.0 |
| | - | - | (0.11) | - | - |
| S - > 14: $B_{14}$ | 0.0 | 0.625 | 0.54 | 0.0 | 1.0 |
| | - | - | (0.08) | - | - |
| S - > 15: $B_{15}$ | 0.0 | 0.5 | 0.54 | 0.0 | 1.11 |
| | - | - | (0.09) | - | (0.21) |
| S - > 16: $B_{16}$ | 0.0 | 0.375 | 0.3 | 0.0 | 0.12 |
| | - | - | (0.09) | - | (0.22) |
| S - > 17: $B_{17}$ | 0.0 | 0.25 | 0.36 | 0.0 | 0.57 |
| | - | - | (0.13) | - | (0.23) |
| S - > 18: $B_{18}$ | 0.0 | 0.125 | 0.17 | 0.0 | -0.67 |
| | - | - | (0.13) | - | (0.36) |
| S - > 19: $B_{19}$ | 0.0 | 0.0 | 0.0 | 0.0 | 0.0 |
| | - | - | - | - | - |
| | | *Latent Means* | | | |
| C - > L: Ml | 20.41 | 18.28 | 17.94 | 19.55 | |
| | (0.21) | (0.37) | (1.37) | (0.31) | |
| C - > S: $Ms_1$ | 0.0 | 4.67 | 5.54 | 2.68 | |
| | - | (0.78) | (1.01) | (1.07) | |
| C - > S: $Ms_2$ | NA | NA | NA | 1.43 | |
| | NA | NA | NA | (0.44) | |
| | | *Latent Deviations* | | | |
| L* - > L: Dl | -2.91 | 1.34 | 0.81 | 2.57 | |
| | (0.29) | (0.69) | (1.37) | (0.31) | |
| S* - > S: $Ds_1$ | 0.0 | 5.53 | -6.12 | 3.97 | |
| | - | (0.6) | (0.8) | (1.6) | |
| S* - > S: $Ds_2$ | NA | NA | NA | 2.99 | |
| | NA | NA | NA | (0.68) | |
| | | *Score Deviations* | | | |
| D* - > Y: $De_1$ | 28.45 | 25.55 | 24.84 | 42.65 | |
| | (1.79) | (1.65) | (1.64) | (5.34) | |
| D* - > Y: $De_2$ | NA | NA | NA | 19.45 | |
| | NA | NA | NA | (1.85) | |
| | | *Goodness of Fit Information* | | | |
| L.R.T. | 135.15 | 81.37 | 54.88 | 76.89 | |
| D.F. | 39 | 37 | 30 | 29 | |
| P-Value | 0.00 | 0.00 | 0.004 | 0.00 | |

(standard errors in parentheses)

*Note*: subscript '1' indicates parameters associated with the first slope factor in dual model and the only slope factor in the linear and latent models;

subscript '2' indicates parameters associated with the second slope factor in the dual model only.

TABLE 11.2B
Covert Scores

| Parameter Estimates | No Growth | Linear | Latent | Dual (Sa_1) | (Sa_2) |
|---|---|---|---|---|---|
| | | | *Model* | | |
| | | *Shape Loadings* | | (Sa_1) | (Sa_2) |
| S - > 11: $B_{11}$ | 0.0 | 1.0 | -0.06 | 0.0 | 0.0 |
| | - | - | (0.18) | - | - |
| S - > 12: $B_{12}$ | 0.0 | 0.875 | 0.02 | 0.32 | 0.0 |
| | - | - | (0.08) | (0.2) | - |
| S - > 13: $B_{13}$ | 0.0 | 0.75 | 0.14 | 1.0 | 0.0 |
| | - | - | (0.07) | - | - |
| S - > 14: $B_{14}$ | 0.0 | 0.625 | 0.55 | 0.0 | 0.53 |
| | - | - | (0.07) | - | (0.08) |
| S - > 15: $B_{15}$ | 0.0 | 0.5 | 0.63 | 0.0 | 0.61 |
| | - | - | (0.08) | - | (0.08) |
| S - > 16: $B_{16}$ | 0.0 | 0.375 | 0.52 | 0.0 | 0.52 |
| | - | - | (0.05) | - | (0.06) |
| S - > 17: $B_{17}$ | 0.0 | 0.25 | 0.51 | 0.0 | 0.5 |
| | - | - | (0.07) | - | (0.08) |
| S - > 18: $B_{18}$ | 0.0 | 0.125 | 1.0 | 0.0 | 1.0 |
| | - | - | - | - | - |
| S - > 19: $B_{19}$ | 0.0 | 0.0 | 0.0 | 0.0 | 0.0 |
| | - | - | - | - | - |
| | | *Latent Means* | | | |
| C - > L: Ml | 11.4 | 10.51 | 10.63 | 1.03 | |
| | (0.14) | (0.23) | (0.18) | (0.02) | |
| C - > S: $Ms_1$ | 0.0 | 1.75 | 1.69 | 0.07 | |
| | - | (0.48) | (0.45) | (0.03) | |
| C - > S: $Ms_2$ | NA | NA | NA | 0.22 | |
| | NA | NA | NA | (0.04) | |
| | | *Latent Deviations* | | | |
| L* - > L: Dl | 2.44 | 0.04 | 0.0 | 0.09 | |
| | (0.14) | (1768) | (1730) | (0.02) | |
| S* - > S: $Ds_1$ | 0.0 | 4.67 | 0.54 | 0.21 | |
| | - | (0.3) | (0.05) | (0.02) | |
| S* - > S: $Ds_2$ | NA | NA | NA | 0.5 | |
| | NA | NA | NA | (0.05) | |
| | | *Score Deviations* | | | |
| D* - > Y: $De_1$ | 8.55 | 7.86 | 0.64 | 0.01 | |
| | (0.54) | (0.57) | (0.05) | (0.005) | |
| D* - > Y: $De_2$ | NA | NA | NA | 0.08 | |
| | NA | NA | NA | (0.01) | |
| | | *Goodness of Fit Information* | | | |
| L.R.T. | 288.17 | 237.34 | 133.1 | 96.46 | |
| D.F. | 39 | 37 | 30 | 29 | |
| P-Value | 0.00 | 0.00 | 0.004 | 0.00 | |

(standard errors in parentheses)

*Note*: subscript '1' indicates parameters associated with the first slope factor in dual model and the only slope factor in the linear and latent models;

subscript '2' indicates parameters associated with the second slope factor in the dual model only.

products matrix multiplied by $1/N$, and augmented by a column of means. Each element of a cross-products matrix can be directly interpreted as the product of two raw scores averaged over all subjects. The elements of these matrices are also frequently treated as mean squares plus covariances, and this interpretation can be employed conveniently to calculate model expectations. In general, then, any problem with $K$ variables requires the preliminary calculation of a $[(K + 1) \times (K + 1)]$ symmetric moment matrix.

The addition of a variable with a constant value of 1 for all subjects is used to separate the means from the covariances in the models that follow. This unit constant variable is represented in Fig. 11.1 by the triangle labeled "1." Arrows from the unit constant represent model mean intercept parameters. For all calculations here, we obtain maximum likelihood parameter estimates, associated standard errors, and an overall likelihood ratio test (LRT) statistic for the evaluation of goodness-of-fit of each model. Each model constraint yields one degree of freedom ($DF$) for testing the fit of the constrained model against some less restricted alternative.

*Fitting No-Growth Baseline Models.* In the first model we restrict the basis coefficients of the slope factor ($S$) to be zero, $B(t) = 0$, to reflect the assumption of no change over time. Furthermore, we restrict $Ms = 0$ and $Ds = 0$. In this model we assume that

$$Y(t,n) = L(n) + E(t,n). \tag{2}$$

Thus, we allow only one mean $Ml$, one common deviation $Dl$, and one unique deviation $De$.

The first column in Table 11.2a is labeled "no growth" and provides parameter estimates for the no-growth model fit to the OVERT statistics. Corresponding estimates for the COVERT scores are presented in the first column of Table 11.2b. For the OVERT scores, $Ml = 20.4$, $Dl = -2.9$, and $De = 28.5$. We interpret these parameters to indicate that: (a) on average all groups obtain a mean score of about 20, (b) individual variation around this group average is relatively small (with a standard deviation of about 3), and (c) the error variance at any one time is large (with a standard deviation of about 29). Because we have forced the shape $B(t) = 0$, the function is flat or level over age. This highly restrictive model fits the data with an $LRT = 135$ on $DF = 39$, suggesting that this model is highly unlikely for these data. We often take this no-growth model as a baseline against which to compare the fit of alternative models.

*Fitting Linear Age-Basis Growth Models.* In a second model, we again restrict the basis coefficients of the shape factor, $B(t)$, but this time we assume that the function is linear with change in chronological age. We write

$$Y(t,n) = L(n) + Ba(t)\, Sa(n) + E(t,n), \tag{3}$$

where $Ba(t)$ is proportional to the age-at-testing $A(t)$ of the groups. Specifically, in our data the average ages at testing are approximately $A(t) = [$ 11, 12, 13, 14, 15, 16, 17, 18, 19 ]. We can define the differences between all ages and the last time point as $dA(t) = A(T)\text{-}A(t) = [$ 8, 7, 6, 5, 4, 3, 2, 1, 0 ]. Typically, we scale these differences in age to be normalized relative to some specific time point. For the Linear model fit here we restrict $B(t) = dA(t)/8 = [$ 1, .875, .75, .625, .5, .375, .25, .125, 0 ] so that each $B(t)$ represents the proportion of total years elapsed between the first and last ages in the data, at that measurement age.

The column labeled "linear" in Table 11.2a displays numerical results for the free parameters for this model fit to the OVERT statistics. The latent mean level for the linear function $Ml = 18.3$ and the mean slope $Ms = 4.7$. The level standard deviation $Dl = 1.3$ is small relative to its standard error and is thus interpreted to be effectively zero, revealing very little reliable individual variation around the group average level. The slope standard deviation, on the other hand, $Ds = 5.5$ is large relative to both its standard error and the mean slope and indicates substantial individual differences in the rate of change in the OVERT scores over age. This model, like the no-growth model is highly restrictive and fits the data with a $LRT = 81$ on $DF = 37$. Although this model still does not fit these data particularly well, it represents a substantial improvement in fit over the no-growth baseline given $dLRT = 54$ on $dDF = 2$.

*Fitting Latent Growth Models.*   Next we fit the first fully latent growth model that, in contrast to the restricted shape bases of the previous models, reflects an optimal patterning over age for the changes in the OVERT scores. The $B(t)$ in this model are estimated from the data and yield a potentially useful, if somewhat unusual, interpretation. The freely estimated $B(t)$ reflect a "metameter" or "latent time" scale (see Rao, 1958; Tucker, 1966) which reshapes the observed time scale so that the latent slopes $S(n)$ are maximally linear. These $B(t)$ thus represent a kind of "rubber ruler" that stretches or reshapes the observed time scale and provides information about the relative rates of change between measured points for the overall function.

The estimation of the $B(t)$ in the latent growth model requires attention to issues of mathematical and statistical identification as is the case in any typical factor analysis. Thus, at least one of the $B(t)$ needs to be fixed at, for example, $B(12) = 1$, and another at, say, $B(19) = 0$. Restricting the $B(t)$ in this manner creates a fixed interval scaling that provides a reference point for the estimation of the other free $B(t)$ parameters.

Results obtained from fitting this latent growth model to the OVERT statistics are presented in the third column of Table 11.2a and are labeled "latent." Here we see that the latent basis coefficients obtained are $B(t) = [$ .3, 1, .77, .54, .54, .3, .36, .17, 0 ]. Their first differences for these coefficients, $dB(t) = [$ 0, -.7, .23, .23, 0, .24, -.06, .19 ], can be compared to the equal age interval step of the linear model presented earlier where $dB(t) = .125$. This comparison reveals rather dramatic increases to about age 12, relatively large increases between the ages of 13 and 17, followed by smaller increases between 18 and 19. The means for this model show a starting point of $Ml = 17.9$ and average change of $Ms = 5.5$. As was true for the linear model, small individual differences in mean level emerge, $Dl = .81$, but considerable individual differences in shape are obtained, $Ds = -6.1$.

It should be noted that although the mean shape for the overall reference curve in this case is $Ms = 5.5$, change is not equal across all ages but instead is proportional to the $B(t)$. In these data the accumulated gain is Gain$(t)$ = $[B(t)^*M(s)]$ = [ 1.65, 5.5, 4.24, 2.97, 2.97, 1.65, 1.98, .94, 0 ]. Thus, the difference in gain is $d$Gain$(t)$ = [ 0, -3.85, 1.26, 1.27, 0, 1.32, -.33, 1.04, .94 ]. The peak gain in these data occurs at age 12, after which time the rate of gain slows down. Note also that the $B(t)$, in general, decrease over age indicating a decrease in the ratio of the common variance to the total variance within each manifest variable as a function of age. This means the individual's growth trajectories become less stable, and hence less predictable, as the individual gets older. This prediction over age is a byproduct of any growth model where decreasing common variance reflects decreasing individual diversity over age.

This model fits the data with an $LRT = 54.88$ on $DF = 30$, not an excellent fit, but the best of the three models fit to this point. The fit of the model represents quite a substantial improvement in fit over the no-growth baseline model, $dLRT = 80$ on $dDF = 9$, as well as over the linear model, $dLRT = 26$ on $dDF = 7$.

*Fitting Dual-Growth Function Models.*    Both the linear and latent growth models are based on the assumption that the patterning of intraindividual change in the OVERT statistics can be efficiently organized into two individual difference components, one representing common sources of individual differences in Level, $L$, and a second representing common sources of individual differences in Slope, $S$. This assumption is just one of many plausible alternatives for these data. A second, depicted in the fourth column of Table 11.2a, labeled "dual," posits the necessity of a second source of individual differences to account for changes the in shape of the developmental function over age. In theory, we can constrain the parameters of this second component in a wide variety of ways to represent numerous testable hypotheses. For example, if we restrict the $B(t)$ of the first slope component to be proportional of age-at-testing, as in the linear model, we might wish to follow a quadratic model and introduce a second slope factor with fixed $B(t)$ determined by squaring the $B(t)$ of the first slope factor.

Here, instead, we explore the possibility that change between ages 11 and 13 years have a common source of individual differences that is distinguishable from the common source of individual differences giving rise to the change between ages 14 and 19. Here we write

$$Y(t,n) = L(n) + Ba_1(t)\ Sa_1(n) + Ba_2(t)\ Sa_2(n) + E(t,n), \qquad (4)$$

where $Ba_1(t)$ is estimated from the data for ages 11 through 13 but restricted to zero for ages 14 through 19, and $Ba_2(t)$ is restricted to zero for ages 11 through 13, but estimated from the data for ages 14 through 19. To ensure unique identifiability and to provide fixed interval scaling of the slope factors we restrict $Ba_1(12) = 1$, $Ba_1(13) = 0$, $Ba_2(14) = 1$, and $Ba_2(19) = 0$.

This model yields a mean level, $Ml = 19.55$, and mean slopes, $Sa_1 = 2.68$ and $Sa_2 = 1.43$. These results indicate that the mean change during the age span 11 through 13 years is larger than that between 14 and 19 years. Individual differences around the mean level are small, $Dl = 2.57$, while those around the means slopes are relatively large, $Ds_1 = 3.97$ and $Ds_2 = 2.99$. In this model two error deviations are estimated, one for the set of variables associated with $Sa_1$, $De_1 = 42.65$, and one for the set of variables associated with $Sa_2$, $De_2 = 19.45$, and indicate greater unexplained variation in the manifest OVERT scores between ages 11 and 13 than between 14 and 19.

The estimates for $Ba_1(t) = [ -.21, 1, 0 ]$ indicate a rapid rise in slope at age 12 relative to ages 11 and 13. Similarly, the estimates for $Ba_2(t) = [ 1, 1.11, .12, .57, -.67, 0 ]$ and indicate relatively rapid rise in slope at ages 14 and 15 compared to ages 16 through 19.

This dual model fits the OVERT statistics with $LRT = 76.89$ on $DF = 29$, yielding a $dLRT = -22$ on $dDF = 1$ compared to the latent growth model fit discussed earlier. This particular dual model does not represent a very likely alternative to the latent model, and the addition of a second source of individual differences in slope of this type does not seem necessary. This is not an inevitable result, however. Indeed, the fourth column of Table 11.2b presents results of this dual model fit to the statistics for COVERT antisocial behavior. In this case, the dual model provides a substantial improvement in fit relative to the latent model, $dLRT = 37$ on $DF = 1$, and provides the best fit to the data of all univariate models fit to the COVERT statistics.

***Fitting a Bivariate Growth Model.***  Our final model expands the univariate foundation of the LGM presented thus far to accomodate developmental functions for both the OVERT and COVERT scores in a single bivariate model. This model is fit to a cross-products matrix that includes both the OVERT and COVERT scores over time. The bivariate model allows the direct comparison of different growth processes. Examination of the "extrinsic" quality of change over time might include testing whether the two curves have the same shape [i.e., does $B_o(t) = B_c(t)$]? Examination of the intrinsic quality of the shape scores might include tests of whether the changes coincide prefectly over both measures; that is, does the correlation between $S_o$ and $S_c$ $(CS_oS_c)$ equal 1? If this model fits the data well, it would suggest that both variables reflect the same intraindividual process. Alternatively, one might ask if the changes are perfectly independent (i.e., does $CS_oS_c = 0$?). These ideas are of interest to researchers wanting to know, for example, whether performance on two tasks represent the same competency over time.

The results of fitting the Bivariate model to the OVERT and COVERT statistics are presented in Table 11.2c. In addition to the basic parameters of the LGM presented thus far, the Bivariate model includes two intervariable factor correlations ($CS_oS_c$, $CL_oS_c$), and one intravariable factor correlation ($CL_o$-$S_o$). The extremely large standard error of the estimate for the level deviation in the latent growth model fit to the COVERT scores ($Dl_c$) posed problems of identification for LISREL in estimating correlations that involved the $Dl_c$. Given that this standard error meant that this estimate was essentially zero, it was restricted to zero in the bivariate model. Also, we allow within time intervariable correlations between the disturbance terms for the OVERT ($D_o$) and COVERT ($D_c$) scores. In this application we allow all parameters to be free between variables.

This model yields results that, within variables, are similar to those obtained from the univariate LGM for the OVERT and COVERT scores. Of particular interest here are the intravariable and intervariable factor correlations. As can be seen in Table 11.2c, there was a large and negative correlation between the OVERT level and slope factor scores ($CL_oS_o$ = -.74). Because the mean OVERT level $Ml_o$ and mean OVERT slope $Ms_o$ scores were positive, this result suggests that the higher an individual's curve in absolute level the smaller was his rate of growth.

The unique aspects of the bivariate model, of course, are reflected in the intervariable factor correlations. Here we see a moderate correlation between the OVERT level and COVERT slope factor scores ($CL_oS_c$ = .50) which we interpret to mean that higher individual OVERT curves in absolute level are associated with faster rates of growth in COVERT scores. The correlation between the slope factor scores, $CS_oS_c$ = -.05, is small relative to its standard error and suggests that there is no reliable relationship between changes in OVERT scores and changes in COVERT scores over time. We interpret this result to mean that the sources of change for these two variable are not the same. This result is of substantive interest as much research has found relatively high correlations between OVERT and COVERT antisocial behaviors over time. These studies did not examine the dynamics underlying change in each of these behaviors and results like those presented here raise important questions about the meaning of the previous findings.

The bivariate model does not fit our data particularly well, $LRT = 241$ on $DF = 70$. This model is presented here merely to illustrate the multivariate flexibility of the LGM approach. Clearly this model might be compared to a broad array of alternatives that place restrictions on various parameters of theoretical interest to those concerned with establish criteria for competence. Moreover, the bivariate model can be expanded to a multivariate form which includes any number of variables.

TABLE 11.2C
Overt and Covert Scores

### Bivariate Model

Parameter
Estimates

#### Shape Loadings

| | | |
|---|---|---|
| $S_O - > 11: B_{O11}$ | 0.26 | (0.09) |
| $S_O - > 12: B_{O12}$ | 1.0 | - |
| $S_O - > 13: B_{O13}$ | 0.69 | (0.08) |
| $S_O - > 14: B_{O14}$ | 0.51 | (0.07) |
| $S_O - > 15: B_{O15}$ | 0.34 | (0.08) |
| $S_O - > 16: B_{O16}$ | 0.29 | (0.08) |
| $S_O - > 17: B_{O17}$ | 0.23 | (0.08) |
| $S_O - > 18: B_{O18}$ | 0.16 | (0.10) |
| $S_O - > 19: B_{O19}$ | 0.0 | - |
| | | |
| $S_C - > 11: B_{C11}$ | -0.08 | (0.15) |
| $S_C - > 12: B_{C12}$ | 0.10 | (0.07) |
| $S_C - > 13: B_{C13}$ | 0.14 | (0.05) |
| $S_C - > 14: B_{C14}$ | 0.56 | (0.06) |
| $S_C - > 15: B_{C15}$ | 0.57 | (0.06) |
| $S_C - > 16: B_{C16}$ | 0.55 | (0.05) |
| $S_C - > 17: B_{C17}$ | 0.52 | (0.06) |
| $S_C - > 18: B_{C18}$ | 1.0 | - |
| $S_C - > 19: B_{C19}$ | 0.0 | - |

#### Latent Means

| | | |
|---|---|---|
| $C - > L_O: M1_O$ | 18.35 | (0.52) |
| $C - > S_O: Ms_O$ | 5.67 | (0.94) |
| $C - > L_C: M1_C$ | 10.68 | (0.17) |
| $C - > S_C: Ms_C$ | 1.68 | (0.41) |

#### Latent Deviations

| | | |
|---|---|---|
| $L^*_O - > L_O: D1_O$ | 3.99 | (0.70) |
| $S^*_O - > S_O: Ds_O$ | 10.24 | (1.31) |
| $L^*_C - > L_C: D1_C$ | 0.0 | - |
| $S^*_C - > S_C: Ds_C$ | 5.31 | (0.40) |

#### Latent Variable Correlations

| | | |
|---|---|---|
| $L^*_O < - > S^*_O: CL_OS_O$ | -0.74 | (0.11) |
| $L^*_O < - > L^*_C: CL_OL_C$ | 0.0 | - |
| $L^*_O < - > S^*_C: CL_OS_C$ | 0.50 | (0.12) |
| $S^*_O < - > S^*_C: CS_OS_C$ | -0.05 | (0.12) |
| $L^*_C < - > S^*_O: CL_CS_O$ | 0.0 | - |
| $L^*_C < - > S^*_C: CL_CS_C$ | 0.0 | - |

#### Score Deviations

| | | |
|---|---|---|
| $D^*_O - > Y: D_O$ | 22.19 | (1.62) |
| $D^*_C - > Y: D_C$ | 6.64 | (0.39) |

(Continued)

TABLE 11.2C
*(Continued)*

*Bivariate Model*

Parameter
Estimates

*Within Time Intervariable Correlations*

| | | |
|---|---|---|
| $D^*_{O11} < - > D^*_{C11}$: $C_{11}$ | 9.24 | (2.33) |
| $D^*_{O12} < - > D^*_{C12}$: $C_{12}$ | 11.14 | (2.22) |
| $D^*_{O13} < - > D^*_{C13}$: $C_{13}$ | 11.46 | (1.27) |
| $D^*_{O14} < - > D^*_{C14}$: $C_{14}$ | 4.64 | (1.40) |
| $D^*_{O15} < - > D^*_{C15}$: $C_{15}$ | 4.85 | (1.23) |
| $D^*_{O16} < - > D^*_{C16}$: $C_{16}$ | 5.71 | (0.95) |
| $D^*_{O17} < - > D^*_{C17}$: $C_{17}$ | 7.02 | (1.05) |
| $D^*_{O18} < - > D^*_{C18}$: $C_{18}$ | 12.37 | (1.63) |
| $D^*_{O19} < - > D^*_{C19}$: $C_{19}$ | 7.55 | (1.59) |

*Goodness of Fit Information*

| | |
|---|---|
| L.R.T. | 241.73 |
| D.F. | 70 |
| P-Value | 0.00 |

(standard errors in parentheses)
*Note*: subscript 'O' indicates parameters associated with the Overt Scores and
subscript 'C' indicates parameters associated with the Covert Scores

## DISCUSSION

The primary advantage of the latent growth curve models illustrated here is
that they allow us to formalize, and therefore directly test, different concepts
of change. Hypotheses about no growth, linear growth, latent growth, and multiple growth functions were illustrated and compared. The graphic representation of various change ideas facilitates communication and thinking in this
area by making explicit the hypotheses and assumptions underlying different
models of change. Obviously, the models illustrated here are neither the only,
nor necessarily the best, way to organize developmental data. They are merely alternatives that we believe have been under-utilized and may provide additional leverage over standard models for examining the dynamics underlying the development of competencies.

The results presented here also illustrate methodology for modeling and testing ideas about the convergence of longitudinal series derived from multiple
staggered groups. Each group provides data on different segments of the age
curve. But because data from the groups overlap, we can treat this as a problem
of multiple groups having different blocks of missing data within a multiple

group structural equation model. This approach provides both practical and statistical efficiency in estimating a single developmental trajectory over all ages represented by the independent groups. Of course, convergence of short-term longitudinal segments across groups is not a necessary feature of the data. But this approach allows us to frame convergence as an empirically rejectable hypothesis.

The bivariate model presented here allows us to examine questions of "convergence of growth curves across separate variables." This model allows direct tests of hypotheses concerning whether different variables seem to follow the same curve over time. In other words, are the curves parallel or synchronous? What is the relative sequencing of multiple growth processes? This model may be particularly useful in debates concerning the competence-performance distinction addressed elsewhere in this volume. Our ability to distinguish fundamental competencies from "performance" factors requires that competencies and performance factors under study not only be conceptually, but also methodologically, independent of each other.

Methodological independence can be modeled in a wide variety of ways. One approach, not often pursued in the literature on competency is depicted easily in the bivariate model. Given the measurement of different variables deemed to represent the competency and performance factors in question, and a theoretical rationale for different patterns of change for these variables over time, examination of the comparability of different growth functions for these variables over time can provide a way to check for the existence of conceptually independent components. In some substantive domains, for example, although one might expect performance factors and competencies to show moderate correlations at any given age, performance functions might be expected to "level off" at ages earlier than the competencies in question. The same logic may also be used to determine whether different tasks, the solutions of which are intended to reflect the same underlying competence, follow the same developmental trajectory.

One limitation, among others, of the models presented here comes from their reliance on a single measured variable to represent the construct of interest. Many of the complex competencies of interest to developmental psychologists cannot easily be represented in this way. Reliance on a single measured variable may be particularly problemmatic for questions of development where the substantive interpretation of a measured variable changes with age. Alternatively, when the construct of interest is represented by a factor at each time of measurement, assumptions of invariance in the pattern of factor loadings across time can be tested directly (see Horn, McArdle, & Mason, 1983; Joreskog, 1971; Meredith, 1964; Nesselroade, 1983). The LGM presented here have been extended in previous work to include such factor analytic measurement models. The curve of factors model (CUFFS) provides extra power to deal with problems of reliability of measurement, and inclusion of complex theoretical constructs, by applying the growth curve methods to latent variables derived from multiple sources of data within each time of measurement (see McArdle, 1988; McArdle & Anderson, 1989, for more details on these models).

Another useful extension of the models illustrated here combines the latent growth curve ideas with more standard causal ideas of path analysis. Exogenous variables measured at one point in time can be added to our LGM. We can then examine the influence of these exogenous variables on any of the change parameters of theoretical interest (see McArdle & Epstein, 1987, and Aber, Lieber, & Mulvey, in press, for examples of these applications).

When trying to measure things that change and develop, one may not want to choose tests with the highest test–retest stability. Nor might one merely be interested in the extent to which variables demonstrate mean differences or normative stability over time. Instead, it may make sense to choose tests with the highest internal consistency reliability together with the "lowest" test–retest stability. The models presented here are consistent with these latter ideas. By moving beyond traditional autoregressive and MANOVA models of change we hope that they may aid researchers interested in thinking about alternative ways of viewing whether a particular developmental milestone has been reached.

## ACKNOWLEDGMENTS

This research has been supported by grants from the Illinois Department of Alcohol and Substance Abuse to the first author, and from the National Institute on Aging (AG07137) to the second author. We thank Dick Bell, Michael Chapman, and Eli Lieber for their support of this work.

## REFERENCES

Aber, M. S. (1989). *Developmental pathways in adolescent antisocial behavior*. Unpublished doctoral dissertation, University of Virginia, Charlottesville, Virginia.

Aber, M. S., Lieber, E., & Mulvey, E. P. (in press). The abandonment of delinquent behavior: New directions in theory and method. In W. A. Rhodes & W. Brown (Eds.), *Why some children succeed despite the odds*. New York: Praeger.

Bell, R. Q. (1953). Convergence: An accelerated longitudinal approach. *Child Development, 24*, 145–152.

Bell, R. Q. (1954). An experimental test of the accelerated longitudinal approach. *Child Development, 25*, 281–286.

Brown, C. H. (1983). Asymptotic comparison of missing data procedures for estimating factor loadings. *Psychometrika, 48*(2), 269–291.

Bryk, A. S., & Raudenbush, S. W. (1987). Application of hierarchical linear models to assessing change. *Psychological Bulletin, 101*(1), 147–158.

Elliot, D. S., Ageton, S. S., Huizinga, D., Knowles, B. A., & Canter, R. J. (1983). *The prevalence and incidence of delinquent behavior: 1976-1980* (The National Survey Report No. 26). Boulder, CO: Behavioral Research Institute.

Glindmeyer, H. W., Diem, J. E., Jones, R. N., & Weil, H. (1982). Noncomparability of longitudinally and cross-sectionally determined annual change in spirometry. *American Review of Respiratory Disease, 125,* 544-548.

Goldstein, H. (1987). *Multilevel models in educational and social research.* London: Oxford University Press.

Horn, J. L. (1972). State, trait and change dimensions of intelligence. *British Journal of Educational Psychology, 42*(2), 159-185.

Horn, J. L., & McArdle, J. J. (1980). Perspectives on mathematical/statistical model building (MASMOB) in research on aging. In L. W. Poon (Ed.), *Aging in the 1980s: Selected contemporary issues in the psychology of aging* (pp. 503-541). Washington, DC: American Psychological Association.

Horn, J. L., McArdle, J. J., & Mason, R. (1983). When is invariance not invariant? A practical scientist's look at the ethereal concept of factor invariance. *The Southern Psychologist, 1*(4), 179-188.

Hultsch, D. F., Nesselroade, J. R., & Plemons, J. K. (1976). Learning ability relations in adulthood. *Human Development, 19,* 234-247.

Joreskog, K. G. (1971). Simultaneous factor analysis in many populations. *Psychometrika, 36*(4), 409-426.

Joreskog, K. G., & Sorbom, D. (1979). *Advances in factor analysis and structural equation models.* Cambridge, MA: Abt Books.

Joreskog, K. G., & Sorbom, D. (1980). *Simultaneous analysis of longitudinal data from several cohorts* (Research Rep. 80-5). Department of Statistics, University of Uppsala, Sweden.

Joreskog, K. G., & Sorbom, D. (1985). *LISREL-VI program manual.* Chicago: International Educational Services.

Kuder, G. F., & Richardson, M. W. (1937). The theory of the estimation of test reliability. *Psychometrika, 2,* 151-160.

McArdle, J. J. (1986). Latent growth within behavior genetic models. *Behavior Genetics, 16*(1), 163-200.

McArdle, J. J. (1988). Dynamic but structural equation modeling of repeated measures data. In J. R. Nesselroade & R. B. Cattell (Eds.), *Handbook of multivariate experimental psychology* (2nd ed., pp. 561-614). New York: Plenum Press.

McArdle, J. J. (in press). Structural models of developmental theory in psychology. In P. Van Geehrt & L. R. Mos (Eds.), *Annals of theoretical psychology* (Vol. 7).

McArdle, J. J., & Aber, M. S. (1990). Patterns of change within latent variable structural equation models. In A. von Eye & M. Rovine (Eds.), *New directions in developmental research* (Vol. 1, pp. 151-223). New York: Academic Press.

McArdle, J., & Anderson, E. (1989). Latent variable growth models for research on aging. In J. E. Birren & K. W. Schaie (Eds.), *The handbook of the psychology of aging* (3rd ed., pp. 21-44). San Diego, CA: Academic Press.

McArdle, J. J., Anderson, E., & Aber, M. S. (1987). Convergence hypotheses modeled and tested with linear structural equations. *Proceedings of the 1987 Public Health Conference on Records and Statistics* (pp. 347-352). National Center for Health Statistics, Hyattsville, MD.

McArdle, J. J., & Epstein, D. (1987). Latent growth curves within developmental structural equation models. *Child Development, 58,* 110-133.

McArdle J. J., & Hamagami, F. (in press). Modeling incomplete longitudinal and cross-sectional data using latent growth structural models. In L. M. Collins & J. L. Horn (Eds.), *Best methods for the analysis of change.* Washington, DC: American Psychological Association.

McDonald, R. P. (1978). A simple comprehensive model for the analysis of covariance structures. *British Journal of Mathematical and Statistical Psychology, 31,* 59-72.

McDonald, R. P. (1985). *Factor analysis and related methods*. Hillsdale, NJ: Lawrence Erlbaum Associates.

Meredith, W. (1964). Notes on factorial invariance. *Psychometrika, 29*(2), 177–185.

Meredith, W., & Tisak, J. (1984). *"Tuckerizing" curves*. Paper presented at the annual meeting of the Psychometric Society, Santa Barbara, CA.

Nesselroade, J. R. (1983). Temporal selection and factor invariance in the study of development and change. In P. B. Baltes & O. G. Brim, Jr. (Eds.), *Life-span development and behavior* (Vol. 5, pp. 59–87). New York: Academic Press.

Perlmutter, M. (1988). Cognitive development in life-span perspective: From description of differences to explanation of changes. In E. M. Hetherington, R. M. Lerner, & M. Perlmutter (Eds.), *Child development in life-span perspective* (pp. 191–217). Hillsdale, NJ: Lawrence Erlbaum Associates.

Rao, C. R. (1958). Some statistical methods for the comparison of growth curves. *Biometrics, 14*, 1–17.

Rao, M. N., & Rao, C. R. (1966). Linked cross-sectional study for determining norms and growth rates: A pilot study on Indian school-going boys. *SANKYA: The Indian Journal of Statistics: Series B, 28*, 237–258.

Rogosa, D., Brandt, D., & Zimowski, M. (1982). A growth curve approach to the measurement of change. *Psychological Bulletin*, 726–748.

Rogosa, D., & Willett, J. B. (1985). Understanding correlates of change modeling individual differences in growth. *Psychometrica, 50*, 203–228.

Rutter, M. (1984). Continuities and discontinuities in socioemotional development: Empirical and conceptual perspectives. In R. N. Emde & R. J. Harmon (Eds.), *Continuities and discontinuities in development* (pp. 41–68). New York: Plenum Press.

Tisak, J., & Meredith, W. (1989). Exploratory longitudinal factor analysis in multiple populations. *Psychometrika, 54*, 261–281.

Tucker, L. R. (1958). Determination of parameters of a functional relation by factor analysis. *Psychometrika, 23*(1), 19–23.

Tucker, L. R. (1966). Learning theory and multivariate experiment: Illustration by determination of parameters of generalized learning curves. In R. B. Cattell (Ed.), *The handbook of multivariate experimental psychology* (pp. 476–501). Chicago: Rand-McNally.

van't Hof, M. A., Roede, M. J., & Kowalski, C. J. (1977). Construction of growth standards from mixed-longitudinal data. *Human Biology, 49*(4), 593–603.

Wohlwill, J. F. (1970). The age variable in psychological research. *Psychological Review, 77*(1), 49–64.

Wohlwill, J. F. (in press). The partial isomorphism between developmental theory and methods. In P. Van Geehrt & L. R. Mos (Eds.), *Annals of theoretical psychology (Vol. 7). Developmental psychology*. New York: Plenum.

# Foreword to
# Further Debate

Michael Chapman
Michael Chandler
*University of British Columbia*

A common way of ending an edited book is to delineate (or if necessary, to invent) some central themes running through the various chapters and to weave them into some tentative, but hopeful conclusions regarding the current state of knowledge about the topic in question. In this instance, we believe that something different is called for. As described in the Introduction, decades of protracted debate over the seemingly elementary procedural question of how best to mark the onset of various cognitive competencies has failed, not only to achieve consensus, but also to identify the routes by which agreement might be reached in the future. Under these circumstances, we believe that it would be inappropriate to end a book on competence with the usual panaceas.

Because of this lack of apparent progress, the problem of how to identify particular competencies when they develop is in danger of being abandoned as unproductive instead of being pursued to its roots. Our goal in editing this book has been to retrace some of the steps that has brought us to this current impasse in the hope of finding some previously unexplored ways around it. It would be premature to suggest that definitive solutions can be distilled from the chapters in this volume, or from any other book on the problem of competence that could have been assembled at this moment in the history of developmental psychology. Instead, we have sought to stimulate our readers to question the old solutions and to search for new ones. For this reason, we wish to to close the book, not merely by summarizing the themes that have been sounded within it, but by drawing out potential implications of those themes, especially those that may have received insufficient emphasis.

## COMPETENCE, CAUSALITY, AND COGNITIVE STRUCTURE

One theme that emerged in several chapters, especially those comprising Part I, is that some further clarification of competence as an explanatory concept is a necessary step toward a resolution of more substantive issues. Thus, Chandler and Overton consider some different ways in which competence has been conceptualized and warn against construing it as a covert efficient cause of outwardly observable performance. Chandler refers to the relation between competence and performance as that between type and token, and both authors see competence as providing a kind of "pattern explanation" of performance. One can easily see Piagetian structures as more particular instances of such "pattern explanations." According to this interpretation, Piagetian structures define the competencies corresponding to the successive stages of cognitive development in terms of characteristic *patterns of performance*. In return, a particular performance can be explained with reference to the overall structural pattern to which it conforms. In different ways, both Chandler and Overton argue for the legitimacy of such forms of explanation and warn against attempts to assimilate them to the notion of efficient causality.

In contrast, Pascual-Leone and Johnson consider such purely structural accounts to be at best "first descriptive approximations" for truly causal explanations and propose an account of dialectical equilibration as a candidate for the latter office. Between these two poles of opinion, other authors in the book make reference to the concept of cognitive structure without examining in detail the issue of its causal status. On the one hand, Smith, Montangero, and Chapman each refer to structures in terms of the formal properties that characterize different levels of competence, a usage that would appear to imply little in the way of causality. On the other hand, Schröder and Edelstein explain the generalization of competence across domains of content as resulting from the "consolidation of a structure," a move that grants at least some minimal causal efficacy to that process.

Although the causal interpretation of cognitive structures is by no means decidable solely on the basis of what Piaget had to say on the subject, the fact that he not only affirmed the objective existence of structures, but also described them as "causally active" (Piaget, 1941, p. 217) is nevertheless of interest. What remains unclear, however, is whether such statements refer only to efficient causes or to formal causes as well.

This dialectic of causal and formal explanation is applicable as well to the kinds of formal models of competence discussed by Aber and McArdle. On the one hand, the most common application of latent variable modeling has been to fit models of causal influence to patterns of interrelationships among observed measurements. On this interpretation, a latent variable is an under-lying cause of variation in the observed measures. On the other hand, some extensions of latent variable techniques lend themselves to questions regard-ing the kind of "pattern explanation" described by Chandler and Overton. Thus, a researcher might be interested in knowing if performances on two or more measures can be construed as belonging to one underlying *type* on the basis of observed similarities, or whether a given sample of children can be represented as composed of a particular *mixture* of underlying types. Such ques-tions can be addressed directly through *latent class analysis* and *finite mixture anal-ysis*, extensions of latent variable methods to qualitative data. The application of latent class analysis to substantive questions of competence and performance is discussed by Rindskopf (1987), and the use of finite mixture analysis in test-ing developmental models is described by Erdfelder (1990).

## THE CONTEXT OF COMPETENCE

A related issue is what might be called the "locus" of competence (or struc-ture) either as a categorical attribute of the individual alone or as a relational characteristic of individuals within a particular social and ecological context. The traditional assumption has been that competence is resident in the individu-al psyche. An alternative, more contextual approach is represented in the chap-ters by Meacham and by Sigel. From a consideration of competence as a legal category, Meacham concludes that competence is best understood, not an at-tribute of individual children only, but of a complex that includes children as well as the social supports available to them. Sigel describes "representational competence" in terms of the mastery of a semiotic system; although children as individuals must learn to master that system in the course of their develop-ment, that mastery by its very nature is shared with an entire community of symbol users.

This point has implications beyond those with which Meacham and Sigel are specifically concerned. Such a contextual approach to competence is a ready antidote to other more common essentialist interpretations, according to which competence is believed to inhere only in individuals. This perspec-tive also creates room for the kinds of social, cultural, and economic factors stressed in Schröder and Edelstein's chapter. Similarly, Dean and Youniss view children's competence for intentional moral judgments as dependent in part on their social-relational context. Finally, Chapman's delineation of an inter-dependence between purely intrapsychic cognitive competence and interper-sonal communicative competence in the domain of children's reasoning is also an effort to view cognitive development within a social context.

## "COMPETENCE" AND THE CONSERVATION
## OF MEANING

We do not wish to act as final arbitrators of the many contentious issues addresses in these chapters. Instead, our central point is that attempts such as these to reflect on the meaning of the concept of competence serve to raise the broader question of how the meanings of such explanatory concepts are determined. In this connection, we believe that much of the confusion surrounding the notion of competence results from insufficient reflection on the constructive role of the scientist in fixing the meanings of explanatory concepts. Even psychologists who otherwise subscribe to a constructivist view of the development of knowledge in children often do not recognize the extent to which the meanings of the theoretical concepts that they employ are circumscribed by their own operational constructions.

The importance of such meaning-giving construction becomes apparent in reflecting on the operational criteria by which competence is attributed. The idea that arguments about the age at which a particular competence develops may hinge as much on the particular measures used as on the facts of development is hardly original, but we believe the significance of this observation has not been fully appreciated. Usually, debate centers on the question of who has the more valid "response criterion" for assessing the competence in question, where the validity of that measure is understood in terms of the ability to make veridical judgments about whether or not that competence is present in a particular case. This measurement-theoretical conception of validity presupposes that the competence as such is indeed present or not, independent of one's efforts to detect it. However, before one can attempt to detect a particular competence, one must have some conception of that which one wishes to detect, and the latter implies in turn that one has some *conceptual* criterion for deciding which instances fall under that concept and which not. (On this Wittgensteinian notion of conceptual "criteria," see Chapman, 1987.)

The problem as we see it is that investigators choosing to use different response criteria in assessing a given competence often commit themselves unawares to different conceptual criteria at the same time. Instead of measuring the same competence with different assessment procedures, they often end up measuring competencies which are conceptual distinct. Much of the sterility of the debate about competence has resulted from the fact that the disputants have often confused the nature of their disagreement. They have argued about empirical questions ("When does Competence X in fact develop"?) or about methodological questions ("Who has the most valid measure of Competence X"?) without always realizing that semantic questions were involved as well (in what *sense* "Competence X" was understood). To borrow Sigel's terminology, the debate has often been characterized by a "nonconservation of meaning." The same terms are invoked, but used in different ways. To consider only one classic example: Borke (1971) argued that young children below the age of 6 or 7 years were not "egocentric," in the sense that they were unable to understand other persons' feelings. In reply, Chandler and Greenspan (1972) countered that, in Piaget's theory, "egocentrism" refers more narrowly to the inability to understand another person's perspective *when that perspective differs from their own,* and they showed that young children are indeed "egocentric" *in that sense.* The point is that the differences that separated Borke from Chandler and Greenspan were as much semantic as empirical in nature and that many controversies about the timing of development involve similar, but often unacknowledged, differences in meaning. Such differences in the conceptualization of terms have often been overlooked, in part because of an empiricist impatience with mere "semantics."

Our view is that debates about competence and its development will remain unproductive unless the participants reflect upon the meanings of their respective concepts and acknowledge conceptual differences when they exist. To the extent that such a goal could be achieved, the focus of the debate would become broadened to include questions of conceptualization and meaning as well as questions of fact and of method. To believe that such a shift in focus would result automatically in agreement would be naive, but we do believe that it would result in progress toward a more incisive identification of the differences which separate the various parties and therefore toward a more productive exchange of views.

## PIAGET AND BEYOND

The importance of considering the ways in which particular competencies are conceptualized becomes especially apparent in evaluating evidence for early competence in relation to Piagetian theory. Most of the interest in research on early competence has stemmed from the claim that a given ability has been detected earlier than was previously reported by some authority. Such claims presuppose that the observed early developing competence is in fact the *same* competence that the authority in question described as emerging only later, and it is therefore not surprising that a frequent counterargument involves a denial of that assumption. Thus, Borke's (1971) report of early development in interpersonal understanding derived much of its novelty and interest from the claim that it was inconsistent with Piagetian theory, and Chandler and Greenspan's (1972) denied that any inconsistency was involved because Borke's "egocentrism" was not the same as that of Piaget.

A similar argument lies at the base of the respective chapters by Montangero and by Dean and Youniss. Montangero argues that some claims regarding the early development of children's understanding of time in fact involved the assessment of different kinds of competencies than those with which Piaget was concerned in his research on that topic. And Dean and Youniss argue that some supposed alternatives to Piagetian theories of mental imagery and moral development are not true alternatives at all, because they address quite different problems than were addressed in Piaget's own work.

We believe that the recognition of such differences in meaning is necessary and essential for further progress. We would only raise the further question of what to do next, once the nonconservation of meaning is recognized. Quite apart from the implications of research on early competence for Piagetian theory, such research often has been successful in identifying some early developing competencies that were previously unrecognized. Beyond the question of whether such research is or is not consistent with Piagetian theory lies a further, and perhaps more productive problem: how to integrate the later developing competencies studied by Piaget with those earlier developing competencies studied by others into a more comprehensive description of children's sequential development. Such a goal is implied in the efforts of Montangero and of Pascual-Leone and Johnson to develop methods of task analysis by which different levels of competence can be unambiguously defined and described. Whereas Montangero pursues structuralist methods of task analysis, Pascual-Leone and Johnson argue that it is necessary to go beyond structural analysis and to develop a method of functional task analysis in which real-time psychological processes are considered as well.

Our main point is that discussions of competence must move beyond the question of the "true age" at which it first develops to the question of *what it is* exactly that develops at different ages. Beyond disputes about whether evidence for early competence is or is not consistent with Piagetian theory is the goal of integrating early developing and later developing competencies in a more comprehensive theory of development. However, little progress can be made toward that goal as long as qualitatively different competencies that happen to develop at different times are confounded with each other in the belief that they are the *same* competence assessed with differing degrees of measurement error. The most urgent task at present is perhaps to develop unambiguous criteria for distinguishing between qualitatively different competencies that may be manifest in a single type of task. We believe that the chapters in this book contain important contributions toward this goal, but also that the issues are too vast to be soluble within the covers of any single book. Our goal will have been accomplished if we succeed in motivating our readers to seek new solutions to these problems and to carry the debate to new and more productive levels of argumentation.

## REFERENCES

Borke, H. (1971). Interpersonal perception of young children. *Developmental Psychology, 5*, 263–269.

Chandler, M. J., & Greenspan, S. (1972). Ersatz egocentrism: A reply to H. Borke. *Developmental Psychology, 7*, 104–106.

Chapman, M. (1987). Inner processes and outward criteria: Wittgenstein's importance for psychology. In M. Chapman & R. A. Dixon (Eds.), *Meaning and the growth of understanding* (pp. 103–127). Berlin: Spring-Verlag.

Erdfelder, E. (1990). Deterministic developmental hypotheses, probabilistic rules of manifestation, and the analysis of finite mixture distributions. In A. von Eye (Ed.), *Statistical methods in longitudinal research* (Vol. 2, pp. 471–510). New York: Academic Press.

Piaget, J. (1941). The mechanism of mental development and the laws of the grouping of operations. *Archives de Psychologie, 28*, 215–285.

Rindskopf, D. (1987). Using latent class analysis to test developmental models. *Developmental Review, 7*, 66–85.

# Author Index

# Subject Index

**L**

Language, 211–212, 215–221, 225–226
Latent variables, 229–230, 233–236
Levels of knowledge, 120–122, 126–127
Logic, 29–30, 32–39, 65, 78, 81

**M**

Meaning, 152, 189, 193, 198, 201, 203, 262–264
Mental capacity, 166–168, 176–182
Mental imagery, 66, 93–94, 96–102, 107, 218, 264
Model estimation, 245–254
Modeling, 102
Moral judgment, 66, 93–94, 102–106, 264

**N**

Nature, 3–4, 44–48
Necessity, 152, 219–224

**O**

Object permanence, 168–182

**P**

Parent-child relations, 48–54

**Pattern** explanation, 2–3, 9, 16, 22–23, 25, 30–32, 260
Performance, ix–x, 1–2, 6–15, 135–136, 154, 163, 195, 199, 225–226
Procedures, 19, 24, 26–30, 32, 40

**R**

Representation, 151–152, 189–199, 202–205, 261

**S**

Scheme(s), 151, 154, 155–163, 165–168, 172–175, 177–182
Signifier, 97
Social class, 65–67, 74–76, 142, 146–148, 152
Stages, 70–71, 153–154
Structure(s), 78, 133–134, 151, 153–154, 158, 164–165, 166, 171, 260
Symbol(s), 191, 196, 204, 215–216

**T**

Task analysis, 151, 163–168, 171–183, 264
Time judgments, 66, 116–119, 120–121, 123–125, 263